I0821855

KINGS MOUNTAIN

KINGS MOUNTAIN

America's Most Forgotten Battle That Changed the Course of the American Revolution

PHILLIP THOMAS TUCKER, PhD

Skyhorse Publishing

Skyhorse Publishing books may be purchased in bulk at special discounts for sales promotion, corporate gifts, fund-raising, or educational purposes. Special editions can also be created to specifications. For details, contact the Special Sales Department, Skyhorse Publishing, 307 5th Avenue, 4th Floor, New York, NY 10016 or info@skyhorsepublishing.com.

Visit our website at www.skyhorsepublishing.com.
Please follow our publisher Tony Lyons on Instagram @tonylyonsisuncertain.

10 9 8 7 6 5 4 3 2 1

Library of Congress Cataloging-in-Publication Data is available on file.

Cover design by Kai Texel

Print ISBN: 978-1-5107-6643-3
Ebook ISBN: 978-1-5107-6644-0

Printed in the United States of America

To Betty Jane Cox-Tucker

Contents

Prologue

Fate and the gods of war were most unkind to Colonel James Williams. Commanding the South Carolina backcountry patriots of the Little River District militia of the Little River Regiment, he was a hero of the key Patriot victory at Musgrove's Mill, South Carolina, on August 19, 1780, and the far more important Battle of Kings Mountain in the South Carolina Piedmont on Saturday, October 7, 1780. However, the colonel's life was tragic because of the surreal horrors of a brutal war that had consumed the backcountry of South Carolina in 1780, after the fall of Charleston, South Carolina, to the British invaders in May.

Most of all, by the fall of 1780 and like so many other backcountry Patriots, Williams was highly motivated, driven in part by vengeance, and for good reason. He had a personal score to settle with Major Patrick Ferguson, who was one of Lord Charles Cornwallis's top lieutenants with the vital mission of conquering the South Carolina backcountry. The Scotland-born commander had occupied Williams's Little River, South Carolina, plantation in the backcountry and forced his wife, Mary Wallace-Williams of Celtic descent, and children out of their home. The colonel's burning desire to meet Ferguson and his command of Loyalists to settle old scores finally became a reality during the bloody struggle on October 7, 1780, for possession of an obscure ridge in the Piedmont of northwestern South Carolina located just below the North Carolina boundary, Kings Mountain.

To this day, James Williams, the highest-ranking American commander who received his death stroke during the most important battle ever fought of the Southern theater, Kings Mountain, has been forgotten in the history books and by the American public, including even by some leading historians: a classic example that is representative of the overall relative obscurity of the Battle of Kings Mountain. Indeed, very few Americans have ever heard anything about Colonel Williams, a devout Presbyterian who helped to win at

Kings Mountain—the decisive showdown of the Revolutionary War. Today, no statue of Colonel Williams can be seen on the top of Kings Mountain, where he received his mortal wound.

In fact, even the remains of Colonel James Williams have no final resting place at the battlefield of Kings Mountain. Instead of having been killed on Kings Mountain, the Virginia-born Colonel Williams died of his wounds on October 8, 1780, at an obscure overnight encampment at age thirty-nine.

At this time, the victorious Patriots were retreating west from Kings Mountain and toward the safety of the heavily forested Blue Ridge Mountains. They had just eliminated the entire task force of nearly a thousand Loyalists—around a third of Lord Charles Cornwallis's Army—in barely an hour of bitter combat. Even more, they also killed the famed Loyalist commander who, ironically, was the only non-American who fought in the battle, Scotland-born Major Patrick Ferguson, during what was America's first civil war, eighty years before the Civil War of 1861–1865. Like no other battle in the American Revolution, the dramatic and climactic showdown at Kings Mountain personified the nightmarish horror of a brutal conflict that pitted brother against brother on an almost unimaginable scale across the South. However, the roles and contributions of the Loyalists, fellow Americans, have also been largely forgotten and ignored because they were the losers in the war over the heart and soul of America.

Unlike the twenty-eight Patriots who were killed on Kings Mountain on the previous day, Colonel Williams was hastily buried by the grieving men of his Little River Regiment on October 8 in a remote grave under a shady chestnut tree beside the dusty road leading toward the safety of the Blue Ridge. After having been finally located and then removed, the grave of Colonel Williams has been marked today by a small, modest monument in the town of Gaffney, South Carolina. Colonel James Williams, a prosperous South Carolina planter, devout leader of the Little River Presbyterian Church, and hard-fighting holy warrior like so many of the Patriots, has served as a representative example of the frightfully high price paid by an entire generation of forgotten Americans in the South in the making of America and the winning of independence.

Unfortunately, these distinguished contributions have been long forgotten, partly because one of the colonel's Patriot rivals unfairly blamed him for a lack of courage and patriotism, although he was mortally wounded in the all-important battle—ugly and unfair charges that were leveled to blemish

Williams's character and reputation, which have been widely accepted by far too many historians in part because the colonel never had a chance to refute them. Nevertheless, the accepted accounts of Williams's influential enemies, especially Colonel William Hill's writings, have long disparaged his contribution at Kings Mountain. This has become part of the standardized version of the Kings Mountain story to this day, while romantic myths and legends have developed to replace other historical facts, while elevating far less deserving individuals into the limelight during the hilltop struggle on October 7, 1781.

In the supreme sacrifice, Colonel Williams gave his life "in defense of my rights and liberties, and that of my children," in his own words, during what was America's first civil war that generations of nationalist historians have overlooked or ignored in their glorification of the American Revolution. Like their father who sacrificed everything for the sacred cause of liberty, Colonel Williams's two oldest sons, Daniel, age eighteen, and Joseph, age fourteen, didn't survive the war. They were hung by the infamous Loyalist partisan leader William "Bloody Bill" Cunningham, of Scotch-Irish descent, and his mostly South Carolina partisans after having surrendered on the false promise that they would receive fair treatment. Both of the colonel's young sons were brutally murdered while serving in South Carolina's Little River Regiment (Daniel was a captain and Joseph a private, and they both had seen action at Kings Mountain in their father's command) on November 19, 1781, barely a year after the October 7, 1780, battle, in cruel revenge for their father's leading role at the Battle of Kings Mountain. "Bloody Bill" had good reason for vengeance because victory at Kings Mountain reversed the course of the American Revolution and placed the British Army, which never completely recovered from the unexpected blow, on the road to Yorktown where America won its independence.

In what had become a very personal war between Colonel James Williams and Major Patrick Ferguson, Williams's wife, Mary Wallace-Williams of Scotch-Irish descent, and their brood of children were thrown out of their home three times by Loyalists. In the South Carolina backcountry in 1780, hundreds of Patriots were similarly abused and victimized by the Loyalists and British. This general historical amnesia about the unmatched cruelty and horrors of America's first civil war in the Southern backcountry has even applied to the Patriots, including the colonel's sons and the men of Kings Mountain, who unfortunately have been forgotten by the nation that they played a large role in helping to save during the darkest days of the American Revolution. These anonymous Patriots sacrificed their all—lives, fortunes, and futures—in the name of America during the struggle for the heart and soul of the new experiment in nationhood, and they deserve full recognition today for what they achieved against the odds.

Introduction

The remarkable story of the dramatic and all-important showdown at Kings Mountain certainly deserves a special place in the American memory and in the annals of American history, because it represented a major turning point of the American Revolution and was America's greatest citizen-soldier success of the entire war. Even more, this climactic battle in the remote South Carolina backwoods of the Piedmont on October 7, 1780, is still important and relevant to this day for a variety of reasons that have nothing to do with the rather remarkable tactical aspects of this crucial engagement. Most of all this long-overlooked battle forcefully demonstrated that it was the most common people of the western frontier, on both sides of the Blue Ridge, who voluntarily rose up to determine their own destiny by winning this turning point showdown at a time when the established leaders, both political and military, of their infant government in Philadelphia, Pennsylvania, had failed them in every possible way.

This dire situation in which life and liberty were at stake presented an emergency situation to the people of the frontier because of the seemingly endless follies of the Continental Congress in Philadelphia and the Army, which had seemingly lost the revolution after the South had been all but conquered by the eventful summer of 1780. The common people of the West were left on their own and unprotected, due to the central government's long list of mistakes and miscalculations, to face a powerful enemy that threatened to destroy their homeland and families, like the Native Americans—especially the Cherokee, whom they had long fought to ensure their survival. As a consequence, and in their common-sense wisdom, they volunteered and then rode forth to fight, despite the omnipresent Indian threat to their settlements and families, to deliver what was necessary for survival: the preemptive strike to catch the enemy by surprise at Kings Mountain.

In the past, generations of American historians have emphasized that the Westerners rode forth toward a rendezvous with destiny because of lofty Age of Enlightenment idealism and nationalism, which was not the case since they had not needed to be told about Age of Enlightenment philosophies or any ideology. Instead, they trekked south through the Blue Ridge Mountains to Kings Mountain in defense of the land that they loved and because of the promise of pushing even farther west in the future to gain even more and richer lands, if independence was won. In this regard, they fought at Kings Mountain on October 7, 1780, for the limitless expanse of this vast land that lay to the West and its sheer beauty and boundlessness.

By this time, the most important and most vital of lessons already had been learned by the hard-pressed people of the western frontier, which came from their knowledge of the Holy Bible's Old Testament and Indian fighting experiences over the years: that when the American people could no longer depend on its own government and its armies, it was time for them to take matters into their own hands. The most important story about the Battle of Kings Mountain was this key decision of the common people of the western frontier that they were actually better off and had a greater chance for success if they depended upon themselves and God as he commanded his true believers—concepts utterly unimaginable, if not entirely not understandable in the minds of modern-day Americans, who have become dependent on their iPhones, modern conveniences, and their bloated government in Washington, DC, in almost too many ways to count.

Significantly, it was this vital decision made by the common people and not the government in Philadelphia or General George Washington that resulted in the reversing of the tide of the revolutionary struggle and saving of the infant republic from his own folly by ultimately paving the way to Lord Charles Cornwallis's surrender at Yorktown, Virginia, barely a year later. This miracle was all made possible by the one-sided victory won by Westerners, who were also Southerners, at Kings Mountain that destroyed Cornwallis's best light expeditionary force in its entirety—a decisive success won by the common people, all volunteers, of the frontier militia, which was a large volunteer force unknown to even exist to General Washington and the Continental Congress.

In this regard, Kings Mountain truly represented the most purely American of all victories, especially in regard to the common people, of the American Revolution because this amazing success resulted from a spontaneously popular uprising of the common people across the Southern frontier just in the nick of time.

In truth and contrary to the standard interpretations that have become popular about the American Revolution in a complete inversion of the facts, especially in terms of overall decisiveness, the crucial Southern theater, and more specifically the war in South Carolina, was the true scene of the Big Show where the war was ultimately won, while the Northern theater, including Washington's campaigns, especially after the miracles at Trenton and Princeton, New Jersey, was nothing more than a sideshow barren of decisive results, except in regard to Saratoga, New York, where victory had been won by the army under Major General Horatio Gates.

In the finest hour of the backcountry and Overmountain militiamen during the war in the South, the bitter and often point-blank struggle that swirled back and forth on the rugged, wooded hillsides of Kings Mountain on that fall afternoon changed the course of the American Revolution. Ironically, this decisive success in the South Carolina Piedmont was not won by conventional military tactics, but by the classic frontier tactics of Indian-style fighting at close range and encirclement to destroy the enemy, fellow Americans. Here, individual citizen-soldiers, who were mostly veteran Indian fighters like most of their popular leaders, won the day. Kings Mountain must be viewed today as a major battle of extreme strategic importance and decisiveness in the annals of the most famous battles in world military history, because this victory saved America in one of her darkest hours.

When compared to other significant engagements of the Revolutionary War, this often-minimized struggle in the South Carolina backwoods was remarkably deceptive at first glance, having lasted barely an hour. Additional obscurity for the fight at Kings Mountain also came from the fact that it was a struggle of Americans pitted against fellow Americans—literally, a true brother's war of America's first civil war. Here, on October 7, 1780, relatives, neighbors, sons, fathers, and brothers of two radically differing militia systems, consisting of family members and relatives who dominated the ranks in familial companies of Patriot volunteers, fought against one another for what they believed was right. In truth, the Patriots were not entirely in the moral right or atrocity free unlike so long presented in the traditional romanticized view of the American Revolution, because of the conflict's seemingly endless complexities and contradictions.

What was most remarkable was the fact that this most dramatic and important victory of the American Revolution in the South was won solely by volunteer militiamen from both sides of the Blue Ridge Mountains, after they had organized behind their own frontier leaders without orders or direction from General Washington, any Continental general officer, state executive, or any legislative or judicial body in the land. The almost accidental creation of a formidable frontier, or ghost, army in record time reaped the astonishing success at Kings Mountain that effectively proved the superiority of the American militiamen to British-trained troops at a time when they were considered decidedly inferior by all the experts and leaders on both sides.

These men, veterans of countless fights with the Cherokee, Creek, Loyalists, and British, wore no uniforms or signs of rank, donning frontier hunting and civilian attire when fighting with backwoods skill like Native Americans, while taking full advantage of the timbered hillsides and rocks along the slope. Even more, they thought much differently about the American Revolution's core philosophical meanings on a much more personal and emotional level—simple biblical, rooted in the Old Testament, and moral laws of basic survival lay at the core of their revolutionary experience and frontier attitudes—rather than on the flowery words of Thomas Jefferson and other founding fathers.

The astounding victory at Kings Mountain all but ensured that the American Revolution was won in the South and that the final showdown at Yorktown was a curtain call to the long, bloody years of America's most savage war, which had consumed the Southern backcountry with horrors that have been seldom revealed in the history books. However, the overall importance of this vicious struggle, which included fierce hand-to-hand combat, on a remote mountain in the backcountry (also known as the up country of the South Carolina Piedmont) by rough-hewn and mostly illiterate men in the Patriot ranks has been long minimized by American historians, especially from the Ivy League colleges of the Northeast, in part because of the victors' lowly, or common, qualities—average Americans who ultimately won this bitter war for the heart and soul of America. Even the top Patriot leaders were rough-and-tumble men of the frontier who knew how to cut the throats of enemies, take their scalps, and hang victims high from the tallest tree.

By any measure, this dramatic showdown was not only the most unexpected battle of the war but also the most unorthodox and strangest one in terms of defying the usual expectations of the experts, because it was the antithesis of a conventional and traditional eighteenth-century engagement in almost every possible way: nearly a thousand Loyalists from New York, New Jersey (Provincial regulars), South Carolina, and North Carolina (militia) held an exceptionally strong position atop Kings Mountain for the supreme tactical advantage, and they were much better trained and equipped, which was simply not enough because they relied on the conventional British tactics that had almost always equated victory—most recently at Camden, South Carolina, on August 16, 1780—the bayonet charge.

If the fight had been a traditional battle on an open field, the undisciplined Patriots would not have stood a chance of winning the day. But the heavily wooded terrain of Kings Mountain and Indian-fighting skills of the Patriots had deemed otherwise. And no large-scale battle of the American Revolution more thoroughly revealed the depths of the hatred and viciousness that existed on each side than on October 7, 1780, including no-quarter warfare and the slaughtering of Loyalists after a white flag was raised in surrender near the battle's conclusion: a tragic and brutal case of hundreds of American fighters on both sides systematically destroying each other in one of the bloodiest battles of the Revolution.

Even more, these frontier and backcountry men never wore fine silk clothing and had no elitist pretensions like upper-class members living on the East Coast, especially in the bustling urban center of Philadelphia: the antithesis of the aristocratic and elitist circles, both colonial and British. Few, if any, of these rough-hewn and raw-boned common men, who were generally tall and lanky, from the western frontier had ever read the words of the Declaration of Independence or English immigrant Thomas Paine's masterpiece *Common Sense* that had helped to revive the revolutionary struggle during the dark days of late 1776.

However, these realities did not matter when it came to hard-nosed Indian fighting against anyone who dared to threaten their frontier communities, families, and distinctive way of life that they cherished. The common Westerners needed no Age of Enlightenment ideals or Patriot propaganda from Philadelphia newspapers to revive their spirits or motivate them to fight against the invaders of their homeland, because the primary motivation of these men was simple survival and to preserve the lives of their communities that they had hacked out of the wilderness. Instead of reading the well-chosen, polished words of the upper-class elites on the east coast, the Overmountain and backcountry men expressed their own personal sentiments about liberty by their combat prowess and desperate fighting at Kings Mountain.

Relying on mobility and stealth, the twin keys to achieving victory in irregular, or guerrilla, warfare when it came to a hard-hitting preemptive strike, it was the swiftness of the mobile force of partisan mounted volunteers of the county militias on both sides of the mountains that ensured that Scotland-born Major Patrick Ferguson was caught by surprise at Kings Mountain. What has been most minimized about the Kings Mountain story has been the Patriots' epic ride across the formidable mountains simply to reach Major Ferguson and his command on their mountaintop to deliver a lethal blow: a frontier odyssey all in itself, when more than a thousand volunteers of the backcountry and Overmountain region trekked south and then east during a grueling ordeal of more than 330 miles in thirteen days, including in the midst of rain and nasty early autumn weather. Well-armed and thirsting for revenge on a hated enemy who had threatened to destroy their home communities, they rode through an uncharted wilderness and across the towering Blue Ridge Mountains, which were part of the Appalachian Mountains, of western North Carolina before reaching the South Carolina backcountry and their ultimate target at Kings Mountain on October 7, 1780.

While fighting Indian-style along the wooded slopes after having stealthily surrounded Kings Mountain on all sides under the unofficial Overmountain leader, Colonel Isaac Shelby, they reaped the most improbable of victories against Provincial regulars, who had been trained like British regulars and wore red uniforms and long-tailed scarlet uniform coats—the best Loyalist fighting men—and hundreds of North and South Carolina Loyalist militiamen who were dressed in typical frontier garb like the Patriots. In striking contrast to Major Ferguson's well-trained Provincials, the victors of Kings Mountain, not even top officers, wore no uniforms and fought in coarse hunting shirts and homespun civilian clothing and wore their hair long and tied in the back in a stylish queue that was popular among the frontiersmen.

Most significantly, these frontiersmen from both sides of the mountains not only prevailed on this bloody Saturday in the South Carolina Piedmont but completely annihilated Ferguson's strong task force by killing, capturing, and wounding every member of the once-thought-invincible command. Lord Cornwallis was depending upon Ferguson to advance north as his left flank for his much-anticipated invasion of North Carolina, then Virginia, and then to eventually confront and crush Washington's Army in a bid to end the war, when Sir Henry Clinton advanced south from New York City. This was a classic pincer movement that promised decisive victory. However, Cornwallis's ambitions of obtaining glory were dashed by the defeat of his largest force of light infantry at Kings Mountain, while conclusively ending the all-important British experiment of relying on newly raised Loyalists to crush the rebels and win the war.

To this day, historians have most often overlooked the complexities of the most crucial theater of operations, which still needs to be fully and better understood today to place the story of Kings Mountain in a proper historical perspective. To a generation of Americans who fought for simple survival and to preserve their families on the western frontier, the American Revolution was most of all an Indian war in what was the largest theater of the war that spanned hundreds of miles of untamed frontier, dwarfing the theaters of General Washington's Continental Army far to the north and witnessing the harshest combat of the war. Historians with a detailed understanding of the complexities of this extremely bitter war in the South can no longer debate the longtime argument whether the American Revolution was truly a revolution or not, because of the existing analogies of America's first civil war, especially in the South, with the horrific "Reign of Terror" of the early 1790s during the French Revolution. It was in the South where the surreal horrors of war truly matched those of the French Revolution, and these extremely dark chapters of the American experience were unleashed by American Patriots and American Loyalists against each other in a savage guerrilla war rather than against British regulars or Continental troops as portrayed in the traditional and mythical American Revolution.

After all, there was no Continental Army in the South by the time that the common people of the backcountry and frontier began to rise up and fight back against the seemingly invincible invaders. The only American army in the South—ironically called the "Grand Army"—had been entirely destroyed by Cornwallis at the Battle of Camden, South Carolina, in mid-August 1780. Then, a miracle occurred when this ghost army of backcountry and Overmountain men, who hailed from the frontier settlements situated in Watauga, Holston, and Nolichucky River valleys west of the mountains, was created by themselves before General Washington dispatched General Nathanael Greene south to create a new army in the South to replace the one destroyed by Lord Cornwallis at Camden. Even more, the Patriot attack force consisted of only 910 men who defied conventional wisdom and tactical thought when they surrounded Kings Mountain and charged uphill against a large and better-trained Loyalist force of more than a thousand men, who held the strategic crest that seemed impregnable: usually the tactical equation that guaranteed defeat for attackers since time immemorial.

The unexpected formation of an entire ad hoc army of backcountry and Overmountain men was an entirely natural development of coming together for urgent self-defense in order to launch an audacious offensive strike to catch the enemy by surprise, partly because it was based on a lengthy historical tradition. The Patriots were mostly Scotch-Irish, Scots, and Welshmen and their descendants—Celts all who still embraced ancient customs and mindsets—who banded together under their own democratically chosen chiefs from both sides of the mountains in times of severe crisis, when either fighting Native Americans or Loyalists, like the gathering of the Celtic and Scottish Highlands clans of old on the Atlantic's other side.

Therefore, there was no centralized or organized command and leadership structure of a traditional army among the victors of Kings Mountain. Then to ensure greater obscurity about the battle to this day, most of these men who won in dramatic fashion on October 7 then continued to move west to new lands, including the Trans-Mississippi and also across the "Father of Waters," and scattered to the winds: a guarantee for greater obscurity in the historical record. As a result, they left behind little collective memory or organized veteran groups in east Tennessee or in the Carolinas, unlike in the case of Civil War veterans, allowing for local historical legacies and memories of the Battle of Kings Mountain to slowly fade away with the mists of time. And because so many of the victors were illiterate, most of the written record was either never penned or simply faded away to be lost forever.

For such reasons, the Battle of Kings Mountain has become America's most forgotten turning point clash of arms of the American Revolution, when Washington's Continental Army hundreds of miles to the north was doing practically nothing to achieve important successes much like America's French allies. In fact, by this time, the French-American alliance looked very much like a flat failure, and the French, including King Louis XVI, became disillusioned by the war and the Americans' excessive demands that seemed to have no end for seemingly everything imaginable. France was headed for bankruptcy—one of the primary causes of the French Revolution that erupted in 1789—because of its massive support for America. As noted and most significantly, it was *not* Washington's Continental Army nor top Continental generals who made the decisions or took actions that turned the tide in 1780 but ordinary Americans, mostly Scotch-Irish of the South, who banded together out of desperation to save homes and families from the British-Loyalist-Native American threat on their own and without support from either the Continental Army or Congress.

When Americans speak today about the Civil War, they fail to understand how the American Revolution in the South was equally as divisive. The best example of this undeniable reality of large numbers of fellow Americans killing Americans on an unprecedented scale was best demonstrated on an obscure hilltop in South Carolina on October 7, 1780. Incredibly and unlike any other battle of the American Revolution, a brutal familial war was waged in full at Kings Mountain. At least seventy-four sets of brothers and twenty-nine sets of father-son fighting teams were among the howling attackers that surrounded the mountain. Indeed, the struggle at Kings Mountain was also the epitome of a fratricidal brothers' fight.

For instance, five brothers of the Goforth family from Tryon County, North Carolina (today's Rutherford County), fought against each other on bloody October 7, 1780: three Loyalist brothers were killed and among the remaining two brothers, one was killed on the Patriot side. Only one Goforth brother survived the battle to tell the tale of the surreal horror of civil war. As was fully demonstrated, these close family connections ensured the most bitter of conflicts of a highly personal and intimate nature in the entire course of American history. No-quarter warfare was commonplace across the South among friends, neighbors, and even family members in a true civil war.

In a striking paradox, these bitter enemies were much the same in regard to class, background, education, and economic standing: primarily small hard-scrabble farmers from the backcountry and Overmountain region of lower- and middle-class antecedents. The men of both sides believed that they were battling in the best interests of themselves and their families: the antithesis of the popular misconception and worn stereotype that the Loyalists hailed primarily from the urban environments of the eastern cities, the upper-class elite, and the educated class, unlike the Patriots.

Here, at Kings Mountain in barely an hour's time, an ad hoc collection of Patriot Westerners without formal military training or having learned any textbook lessons about the advantages of fighting on foot Indian-style with the deadly Long Rifle, or the Pennsylvania Rifle, to completely eliminate the entire left-wing strike force of Lord Charles Cornwallis, who was thought by King George III and ministers to have been on the verge of winning it all and ending the revolution. The enemy force of Loyalist Americans was swiftly vanquished by 910 backcountry and Overmountain men to sabotage the entire British plan, the so-called Southern Strategy for winning the war. Around half of Patriots at Kings Mountain were backcountry men of South Carolina from the region, which was remote and frontier-like, located around seventy-five miles from the coastal lowlands filled with rice plantations and from the wilder frontier west of the mountains from where roughly the other half of the Patriots hailed.

Most important and as noted, this remarkable October victory in 1780 led to Yorktown in part because Cornwallis's Army never recovered from the elimination of Ferguson's entire command in the most unexpected tactical development of the war. For such reasons, more than 240 years after this all-important battle for the heart and soul of America was fought, it is time to take a new and fresh look at this remarkable clash of arms and the equally remarkable men on both sides who fought at Kings Mountain and well beyond the traditional layers of popular myths, fiction, and familiar stereotypes that have obscured fundamental truths for generations. In consequence, the overall purpose of this book is to present as many new views and fresh perspectives as possible to replace the old myths and stereotypes that have existed since the battle was fought so long ago.

This book seeks to understand the spirit, heart, and soul of the American Revolution by looking more closely at the ordinary Americans who rose to the fore at Kings Mountain—basically, a most revealing analysis of the American Revolution from below at the common soldier level. And no single battle from 1775 to 1783 was won more exclusively by average Americans—citizen-soldiers of the Southern frontier militia—than Kings Mountain, which represented the most democratic battlefield success of the American Revolution. These average men of the frontier, including many volunteers who had been born in Ulster Province, north Ireland, were the ones who ensured that a true common people's revolution would be won in the end. Even more, the American Revolution was a rich man's war and a poor or average man's fight, with no battle better representing this fundamental truism on both sides than Kings Mountain.

Every man among the attackers fought on his own hook in repeatedly advancing up the hill through the trees and then in prudently withdrawing back down when the Loyalists unleashed repeated bayonet attacks, and then the Patriots resumed the advance up the wooded slopes in a highly effective buddy system of two friends (basically one fired while the other loaded at intervals), who fought together as formidable teams at Kings Mountain.

In New England and in the mid-Atlantic states, the romantic image of the yeoman farmer-citizen-soldier, or the so-called "Minute Man," was largely a myth beyond the first eighteen months of the war, unlike in the South. Here, in the South, the average yeoman farmer—unlike the poor, immigrants, youths, unmarried men, free Blacks, and slaves on society's margins—primarily served as a lower-class foundation of the Continental Army's enlisted ranks. Most important, the local militia in the backcountry and Overmountain region of the South made a more significant contribution to winning the war as demonstrated at Kings Mountain as opposed to farther north. Serving in regiments that represented counties in Virginia and North Carolina and districts in South Carolina, many backcountry militiamen had served from the beginning in the Cherokee War of 1776 and to the war's end, including at Yorktown.

Indeed, another one of the great myths of the American Revolution was that the Southern Patriots of the militia—to coincide with the myth of the militia's much-emphasized ineffectiveness and ineptness, which was far more the case in the North than in the South—in the backcountry were generally inactive and nonparticipants in the struggle after the fall of Charleston to Sir Henry Clinton on May 12, 1780. However, nothing could have been further from the truth, because Patriots in the backcountry, Overmountain region, and the Eastern lowlands began to rise up almost immediately to defend families and the land they loved.

Contrary to the generally poor performance of the American militia in New England and the mid-Atlantic states except in the war's beginning and during the 1777 Saratoga Campaign where the New England militia shined in conjunction with Continental troops, it was the Southern militia of backcountry Virginia, North Carolina, today's east Tennessee, and South Carolina that primarily reversed the war's course, especially at Kings Mountain, and won the war in the South against British regulars, Royal Provincial regulars, Native Americans, and Loyalist militia and not the Continental troops, who generally performed poorly in the South when mixed with militia. Ironically, there was not a single Continental soldier or officer at Kings Mountain.

In the annals of the American Revolution and in a most unfortunate development, the generally unreliable performance of the militia in Washington's Army, with notable exceptions like the Trenton-Princeton campaign, has long stained the far higher reputation of the Southern militia, especially of the backcountry, in an entirely unfair and erroneous judgment that has endured to this day. Ironically, the mythical revolution has long glorified the Patriot militia of the North, especially from New England, thanks to the early dominance of regional historians in American Revolutionary historiography, while basically ignoring the far more important, if not decisive in the end, contributions of the South's hard-fighting militia of the backcountry that compiled a dramatic list of victories in 1780. All in all, by relying on the wisdom of Indian tactics and experienced popular leaders, the success of the militia of the South went a long way toward the winning of the American Revolution.

Quite simply, it was Southern militia—highly mobile fighting men who relied on swift movements on horseback, basically light cavalry or mounted infantry, to surprise the enemy and then fought dismounted with deadly long rifles in a winning tactical formula, instead of attempting to fight in the conventional manner (a recipe for disaster as Major Ferguson discovered to his dismay) by European rules of warfare—of the backcountry and Overmountain region that not only saved the day by winning on October 7, but also set the stage for Washington's Continentals, along with their French allies, to reap the lion's share of the glory by marching south to win victory at Yorktown in the following October. But without the Patriot militia's great victory at Kings Mountain and other lesser-known places in South Carolina, including Musgrove's Mill where the tactically astute Isaac Shelby prevailed, then there would have been no dramatic victory at Yorktown that changed the course of not only American history, but world history.

Significantly, in an overlooked ethnic analysis, it should not be surprising that the backwater, Overmountain, and frontier Patriot militia proved so effective by 1780 because these were mostly hardy Scotch-Irish, who hailed from an embattled native homeland across the Atlantic and from some of America's most remote and isolated areas, where they had made their homes in the untamed wilderness. The Scotch-Irish people continued a lengthy tradition of battling the oppressive forces of England. The British first began to create a vast colonial empire by denying the Celtic people in various lands, beginning in Ireland that became an English colony by way of a brutal conquest in the 1500s, the right of self-determination by crushing one common people's revolt after another, going back to ancestors who fought in doomed Celtic independence struggles, including under nationalist leaders such as William Wallace in Scotland and Owain Glyndwr in Wales. Most of all, it was the Scotch-Irish who had been most recently oppressed in Ulster Province, north Ireland, by the autocratic dictates of the British government and greedy landlords, which ensured that they had ample old scores to settle with the British during the American Revolution.

Most important, the mostly Scotch-Irish frontiersmen of Kings Mountain possessed the most thorough battle experience of any fighting men in America by 1780. Most Patriots who won one the American Revolution's most remarkable and unexpected victories at Kings Mountain did so because they were hardened veterans of a half-decade of bitter, exceptionally bloody, and often no-quarter conflict against Native Americans and Loyalists. These were the common men who rose magnificently to the fore while serving under their own elected officers, fought in their own way with the same hunting rifles that had long provided food for the table and had vanquished the Cherokee, rode their own trusty war horses, made their own tactical decisions on the fly as tactically astute individuals, and battled on their own terms to save their cherished homeland, way of life, and families from the enemy: a truly astonishing success on October 7 at a time when there was no state legal authority or government to help them in their vital mission.

Even more, these Patriot men of lowly origins were also inspired and motivated by a sense of an early spirit of Manifest Destiny that always pointed west toward new lands and the setting sun, where the future lay for them and their families. While the Loyalists and British looked to the old ways of the past and a future within the British Empire, the backcountry men, especially those hardy pioneers who had settled west of the Appalachians, were more forward-thinking idealists, because they possessed a vibrant, expansionist continental vision, which fueled western expansion and was not understood or appreciated by their foes: another forgotten aspect of the battle that made Kings Mountain so different and unique from other Revolutionary War battles.

Indeed, the case can be made that this astonishing victory when least expected was won partly because of the vibrancy of America's early sense of

Manifest Destiny that existed in the hearts and minds of the frontiersmen, because the British, personified by Major Ferguson, posed a barrier to future westward expansion if they won this war for the heart and soul of America, because Great Britain envisioned a vast Indian reserve west of the mountains and a halt to westward migration. This deep-seated fear infused the backcountry Patriots, who fought in part to fulfill both a personal and national destiny that lay in the limitless opportunities in the seemingly boundless west. Such an intoxicating futuristic vision that more fertile lands for the taking lay open for them to the west—in the Ohio and Mississippi Valleys and all the way to the Mississippi River—made them even more highly motivated to fulfill a historic mission of the American people by eliminating the British: boldly leading the way ever-westward into the lands of the fertile Mississippi Valley and then all the way to the Pacific Ocean.

Precisely because they were ordinary men of the remote frontier, these extraordinary individuals fought with their hearts and souls, while risking all in perhaps the most remarkable battle of the American Revolution at this key turning point, even while their homeland was still under Indian threat and the nation's future could not have seemed more bleak. And by far the most forgotten frontier Celtic leader was Colonel Isaac Shelby, who played the decisive role in winning victory not only at Kings Mountain but also in all of the South in the turning point year of 1780. He was the rawboned and unorthodox son of an immigrant from Wales, which had been conquered by the British like Ireland and Scotland centuries before. Shelby hailed from the South Holston River settlement located in the pristine lands west of the mountains, emerging as the finest leader produced in the Overmountain region. By any measure, Shelby was the most extraordinary of the common men from the western frontier. He became the top tactical expert in the frontier art of Indian fighting and the real inspirational and moral leader of the far-flung expedition to Kings Mountain and the remarkable, one-sided victory. In leading his Overmountain men from west of the Blue Ridge Mountains with consummate skill, Shelby made the key leadership decisions that led to the war's most surprising victory in America's darkest hour, becoming the forgotten "father" of the remarkable October 7 success. Quite simply, without Colonel Shelby, there would have been no victory at Kings Mountain and no key turning point of the American Revolution in the early fall of 1780. Indeed, the long-forgotten and ignored Shelby truly deserved the lion's share of the credit for this most surprising victory of the

American Revolution. The common omission of Shelby's name from the list of the most distinguished and capable South Carolina partisan leaders of the war, such as Francis Marion, Thomas Sumter, and Andrew Pickens, is certainly not only one of the great ironies but also one of the great injustices of generations of American Revolution historiography.

It was the astute Colonel Shelby who made a series of smart Solomon-like leadership decisions from the beginning to end of this campaign and led by example both on and off the battlefield, ensuring the reaping of perhaps the war's most dramatic victory. It was Shelby's relentless driving force, never-say-die personality, and sense of determination, which had been forged by years of battling Native Americans, that made him an irrepressible force of nature throughout the most grueling of campaigns, guaranteeing victory in the final showdown at Kings Mountain.

Most important, their victory at Kings Mountain significantly reinvigorated the overall resistance effort and spirit of the revolutionary struggle, especially in the South, by demonstrating most convincingly that ordinary Americans of the militia could defeat even the best-trained Loyalists to boost pride and confidence. Kings Mountain, therefore, was a most decisive battle in multiple ways, and, without this victory in the middle of nowhere, America would be a much different nation today because this backwoods success cast a giant shadow that ensured the winning of America's independence. In the words of one historian who emphasized what the Battle of Kings Mountain actually represented in a larger historical perspective, it was "the grave of the last British hope of subduing the United States."

In the end, the British came closer to winning the war in the South—it could not be won in the northern and middle states because of strategic stalemate as had been repeatedly demonstrated by years of indecisive British victories, including even the 1777 capture of America's capital of Philadelphia—than has been generally recognized by historians. While Washington's Continental Army failed to achieve decisive victory and merely fought to survive during a lengthy war of attrition, and because of the ineptitude of the Continental Congress, it was largely left to the common people to rise up as one at the last minute and *on their own* in the South like nationalistic Celtic rebels of one of the many Scottish, Welsh, or Irish rebellions of old (which all failed because of superior British might, organization, and arms) without Continental officers or troops, without funds and arms, without military maps, without a central headquarters, without formal military educations or training, and without any authorization or knowledge of either George Washington, the Continental Army, or the United States Congress to thwart the most ambitious and best British military plan of conquest during the course of the American Revolution.

After having successfully contained the threat posed by the northern and middle colonies by effectively neutralizing Washington's Army and then easily subduing South Carolina in 1780, Cornwallis then planned to push north to conquer North Carolina and Virginia before descending on Washington's Army to deliver the decisive death stroke of the war: a tactical master plan of the conquest of America that was proven not feasible because it was largely undone by the unimaginable Patriot victory at Kings Mountain.

However, what was most remarkable was exactly how close the British plan came close to succeeding in winning the Southern war and then capitalizing on that success farther north. In formulating their ambitious plans of conquest, British strategists on both sides of the Atlantic completely forgot about the tough fighting men, especially the Scotch-Irish, of the Southern backcountry and the frontier on both sides of the mountains who had already won a two-front war against the Cherokee to the west and the Loyalists to the east in masterful fashion by the end of 1780.

Lord Cornwallis was shocked by this unknown enemy from the wilderness who had suddenly crossed the mountains from west to east and emerged from the backcountry to destroy his crucial left flank task force of Loyalists with an astonishing swiftness seldom seen. He wrote with some shock how a "numerous and unexpected enemy came from the mountains [and] As they had good horses, their movements were rapid," unlike the overconfident Major Ferguson, who had decided to make his ill-advised defensive stand atop Kings Mountain because he naively believed that he could defeat the best and most experienced fighting men in America—a fighting force that was destined to badly outclass him and his men in a fight to the death with a savagery seen in no other Revolutionary War battle of importance.

Basically, two victories, tactical and strategic, were won there when they were needed the most by a hard-pressed America: First, the October battle itself in tactical terms and second in strategic terms with the spread of the people's uprising and heightened resistance across the South when the astonishing news of the war's most unexpected victory spread far and wide. The rejuvenated resistance efforts led to other Patriot victories in the backcountry, including at Cowpens, South Carolina, on January 17, 1781, where many Kings Mountain veterans fought, dwindling Cornwallis's numbers and the morale of his increasingly exhausted men, because the Loyalists' spirit and resolve had been broken forever by the decisive victory on October 7. After that success orchestrated by Colonel Shelby and the grim lesson that resulted from the hanging of nine captured Loyalists by the Kings Mountain victors not long afterward, the Loyalists were effectively demoralized and taught a bitter lesson. In this sense, the most potent fuel to the Patriot resistance effort that ultimately succeeded and paved the way to Yorktown began at Kings Mountain.

If not for what these most ordinary of men achieved on October 7, America's most celebrated men, including George Washington and Thomas Jefferson, would have been hung as traitors, and America today would be governed by a constitutional monarchy across the sea. Therefore, this book is dedicated to these average and ordinary Americans who rose up on their own in the frontier tradition—although their homeland, especially west of the mountains, was still under Indian threat—to unite and strike as one to completely undo British strategic planning by winning an all-important battle in which glory, colorful flags, martial music, fancy uniforms, proper training, military organization, and the traditional rules of waging war were entirely absent on the Patriot side.

In separating myths from realities, this book has been written to shatter the enduring popular romance and enduring legends about this relatively obscure battle, the war in general, and the men who won it to bring new insights and a fresh understanding to the least appreciated story of the American Revolution, and to demonstrate that the great dream of independence was actually decisively won in the forgotten struggles of the Southern backcountry. Lord Cornwallis received one of the greatest shocks of his life "when the numerous and formidable body of the Back Mountains men came down to attack Major Ferguson and shewed themselves to be our most inveterate enemies" in this war at a time when it seemed that England was about to win back its wayward thirteen colonies because of a faltering resistance effort and the misfires of American and French collaborative efforts that brought this crucial alliance to the verge of extinction. Instead of Great Britain winning it all as already confidently assumed in London, the sparkling Patriot success on October 7, 1780, drove a stake through the heart of the entire foundation of the British strategy of winning the war by having Americans vanquish their fellow Americans.

In the end, perhaps Thomas Jefferson said it best about the supreme importance of the bloody showdown at this remote hilltop in the South Carolina Piedmont: "I remember well the deep and grateful impression made on the minds of every one by the memorable victory [at Kings Mountain]. It was the joyful annunciation of that turn of the tide of success which terminated the Revolutionary War, with the seal of our independence" of a new nation, the United States of America.

Most important, I also have told the incredible story of the common soldiers, who were almost all poor but incredibly rich in self-reliance, resourcefulness, and democratic leanings, as much as possible, despite the fact that this is very nearly an impossibility because of the absence of soldier letters, diaries, and memoirs—more than in any other war in America partly because of the high rate of illiteracy, especially in the Southern backcountry and frontier. Even accounts from the British side, especially among the common Loyalist soldiers from the Carolina backcountry who were basically from the same class as the Patriots at Kings Mountain, are rare for the same basic reasons.

Consequently, the forgotten stories, brief but insightful, of America's common soldiers in the South from 1775 to 1783 have been lost for the most part and remain glaringly absent in most books, especially accounts from men of the backcountry and on the frontier, and most specifically in the case of citizen-soldiers from west of the mountains. Most of all, in this author's opinion, these men need to be rescued from an undeserved oblivion.

After nearly 250 years, it is certainly time for a fresh, new look at this decisive battle that forever altered America's fate and destiny. Consequently, I have heavily focused on placing the overall story of Kings Mountain in a proper historical perspective. And the story cannot be fully understood without first understanding the history of the Scotch-Irish and Indian conflict—basically a bloody forge and training ground that created first-class fighting men by the time of the climactic showdown at Kings Mountain, thanks to the horrors of the savage war in the backcountry.

Without a hint of the traditional romance and myths that have so long distorted even the most acclaimed books about the American Revolution, I have also presented the darker and uglier side, but a more honest and accurate one, of the American Revolution with all its warts and blemishes. In consequence, the story of Kings Mountain is also a story of sheer brutality and savagery on multiple levels and on a scale not seen anywhere else during the American Revolution. Even more than the conflict with Native Americans, the war's greatest evils evolved from whites destroying fellow whites—Americans all—which appalled leaders, especially the British, on both sides to a degree not previously seen in this war.

Almost all books devoted to the American Revolution have long rehashed in ever-predictable fashion the same old standard analysis and interpretations that have become exceedingly stale for the last nearly 250 years. And in these popular and widely acclaimed traditional books by first-class authors, what has been most absent have been the stories of the forgotten common soldiers, especially the men of the Southern theater. To a degree that is truly astonishing, they—the most important players in the most overlooked story that made America—have been left out of most traditional historical narratives as if they were unimportant or even nonexistent, and this was especially the case in the war in the South. Consequently, the names, backgrounds, hopes, and fears of these forgotten Patriots of lower- and middle-class status will be explored in detail, especially Irish immigrants and most notably the Scotch-Irish who were truly the forgotten men of the American Revolution, despite their disproportionate and crucial role throughout the struggle.

Consequently, for the first time in a book devoted to a remarkable short campaign in the most overlooked theater of the American Revolution, the experiences of the forgotten common soldiers, who were the anonymous "Sons of the Mountains" and the isolated Southern backcountry, will be told as much as possible.

In walking today through the oak, hickory, and pine woodlands of Kings Mountain National Military Park, which is far off the beaten path and one of the least visited national military parks in America, it is still as pristine as it was on the fateful and bloody afternoon of October 7, 1780. It is quite amazing to realize how this sacred ground in the middle of nowhere was the dramatic scene of the greatest Patriot militia victory of the war and where the tide of the American Revolution was turned in a most decisive way in one of America's darkest hours. Most important, this long-forgotten battle in the South Carolina Piedmont was not a contest between well-educated men, aristocrats of the elite, or revered leaders who had been trained at military. Instead, the all-important victory at Kings Mountain in the sixth October of the war was orchestrated by the inhabitants of the Southern frontier and backcountry and was won by the resourcefulness, faith, courage, skills, and character of the common people.

—Phillip Thomas Tucker, PhD
Central Florida
September 1, 2024

Chapter I

Major Patrick Ferguson's Greatest Mistake and the Bluff That Disastrously Backfired: Threatening the Overmountain Men with Destruction

The stately hardwood trees, especially the towering cottonwoods along the rivers and creeks of the Southern backcountry, were already beginning to turn to their beautiful autumnal colors with the arrival of an early fall in late September 1780. After more than five years of war waged by America's rustic revolutionaries against the might of the British Empire, this was no ordinary autumn in the life of the young United States of America. The fall of 1780 was destined to be the most decisive one to date in the history of the infant American republic, which was battling for its life in a lengthy war of attrition against one of the world's most powerful nations.

To date, the war effort of the fumbling and inept American revolutionaries had proved disastrous, especially in the South after the fall of its most important city of Charles Town (Charleston, South Carolina) on May 12, 1780, and a frustrating stalemate in the North. This stalemate had presented the golden opportunity in 1780 for the British Army to take the initiative in the South, where they envisioned that decisive victory could be won to restore the thirteen colonies back to their "rightful" place in the British Empire.

Only one obstacle now stood in the way of Great Britain achieving decisive victory in the South: the Scotch-Irish people who were Patriots and anti-British to the core, because of the cycles and contours of history that had long been tragic ones in Scotland and Ireland, thanks to generations of British conquerors. A good many searing past and present Celtic memories—especially of the Scotch-Irish who were the majority of Patriot settlers in the South Carolina backcountry and also west of the Blue Ridge—of British conquest in Ireland and Scotland were about to be rekindled by the looming threat of Scotland-born

Major Patrick Ferguson, who was the top lieutenant of Lord Charles Cornwallis now leading the invasion of the South. A capable and talented commander, Ferguson had boldly penetrated deep in the North Carolina backcountry with impunity like invading British troops in the ancestral Scottish and Irish homelands for centuries. Overconfidence (if not hubris), the lack of Patriot resistance, and the desire to organize new Loyalist units had drawn Ferguson ever deeper into western North Carolina like a magnet and ever closer to the remote and isolated Overmountain settlements west of the Blue Ridge Mountains, as part of Lord Cornwallis's overall invasion of North Carolina.

Nestled in a pristine wilderness and lush river valleys of incredible beauty, these remote settlements of mostly Scotch-Irish were full of experienced county militiamen with abundant Indian-fighting skills who were experts in the use of firearms. Virtually every male of age was an experienced militia member of his respective county and possessed a deadly long rifle, which had already proven highly effective in the successful 1776 campaign against the Cherokee. Revealing a recklessness and gambler's instinct for which he was well known, Ferguson had taken an advanced position far to the west—too far and to nearly the forest-covered foothills of the Blue Ridge Mountains—at Gilbert Town, North Carolina, while serving at the far left, or western, flank of Cornwallis's British Army to the east that had invaded North Carolina. With his main force that served as the center of his invading army, Cornwallis had captured Charlotte, North Carolina, on September 26, 1780, after a hot skirmish that had been skillfully conducted by the feisty band of Patriot defenders who were badly outnumbered.

Major Ferguson, a veteran commander who had battled Washington's Continental Army to the north in the past, including at Brandywine, Pennsylvania, on September 11, 1777, where he had been wounded in battle, was now situated farther away from Cornwallis's main force at Charlotte. Clearly, much like Ferguson, Cornwallis was a gambler who was going for broke, after the conquest of South Carolina and Charles Town's fall before mid-1780, which had paved the way to the ambitious invasion of North Carolina: a dangerous situation for an isolated task force deep in the unfamiliar territory of a sprawling land populated mostly by the Scotch-Irish.

At Gilbert Town, beginning to realize that he was out on a limb because he was too close to the Overmountain settlements, Ferguson devised a scheme that he hoped would keep the Overmountain militia at bay in their stationary place west of the Blue Ridge Mountains. He hoped that they would stay there after what Colonel Isaac Shelby, a primary frontier commander from west of the majestic Blue Ridge and of Welsh, or Celtic, descent, had demonstrated in the victory at Musgrove's Mill, South Carolina, on the chocolate-colored Enoree River just after mid-August 1780. All the while, Ferguson continued to perform his mission of guarding Cornwallis's left flank, watching for the irrepressible Elijah Clarke and his Georgians, and raising Loyalist militia in the backcountry. For ample good reason, Major Ferguson was naturally concerned about receiving an attack from the west on his own left flank, because the Overmountain men from the scattered frontier settlements west of the imposing Blue Ridge had crossed the mountains to strike hard-hitting blows in South Carolina during the summer of 1780.

The Scottish major's scheme to eliminate this threatening potential west of the mountains came in the form of a direct threat that was a bold outright bluff: an ill-fated decision that was destined to backfire on him with disastrous consequences, primarily because he had failed to understand his opponent's inherent nature and psychology, Colonel Isaac Shelby's character, and his enemy's predominant ethnic composition, Scotch-Irish, and their traditional defiance in the face of threats, especially from a menacing foreign invader on their doorstep.

As a Scottish aristocrat and professional officer of the British Army dominated by upper-class values and elitist mentalities, Ferguson was unable to appreciate the fact that the Overmountain leaders were the least likely of any men in America to be bluffed by harsh words. In such a situation in a harsh environment in which simple survival of the settlers west of the mountains was based on the laws of nature that were Darwinian in the extreme, Ferguson's decision to issue threatening words were about to strike the rawest of nerves among the Overmountain men. From his comfortable headquarters at Gilbert Town, Ferguson was shortly about to send forth his ill-conceived verbal message to Colonel Shelby, the victor of Musgrove's Mill, South Carolina, in August 1780 and other hard-fought small-scale actions east of the mountains. As events at Kings Mountain would demonstrate, this was the Scottish major's ultimate mistake, because this threatening message "instructed him [the messenger] to inform the officers of the Western officers, that if they did not desist from their opposition to the British arms, and taken protection under his standard, he would march his army over the mountains, lay their country waste with fire and sword."[1]

Indeed, Ferguson's ill-fated message would be most serious, full of devastating intent and the promise to unleash a brand of total warfare on the Overmountain settlements just like Native American warriors, especially because, in the words of Ireland-born Colonel William Hill, "the greatest part of the Tories with him were well acquainted with every gap in the [Blue Ridge] mountain[s], every ford of the rivers or creeks."[2] Clearly, this was no ordinary threat that would be forthcoming from Ferguson's headquarters at Gilbert Town, located just on the other side of the mountains, and one that Colonel Shelby, an experienced Indian fighter and the primary orchestrator of the concept of an immediate forceful response with a hard-hitting preemptive strike, took most seriously. If Ferguson's bluff succeeded, then it would help to ensure that not only would the brash Scotsman succeed in his daunting mission of protecting Cornwallis's left flank, but also all but ensure the overall success of Cornwallis's campaign of invading North Carolina and even farther north in what he and other British leaders, both military and civilian, believed would be the war's most decisive campaign.[3] Demonstrating a degree of wisdom, however, Ferguson was right on target in his growing concern because he was now situated so near to the heavily forested ranges of the Blue Ridge Mountains and the rebels west of the mountains. After all, the Overmountain men had already demonstrated their formidable war-waging capabilities on both sides of the mountains, especially as mounted infantrymen armed with deadly long rifles. With insightful vision, Shelby, coming off his remarkable victory at Musgrove's Mill and understanding how the initiative and momentum must be maintained in 1780 to win the backcountry, had already wisely "proposed that an army of volunteers be raised on both sides of the mountains for the purpose of resisting Ferguson's advance" west and ever-closer to the Overmountain settlements that were isolated and vulnerable.[4]

But Colonel Shelby's timely tactical vision and dream of attacking "the lion in his den" east of the mountains to eliminate Ferguson and any other British leader sent forth by Cornwallis were simply not to be in the summer of 1780, since it had to be delayed because of the harvesting of crops in September upon which the frontier families and communities depended to survive the upcoming winter. However, because Shelby's forward-thinking proposal had been favorably received by other Patriot leaders primarily because of the continued Cherokee threat, the seed had been planted and the wheels were already in motion to create a frontier army of citizen-soldiers from the existing county militias that eventually won the day at Kings Mountain. In fact, Shelby, only twenty-nine and an experienced frontiersman, was already planning to cross the mountains and strike Ferguson's roving patrols after the fall harvest, when all of the necessary work on the settlers' small farms for the upcoming winter had been completed so that he could tap into all available manpower.

Because of the wide dispersal of Colonel Charles McDowell's Burke County, North Carolina, militia command, including those refugees who had fled west of the mountains after their defeat at Cane Creek, North Carolina, which had resulted in his aggressive pursuit, Major Ferguson's daunting mission was now actually beyond his capabilities for a relatively small independent command located too far from the main army. Hence, raising thousands of Loyalist militiamen to compensate for Ferguson's weaknesses was now the only solution. Despite commanding more than a thousand Loyalists, including recent recruits from Gilbert Town and Tryon County, North Carolina, Ferguson was already over his head because of his limited capabilities and vulnerable personal qualities, especially when so near to the Overmountain region. Most of all, this now involved a guerrilla war in which the winning of hearts and minds was crucial: the impossible objective of the British in crushing the revolutionary spirit because it existed deep inside the hearts and minds of a majority of the people of the backcountry, especially in western North Carolina, and simply could not be destroyed, especially among the Scotch-Irish. In fact, at this time in late September, Ferguson was not focused on the main threat west of the mountains, despite his location. He was far more worried about eliminating that persistent threat presented by Colonel Elijah Clarke and his hard-fighting Georgia partisans that consisted of a relatively small band of men. Ferguson continued to hope that he could succeed in intercepting and "cutting off" the Georgian's retreat northwest to the safety of North Carolina's mountains and Overmountain settlements after his defeat when the British had captured Augusta, Georgia, while ignoring the reality of the nearby presence of the Overmountain men just across the mountains: a glaring, inexcusable mistake made by Ferguson. Unfortunately for him, Ferguson had taken his eyes off what should have been his top priority, which played a large role in his undoing at Kings Mountain. Indeed, as fast-paced events shortly demonstrated, he should have been focused on the potential threat to the west because it far outweighed that posed by Clarke and his small band of Georgians.

Characteristic of his fiery nature and natural aggressiveness, Ferguson's movement deep into western North Carolina and pushing through hostile country all the way to Gilbert Town at the picturesque foothills of the Blue Ridge Mountains had been too bold for his own good. The Scottish major had fully realized that nothing could stop him, and he had met with almost no resistance during his push through North Carolina, which emboldened him and made him more confident. In fact, Ferguson seemed to think and act like Clarke's force of diehard Georgians was the only sizable force left in the entire backcountry. Even more, he almost seemed to have a personal grudge against the elusive Clarke, because he was consumed with a burning desire and obsession to cut off the refugee Georgians, who were reported to be fleeing north for the safety of the mountains and the Overmountain settlements.

Worst of all for British fortunes, Ferguson was not interested in winning hearts and minds, because this goal—the key to winning any insurgency from time immemorial—was simply not part of official British policy. Cornwallis's priorities were revealed in his harsh orders issued in the past, helping to make the South Carolina war even more murderous and desperate. Because he was a faithful officer, the Scotsman in a major's uniform had fully embraced Cornwallis's harsh brand of warfare. For example, Ferguson's troops burned and looted wide stretches of the backcountry side to ensure plenty of enemies in his wake; thus making his name infamous to the Overmountain men. The people west of the mountains had already learned shocking details about the savage nature of the war east of the mountains. While Cornwallis demonstrated caution when it came to advancing farther north from Charlotte toward Salisbury and into even more unfamiliar North Carolina territory because of increasing signs of trouble, Ferguson was more eager and aggressive, throwing caution to the wind. The Scottish "Bulldog," who possessed a distinctive Celtic swagger of a privileged aristocrat with the common touch, should not have lived up to his well-deserved nickname as a true dog of war when situated at his Gilbert Town headquarters so far from Cornwallis and support in hostile country, which was populated by so many Scotch-Irish. To be fair to Major Ferguson, he was only the blunt instrument of Lord Cornwallis and King George III, who was known for this hatred of the Irish and Scotch-Irish on both sides of the Atlantic. All the while, British leaders were only repeating the same kind of fundamental mistakes that had fueled popular uprisings in Ireland and Scotland for centuries.

By late September, Ferguson had advanced so far west into the rolling hills of Tryon County that he spent the last days of the month in complacency at his headquarters at Gilbert Town within only a few miles of the Blue Ridge to the west. This picturesque hamlet was located less than fifty miles from the Holston River Valley and the homeland of the Sullivan County militiamen west of the mountains, Colonel Shelby's beloved homeland. He was now within striking range of the Overmountain settlements. At this point, Ferguson needed to be cautious and careful, especially in regard to not doing anything to stir up the hornet's nest in the Overmountain settlements. Instead, the major's roving parties of Loyalist troops were as abusive in Tryon County as they had been in the backcountry during the advance north, almost as if attempting to spark an uprising.

But the ever-unpredictable Ferguson proceeded to do exactly what he should not do at all costs to fulfill his crucial mission when vulnerable at Gilbert Town. Against all good sense and sound judgment for anyone who possessed even a slight understanding of the psychology of his opponent west of the mountains, he proceeded to make the most fateful of decisions. Indeed, like a mistake-prone rookie commander, Major Ferguson made the worst of all decisions in a high-stakes game of bluff in the hope of keeping the recently active Overmountain men inactive by issuing the ill-fated threatening proclamation to them. Ferguson's disguised fear of the Overmountain men in part prompted his decision to play this risky game of bluff, when the stakes were exceptionally high.

To ensure that the Overmountain men received his threatening message "to march over the mountains, hang their leaders, and lay the country waste with fires and sword," Ferguson went out of his way on September 10. He paroled a Patriot prisoner—a distant relative of Isaac Shelby from the South Holston River Valley—to set his harebrained scheme in motion: an impetuous decision that revealed his poor judgment and ignorance of the Scotch-Irish frontiersmen, whose values and sensibilities were opposite to those of the upper-class elite in Great Britain and America's coastal regions.

A lone rider on a fast horse departed the major's headquarters in the western Piedmont and the community's largest house at Gilbert Town. He headed northwest for the imposing Blue Ridge Mountains that dominated the western horizon as far as the eye could see. Without much serious deliberation or Cornwallis's more mature, wiser advice, Ferguson sent his threatening missive with paroled prisoner Samuel Phillips. He was "a distant connection [relative] of mine" in Shelby's words and knew exactly where the colonel of the Sullivan County, North Carolina, militia could be found. On his increasingly exhausted horse, Phillips rode at a brisk pace up the steep trail ascending the imposing mountains as temperatures grew colder. Day after day, he toiled through an uncharted wilderness and rode through the main pass to cross to the west side in today's east Tennessee with Ferguson's threatening message.

Once west of the mountains in the pristine lands of western North Carolina where the rivers flowed southwest through the virgin wilderness, Phillips knew what he had to do to guarantee the most forceful Patriot response. He, therefore, rode directly to Colonel Shelby's home without hesitation. Here, he presented the astounding news of the most outlandish of threats to Shelby—the threatened destruction of the Overmountain homeland with fire and sword. Ferguson had made a grievous error in having singled out Shelby, who immediately thought of only one thing—orchestrating a hard-hitting retaliation calculated to destroy Ferguson. Shelby immediately saddled his best horse after Phillips had presented the shocking news and departed his Sapling Grove home (located near today's Bristol, Tennessee) in the wilderness of the South Holston River country, and headed at a rapid rate straight for the Watauga settlement to the southeast.

Burning with rage at Major Ferguson's sheer audacity in having attempted to scare and intimidate him—which even a good many Native American warriors of multiple tribes had been unable to accomplish for years—Colonel Shelby had already developed a master tactical plan in his head to destroy Ferguson once and for all. He consequently rode straight for the frontier home of Colonel John Sevier, his old Indian-fighting comrade-in-arms and the son of a French Huguenot immigrant who now commanded the Washington County militia of the Watauga settlement. Clearly, these kind of tough western frontier leaders and old Indian fighters simply could not be bluffed or intimidated by an upper-class Scotsman in a red uniform. Shelby and Sevier were frontier kindred spirits—experienced fighters who valued the tactical merits of the hard-hitting preemptive strike—two of the most respected and successful Indian fighters west of the mountains, who were more than a match for Major Ferguson. This, of course, was the very reason that Shelby had decided to hurriedly meet with Sevier and present the boldest of ideas: to cross the mountains with a large force of mounted volunteers and launch an immediate pursuit of Ferguson, seek him out, and destroy him and his command once and for all in a classic preemptive strike.

In consequence, what was in the process of being forged was the resurrection of a truly unbeatable team of Shelby-Sevier and their Sullivan County and Washington County militias, respectively, around which an entire Overmountain and backcountry army was destined to rally in record time. Indeed, what also was about to be reconstituted was Shelby's original heady vision of uniting the frontier militias of Virginia, South Carolina, and North Carolina, including the Overmountain men, and for their popular leaders to work closely together, which he had already wisely first proposed after his astonishing victory at Musgrove's Mill. Like a man possessed because he was convinced that his audacious plan would pay immense dividends, Shelby continued to dash rapidly southeast along a dusty road, which more resembled an Indian or game trail, that had been hewn through the wilderness and was about forty miles distant in the Nolichucky settlement nestled in the pristine Nolichucky River country. Originating in the wilds of western North Carolina, the picturesque Nolichucky River, which meant "rushing waters" to the Cherokee, cut through the high, forested mountains in deep gorges and through today's east Tennessee, flowing southwest toward America's seemingly endless expanse.

The veteran frontier colonel of Welsh heritage knew that the highly effective team of the two hardest-hitting Indian fighters west—or east for that matter—of the mountains had to be resurrected as soon as possible. After all, he had to take Ferguson's threat seriously, because too much was at stake: a free way of life, the blessings of liberty, and the very existence of the vulnerable settlements west of the mountains. Clearly, these Overmountain men, especially an old Indian fighter like Shelby, although young and still in his twenties, and other experienced frontier leaders could never be bluffed by either the most warlike Cherokee or Creek war chief or even the aristocratic Lord Cornwallis himself. Instead, Ferguson's message of imminent destruction of the frontier settlements west of the mountains was guaranteed to prompt the most vigorous of responses because it challenged the manhood of these tough fighting men, who had already conquered not only the wilderness but also the Cherokee to win this land that they loved. It was almost as if Major Ferguson possessed a secret desire of a subliminal nature not to prevail.

All in all, these mostly Scotch-Irish were emotionally, physically, and psychologically hardened by the toughening wilderness experience and years of battling and beating the most powerful tribe in the South, the Cherokee and their allies, the Creeks, who lived farther to the southwest. Any kind of bluff directed at them was sure to have the same effect as throwing a tub of whale oil from New England onto a bonfire. The Scotch-Irish had only survived for so long against the odds on both sides of the Atlantic because they harbored no illusions or delusions whatsoever when it came to their enemies. They eliminated any suddenly emerging threat as quickly and as efficiently as possible. Therefore, Major Ferguson did exactly what he definitely should not have ever done, which was threatening not only the Overmountain men, but also their homes and families with destruction. In the end, Ferguson's bluff ensured that Colonel Shelby would not waste a moment in organizing a most forceful response.

What Ferguson, without much thought, committed in his high stakes game of bluff was a certain recipe for disaster because the naive major, who was the antithesis of a master of psychological warfare, without knowing his opponent's mentality, which is all-important in the art of war, had handed a golden opportunity to the hard-hitting and highly experienced team of Shelby and Sevier. Such threats that had emitted from Ferguson's Scottish old-world mind, which ignored fundamental new-world realities, may have worked with the people of the South Carolina low country or the firearm-short peasants of Ireland or Scotland, as in past centuries. But now there was absolutely no way on earth that this kind of unrealistic plan based on bluff and bluster would ever work with the new-world Scotch-Irish living west of the mountains.

After all, they had only survived because they repeatedly met such threats from Native Americans head-on, turning the aggressor into the vanquished: the longtime tactical formula of the preemptive strike to ensure not only a people's survival, but also for achieving decisive success in wartime to keep possession of the land.[5] Clearly, in his hubris and folly, Major Patrick Ferguson had committed a fatal mistake. His ill-advised "ultimatum to a proud [and mostly Scotch-Irish] people seeking freedom from tyranny and despotism [now] made himself the target of their frustration. Through his words and deeds, Ferguson became the embodiment of everything the American Patriots abhorred."[6]

The Beginning of the Gathering of the Celtic Clans

After the lengthy ride of around forty miles southeast through the wilderness of the Overmountain region, Colonel Isaac Shelby was in for a shock. He was utterly astounded to encounter a festive gathering of friends and neighbors at Sevier's sprawling farm in the Nolichucky River country of Washington

County, North Carolina. A large crowd of frontier families from the surrounding area had gathered for a horse race and a barbecue of a freshly killed steer or hog—a case of enjoying themselves by eating "high on the hog"—at the Sevier farm. As usual, an expert fiddler, perhaps a Black man or Irishman with talent from the Celtic land across the sea, was no doubt present for the festive gathering that included dancing to the ancient Celtic-Gaelic tunes of old Ireland, especially from north Ireland.

This joyous atmosphere and fun-loving ease that dominated a traditional western frontier gathering thoroughly upset Shelby to no end. After all, he fully realized that Major Patrick Ferguson's sword of Damocles was now hanging over the remote frontier settlements, yet waging the necessary war for survival was far from these mostly Celtic people's minds and interests. The combination of Ferguson's threat and the sight of the festive atmosphere at a time when the western settlements in the Overmountain region faced their greatest adversary was truly alarming to Shelby. Consequently, after shaking hands with his old friend Sevier, who was slightly older and clearly saw that his frontier Indian fighting friend of Welsh heritage was highly upset, Colonel Shelby now "vehemently declared that this was a time, not for a frolic, but for a fight."[7]

Obsessed with the thought of destroying Major Ferguson and his Loyalist command, Shelby was so upset that he was fairly "shaking with rage" from the words of Ferguson's threat and the shocking nonchalance of so many Washington County people, who were now in harm's way and acted as if no war existed at all. The two frontier leaders immediately departed the festivities in a hurry to privately discuss the wisest course of action. To establish the central foundation for what was ultimately needed to vanquish Ferguson and his legions of Loyalist Americans, Colonel Sevier could not have been more receptive to Shelby's audacious proposal of almost immediately trekking over the mountains to hunt down Ferguson, despite the distinct possibility of the Overmountain settlements coming under Indian attack once they had departed to serve east of the mountains for an extended period of time. Shelby and Sevier decided to rally their respective militias for a unified effort to destroy Ferguson as soon as possible and with as many men as they could gather together in an emergency situation. On every point, Sevier enthusiastically agreed with Colonel Shelby that now was the time to not only rally the Overmountain men but also to attempt to link with any other Patriots east of the mountains so as to wipe Ferguson out once and for all to forever end the threat to their homes, communities, and families. Fortunately for America's sagging fortunes, Shelby and Sevier had been perfectly shaped for this supreme challenge in defending the vulnerable homeland, ensuring that they saw eye to eye on all matters.

In short order, Colonels Shelby and Sevier also conferred with the revenge-seeking leaders of the refugee North Carolinians, under Colonel Charles McDowell's command, who had fled west of the mountains for safety after their defeat by Ferguson's troops at Cane Creek in Burke County. With plenty of old scores to settle, the refugees readily agreed to unite with Shelby's and Sevier's Overmountain militiamen to wage an aggressive holy war. Even more, Sevier prepared to contact other top North Carolina officers to gain their support, while Shelby embarked upon the vital effort of contacting Virginia militiamen of Washington County, just to the northeast, under the command of Colonel William Campbell, to gain the Virginians' support. As the hard-driving mastermind and prime organizer of this ambitious expedition, Colonel Shelby was in the process of creating the most formidable army of citizen-soldiers ever seen on either side of the mountains in the South. Even if they failed to locate the hated Ferguson east of the mountains, their efforts would not be wasted because they then "would attack whoever they could find."[8] Wasting no time whatsoever, Shelby and Sevier were busily orchestrating the crucial all-out effort to "attempt to surprise Ferguson by attacking him in his camp, or at any rate before he was prepared."[9]

Captain David Vance, a North Carolina militia officer of Scotch-Irish descent and a veteran of Shelby's success at Musgrove's Mill along the Enoree River, described the swift evolution of the vital decision that was destined to change the course of the American Revolution: "Then it was suggested by Shelby, that a sufficient force could be raised over the Mountains, with the assistance from Wilkes and Surry counties [in the foothills and backcountry of southwest Virginia and adjacent to Sevier's Nolichucky River country community on the mountain's west side], to defeat Ferguson. This was agreed to by all officers present [and therefore] The troops were raised without Government orders; each man had to furnish his own provisions, arms, ammunition and horse, and all his equipage without the value of a gun flint from the public; without pay, or expectation of pay or reward [because] They were all volunteers."[10]

Indeed, in one of the war's great ironies, Major Ferguson had set the stage for his own demise and that of his Loyalist command in the most efficient fashion possible by having dispatched Samuel Phillips, the distant relative of Shelby and a paroled prisoner, from Gilbert Town in the most personal of messages whose dark intent was clear and the genesis of the war's most surprising victory at Kings Mountain.[11]

Having learned their lesson from years of Indian warfare of the most bitter nature, Shelby and Sevier immediately rallied the men of their Overmountain communities in Sullivan and Washington counties to defend their frontier settlements by way of a bold preemptive strike. Even more, these two most respected men living west of the mountains harbored no illusions or delusions whatsoever when it came to the enemy and his sinister intentions as threatened, because only one mistake or miscalculation might result in the deaths of themselves, their communities, their families, and all their dreams. Indeed, with so much at stake, they could literally lose everything that they knew and loved; doing nothing to prevent the worst-case scenario was fatal. On the harsh western frontier where survival of the fittest was the supreme law of the land, one wrong move or incorrect decision might result in the complete destruction of the frontier worlds they had created by their own hard work and ingenuity. Fortunately for America, the upcoming bid to destroy Major Ferguson and his command was now in the best of possible hands.

During their personal conference for two days in Washington County, Shelby and Sevier even devised a contingency plan in case of a dire emergency situation, especially if they were defeated east of the mountains. After all, the lives of a good many women and children on the frontier were at stake if they failed or if the Native Americans struck in their absence. In consequence, absolutely nothing was left to chance, because "in the event of failure, with the consequent desolation of their homes, [they planned] to take water, float down the Holston, Tennessee, Ohio, and Mississippi rivers and find a home with the Spaniards in Louisiana."[12]

However, Shelby and Sevier were now entirely focused on conquering Major Ferguson and his Loyalist command until not a trace remained, an obsession second to none. Therefore, the two frontier commanders had issued the call for the Sullivan and Washington County militias to assemble on Monday, September 25, at a well-known place on the Watauga River, Fort Watauga at Sycamore Shoals or Flats. The broad open meadow of Sycamore Shoals, surrounded by forested hills in a most picturesque setting, was where Patriot refugees from east of the mountains had already collected. With horror stories about what they had suffered at the hands of the vengeful Loyalists and British, these North Carolina men from Burke County were experienced members of the militia command of Colonel Charles McDowell and Colonel Andrew Hampton, who had fled to the safety of the Overmountain region. They were now eager for revenge for the many wrongs inflicted on them and their families east of the mountains.[13]

Knowing that he also had to secure the aid of the Virginians, Shelby's careful calculations and sound reasoning continued to be right on target. In his own words: "without the aid of the militia under Col. Campbell's command, I feared that we could not otherwise have a sufficient force to meet Ferguson."[14] Indeed, Colonel Shelby wisely realized that they could not succeed in fulfilling his bold mission and ambitious vision without the large number of Virginians of the Washington County militia from the east side of the mountains in southwest Virginia. Shelby's old post-Musgrove Mill plan of uniting the mountaineers with militiamen of the backcountry to create a formidable group of fighting men from both sides of the mountains now needed to be resurrected in full, because he knew that it was the key for achieving any decisive success over Ferguson and his large command. However, securing Campbell's support would not be easy. The better-educated Campbell was a different kind of man from Sevier and Shelby, who were younger, in an entirely different situation in a different state, while burdened with more community responsibilities, especially in terms of defense, and civil positions. This naturally meant that his views were more locally based, especially because Cornwallis had targeted not only North Carolina but also Virginia for conquest, although Campbell also was a frontiersman and Indian fighter to the core.

Hoping for the best in a desperate situation, Colonel Shelby dispatched his trusty brother, Captain Moses Shelby, with an urgent message to Colonel William Campbell, who had been born in the Shenandoah Valley of Virginia. Campbell commanded the militia of the neighboring Virginia county of Washington located about twenty miles to the northeast of Shelby's Holston River settlement. When Campbell, who naturally had other plans for protecting Washington County, especially in regard to confronting the threat of Cornwallis's push north, refused to comply, Shelby was placed in a serious dilemma. After all, young Isaac Shelby had realized early that it was absolutely crucial to gain Campbell's support. Adequate manpower—older and mature Washington and Sullivan County men with Indian fighting experience rather than rookie teenagers—had to be left behind to guard the still threatened homeland from the Cherokee when they departed on their expedition, which reduced the number of available Overmountain men for the upcoming expedition east of the mountains.

In this emergency situation, Colonels Shelby and Sevier realized that every good fighting man would be needed in the ranks to vanquish Ferguson, knowing that the backcountry boys of the southwest Virginia militia—larger than each of Shelby's and Sevier's command separately but not combined—were as fierce fighters as the Overmountain militiamen. But Colonel Campbell, who was known for his Celtic stubbornness, had just returned home from battling ever-troublesome Loyalists. Focused on defending his own homeland from Native Americans, Loyalists, and the British, Campbell's refusal to unite his forces with the Overmountain men and Colonel McDowell's refugee command of North Carolinians now encamped among the grassy shores of the Watauga at Sycamore Shoals was reasonable under the circumstances. As noted, Colonel Campbell's strategic thinking based on local concerns now had him primarily wanting to oppose the march of Cornwallis's main force north to the Virginia-North Carolina line, where the frontier colonel and his men almost certainly would have been crushed, which would allow the redcoats to secure all of North Carolina.

What could Colonel Shelby now do in such a vexing no-win situation because Campbell had made up his mind? Shelby desperately needed the capable Campbell and his around two hundred Virginia boys, because they would represent the largest single contingent of the entire expedition. Married to Patrick Henry's sister Elizabeth, Campbell was every inch of a Celtic fighter, who had battled Loyalists in North Carolina and Virginia since the summer of 1779. He was the well-established and educated son of a Scotch-Irish immigrant, in his mid-thirties, who had been on the Virginia expedition in Lord Dunmore's War that ended in victory on the Ohio River at Point Pleasant (in today's West Virginia) in 1774, where Shelby had fought with distinction as a young officer. Although twenty-nine, Shelby possessed diplomatic skills and some clout of his own, because he had succeeded his own father, Evan, in April 1780 as the colonel of the Sullivan County militia.

As when he captured the Loyalist bastion in the South Carolina backcountry known as "Thicketty Fort" at the end of July 1780 when the fort's tough-minded commandant had first refused his surrender summons and later changed his mind thanks to a series of clever ruses, Shelby was not deterred in the least by Campbell's curt refusal. As a natural problem-solver and flexible thinker, he had developed a smart solution to the dilemma at Thicketty Fort, which had called for a masterful game of bluff. He had his troops ease closer to the fort and repeatedly maneuver in menacing fashion to present the appearance of far larger numbers than was actually the case, as if preparing to attack. Colonel Shelby's tactical finesse and ruses had worked to perfection. Ignoring the fort commander's first refusal, Shelby then dispatched a second surrender summons to Colonel Patrick Moore with the grim promise of no quarter if refused. Feeling that he had been granted a reprieve from certain death or worse at the hands of Overmountain "barbarians," the unnerved commander had only then agreed to surrender his nearly ninety-five Loyalists. In masterful fashion, Shelby had captured the little fort on Thicketty Creek without the loss of a single man when manpower was in short supply, and not a single Patriot life had been squandered.

Drawing upon this key lesson of backwoods warfare that revealed the importance of flexibility and open-mindedness in the art of war, Shelby once again sent another message to Campbell, who was now far more concerned about fighting his own war protecting his Virginia homeland than joining the Overmountain men on a far-flung expedition. But this time, Shelby smartly placed more emphasis on urgency and how Virginia manpower was desperately needed for succeeding in the daunting dual mission of protecting the settlements from the Cherokee and then attacking Ferguson east of the mountains. This more desperately worded initiative revealed Shelby's own stubbornness and refusal to take no for an answer in a critical situation. For Shelby and Campbell, both of Celtic heritage and known for their hard-fighting ways, the memory of how the British had eliminated the hopes and dreams, especially nationalist aspirations, of generations of Celts in Wales, Scotland, and Ireland was never forgotten by them. As Shelby had envisioned, this time Campbell would be more open to linking his larger Washington County, Virginia, militia with the Overmountain men in one of the most crucial missions of the war. Once again, Shelby demonstrated his considerable skills of persuasion behind the scenes that were so vital for any possibility of success like at Thicketty Fort.[15]

For his second all-important plea to the Virginians, Colonel Shelby once again dispatched Moses Shelby but this time with the mission of visiting Colonel Arthur Campbell, who was the top county lieutenant of Washington County and also William Campbell's cousin and brother-in-law. In this second effort, Shelby had smartly decided to apply a little family pressure on the stubborn Scotch-Irish colonel. Shelby's clever plan worked, and he finally received an affirmative response from the two Campbells, who were now, as of September 22, eager to cooperate with the Overmountain men to save their country. They agreed to link their Washington County militia from the eastern slope of the mountains with Sevier's and Shelby's militias from the wild lands west of the mountains and Colonel Charles McDowell's refugee militiamen, who had been driven out of their backcountry Piedmont world of Burke County, North Carolina. Fortunately for American forces and although not realized by him at the time, Colonel William Campbell, who was fated to die of disease less than a year later in the summer of 1781, had just made his best decision to greatly assist the overall war effort and cause of American liberty by agreeing to make this invaluable contribution.[16]

Then to rally more troops, on September 22, a fast-riding messenger was dispatched from "Colonel William Campbell, who commanded the Washington County, Virginia, militia, to Colonel Benjamin Cleveland of Wilkes County, North Carolina, and who led the Wilkes County militia to [rally to] the plan; and Cleveland was also urged by an 'express' [carried by Colonel Charles McDowell] from [Major Joseph] McDowell [Jr.] to join the 'over-mountain men' on the east side of the mountains [at Quaker Meadows in North Carolina, to the southeast and near the modern day community west of Hickory, North Carolina] with as large a force as he could raise."[17] Significantly, the Campbell leadership clan had previously worked together with Colonel Cleveland in their war against the British and the Loyalists east of the mountains, becoming an experienced team of tough fighters: a boon to Shelby and Sevier and their Overmountain men from North Carolina.[18] Not long after Campbell made his momentous decision to join the expedition to attack Ferguson with his Virginians, he issued his call for his Washington County boys to assemble at a grassy pasture known as Dunn's Meadow in today's Abingdon, southwest Virginia. Located in the Great Appalachian Valley and nestled between the middle fork and the north fork of the Holston, Abingdon served as the county seat.[19]

As subsequent events demonstrated, especially the behind-the-scenes necessary actions of a political and diplomatic nature that paved the way to victory at Kings Mountain and proved that he was far more than a hard-nosed fighter, Colonel Shelby was the timely master organizer and administrator of the creation of a formidable frontier army of volunteers in one of the hours of greatest crisis for America: the antithesis of the one-dimensional and simplistic Indian hater (contrary to today's general assumptions and popular beliefs about Shelby, who has faded from the pages of history) from the most remote backwoods. A model frontier and popular leader, Shelby was an intelligent and insightful visionary blessed with a host of skills. For such reasons, Shelby had earlier served as a capable officer of the army's commissary department on the frontier, when his many talents had been recognized by higher authorities. Earlier in this war, he had already been in charge of sending supplies to the Continental Army, an expedition directed against northwestern tribes of the Ohio Valley, and other frontier expeditions against Native Americans: an invaluable set of well-honed skills and experiences that were destined to pay high dividends in the Kings Mountain campaign, which he skillfully orchestrated with equal ease and competence. Governor Thomas Jefferson had also appointed Shelby to supply the 1779 expedition led by his father, Colonel Evan Shelby Sr., against the Chickamauga warriors of the Cherokee nation near today's Chattanooga, Tennessee. This was no small challenge, because "not one cent could be advanced by the government and the whole expense of the supplies and transportation was sustained by his own individual credit." As usual, Shelby had been forced to rely on his own considerable talents, ingenuity, and resourcefulness for successfully outfitting a large expedition of frontiersmen, who had eliminated the most diehard warriors of the Cherokee Nation, the Chickamauga, during the most challenging of wilderness campaigns.[20]

By any measure at this crucial time in September 1780, Colonel Shelby had become a master organizer and administrator blessed with a host of special talents that made him the ideal man for the job of orchestrating an overpowering response to meet Major Ferguson's threats. In fact, given the special demands and disadvantages of the frontier war and challenging western environment, Shelby might have been described as a logistical genius by what he was able to accomplish both in the past and present. Without formal military training or an education at a military school or academy, he mastered the complex art of understanding how to supply a large expeditionary force bound to cover long distances through the wilderness by relying on his own talents even better than the much-touted Cornwallis, although his lordship possessed all of the advantages of the army's well-organized bureaucratic system and England's finest educational systems, both civilian and military. Most of all, frontier flexibility and innovative adaptability were the keys to success outside of traditional military channels and bureaucratic networks, making Shelby a master at this art. Shelby had long relied on unorthodox ways to secure what was needed by the frontiersmen for far-flung expeditions deep into the wilderness, like the Kings Mountain campaign.

Indeed, in the most challenging of environments in a backward region with few resources, Shelby had to be exceptionally resourceful, which called for drawing upon whatever could be secured in record time by almost any means with his own ingenuity and frontier savvy. Although never trained in the quartermaster or logistical fields like British officers, Shelby possessed an uncanny ability to improvise and innovate in key situations: the forgotten success story that played no small, but often overlooked, part in the upcoming success at Kings Mountain. Shelby played the leading role in not only securing additional manpower in regard to Colonel Campbell and his Virginia men, but also acquiring adequate supplies, including a small herd of cattle, which was food on the hoof for the large concentration of volunteers: all achievements that required considerable expertise and experience. Of course, the idea of providing more than a thousand expeditioners with beef was necessary because there was now no time to slaughter cattle, especially for making nutritious beef jerky from sun-dried meat, when time was of the essence, if they were going to catch Ferguson before he withdrew back to Cornwallis or received sizable reinforcements. But the herd of cattle was eventually abandoned out of necessity during the rough and long ride over the mountains, because it slowed the relentless push south, after having provided much-needed nourishment on the march.[21]

But the irrepressible Colonel Shelby, who excelled in overcoming obstacles in his own unique way, was also the masterful wizard behind the scenes in regard to securing finances for the lengthy expedition across the Blue Ridge and into the Piedmont east of the mountains. On the isolated and remote frontier, money was virtually nonexistent, largely because settlers, mostly lower-class individuals, had already spent their savings on purchasing land. After having failed to borrow funds from the usual sources because money, both Continental currency and specie, was scarce on the remote frontier, Shelby and Sevier requested funds for the expedition from the only person and single existing source on the frontier with any available cash—John Adair, the tax collector of Sullivan County. After having recently convinced Sevier,

Campbell, and other leaders to join the upcoming expedition east of the mountains, Colonel Shelby was able to convince Adair, who had been born in County Antrim, Ulster Province, north Ireland, to exceed his authority and responsibilities by providing full support. Of course, it helped when Shelby, who was known far and wide as a man of his word, pledged his personal fortune for a possible reimbursement in the future. Adair, a true-blue Patriot who spoke with a distinctive North Irish brogue, solemnly answered the audacious request: "Colonel Sevier, I have no authority by law to make that disposition of this money. It belongs to the impoverished treasury of North Carolina, and I dare not appropriate a cent of it to any purpose. But, if the country is overrun by the British, liberty is gone. Let the money go too. Take it. If the enemy, by its use, is driven from this country, I can trust that country to justify and vindicate my conduct. Take it."[22]

During this crisis situation, Sevier's self-sacrificing patriotic wife, Catherine Sherrill-Sevier, or "Bonnie Kate," shortly told her husband in regard to the all-important mission to vanquish Ferguson, "Here, Mr. Sevier, is another of your boys who wants to go with his father and brother Joseph to the war."[23] Most important, Adair's timely contribution, a total of $12,735, proved invaluable in supporting the men with an adequate amount of black powder, lead for bullets, and other precious supplies. The two colonels solemnly "pledged themselves to see it refunded or its use legalized by an act" of the North Carolina legislature: a solemn trust that was fulfilled in the end. But in essence and with finesse, "Shelby and Sevier [had successfully] raided the county treasury that yield just enough money" for the expedition's seemingly endless needs.[24]

At breakneck speed along a narrow wilderness road, Colonel Shelby then rode back northwest to the Holston River country and began raising around 240 militiamen of Sullivan County. In the Celtic clan tradition of generations of fighting men from Ireland, Scotland, and Wales, the Shelby family of Welsh antecedents was well represented in the ranks. Isaac's younger brothers, Evan Jr. and James, both served on this expedition. James was a major of the militia, while Moses, his teenage brother, held a captain's rank. In addition, Isaac's uncle John Shelby, now a major, was more than ready for a fight like his two sons, David and Thomas, teenagers who also served in the ranks. Private Thomas Shelby was only fifteen, while David was two years older.[25] With the life of his community at stake, Colonel Shelby described how he had become so incensed to provide the key catalyst for all his efforts, because he had been informed that if he "did not surrender [then Ferguson] would come over the mountains and put him to death, and burn the whole country [and] no further taut [was now necessary] to arouse [his] patriotic indignation [and] to make the effort to raise a force, in connection with other officers, which should surprise and defeat Ferguson."[26]

But, of course, it was much more that galvanized the Overmountain men than just a few words from Major Ferguson. Most of all, it was the frontier and patriotic spirit that had risen to the fore, because America's fortunes had reached a new low and now each citizen-soldier must make his own personal sacrifice for the good of the new republic. After all, the very "people Ferguson was trying to intimidate were exactly the kind of people that such demonstrations of bravado failed to impress. The population of this area of [western] North Carolina were predominately Scotch-Irish, who lived on the bleeding edge of what could loosely be described as civilization. They [had] carved a living out of the forests, fought Indians, survived illness and lived their lives free from outside interference or outside help. They detested authority that was not of their own making or choosing and looked on all forms of government with a decidedly skeptical eye."[27]

The Forgotten Personal Feud That Altered America's Destiny

Clearly, Colonel Shelby was so highly motivated, if not obsessed, with the thought of destroying Ferguson also because this had become a very personal kind of war between the two Celts.

The antecedents of the upcoming Kings Mountain success were rooted in disaster. After having won his sparkling success at Musgrove's Mill along with Georgian Elijah Clarke, who was a diehard popular leader of the Deep South, Shelby knew that he had to take forceful action after having learned how General Gates and his ill-fated army had been annihilated at Camden in mid-August 1780. At that time, the victors from the Overmountain region had only then belatedly realized that they were in a bad fix, because Major Ferguson was almost certainly in pursuit of them, after having been emboldened by the one-sided Camden victory. Quite simply, the situation had become extremely dangerous for Colonel Shelby, because "Ferguson could easily bring his entire force [upon them because] he might have started the day before. If he had and if they delayed [at Musgrove's Mill after the astounding victory that had been hard-won then] they would be cut off and destroyed."[28] Consequently, the victors of Musgrove's Mill had suddenly become the prey during the dash west toward North Carolina in a desperate race to reach safety, while risking getting cut down by slashing sabers and annihilated by Ferguson's cavalrymen. All the while, Shelby had kept everyone moving onward at a fast pace to outdistance Ferguson's pursuit, after the sharp clash at Cedar Springs, South Carolina, during hot summer weather. Shelby and his men had finally reached the safety of Gilbert Town, North Carolina, and then the frontier settlements situated just beyond the imposing parallel ranges of mountains covered in dense forests. Shelby's rapid withdrawal had covered more than a hundred miles through the backcountry before safety was finally reached. By this time, the Scottish major "was turning into his personal enemy [and by September 1780, Shelby] intended to get Ferguson."[29]

Ironically and in symbolic fashion, this personal feud that existed between Shelby and Ferguson revealed a larger feud between King George III and the Scotch-Irish and the ancient one between Celtic peoples and England that had lasted for centuries. For these reasons, which now especially applied not only to the war in the South but also the Kings Mountain campaign, "Those pestiferous Presbyterians, they are always in unrest and will be until they are wiped out."[30]

Meanwhile Colonel Shelby and other Patriot commanders continued to make all the right timely decisions to set the all-important pattern of exceptional leadership demonstrated throughout the course of the Kings Mountain campaign. In contrast, Major Ferguson, the consummate professional military man whose life had been long devoted to the military arts, continued to make key mistakes of a grievous nature on the eve of engaging in his most important and last battle. While at Gilbert Town, Ferguson still remained so supremely confident that he continued to diminish his strength in bad decisions that were destined to come back and haunt him on October 7. First, the overconfident Ferguson began to issue furloughs to his men. For reasons unknown, he continued this ill-timed policy for an extended period. Then, to deprive himself of more good fighting men, he was destined to then "send out a battalion-sized foraging party (around 200 men) on the [Saturday] morning of the battle [which] seriously weakened his combat power at a critical moment."[31]

And Major Ferguson's attention to his crucial mission on Cornwallis's west flank and situation in a hostile land was too often almost certainly diverted, especially at night, by the two women at headquarters who were said to have been his attractive mistresses, Virginia Sal and Virginia Paul—if so, then this was a classic case of sex befuddling the mind of still another military man while on active campaigning, which was a development only too common among high-level British leadership in America. Despite bestowing Ferguson with the key mission of guarding and protecting his west end, or left, flank during the ambitious push into North Carolina and being an excellent judge of the strength and weaknesses of his top lieutenants, Lord Cornwallis was destined to prove eerily prophetic when he wrote about Ferguson to Lieutenant Colonel John Harris Cruger, who commanded at the forward outpost of Ninety-Six, South Carolina, located directly south of Gilbert Town, on July 3, 1780: "I am afraid of his getting to the [western] frontier of N. Carolina and playing us some cussed trick."[32] Of course, this "cussed trick" was destined to be played out in full during the crucial showdown at Kings Mountain on the decisive afternoon of October 7, 1780.

Chapter II

A Special Place in the Watauga Wilderness Called Sycamore Shoals

Along the fast-moving, clear waters of the Watauga where it grew shallow passing over rocky shoals, and where this wild river in the wilderness became a stretch of white water in a picturesque valley surrounded by blue-hazed mountains, lay the broad grassy meadow of Sycamore Shoals. Nestled amid the Great Smoky Mountains that had once been the sacred homeland of the Cherokee, this special place located amid the hardwood forests was known for its pristine beauty. It had long served as a gathering place for America's foremost settlers on the western frontier because of the comforting presence of Fort Watauga—Sycamore Shoals and Sycamore Flats. Daniel Boone had departed Fort Watauga with the first hopeful settlers bound west for the promised land of Kentucky. Thriving pioneer settlements now filled the fertile and picturesque river valleys of the Watauga, Nolichucky, and Holston Rivers. The beginning of Overmountain life in the wilderness—a land they believed God had chosen for them—was a relatively recent development, beginning in the 1760s. Then, in 1772, the settlers created the Watauga settlement in the fertile Watauga River Valley, after the largest party had been earlier led to this "Land of Canaan" by James Robertson and John Sevier.[1]

Incredibly, the gathering of the Celtic clans at Sycamore Shoals in the pristine Watauga River Valley rapidly came together at the right time and place for the stern challenge of eliminating the ominous threat of Major Patrick Ferguson. The great gathering took place in this beautiful setting on Monday, September 25, when the nights had already begun to cool off and the leaves on the hardwood trees, especially the stately cottonwoods lining the banks of the Watauga River, were already beginning to turn a lighter color as the first trees to do so in early fall, after most of the work for the farm harvest had been completed. This most timely gathering of hundreds of armed citizen-soldiers, who had answered the call and volunteered on their own in this crisis situation, was almost a minor miracle that had been fueled by a sense of desperation and urgency that had surged across the frontier on both sides of the mountains like electricity. These eager volunteers, who meant business and were in deadly earnest, of the county regiments of Sullivan (Shelby) and Washington (Sevier) from the Overmountain region were determined to protect themselves and their families with their lives. Most important, they possessed good horses, healthy and fresh, which made the early rendezvous date at the shoals possible for these hard-riding volunteers from across the sprawling untamed frontier west of the mountains.

For this vast assembly of mostly young militiamen along the Watauga, whose clear waters followed the timbered base of the Blue Ridge Mountains, Colonel Shelby had ridden southeast from the Holston River country with 240 men, following the Watauga River through the wilderness and all the way to Sycamore Shoals, while Colonel Sevier's band of 240 warriors from the Nolichucky River country rode east and reached the rendezvous site in the nick of time: nearly five hundred experienced mounted riflemen, who were determined to protect their beloved homeland at all costs. Already encamped in the grassy fields in the picturesque valley of Sycamore Shoals, Colonel Charles McDowell's 160 militiamen from east of the mountains in Burke County, North Carolina, were determined to regain their homeland, after they had been driven away in a tragic exodus.

At this time, the North Carolina boys were without their beloved Winchester, Virginia-born Colonel McDowell, who was still absent. He had prudently ridden back across the mountains to rally additional men from the North Carolina backcountry with the news that the much-touted Overmountain men were shortly to be on the way to the east side of the mountains. When least expected, Colonel Arthur Campbell, who had been born in Virginia's Shenandoah Valley in 1743, suddenly rode into Sycamore Shoals to a chorus of cheers with another two hundred riflemen from southwest Virginia. All in all, this was a true gathering of the Celtic clans of old like in the beautiful Scottish Highlands to confront invading redcoats, when nationalist freedom fighter William Wallace had led a fiery Celtic people's rebellion against the British. However, Arthur Campbell also shortly returned home because the southwestern Virginia frontier was also under the threat of Cherokee attack like the Overmountain settlements at this time. Clearly, the upcoming pursuit of Ferguson was risky business on the east side of the Blue Ridge Mountains, and everything had to be accomplished quickly because the Cherokee would almost certainly attack if they discovered that most manpower of the Overmountain and southwest Virginia settlements was absent and a long way from home.

The lengthy trip across country for the golden opportunity to catch Major Ferguson by surprise and destroy his command had been extremely difficult for Colonel Campbell's Virginians. They had departed the frontier of southwest Virginia—located just northeast of the Holston River country where Shelby's citizen-soldiers lived and farmed the land in the creek and river valleys—and had ridden south to cross the Virginia-North Carolina line to reach the chosen meeting place of Sycamore Shoals amid the uncharted wilderness. But the most reliable and experienced backbone of the assembled task force was Shelby's and Sevier's Overmountain men who possessed lethal long rifles and plenty of Indian-fighting experience. Symbolically, one of the rallying cries that had united the Overmountain men of Colonel Sevier's Washington County militia regiment at Sycamore Shoals based on Colonel Shelby's deadline date for the rendezvous of Monday, September 25—that had drawn fighting men from far and wide and their friends and families to see them off—had been "Rally for Chucky Jack and freedom!" as the popular John Sevier was known as "Nolichucky Jack."[2]

Here, along this rocky, shallow stretch of river where the wooden walls of little Fort Watauga stood in protective fashion, the various groups of militiamen, who looked like anything but legitimate soldiers in the traditional sense, had faithfully answered the call. Never before had such a large gathering of citizen-soldiers been seen west of the mountains. As mentioned, a good many relatives, including older men now past their prime but who could still defend the homeland, now had their key assignments if the Cherokee struck, and close friends and family members from the frontier settlements had accompanied their boys to Sycamore Shoals to encourage them on their all-important mission. Playing their part, mothers and daughters had packed provisions for the lengthy journey of the young volunteers. They had also sewn and mended hunting clothes and other apparel now worn by the eager citizen-soldiers, who felt that they were about to embark on an exciting adventure. Disguising the fact that these men were going to war and some of them would never return, the festive mood along the picturesque Watauga was much like at a popular barbecue, a traditional Irish market day, or a day-long wedding on the Emerald Isle, when the entire community traditionally turned out to dance Irish jigs and hear the lively tunes played by fiddlers.

Old Indian fighters, including French and Indian War veterans, and friends who had led their Overmountain men in vanquishing the Cherokee were now together once again. This gathering consisted of an elite force of experienced frontier fighters, who were masters in the art of Indian warfare. These were highly motivated fighting men, from their county regiments from both sides of the mountains, who had gathered as one in the valley along the Watauga, and they were itching for a fight. As mentioned, Shelby led the Sullivan County militia of around 240 men and Sevier led around the same number of Washington County militiamen. The third group of frontier militia consisted of Colonel Charles McDowell's around 160 militiamen, who had fought Loyalists in a bitter civil war in the Piedmont and were already encamped at Sycamore Shoals, after having fled from North Carolina east of the mountains to safety west of the mountains to escape persecution, including death by hanging. And thanks to Colonel Shelby's persuasive skills, Colonel William Campbell and his two hundred Virginians from the Old Dominion backcountry lands situated just northeast of Shelby's home of Sapling Grove were destined to make an invaluable contribution. All these men, in hunting clothes and wearing long hair, were now ready for action in what they deemed as the most righteous of crusades to vanquish evil in the hated form of a swashbuckling Scottish major.[3]

These revered frontier colonels, Shelby, Sevier, and Campbell, were the finest militia leaders in the land, and they always led by example, especially in battle where the bullets and arrows flew thickest. These popular leaders and their men were ready to strike a blow to eliminate a serious threat, as they had when they vanquished the Cherokee in 1776 and 1779: the old frontier tactical formula that called for the preemptive strike to catch the enemy by surprise.

Here, in late September when the first early autumn cool had already begun to descend upon this picturesque valley, surrounded by green hills of virgin timber, along the south bank of the Watauga River where the spring-fed waters grew shallow at Sycamore Shoals, more than a thousand fighting men and perhaps as many friends, neighbors, and relatives gathered in a carnival-like atmosphere to fill the grassy meadow. In this natural pasture along the river that had already begun to turn slightly brown in its cloak of an early autumnal hue, a formidable frontier army took shape and fused together. As if to mask the seriousness of the upcoming effort to destroy Ferguson, this festive gathering was made livelier by frontier fiddlers playing music that echoed the traditional melodies and revolutionary tunes of old Ireland, while others played popular tunes with "Jew's harps" and an occasional banjo. They knew that Major Ferguson and his Loyalist command had terrorized the South Carolina and then the North Carolina backcountry and now threatened to inflict the same evils west of the mountains. Barely more than half of the gathered citizen-soldiers at the shoals were Overmountain men, while the remaining fighting volunteers hailed from the rugged backcountry. Large numbers of women and children were about to see their fathers, sons, and brothers off to war, while knowing that they might never return to the broad pasture around Fort Watauga in this lifetime.[4] However, some volunteer citizen-soldiers had no relatives to see them off. Burt Moore, who had been born in Halifax County, Virginia, was a refugee from the war that had fiercely raged east of the mountains in the South Carolina backcountry. Indeed, "when Ferguson overran the backcountry, he crossed the mountains and joined Cols. Sevier and Shelby" in time for the dramatic showdown at Kings Mountain.[5]

By this time, the desire was so strong to defend the endangered homeland that a feeling of confidence was in the air after every able-bodied man of the settlements had turned out with his own rifle or musket, provisions, best horse, and complete fighting gear, which was light like during Indian campaigns far from home.

Catherine "Bonny Kate" Sherrill-Sevier, who was married to Colonel John Sevier, knew what was now at stake—their lives, future, and very existence—if Major Ferguson carried out his ominous threats to destroy the Overmountain homeland. While Colonel Sevier and his son Joseph, eighteen, prepared to ride out to face Ferguson and his well-trained Loyalists, the feisty "Bonnie Kate" (Bonnie is a Celtic name for an attractive, fair woman) appeared with son James, who was only sixteen. On her own and instead of being concerned about her personal protection if the Cherokee once again struck the Watauga Settlement when the fighting men were east of the mountains, she delivered James to his father with no tears in her eyes and the words "that would have honored a Spartan mother" before the famous showdown at Thermopylae in 480 BC by imploring her husband to take James with him to vanquish Ferguson and his men.[6]

At this time, the fear of a Cherokee strike was alive and well. "We had received information that they [the Cherokee] were planning an attack upon us in the course of a few weeks," in Colonel Shelby's words.[7] In consequence, a good many older men would have to be left behind to protect the settlements just in case. However, the unbridled hatred of Ferguson, who was known for raiding the homes of Patriots and wreaking havoc, was so intense and his threats taken so seriously that launching a far-flung expedition east of the mountains was well worth the risk: a desperate situation that explained why so many Patriots had congregated with considerable enthusiasm at Sycamore Shoals for the express purpose of destroying Ferguson as quickly as possible, while knowing that the Indian threat was as real as that posed by the Scotland-born major.[8]

Most important, this ad hoc expedition formed at the last minute was led by experienced men who knew the key to success: the old concept of divide and conquer, which emphasized the necessity of striking and defeating one opponent at a time before they had the chance to unite and then be insurmountable. Most of all, the frontier wisdom of the preemptive strike was adhered to almost instinctively by these experienced men, who had been primarily focused on the art of daily survival in a hostile land and natural environment for as long as they could remember. The hundreds of volunteers who had gathered in the pastures of Sycamore Shoals on September 25, 1780, possessed the most important ingredients for eventually winning victory: a good horse for swift movements, a trusty rifle that had long put food on the table, plenty of black powder, a strong religious faith to persevere against the odds, and courage to face seemingly insurmountable challenges and hardships of an almost unimaginable nature. Contrary to romantic myth, it was not a spontaneous uprising of a band of fighting frontier farmers who united as one in this emergency situation. Instead, the men who prevailed at Kings Mountain were for the most part veteran Indian fighters and members of a highly effective and well-organized militia system (a county system in North Carolina and Virginia and a comparable district system in South Carolina) that had been born in defending the homeland from Native Americans, which had created an experienced and highly skilled soldiery and talented officers.[9]

Like the frontier settlements situated west of the mountains, each South Carolina district and North Carolina and Virginia county possessed its own militia regiment as a primary defensive force, because centers of government on the East Coast were located so far away. These were not infantry regiments in the traditional sense, but highly mobile strike forces of basically light cavalry that bestowed a significant tactical advantage when it came to the stern demands of frontier warfare, especially in swiftly covering long distances to catch the enemy by surprise. As noted, every man on the frontier and in the backcountry needed not only his long rifle, but also a good horse to protect the vulnerable homeland and families: an almost unbeatable tactical combination as the Native Americans had discovered.[10]

Late arrivals from North Carolina and Colonel Arthur Campbell, who had worried that an insufficient number of fighting men had gathered at Sycamore Shoals, had ridden to the Watauga settlement with a force of around two hundred additional Washington County militiamen. Most of all, Campbell was a savvy survivor and seasoned leader. At age fifteen, Arthur Campbell had been captured by a Wyandotte raiding party and carried around six hundred miles northwest to the British outpost of Detroit on Lake Michigan, where he had remained a captive of the tribe for two years before escaping. He departed the great gathering at Sycamore Shoals in late September to return east of the mountains to galvanize a defense for fear that the Cherokee and Creek were about to strike his own homeland.[11]

The timely support of the hard-fighting Campbells, including Ensign Robert Campbell who was the younger brother of Colonel Arthur Campbell, of southwest Virginia had been crucial for future success at Kings Mountain, as Colonel Shelby had fully realized from the beginning. He wrote how everything had hinged on gaining the support of the Virginians, who had the largest contingent of troops, to boost numbers sufficiently to have a decent chance of defeating Ferguson. In Shelby's words:

> It surely cannot distract from the merits of Col. Campbell, that this expedition was not set on foot by him, but by others [primarily Colonel Shelby]. He lived in Virginia, in a state of comparative security, and was preparing to aid his own State when she should be invaded [by Cornwallis and other British leaders, including Brigadier General Benedict Arnold on the Chesapeake Bay]. We lived in North Carolina, a great part of which State was prostrate before the British arms. We were nearer to the enemy, and we were threatened. We, therefore, determined to anticipate the invasion and vengeance mediated against us, and to strike the first blow. To do this effectively, we asked for and

> received the aid of the nearest County [Washington County, Virginia] in a neighboring State.[12]

The memories and lessons of history were never far from the minds of realistic-thinking and practical men like Shelby and especially the Scotch-Irish. At this time, the typical mindset of the Scotch-Irish along the frontier on both sides of the mountains was a faithful adherence to the backwoods philosophy of striking your enemy first before he struck you, as the Cherokee had learned the hard way. And they had never forgotten how:

> Many of us and our forefathers left our native land [of Ulster Province, north Ireland], considering it as a Kingdom subjected to inordinate power, and greatly abridged of it liberties; we crossed the Atlantic, and explored this then uncultivated wilderness, bordering on many nations of Savages, and surrounded by Mountains almost inaccessible to any but those very Savages, who have incessantly been committing barbarities and depredations on us since our first seating the country. These fatigues and dangers we patiently encountered, supported by the pleasing hope of enjoying those rights and liberties . . . denied us in our native country [and we now enjoy] liberty and property with which God, nature, and the rights of humanity have vested us.[13]

Consequently, the Overmountain and backcountry men were determined not to surrender what they believed God had blessed them with in America. They had carved out homes for their families and had already fought to defend them against the British, Native Americans, and Loyalists. These highly motivated citizen-soldiers wore no uniforms or even badges of rank, but they possessed war-fighting skills and a diehard resolve in great abundance. What the fighting men at Sycamore Shoals now wore instead of any kind of uniform had been handmade by wives and daughters on family wooden spinning wheels: coarse homespun clothing and hunting shirts called linsey-woolsey, which had been made from wool sheared from small flocks of family sheep and the crop of flax that they had grown in the fields. Woolen hunting shirts of the Overmountain and backcountry men were fringed around the edges, which allowed for rapid drying of wet clothing after a rainstorm or crossing a river, when campaigning far from home. These volunteer citizen-soldiers also wore wool breeches and leather leggings like Native American warriors and donned loose and light wool coats for protection when the nights grew cooler.

Instead of the fashionable tricorne hats of the aristocratic class of the eastern lowlands and the North and South Carolina Loyalists of Ferguson's command, these citizen-soldiers wore practical broad-brimmed felt hats that protected their heads and necks from rainfall and a hot, blazing sun. And instead of wearing a revolutionary cockade or plume like Patriots to the east, the frontiersmen from west of the Blue Ridge wore eagle feathers, fox tails, or the tails of white-tailed bucks in hats angled in a jaunty manner. Their long hair was tied behind their backs in a long queue that hung down the back of hunting shirts in the popular frontier style of the day. Some backcountry and Overmountain men wore fur hats, including Private John Warnock, who had been born in Ireland in 1757 and was a savvy veteran of two campaigns against the Cherokee. Like some of his comrades at Sycamore Shoals, Warnock wore a "racoon hat." Besides a sharp hunting, or scalping, knife that had been made from a frontier forge by a capable local blacksmith, these men also carried the weapon of choice adapted from Native Americans because of its utility and practicality in both peace and war—the iron- and steel-bladed tomahawk with a sturdy hickory or oak handle.[14]

As noted earlier, with the call to arms there was no time to slaughter beef and make jerky by drying strips of meat for the long journey to hunt down Major Ferguson and destroy him. However, these volunteers had brought rations of bread or parched corn with them for nourishment because it was light and easily carried in small pouches or even pockets. It is not known, but some men almost certainly carried apples or dried fruit taken from rock-lined cellars in the ground at home and tasty cornbread baked by wives, sisters, and mothers. But whatever provisions they brought with them from home, these meager rations would not last during the long journey across the mountains and into the lower lands of the Carolina Piedmont. Consequently, for the most part, the citizen-soldiers now concentrated at Sycamore Shoals and about to embark on their greatest challenge would have to live off the land as best they could during a long, grueling journey full of uncertainties, because nothing was more important than moving light and fast in the pursuit of the Scotland-born major and his Loyalist task force, which were now sitting ducks east of the Blue Ridge.[15]

And, of course, there was no longer a state government to provide tents, ammunition, food, clothing, or shot from the supply depots of the Continental

Army located many miles away. In consequence, these men would have to sleep on the ground in their hunting clothes with only a light woolen blanket to cover and protect them from the autumn rains, cold nights, and heavy dews of early fall in the Blue Ridge Mountains. Most important when campaigning against Native Americans, British, and Loyalists, experienced militiamen often smartly slept with the firing mechanisms of their rifles and smoothbore muskets tucked between their legs for protection against rainfall and heavy dews that dampened everything except the fighting spirit of the Overmountain and backcountry men.[16]

In many ways and by any measure, this was the most remarkable and unorthodox force of Patriot fighting men ever collected not only in the history of the American Revolution but also in the annals of American military history. These citizen-soldiers, in one officer's words, knew that they would serve and fight "without pay, or expectation of pay or reward, even to the amount of a Continental dollar depreciated to 800 to 1 [and as volunteers], they were under no compulsion to go, but each man in advance consulted his own courage, well knowing he was going to fight before his return," if he ever returned at all.[17]

The Overmountain and backcountry volunteers fortunately possessed plenty of black powder, which often meant the difference between life and death—like being a good shot with a reliable rifle—on the western frontier when battling enemies that seemingly came from every direction. The American Revolution had been originally sparked partly by British leadership attempting to deny black powder reserves to the New England patriots, which had led to the first clash of arms at Lexington and Concord, Massachusetts, on April 19, 1775. At this time, the black powder capabilities of the non-industrialized thirteen colonies were nearly zero, while England, a manufacturing nation in the first phases of the Industrial Revolution, possessed seemingly endless means of creating gunpowder like other basic instruments of war. Therefore, British military leaders had first relied upon the strategy of nipping the revolution in New England in the bud by confiscating powder reserves, including storehouses of the king's black powder. After all, the crushing of the Irish and Scottish people's Celtic rebellions against England in centuries past was far easier because of the lack of black powder, firearms, and munitions of the insurgents, who were doomed in consequence.[18]

The volunteers at Sycamore Shoals were most fortunate when it came to their own supplies of black powder. Mary McKeehan Patton, of Celtic heritage, won well-deserved recognition as having "made [the Battle of Kings Mountain] even possible" by having manufactured the large reserves of black powder that supplied the expedition.[19] Mary McKeehan Patton was a true heroine and one of the forgotten authors of the remarkable Patriot victory on October 7, 1780. Mary's knowledge of black powder-making had been early gained from her enterprising father, David Patton, in England, before the family immigrated to Pennsylvania in the 1760s. Mary and her husband, who was also in the powder-making business, prudently moved west of the mountains and out of harm's way when the revolution was brewing and about to erupt in full fury. Here, they established a black powder mill on a fast-flowing stream to supply the Overmountain settlements not only for their defense, but also for taking the war to the British and Loyalists east of the mountains. The Patton family produced a high-quality and fine grade of black powder that sold for $1.00 a pound. The Patton black powder mill provided an estimated five hundred pounds of black powder that fueled much of the fire power from the mostly long rifles of the Overmountain men at the Battle of Kings Mountain.[20]

In overall terms, Mary McKeehan Patton's timely contribution was invaluable, ensuring that the Patriots from west of the mountains possessed plenty of black powder at the moment of truth at the end of first week of October. Unfortunately, this had not been the case with Colonel McDowell's band of partisans who had sought in vain to defend their native homeland of Burke County, North Carolina, on the east side of the mountains with only limited supplies of black powder against Major Ferguson's invaders, who had easily overwhelmed them.[21]

Paying invaluable dividends, the hardworking Mary "supplied the partisan army [bound for Kings Mountain] with 500 pounds of gunpowder that she personally prepared. This was a risky endeavor because of not only the inherent dangers of mixing gunpowder, but also since British authorities had deemed it illegal. Sweating over a large cast iron kettle, Mary's difficult and meticulous labors filled the Patriots' powder horns with high-quality, fast-burning gunpowder."[22] Of course, full powder horns of hundreds of zealous volunteers meant nothing if each man did not possess plenty of lead balls in his leather or deerskin shot pouch. Private Leonard Hice, who served with his fellow Virginians of Colonel Campbell's command, would enter the Battle of Kings Mountain "with 100 bullets and after the battle missed sixteen," which were fired as rapidly as possible before he fell with multiple wounds.[23]

The Most Lethal Widow-Maker in the Land—the Pennsylvania, or Kentucky, Long Rifle

However, it was far more than an ample supply of black power and lead balls that was destined to play a key role in winning the day at Kings Mountain. To greatly enhance combat capabilities and prowess, the Overmountain men carried long rifles, the hunting weapon of choice to put food on the table and eliminate Native American threats, and not smoothbore muskets like most backcountry Patriots.

While the Patriots of the low country were mostly armed with smoothbore muskets, the most technologically advanced and lethal firearm, the Pennsylvania, or Kentucky long rifle—sleek, lengthy, graceful and elegant—was the most deadly small-caliber weapon of the Overmountain men and of the backcountry men to a lesser extent. Distinguished by an octagonal barrel with spiral grooves, or rifling, the long rifle, unlike a flintlock musket like the British "Brown Bess," was an especially deadly weapon at long range. These magnificent long rifles were light and ideal for carrying over long distances, especially in the upcoming long-distance pursuit of Ferguson. This magnificent weapon was known as the Kentucky Rifle, which was a misnomer because most of these long rifles were made in Pennsylvania, not Kentucky, which was a thinly settled backwater far to the west since shortly before the Revolutionary War years. The long rifle was produced by master gunsmiths on both sides of the mountains with loving care and skilled workmanship. The British and Loyalists, of course, painfully learned the fundamental lesson about the lethality of the long rifle, which came as a great shock, because they were convinced that the .75 caliber Brown Bess—the principal flintlock musket of the British Army during the eighteenth century—was a superior weapon, but only if used with the lengthy socket bayonets. However, this smoothbore weapon was limited because of its inaccuracy and short range. Especially at long range, the Brown Bess was vastly inferior to the weapon of choice on the frontier, the graceful long rifle. After all, this fine weapon of master craftsmanship could take off a squirrel's or turkey's head in the hands of an experienced settler to avoid damage to the meat bound for the family's kitchen table. This frontier weapon was deadly at two hundred yards and even at three or four hundred, when fired by an expert marksman.

Compared to the long rifle, the Brown Bess was notoriously inaccurate at more than 150 yards, while the long rifle was accurate in firing a small-caliber round ball of lead or pewter at long distance. Even volley firing by dense British formations of well-trained regulars often produced minimum results, including hitting no one at all in some cases. Even more, the Brown Bess was stocky, heavy, and cumbersome to load, costing precious time in the heat of battle. And it lacked something extremely important that seriously hampered its accuracy, the notable absence of which almost certainly raised howls of laughter among the sharpshooting frontiersman—the lack of a rear sight. Of course, the long rifle possessed a blade sight near the barrel's end and a rear sight not far beyond the firing pan of the flintlock to ensure great accuracy in the hands of a skilled shooter.

Talented German gunsmiths were the forgotten backwoods mechanical geniuses behind the creation of the long rifle. An amazing technological revolution had resulted from the gradual evolution over time of the German Jaeger or hunter rifle, which led to the creation of a distinctive frontier masterpiece. These skilled gunsmiths were indeed miracle workers when it came to creating masterful firearms. On the western frontier, German immigrants and those of German descent (sons and grandsons) were the majority of these artful makers, including Mathew Roesser, but also Anglo-Saxons such as William Henry and the Hawkins family of Dutch origins. In the beginning, these innovative gunsmiths had created something special from the Jaeger rifle in the rustic log gun shops in the remote valleys and hills of western Pennsylvania before the American Revolution: the Pennsylvania long rifle. Other well-known German makers of the long rifle included such skilled men as John Moll, Peter Brong, Jacob Newhardt, John Lassler, Daniel Kliest, Frederick Zorger, and others who have been forgotten by history with the passage of time.

This superior firearm technology had been first brought to America by enterprising immigrants not only from Germany but also from Austria and Switzerland. Masterful gunsmiths in the Lancaster region, west of Philadelphia, had provided more of these legendary rifles than anywhere else in America, and it was here that the greatest number of Pennsylvania long rifles were produced for the longest period of time. These versatile German gunsmiths in the Lancaster area first developed the novel concept of the "grease pad" technique for loading small-caliber firearms. The Overmountain men used a small piece of fabric or deerskin dipped in bear grease to wrap around the small-caliber lead bullet for an easy fit (the ball was slightly smaller than the barrel's caliber) for more easily ramming the ball down the lengthy barrel: a guarantee of more accurate firing, thanks to the barrel's spiral rifling, than a smoothbore musket without rifling, while also saving precious time, which was crucial in the heat of battle.

Naturally, after moving south from Pennsylvania with the flowing tide of migrants, these newly arrived gunsmiths had opened up their businesses in the backcountry and along the frontier on both sides of the mountains, continuing the tradition of creating beautiful rifles with sleek and graceful stocks, long barrels, and carefully selected wood, mostly maple but also cherry, black walnut, and applewood, stained dark to present the most appealing appearance. The Bean family, father and sons, of the Watauga settlement built beautiful long rifles that were eagerly sought by the settlers. The elder Bean had moved across the mountains from Virginia in 1768 or 1769. But these innovative western gunsmiths did not duplicate the Pennsylvania long rifle; instead they added their own personal touches and flourishes that led to the creation of what became known as the "Tennessee rifle" and the "mountain rifle."

This accurate weapon of choice was ideal for the mounted riflemen of the Sullivan and Washington County regiments. Indeed, the long rifle was a perfect match for the relentless push west and battling enemies regardless of color or race and in the elimination of threats, from Native Americans to Major Patrick Ferguson and his Loyalists, because it was light with its small caliber and sleek design. The superior rifle's long barrel provided a sighting radius that guaranteed its legendary lethality and often meant the difference between life and death. For such reasons, the deadly Pennsylvania long rifle became "as part of each patriot as was his good right arm." When Kentucky was first settled in 1774 by Virginians and Carolinians just before the outbreak of the American Revolution, the favored weapon of the frontier gained a new name: the Kentucky rifle. The long rifle also possessed the name of its original maker, Jacob Dickert of Lancaster, Pennsylvania; most of the Overmountain men carried this lethal weapon with them at Sycamore Shoals and into the fighting at Kings Mountain. Then and even today, the long rifle has become known as the Deckhard rifle, which is a corruption of Dickert. According to existing sources, the so-called Deckhard rifle was second to none in regard to overall quality and accuracy. The long rifle possessed the potential to prove invaluable in winning the day if these frontiersmen eventually located Major Ferguson and his Loyalist command of Provincial regulars and Carolina militia, especially on a timbered battlefield on rugged terrain, where they could rely on the superior advantages of the long rifle and natural cover combined with Indian warfare tactics to overcome the best British conventional tactics: an unbeatable combination that ultimately prevailed at Kings Mountain, the most ideal of situations.

Each common soldier also carried a small handmade bullet mold to manufacture round bullets of small caliber by the melting down of lead strips or the family's pewter plates and cups. Homemade hinged bullet molds, less than six inches in length with the two small halves held together by a single wooden peg at one end, were small, having been made of locally carved soapstone, which was also light.

In the end, the famous long rifle was destined not only to win the day at Kings Mountain, but also to play a large role in winning the war in the Southern backcountry against the British and Loyalists to the east and the Native Americans to the west. In contrast to generations of nationalist historians who have long maintained that it was the moral superiority of the idealistic concepts of personal liberty and lofty republican principles that were the keys to Patriot victory, it was actually the technical superiority of the long rifle that ultimately carried the day and won the struggle for the Southern backcountry, where the war was ultimately won for good. Of course, the Battle of Kings Mountain provided the best example of this undeniable reality. The harsh frontier experience, Darwinian in every way on both sides of the mountains, had created an extremely hardened professional killer, who was second to none in delivering severe punishment by way of the day's most technologically advanced weapon. And it was the long rifle that was destined to unmercifully slaughter a large number of Loyalists in record time at Kings Mountain to ensure the critical victory that reversed the course of the American Revolution.[24]

Highly skilled gunsmiths on both sides of the mountains ensured that weapons, both smoothbores and long rifles, were in excellent working order for the fighting men who defended their isolated rural communities with their lives. For instance, near the Blue Ridge Mountains in western North Carolina, the Gillespie brothers, of Scotch-Irish descent like most of their customers, were some of the most respected gunsmiths and long rifle makers in their backcountry region.[25] In a striking paradox, the Winchester repeating rifle has long been acclaimed by generations of American historians as the gun that won the West and fueled America's expansion to the Pacific's shore after the Civil War. However, historians have overlooked how it was the long rifle that turned the tide of the American Revolution at Kings Mountain to allow that historic push to the sea to fulfill a national destiny of the American people.[26]

However, many backcountry men at Sycamore Shoals possessed smoothbore muskets, which were made more deadly by the use of "buck & ball" rounds (one large caliber ball and several buckshot of a small caliber) for a shotgun-like effect, especially at close range. And some citizen-soldiers, like James Collins, carried fowling pieces that fired buckshot of a smaller caliber than the traditional "buck & ball."[27] The gathered men at Sycamore Shoals were about to embark upon the long journey to Kings Mountain with high hopes and only a bare minimum of supplies. For the long trip to the east side of the mountains, they carried everything that they needed on their person or hung from leather saddles of their favorite mounts in a logistical system on horseback. Older men, such as leading officers, wore leather boots if they could afford them. However, most of these citizen-soldiers, especially the Overmountain men, wore moccasins for comfort and for easing silently through the forests. Some younger men, especially the teenagers, of limited means were destined to fight barefoot, which was the case of Private Thomas Young, and wore saggy manes of long hair, which was the popular style of the frontier, that made them almost look like Native American warriors.[28]

Ironically, no soldiers in all of America were held in greater contempt by the British than the crack fighting men of the Overmountain region, despite their formidable and lethal qualities that had already been long demonstrated against Native Americans. But this gross underestimation of the heightened capabilities of the frontier citizen-soldiers, especially the Scotch-Irish who British leadership, including Ferguson, considered the "dregs of mankind," had more to do with matters of class, race, and societal views rather than combat prowess—a fatal mistake made by the British. Major George Hanger of Lieutenant Colonel Banastre Tarleton's British Legion reflected the typical British mindset about this mysterious foe from west of the mountains: They knew practically nothing about life in the backcountry. When the aristocratic Hanger, who was amazed that "you might travel sixty or seventy miles, and not see a church," attempted to learn more from the freedom-loving inhabitants of an isolated cabin in the South Carolina backcountry by asking, "Of what religion are you?" he was astounded by the curt no-nonsense response: "Religion does not trouble us much in these parts."[29]

Hanger expressed his utter contempt by concluding in no uncertain terms how this "race of men are more savage than the Indians and possess every one of their vices, but not one of their virtues." Clearly, the utter British contempt of the Overmountain men, who were viewed as a "set of mongrels," could not have been greater.[30]

In the end, these were the kind of endlessly derided common men of the most humble origins who would defeat Ferguson in one of the most one-sided and decisive victories of the American Revolution. In perhaps the greatest irony of the Battle of Kings Mountain, Major Ferguson, who was known as "the best rifle shot in the British Army," was destined to be vanquished by these much-maligned Overmountain and backcountry men, whose skills with the deadly long rifle far surpassed what Ferguson or anyone else in the highly professional British military establishment, which was considered the finest in the world at this time, could possibly imagine.[31]

Reverend Samuel Doak's Inspirational Sunday Benediction on September 26

Here, on the early morning of Tuesday, September 26, the second day at this rendezvous site in the picturesque valley of the clear waters of the Watauga, the festive atmosphere of the large gathering of fighting men and their families, friends, relatives, and neighbors at Sycamore Shoals finally lost its Irish market day and carnival-like atmosphere. Family members were saying heartfelt goodbyes to the militiamen, who were about to mount up and ride off to war on a true epic journey that covered today's four states of Tennessee, Virginia, North Carolina, and South Carolina. However, just before they departed on their odyssey across the formidable Blue Ridge Mountains, a strange silence suddenly fell over the large crowd gathered together at Sycamore Shoals. People instinctively ceased talking when Reverend Samuel Doak, wearing a solemn look, suddenly made his appearance.

The Virginia-born Reverend Doak was the revered preacher of the Watauga settlement that consisted of hundreds of rustic log cabins. He stepped forward and prepared to speak as if about to give a Sunday morning sermon. Looking grave while wearing a long frock coat of black, the outsized respect for religion and men of God in general, especially if they were Presbyterians, also gave the sudden eerie silence a special air of spirituality and reverence that descended over Sycamore Shoals.

Just under 1,400 citizen-soldiers bowed their heads in anticipation of the inspirational words that they were about to hear, after dropping to their knees in respect to God and Doak, as if this setting in the grassy river bottom was the open air of an outdoor church. This revered Scotch-Irish man of God was no backwoods cracker or circuit rider as was usually the case on the remote frontier, especially west of the mountains. Instead, Doak was a graduate of New Jersey's Princeton University and a product of a cultured and sophisticated world. By this time, all was ready for the departure from Sycamore Shoals because the men had instinctively gotten up before daylight on this Tuesday morning to make final preparations for the long ride across the Blue Ridge Mountains.

Meanwhile, the women had earlier cooked breakfast of venison, pork, and beef, and this food had already been packed in the saddlebags or leather pouches of the volunteers. In addition, a supply of parched cornmeal, when mixed with water, would provide some nourishment for the militiamen during their lengthy journey east of the mountains. Instead of relying on the army commissary department that was nonexistent in this ad hoc task force, each man basically served as his own commissary department.

Reverend Doak was the only Scotch-Irish minister and Presbyterian west of the mountains and the spiritual voice of the largely Scotch-Irish communities along the Holston, Watauga, and Nolichucky Rivers. In past sermons, he had long made biblical analogies between the plight of settlers west of the mountains in having to face fierce Native American enemies and the ancient Israelites in facing Godless barbarian tribes in their own struggle to retain possession of the Promised Land of Canaan and the sacred privilege to worship one God. With the traces of his Scotch-Irish brogue from north Ireland, Doak was about to preach to the largest number of assembled people that he had ever seen from both sides of the mountains. Thinking ahead, Colonel John Sevier had asked his favorite Presbyterian minister to speak to the great throng of fighting men to instill the proper moral and spiritual guidance to these militiamen, who were fighting not only for their homeland and families, but also their God.

In the crisp autumn air while bright morning sunshine illuminated the expansive meadow that lay beside the Watauga River, thirty-one-year-old Reverend Doak prepared to speak heartfelt words of faith with the promise of victory during this time of crisis. Appropriately, the Scotch-Irish man of God knew that he would be speaking to a largely Presbyterian soldiery at Sycamore Shoals. The eyes and attention of Colonel Isaac Shelby's and Colonel John Sevier's Overmountain men, Colonel McDowell's Burke County boys, and

Colonel William Campbell's citizen-soldiers from the backcountry of southwest Virginia were concentrated on Reverend Doak. Symbolically, Shelby, Sevier, McDowell, and Campbell were all Presbyterian elders of the church that they loved as much as their pristine homeland.

The Augusta County, Virginia-born Doak had been transformed by the wilderness experience west of the mountains, after having shared the dangers and hardships with the settlers since arriving west of the mountains around 1778.[32] Reverend Doak was now thinking about the common Israelite farmer-turned-holy warrior leader named Gideon from ancient biblical days, when the Israeli people faced a comparable crisis that had threatened their existence. In liberating his Hebrew people to ensure a long life for ancient Israel, he had raised an army of his "Valiant Three Hundred" Jewish fighters, pitifully small in numbers and without experience, but high in moral courage and faith in God. Gideon had organized these Hebrew citizen-soldiers, not unlike the men of Kings Mountain in fundamental ways, to fight the vastly superior might of the heathen Midianite army to defend the "Promised Land." Doak knew that an all-powerful God would assist in leading them to victory, and he realized that it was important for the assembled men to be reminded that a loving God was now on their side and would be beside them on their holy mission to vanquish Major Ferguson and his command.[33]

By this time, Reverend Doak decided to focus on the wise words found in Judges 6 and 7 of the Holy Bible for his upcoming solemn prayer for victory. He recalled how Gideon had been chosen by God to deliver his people, because "the children of Israel did evil in the sight of the Lord [and] So the Lord delivered [them] into the hand" of their enemies and they had been forced to live in the mountains like the Overmountain men.[34] The Midianites had repeatedly attacked the Israelites' croplands until the ancient Hebrew nation became "greatly impoverished because of the Midianites, and the children of Israel cried out to the Lord." To save his chosen people, the Lord sent an Angel to Gideon while he was threshing wheat in the sun-baked fields of ancient Israel, saying, "The Lord is with you, you mighty man of valor!"[35] Then, the Lord spoke to Gideon to comfort him in preparation for the arduous task that lay ahead: "Surely I will be with you, and you shall defeat the Midianites as one man," and so these words proved true by the heroic actions of Gideon's Valiant Three Hundred, who were the best warriors out of thousands. Against the odds, they had then reaped a dramatic victory with a surprise night attack on the sizable

Midianite encampment that contained vast numbers of lethal warriors who lusted for Hebrew blood and Israel's destruction, after first blowing trumpets loudly at once on every side of the enemy's position and shouting, "The sword of the Lord, and of Gideon!": the righteous war cry that routed the enemy and led to the subsequent slaughter of the Midianite hordes.[36]

Despite never having spoken to such a large crowd in his entire life, Doak knew that nothing was more important than instilling greater faith in the ultimate victory among these young men and boys who were about to go to war, especially those youngsters who were about to engage in their first battle. Most of all, the dignified Presbyterian reverend realized that many of these citizen-soldiers would never return to their beloved families and river valleys. In stirring words spoken with an Irish brogue since he was the son of Ulster Province immigrants, while he raised arms toward the heavens in invoking God's blessings, Reverend Doak finally spoke on the early morning of September 26, 1780. This inspirational sermon was never forgotten by the men who hung on Doak's every word:

> My countrymen, you are about to set out on an expedition which is full of hardships and dangers, but one in which the Almighty will attend you. The Mother Country has her hands upon you, these American Colonies, and takes that for which our fathers planted their homes in the wilderness—OUR LIBERTY. Taxation without representation and the quarters of soldiers in the homes of our people without their consent are evidence that the Crown of England would take from its American Subjects the last vestige of Freedom. Your brethren across the mountains are crying like Macedonia unto your help. God forbid that you shall refuse to hear and answer their call—but the call of our brethren is not all. The enemy is marking hither to destroy your homes. Brave men, you are not unacquainted with battle. Your hands have already been taught to war and your fingers to fight. You have wrested these beautiful valleys of the Holston and Watauga from the savage hand. Will you tarry now until the other enemy carries fire and sword to your very door? No, it shall not be. Go forth then in the strength of your manhood to the aid of your brethren, the defense of your liberty and the protection of your homes. And may the God of Justice be with you and give you victory. Let us pray. Almighty

> and gracious God! Thou hast been the refuge and strength of Thy people in all ages. In time of sorest need we have learned to come to Thee—our Rock and our Fortress. Thou knowest the dangers and snares that surround us on march and in battle. Thou knowest the dangers that constantly threaten the humble, but well beloved homes, which Thy servants have left behind them. O, in Thine infinite mercy, save us from the cruel hand of the savage, and of the tyrant. Save the unprotected homes while fathers and husbands and sons are far away fighting for freedom and helping the oppressed. Thou, who promised to protect the sparrow in its flight, keep creaseless watch, by day and by night, over our loved ones. The helpless women and little children, we commit to Thy care. Thou wilt not leave them or forsake them in times of loneliness and anxiety and terror. O, God of Battle, arise in Thy might. Avenge the slaughter of Thy people. Confound those who plot for our destruction. Crown this mighty effort with victory, and smite those who exalt themselves against liberty and justice and truth. Help us as good soldiers to wield the SWORD OF THE LORD AND GIDEON, Amen.[37]

As one, the bowed men answered in a spontaneous unleashing of emotion that echoed across the picturesque river valley, "the sword of the Lord and of our Gideons."[38] After responding in unison to Reverend Doak's solemn prayer that inspired one and all, the men of the mountains and backcountry then revealed their fiery fighting spirit when they raised their own war cry that echoed across the valley of the Watauga.[39]

Most important, the men now placed their faith not only in Reverend Doak's inspirational words of prophecy that promised assistance from God but also their trusty long rifles and their well-honed Indian fighting skills. Clearly, in strictly moral terms, this was a holy war in which they were determined to bring God's wrath down on the head of Major Patrick Ferguson and his Loyalists. Ferguson, despite his high rank in the British Army, was now viewed as little more than a common criminal—a contemptable horse thief or murderer—who wore the fancy red uniform of a British major. In the minds of the Overmountain men and as Reverend Doak had emphasized with his inspiring words, Ferguson was also much like an ancient pagan Midianite leader, who Gideon and his small band of ancient Hebrew farmers-turned-warriors had vanquished long ago because God was on their side. To the thinking of the Overmountain men and from what they had learned of the Loyalist outrages, murders, and criminal activities, including the systematic looting of Patriot homes and murder of prisoners east of the mountains, Ferguson was nothing more than a Godless invader and "blatant criminal."[40]

In a striking paradox and despite the frontier leaders including "men of some education, many had only the most distant notion of the war's political aspects. An appeal to ride south and die for something called the United States would have fallen on deaf ears, but when these thousand men [heard the inspiring words of Doak's] ringing sermon on the biblical tale of Gideon's people rising up and defeating their oppressors," the moral message of faith was warmly embraced. After all, in "many a frontier cabin the Bible was the only book; men who could not have quoted a line of Thomas Paine's *Common Sense*, men who knew nothing of the Declaration of Independence, had no trouble identifying themselves as actors in a contemporary biblical epic."[41]

These frontier people were extremely devout, and they had long looked to God for deliverance rather than to any man or government—partly because their daily lives on the frontier were so challenging, even in peacetime. With the belief that God was with them, these rough-and-tumble citizen-soldiers with hardened hearts for the enemy now kissed and hugged loved ones in tearful farewells. They mounted up, and as far as the eye could see, a lengthy column of citizen-soldiers rode southeast along the banks of the Watauga River. They continued southeast, climbing ever higher up the towering height of Yellow Mountain in the Blue Ridge, crossing the spring-fed waters of Little Doe River and passing through Doe River Gorge on September 26. The trekkers on their righteous mission to save their endangered homeland moved faster on their long journey after slaughtering the balking cattle, which had slowed up the march, to provide fresh meat: a timely decision that would unleash them from all logistical connections and restraints to increase the speed of their journey across the mountains. The sojourners felt their breathing come harder at this high altitude as they trekked around twenty miles on the first day.

Then, on Wednesday, September 27, the nearly 1,400-man task force, commanded by their respective colonels leading their militia regiments, pushed past Mount Fork on the left, or east, and Roan Mountain, which was located southeast of Fort Watauga and topped with snow. Beyond the mountains ran the Nolichucky River, on the right, or west, farther southeast and roughly parallel to the trekkers. These men—perhaps the most motley army in American history—wore buckskin civilian clothing, hunting shirts, and heavy linsey-woolsey coats or blankets for extra warmth at high altitudes. After several days in the saddle, the citizen-soldiers, now distinguished by a thin growth of beard from having no opportunity to shave in a day when the clean-shaven look was popular even on the frontier, had become perspiration-stained and grimy from their physical exertions.[42]

Ensign Robert Campbell, of Colonel William Campbell's Virginia command and the colonel's brother, penned in his diary how "no provisions were taken but such as each man could carry in his wallet or saddle-bags."[43] While rising to imposing heights of five thousand to six thousand feet through the mountains, which were covered in virgin hardwood timber of a breathtaking wilderness, the Overmountain men were reminded of the pristine beauty of this magnificent land—something well worth fighting and dying for—which they believed that God had created expressly for them. Riding in thoughtful silence along the forested Indian trail that cut through the wilderness and could be barely ascertained with the naked eye, no joyful whistling or singing of songs erupted along the lengthy column of riders because the mood remained serious and solemn like at a funeral.

These volunteers, including a good many teenagers, had plenty of time to marvel at the sheer beauty of these mountains and pristine high country meadows that surrounded them in an autumnal shroud of light brown and early fall colors, while they ignored their weariness and steadily rode onward: the clear mountain streams and spring-fed creeks, full of rainbow trout, cascading down over boulders in dramatic waterfalls; tall, virgin timber that kissed the blue skies of the remarkably pure air of the mountain's high altitude; the refreshing cool of the early autumn afternoons that grew so cold at night that a light frost formed in these pristine high places; the grassy meadows, including those covered in colorful mountain flowers, nestled in the rugged mountains; parts of this country never seen before by man, neither whites nor Native Americans; and, most of all, the promise of this beautiful land and what these mountains symbolically meant to them—living as free men far from a fumbling central government in Philadelphia and controlling their own destiny and futures. The endless series of high ridges that lay before them seemed to beckon each man onward toward an unknown personal destiny. They knew that Major Ferguson and his command lay somewhere in the wide river valleys of the sprawling Piedmont far below them somewhere to the east.

On September 29, the men descended the commanding Blue Ridge in two columns along old Indian trails—one easing through McKinney's Gap and the other through snowy Gillespie Gap, about halfway between Roan Mountain to the north and Quaker Meadows to the south. From there, they could see the Catawba River's green valley below. The descent from the imposing mountains was precarious, with only a single-file column of horsemen able to descend through rugged, sharp ravines filled with tall, virgin timber. From Gillespie Gap—named after an early Scotch-Irish pioneer like McKinney's Gap—they continued south toward the fertile pasturelands of Quaker Meadows, which lay ninety miles to the south, in two separate columns for safety's sake, just in case one column was ambushed.

Quaker Meadows and Colonel Sevier's Loyalist Deserters

In two groups on September 30, the frontier and backcountry men of the task forces followed the clear waters of the Catawba, riding on each side of the river during the relentless push toward Quaker Meadows. After continuing southeast past Paddy Creek that flowed southeast and had been named after an early Irish settler and located just south of Gillespie Gap, the trekkers then rode east until they reached the picturesque setting of Quaker Meadows, North Carolina, after journeying five days through the mountains from Sycamore Shoals. This pristine place located on the upper waters of the Catawba River near today's Morganton, Burke County, North Carolina, was situated about forty miles northeast of Gilbert Town. Major Ferguson and his men were last known by the sojourners to have been at their westernmost forward base at Gilbert Town, which served as the seat of Tryon, North Carolina. Everything had gone relatively well on the journey until an ad hoc muster revealed that two of Colonel Sevier's Washington County militiamen, who were secret Loyalists and knew the exact course of the task force's route, had deserted from the encampment atop Yellow Mountain in a bid to warn Major Ferguson about the new threat. Therefore, Patriot leaders, who now had reason to fear a possible ambush by Ferguson's alerted men, had prudently taken more obscure routes through the mountains that the deserters did not know about.

After a five-day journey through the wilderness into an "atmosphere of summer mildness," in the words of Ensign Robert Campbell, the Patriots finally found an opportunity to rest and gain shelter from the falling rain on September 30 in the broad, grassy fields of Major Joseph McDowell Jr., who owned Quaker Meadows and commanded the Burke County men. The McDowell family home was located deep in the North Carolina backcountry under the Blue Ridge's shadow. McDowell, therefore, was known as "Quaker Meadows" McDowell to separate him from his politician-cousin of the same name, Joseph "Pleasant Garden" McDowell. Located south of the mountains and just north of the fast-flowing headwaters of the Catawba River, Quaker Meadows was a fine farm, including a wide stretch of grazing lands nestled amid a virgin wilderness.

However, it was not the sheer beauty of Quaker Meadows—a natural oasis in the seemingly endless forests—that was important, because the sprawling pasture land of this well-developed farm was another key rendezvous site like Sycamore Shoals. Here, the trekkers were greeted and welcomed to Quaker Meadows, including a generous offer to use the fence rails for firewood, by Major McDowell. The McDowell family was a hard-fighting Scotch-Irish clan like so many other Celtic families living west of the mountains. But more important, around 350 North Carolina militiamen from Surry County, under Major Joseph Winston, and Wilkes County, under Colonel Benjamin Cleveland, were encamped on McDowell's fields at Quaker Meadows, which was named in honor of an early pacifist pioneer, to unite with the newcomers. These were no ordinary fighting men. The Wilkes County militiamen were "the hardly followers of that fierce and blood-thirsty fighter, Colonel Benjamin Cleveland, 'Old Roundabout,' who called themselves 'Cleveland's Bulldogs,' the stalwart riflemen of [Brigadier General Griffith] Rutherford under Colonel Andrew Hampton, and the flower of the militant citizen shop of Surry [County, North Carolina] led by a born leader of men, a cousin of Patrick Henry, Colonel Joseph Winston."[44]

Colonel Cleveland's nickname described his considerable girth that failed to translate into the stereotypical jovial and merrymaker type of commander. The war-hardened Cleveland possessed a well-deserved reputation as a notorious loyalist killer and an especially brutal one who showed no mercy or pity. Of course, the Loyalists had other sobriquets for Cleveland that were much less flattering. Because he was also an old Indian fighter with hard-hitting ways, the Cherokee likewise no doubt possessed an even less flattering nickname for the ruthless Cleveland. Born in 1738, Colonel Cleveland was six and a half feet in height and weighed as much as 350 pounds. With little education that was typical of frontiersmen and hunters of the Yadkin River country, Cleveland was beloved by his men of the Wilkes County, North Carolina, militia. He was a natural leader and professional killer whose immigrant father had migrated from the North Riding of Yorkshire, England.

Ironically, Major Joseph Winston from Surry County, North Carolina, likewise possessed Yorkshire roots in old England, while having considerable Indian fighting experience going all the way back to service as a ranger during the French and Indian War. At this time, a lead ball from a distant battle with England's enemies was still in his body, which failed to slow Winston's exertions in leading his Surry County boys during the Kings Mountain campaign. Like Cleveland, Winston fought Loyalists with the same intensity as he had battled Native Americans during the French and Indian War, because they were the enemies of his people, and race and skin color were not serious considerations, as so often assumed today, in a basic struggle for survival.

Like his hard-fighting Bulldogs from the backcountry, Colonel Cleveland now had no trace whatsoever of any love for King George III or anyone who favored the Crown, especially if he was an American, which was a double curse to his way of thinking and deserved harsh retribution. He relentlessly pursued Loyalists like the Overmountain men pursued white-tailed deer or turkey through the forest to then place on the dinner table except that he had hanging on his hate-filled mind.[45]

The rotund Cleveland also possessed a hot temper that often erupted. However, he was best known for his undying hatred of Loyalists that was most often expressed by his own swift brand of frontier justice, relentlessly hunting down and "quickly dispatching his opponents," especially by hanging from the highest tree.[46] In no uncertain terms, Colonel Cleveland described Major Ferguson to his men as "Your enemy and the enemy of mankind."[47] For such reasons and as he would shortly demonstrate in full at Kings Mountain, Cleveland was a perfect "Terror of the Tories," especially in the Yadkin River country.[48] Hardened from the dual frontier and Indian fighting experiences, Colonel Cleveland was not the only seasoned Loyalist killer who had evolved into a popular leader of note. Equally ruthless and cold-hearted when it came to his country's enemies, especially if they were fellow Americans, Colonel William Campbell was known far and wide as "the bloody tyrant of Washington County" for his extremely harsh dealings with the Loyalists that included the most popular form of administrating frontier justice, which was hanging Tories high from a sturdy oak limb.[49] Clearly, these were some exceptionally tough and hardened frontier leaders, who had already vanquished the Cherokee warriors and a good many Loyalists in their home area, who were about to descend upon Major Ferguson and his Loyalists in a righteous rage, which had been simmering and building up for years. Ferguson had seriously underestimated the combat qualities and capabilities of the men who he held in such contempt and low esteem.

Frontiersmen from the Backwoods

Leading 450 South Carolinians, including the veterans of his Little River Regiment, was Colonel James Williams, who was destined to join the task force at the Cowpens on October 6 during the long trek to strike Ferguson a lethal blow. In what had become a very personal war, he was itching to deal a measure of frontier justice to Ferguson and his command for having invaded his home and abused his family. As he penned in an October 2 letter to Major General Horatio Gates, of the exciting news about the uniting of the Overmountain and backcountry clans: "And this Moment another of my Expresses is arrived from Cols. McDowell and Shelby: They were on their way near Burk[e] Court House [Burke County, North Carolina], with 1500 brave Mountain Men, & Col. Cleveland was within 10 miles of them with 800 Men, and was to form a Junction with them this day [and] I expect to Join them tomorrow, in pursuit of Col. Ferguson, and, under the direction of Heaven, I hope to give a good account of him in a few days."[50]

A homespun frontier army of Overmountain and backcountry men had seemingly emerged out of thin air, which ensured that they were about to catch British leadership by surprise. Later comments by the British revealed the utter astonishment at the emergence of this ghost army from some of America's most remote corners. However, many enemy voices, especially those of Major Ferguson and his men, were never recorded because they became the ultimate victims of this latest popular backwoods uprising that had mysteriously erupted out of nowhere so suddenly. In an October 24, 1780, letter, an incredulous Lord Francis Rawdon, who commanded at Camden, wrote in utter amazement how "a numerous army now appeared on the frontier, drawn from Nolichucky, and other settlements beyond the mountains, whose very names had been unknown to us."[51] In no uncertain terms, Lieutenant Colonel John

Harris Cruger, the aristocratic scion of the wealthy Cruger family of New York merchants who commanded the forward western outpost of Ninety-Six south of the Cowpens, warned Major Ferguson about the undeniable truth, how the Loyalist militiamen were simply "not equal to the mountain lads" in this war.[52]

Indeed, the "wild and fierce inhabitants of [numerous] settlements westward of the Alleghany mountains assembled suddenly and silently" like no other military force in America and like no other chapter in the annals of military history.[53] Suddenly emerging from the dark, uncharted forests, these were some of the most experienced and best Indian fighters not only in the South, but also in America. By any measure when it seemed like South Carolina and Georgia had been already conquered by the British war machine, these were some of the revolution's darkest days in ill-fated 1780. Indeed, across the land "heard in the first days of autumn was the prediction that the Patriots could not last out the winter, that Britain's Southern strategy had at last began to pay off and that Cornwallis was prepared to offer acceptable peace terms. To all these rumors, Patriot guerrillas, shivering in the swamps and back-country hideouts, turned deaf ears [like the Overmountain men]. It was time of hanging on, of hoping for a miracle."[54] And that miracle was about to come when least expected at an obscure place called Kings Mountain in a remote part of the South Carolina backcountry.

Even more and in most convincing fashion, the sudden formation of a frontier army of more than a thousand backcountry and Overmountain men shortly demonstrated the fallacy upon which the entire Southern Strategy of King George III and his ministers was based: the fatal illusion that the vast majority of Americans still loved Great Britain, like during the unified American-British effort of the French and Indian War, and that the Patriots' popular uprising had been only due to a sinister "conspiracy of a minority" of rebels, who had led the so-called deluded common people into a foolhardy bloodletting. This was a myth warmly embraced by British leadership on both sides of the Atlantic. Thanks in part to the ceaseless, influential voices of Loyalists and exiled Southern Royal governors who desired to regain their old lofty positions, neither the king in Windsor Castle nor his aristocratic ministers, especially Lord George Germain who was the secretary of state for the Colonies, ever grasped that an irreversible sense of a nascent American nationalism had developed and taken deep root among a politically maturing people, which had now made them far more American than British. Nothing in the world could possibly turn back the clock of that evolutionary process, especially when it had been born of the searing frontier, Indian fighting, and wilderness experiences.[55]

Now the fruits of this evolutionary process of Americanization and democratization on the frontier were on the march toward a rendezvous with destiny on October 7, 1780, to show England's obsessive, single-minded King George III that raising a large army of Loyalist militiamen to win the war in the South was nothing but a "Fatal infatuation."[56]

Enduring Myths About Major Patrick Ferguson

Meanwhile, at the small Tryon County, North Carolina, community of Gilbert Town during the last week of September when the hardwood trees had already begun to turn to the autumnal colors, Ferguson continued to remain far west of Cornwallis's main force at Charlotte, serving as the main army's west flank guardian with the key mission of raising Loyalist militia in western North Carolina. To his liking, Ferguson possessed independent command, while still on the hunt for the elusive command of Colonel Elijah Clarke and his Georgians, who had been recently repulsed at Augusta in the Georgia backcountry slightly northwest of the strategic Atlantic port of Savannah, now held by the British after its capture in December 1778. The Scottish major, who detested rebels with a passion, still was not aware of the precarious situation that he was in, while hundreds of Patriots were gradually converging on his exposed position at the picturesque edge of the Blue Ridge Mountains.[57]

In regard to recruiting, Ferguson's special mission was of supreme importance and a central part of the overall strategic plan of winning the war in the South—the "Americanization" of the war effort or the Southern Strategy. Lord Cornwallis at Charlotte was depending heavily on Ferguson to the west to reap success in what he believed would be the war's most decisive campaign by taking the war ever farther north. Cornwallis's May 1780 instructions to Ferguson outlined his extensive responsibilities for the summer and fall campaign, which were spelled out in some detail: "By virtue of the commission of Inspector of Militia, with which you are vested, you will use your best endeavors, without loss of time, to form into corps all the young or unmarried men of the provinces of Georgia and two Carolinas as opportunity shall offer [and] Beside this body of militia to act offensively with the army you will promote the establishment of a domestick [sic] militia for the maintenance of peace and good order throughout the country."[58]

Layers of romance and myth have long shrouded the real Major Patrick Ferguson because of the embellishments of generations of American writers and historians who have created the perfect foil. In a thorough demonization of Ferguson, he has been long portrayed as the epitome of evil by American writers and historians in one book after another. In truth, he was not only a humane officer, but also one of the most remarkable British leaders of the American Revolution. As mentioned, he had been presented with a crucial assignment by Lord Cornwallis while commanding his Loyalist militia and crack American Volunteers (Royal Provincials), and his faith was well placed because no one was better at raising and leading Loyalist troops in America than Major Ferguson.

Contrary to general assumptions, Major Ferguson, born in 1744, fit the very definition of a proper "officer and a gentleman." Even more, he was aggressive and every inch a fighter, despite having begun life in poor health and cursed with a frail disposition. He was the privileged son of a prosperous Aberdeenshire, Scotland, laird and attorney of the upper-class elite. However, Ferguson had earned the affectionate sobriquet from his men of "Bulldog" because of his tenacity, despite his slender and delicate frame. This most revealing nickname entirely pertained to his diehard qualities as a highly respected British Army officer, who was now directing his efforts at wiping out this "damned banditti," but without compromising his integrity and high soldiery values, unlike so many other British officers, who had been corrupted by the horrors of guerrilla warfare. Lord Cornwallis had placed his faith in an aggressive commander to protect his western flank who he did not completely trust, however. Contrary to the popular stereotypes, Ferguson, thirty-six, was not only a model officer but also a gifted one much like Banastre 'Bloody Ban' Tarleton but in different ways. Even more, the red-haired and blue-eyed (like Tarleton) Scotsman was a humane man (unlike Tarleton), with polished manners and a host of other talents and personal gifts. A member of the Scottish gentry, Ferguson was the son of a senator of the College of Justice and one of the lords commissioners of Scotland's justiciary, hailing from the elite of Scotland. His mother was the daughter of the fourth Lord of Elibank, and her upper-class family possessed respected military connections, while his father's family boasted high-level political connections.

Most of all, Ferguson knew the business of soldiering and was a true "son of Mars," having begun his military career at age fifteen. The former commander of the American Volunteers, which were now his elite troops who formed the nucleus of his task force, Ferguson had served in the Middle Colonies during the frustrating campaigns that had been waged against General George Washington. The young Scotsman was known for his fearlessness both on and off the battlefield, and he continued to demonstrate his heroics in campaigns across the South. After the fall of Fort Sullivan in 1780, for instance, he had been one of the first British officers of the army's assault vanguard who first touched South Carolina soil to tighten the noose around Charles Town. Like at the Battle of Brandywine, Pennsylvania, where he had been wounded and left with a disabled right arm on September 11, 1777, Ferguson's achievements in the South were well documented and printed in colonial newspapers, especially Royalist periodicals, and he was well-known to the Loyalist community, both military and civilian.

The talented Scotsman, who had invented the Ferguson rifle, which was an advanced breechloading weapon ahead of its time, was on the fast track, while serving under Sir Henry Clinton's admiring eye and enjoying his enthusiastic support. He had won promotion to major of the 2nd Battalion of Simon Fraser's Scottish Highlanders, or the 71st Regiment of Foot, in October 1779, even before embarking on Clinton's expedition to South Carolina that resulted in Charles Town's fall. Appropriately, the fighting men of the 71st Regiment of Foot wore traditional Scottish tartan, or plaid, on their distinctive headgear. At that time, Ferguson commanded hand picked soldiers of his beloved American Volunteers from New York and New Jersey, which consisted of excellent fighting men. And now Ferguson was extremely effective as the Inspector of Militia of the Carolinas and Georgia, as named on May 22, 1780, by Clinton and not Cornwallis, who had nothing to do with the promotion.

In overall political terms in regard to his special place in the British Army, Ferguson was a devoted Clinton man. Recognizing his talents, Sir Henry Clinton had even employed him in intelligence work, while Ferguson was mending from his Brandywine wound, unlike Cornwallis's other top lieutenants like Tarleton and Nisbet Balfour, who, despite being a fellow Scotsman, saw relatively few redeeming qualities in Ferguson.

However, the wisdom of Major Ferguson's appointment by Clinton as the inspector of militia had been nicely repaid by the Scotsman's energetic efforts that resulted in the creation of no less than seven Loyalist Militia regiments of around 1,500 men, including the Cane Creek Regiment, Dutch Fork Regiment, and the Fair Forest Regiment (all three units fought at Kings Mountain) from the Ninety-Six District, while playing a key role in the overall process of pacifying the backcountry of South Carolina from his headquarters at the forward western base of Ninety-Six during the summer of 1780. As a dynamic Provincial officer who was extremely proud of his men, Ferguson succeeded in creating an elite corps of Loyalist fighting men in the Provincial regulars or American Volunteers, which threatened the status quo of the already established, strictly structured military caste and tradition-bound hierarchical system and thus sparked resentment and jealousy among regular British officers, including Lieutenant Colonel Nisbet Balfour and Lord Francis Rawdon, who were both Cornwallis's young golden boys. Never having married because he had dedicated his life to the military, and six years younger than Cornwallis, Ferguson was barely more than a decade older than the Cornwallis favorites, especially Tarleton and Rawdon who were his "bright stars," while possessing two decades of service for the king and country.

Unfortunately for him in 1780 and despite his impressive achievements, Ferguson remained uncomfortably on the outside of this tight old boy network of the regular army establishment of Cornwallis. Through no fault of his own, this was an inevitable development partly because Ferguson had been one of Clinton's golden boys, and partly because he was unorthodox and had accomplished what had not been previously done like inventing the Ferguson rifle, which he had introduced to the British government in 1776. The weapon was ahead of its time by nearly a century—a breechloader capable of firing a half dozen shots a minute, which was a revolutionary technical development because it would have given the British military a modern weapon with superior capabilities, if it had been accepted. Naturally and as could be expected, the tradition-bound and ultra-conservative British government and military establishment would have nothing to do with Ferguson's technological masterpiece and the smart futuristic concept: a victim of the fossilized thinking of the old system and the traditional military establishment. Ironically, Ferguson would certainly have prevailed in the upcoming showdown at Kings Mountain if all of his men would have been armed with the Ferguson rifle—the first breechloader ever used in America, including by Ferguson himself at the Battle of Brandywine that had been fought just outside Philadelphia and lost by General Washington.

Compared to the average British commander who was a consummate political player and thoroughly immersed in the upper-class status value structure both inside and outside the army, Ferguson was still an outsider partly because he was an independent forward thinker, who envisioned the future with clarity, unlike so many of his more conservative peers: a rare gift that naturally engendered envy and even hatred from the less talented officers of the old traditional school of British regular officer corps, especially in South Carolina. Unfortunately for him and his future aspirations in the military establishment, Ferguson had been left in a lurch when Sir Henry Clinton had sailed back to New York City, after the capture of Charles Town, because he lost his highest-level supporter to severely diminish his future prospects. The most prejudiced colonel in the regular army against the Scottish major, Lieutenant Colonel Nisbet Balfour, 23rd Regiment of Foot, knew how to cater to Cornwallis's low opinion of Ferguson and make himself look better. In the omnipresent game of backdoor army politics so prevalent in the British military establishment, the sneaky Balfour had the smug audacity to unfairly pen that "we can expect but little assistance from him [Ferguson] further than bare inspection," which was a gross distortion of Ferguson's true abilities and achievements, especially his organizational skills. Ferguson was best at this, especially because of his talent in developing his own personal initiatives and acting upon them, which suited his temperament and free-thinking nature when in independent command of his own force of well-trained Loyalists. In this role, he warmly embraced the opportunities presented by freedom of action, including the chance to make a greater name for himself by way of achievements both on and off the battlefield. Even more, the brave Scotsman with a widespread reputation still possessed an uncanny ability to raise large numbers of Loyalists seemingly wherever he went, including at Gilbert Town and Tyron County, North Carolina, while keeping the Carolina backcountry under control and quiet—no small accomplishment under challenging circumstances.

Heroic Patriot Women Forgotten by History

Patriot women were often treated as harshly by Loyalists as the men, especially in the remote backcountry where America's first civil war reached its ugliest form. For instance, Ireland-born Christina Patterson Henderson paid a price for having been married to Patriot Private Charles Tuclon, who was wounded in one South Carolina skirmish. Christina "was wounded by a bayonet because she refused to tell Tories where her husband was."[59] Hannah Ogden Caldwell was killed when a soldier's bullet "tore open her chest and punctured her lung."[60] In his diary, a French officer in the Southern theater wrote how the British "captured a pregnant woman near Portsmouth [Virginia] and hanged her with this inscription: 'You will no longer give birth to rebels.'"[61]

Loyalists had good reason to hate Patriot women of the backcountry of South Carolina, especially if Scotch-Irish, because some British officers considered them even more militant and radical than their husbands, sons, and fathers.[62] Sarah Hawkins Sevier, the first wife of Kings Mountain leader John Sevier, was one such Patriot woman of strong character and feisty nature. Sarah was as much of a pioneer as her husband, having been born on the Virginia frontier of the Shenandoah Valley in 1746. After marrying John in 1773 at fifteen, Sarah bravely withstood the hardships of migrating across the imposing mountains to the beautiful Watauga Valley and boldly faced the dangers of Cherokee attack. She also saved her husband from a revenge-seeking Loyalist partisan leader after she had early learned of the dire threat.[63] Rachel Denny was an Irish Patriot whose husband, a "strict" Presbyterian of Scotch-Irish heritage, was away from home battling for liberty, leaving her vulnerable. She sat in stoic defiance and disgust while raiding Loyalists looted and plundered her home in the North Buffalo Creek country of South Carolina. When a British officer asked her if she was afraid that her husband would be caught and then hung as a traitor, Rachel responded in defiance: "as he was engaged in a good cause, he was in good hands, and she hoped he would be protected." The incensed British officer, unleashing a string of curses at her, responded with a fundamental truth about the war in the Southern backcountry by declaring: "the women in that part of the country [were] as damned rebels as the men, and that one-half of them, at least, ought to be shot or hung."[64]

The highly capable Joseph McJunkin, a diehard Scotch-Irish officer of South Carolina's 2nd Spartan Regiment who had been born in 1755, described how a Loyalist raiding party came "to my father's house [Samuel McJunkin of Union District, South Carolina, when] there being none but females at home [and stayed all night and then when] going off in the [next] morning, began to pillage & take all they could [and Loyalist] Bill Hanesworth, seeing a bed-quilt took & started to put it on his horse, when one of my sisters, Jane, seized it, & they began to pull [and Bill slipped and fell when Jane] putting one foot on him, pulled it away from him. Their Colonel having sworn during the scuffle that if she could get it from him, she should have it."[65] To their credit, Loyalist soldiers caught the spirit of Jane's spirited defiance and surprising strength, yelling, "Well done, woman!"[66]

Nancy Jackson was another feisty Scotch-Irish woman, who was described as "the heroic girl" because of her spunky defiance toward the enemy.[67] She was ready to take on Loyalist raiders when they suddenly descended like locusts upon the family home that was located near Fair Forest Creek in the South Carolina backcountry. When the Loyalist raiders began ransacking the home and stealing prized family possessions, she "kicked a Tory down the stairs as he was descending, loaded with plunder."[68] Colonel James Williams, who was destined to lead South Carolina's Little River Regiment into the vortex of the Battle of Kings Mountain, felt guilty because of his long absences from home in battling for liberty. He penned in a June 12, 1779, letter to his son, Daniel, who also fought at Kings Mountain: "When I reflect on my own distress, I feel for that of my family, on account of my absence from their midst; and especially for the mother, who sits like a dove that has lost its mate, having the weight of the family on her shoulders."[69] God's mercies were destined to not help the hard-luck Williams family of the South Carolina backcountry in this cruelest of wars. The respected South Carolina colonel would be mortally wounded at Kings Mountain and the highest-ranking officer to die, and sons Joseph, a teenager, and Daniel, while serving as a captain of the Little River Regiment, would be hung by "Bloody" Bill Cunningham barely a year later in November 1781.[70] To the end and despite all of the sharp setbacks and hardships, Colonel James Williams never lost his faith in God, informing his wife in a September 30, 1779, letter: "I beg that you may bear with fortitude my absence; and let us with humble confidence rely on Him that is able to protect and defend us, in all danger, and through every difficulty; but, my dear, let us, with one heart, call on God for his mercies."[71]

When Colonel John Sevier had embarked on one of his Indian campaigns to protect the frontier settlements, wife Sarah and her brothers remained behind to defend the family and their log cabin fort in the Watauga Valley, molding bullets from pewter plates in preparation for a future Cherokee attack, after the expeditioners had taken all lead shot with them in their preemptive strike upon Ferguson.[72] Perhaps the finest tribute paid to Patriot women in the South came from one of Cornwallis's officers who swore "that he believed if he had destroyed all the men in North America, we should have enough to do to conquer the women."[73]

The Real Major Ferguson

Despite the surreal horrors of guerrilla warfare and unlike so many other fighting men on both sides, Major Ferguson remained true to his principles and humanity with a stubborn tenacity, which was no small achievement. In the fight against Isaac Shelby and Elijah Clarke at Cedar Springs on August 8, 1780, Ferguson made sure that the fallen Patriots were decently buried in the little peach orchard where much of the battle was fought. New peach trees sprouted in the spring from the peaches (seeds) that had been left in the pockets of the dead Patriots, who had unwittingly enjoyed a last supper when they had no idea that they were about to meet their Maker while enjoying fresh peaches.[74] Complimentary evaluations of Major Ferguson by the experts were correct and right on target, because he was "a fit associate for Tarleton in hardy, scrambling, partisan enterprise; equally intrepid and determined, but cooler and more open to impulses of humanity," earning him his "bulldog" sobriquet.[75] By the summer of 1780, Major Ferguson was not only in his prime but also at the zenith of his splendid military career, which had been most impressive. He was not like most British commanders in the remote backcountry who "were not backward in their severities against the unhappy citizens, many of whom they hung up or otherwise cruelly treated or put to death in a wanton manner," in the words of Patriot General William Moultrie, who recognized Ferguson as a decent man trapped in the horrors of an indecent war and guerrilla conflict.[76]

When one of Ferguson's soldiers stole a chicken to supplement dreary army rations, the offended lady of the victimized residence reported the thief to the indignant major, who promptly had the man punished. In even more gallant fashion, Ferguson then paid the lady a dollar for her loss. Clearly, this generous "act was certainly creditable to Ferguson's sense of justice; but it was, like an oasis in the desert, a circumstance of very unfrequent occurrence."[77] However, Major Ferguson was also tough as nails and obeyed orders to the letter because it was his duty to God and country. In his diary, Lieutenant Anthony Allaire wrote how near the end of March 1780, "Ferguson got to the rear guard in order to do his King and country justice, by protecting friends, and widows, and destroying Rebel property; also to collect live stock for the use of the army . . . destroying furniture, breaking windows, etc."[78] During the Egg Harbor Expedition of early October 1778, Ferguson led a surprise attack on Count Brigadier General Casimir Pulaski's small force and a slaughter ensued. Ferguson had defended the brutality inflicted on the command of the

Poland-born Pulaski, who was mortally wounded at the Battle of Savannah on October 9, 1779, by casually writing how during the "night attack, little quarter could, of course, be given."[79]

Ferguson was one of Cornwallis's most promising officers of distinction, even if his lordship was not fully aware of that undeniable fact because of his lack of confidence in the Scotsman in part because he was a Clinton man and a Celt. In addition, Ferguson was young and vigorous, beloved by his American fighting men who were devoted to him. At age thirty-six but around ten years older than "Bloody Ban" Tarleton, the dashing Scottish major was handsome and athletic with a trim, erect figure. Ferguson's striking appearance was fitting for his lofty status as Cornwallis's inspector of militia, which was a misleading title because his main responsibility was raising Loyalist regiments for the king during the "Americanization" for the fulfillment of the ambitious Southern Strategy. He was also described as having been "of middle stature, slender make and possessing a serious countenance, yet it was his peculiar characteristic to gain the affections of the men under his command."[80]

General Moultrie, despite the fact that his beloved state of South Carolina was overrun with British and Loyalists, had glowing words for Ferguson, calling him "an experienced, brave, active partisan officer."[81] Throughout the war, Ferguson adhered to his core belief of a rare value system in this war: "We came not to make war on women and children, but to relieve their distresses."[82] Ironically, General Moultrie's view of Ferguson was higher than that of a jealous and backstabbing Lieutenant Colonel Nisbet Balfour, who wrote to Cornwallis how "as to Ferguson, his ideas are so wild and sanguine [that] it would be dangerous to trust him with the conduct of any plan."[83] Indeed, like Tarleton, Major Ferguson had his weaknesses that were partly hidden by his string of successes that had allowed him to reach the peak of his distinguished career. However, he was overly ambitious and possessed a reckless streak in consequence—a bad combination in an unpredictable guerrilla war and one that played a large role in spelling his doom at Kings Mountain. In Lord Cornwallis's harsh words, which reflected a tainted view but were destined to prove prophetic in regard to the fast-approaching showdown at Kings Mountain: "I find it impossible to trust him out of my sight."[84]

Most of all, Ferguson committed the folly of significantly underestimating his opponent, especially the Scotch-Irish who he viewed as "a set of mongrels." However, he understood that it was:

> a great error to suppose [that his opponents] were new to the exigencies and dangers of battle. Their fighting qualities could not be regarded as otherwise than respectable by professional soldiers [having] been acclimated to something like regular war by engagements, skirmishes and collisions with loyal uprisings and regular forces. They were of totally different and far better stuff than the militia [like at the Battle of Camden] who threw down their arms after a single scattering discharge, or without firing at all [and] If they were not regular soldiers they were brave men and stalwart adversaries, and if they did not understand the tactics of the Continentals, they had tactics of their own which suited the region in which they had to operate. The tactics of the [Overmountain and backcountry] colonels [were in fact] far superior to those of Ferguson.[85]

And now, Major Ferguson was too far removed to the west from Cornwallis and the main army at Charlotte—literally out on a limb at Gilbert Town, situated at the foothills of the Blue Ridge Mountains during the last week of September 1780. For a variety of reasons, Ferguson was in the process of committing absolute folly, partly because of the disconnect between the unorthodox Scotsman and his tradition-bound commander, who was held in such high esteem by King George III. In Cornwallis's words in a letter to Lieutenant Colonel Nisbet Balfour that revealed his lack of confidence in Ferguson and his men whom he had trained and disciplined, after the Scottish major had boasted of the prowess of his Loyalists: "I am sorry to say that his own experience as well as that of every other officer is totally against him."[86]

A Most Perfect Harmony When Most Needed

In striking contrast to British leadership, perhaps the most important ingredient in the one-sided victory at Kings Mountain that reversed the American Revolution's course was the smooth working relationship and ideal harmony that existed between top Patriot leadership from beginning to end that proved invaluable. Although these were tough, strong-willed men of the Western frontier, the urgency of the hour and the dire situation called for none of the usual bickering and arguments among leadership based largely on inflated egos, strong wills, and lofty reputations. Despite his youth, Colonel Isaac Shelby was the ultimate diplomat and master frontier psychologist who served as the vital glue that kept everything about this expedition together, from logistics to divergent personalities that sharply clashed, while serving as the expedition's real undisputed leader. Indeed, the case could be made that success at Kings Mountain would never have become a reality without the key contributions of Shelby's many talents, including tactical, logistical, and leadership abilities on multiple levels. In striking contrast, arguments, gossip, and bickering had long dominated the top of the British command structure to reduce effectiveness and chances for winning decisive victory in America. And this internal division and conflict existed at the highest levels in the South between Sir Henry Clinton and his top lieutenant Cornwallis to the overall benefit of the often-defeated Patriots. The deep divide that existed between the two aristocratic men, which ensured a constant running feud between them during the war years in the South, began at an early date to sabotage the much-needed working relationship of the chain of command assigned the main responsibility of conquering the South.

Despite the fact that both men had been members of Parliament and part of a military oligarchy deeply entrenched in tradition and upper-class values, the amount of bad blood that existed between Clinton and Cornwallis was no longer reconcilable, especially because the senior commander in New York City was nothing less than neurotic and excessively paranoid. The source of the trouble between the two aristocrats had begun years before. In a rare lapse of his usual good judgment, or in an ill-advised attempt to curry favor with Sir William Howe, who had been the supreme commander of British forces in America in the war's beginning before Clinton replaced him, Cornwallis had let slip Clinton's negative comments about Howe in a betrayal of Clinton's trust and friendship. Clinton later learned as much, and it led the ever-suspicious and excessively wary Briton to suspect the worst of Cornwallis's motives during the war in the South.

Even more, Cornwallis hailed from a privileged and wealthy family, which had been long favored by King George III, of an elevated social position higher than that of Clinton—another guarantee of friction, jealousy, and conflict. And Cornwallis possessed a superior education to Clinton, including at Eton, which was the prestigious school of the upper-class British elite. And unlike most British officers, including Clinton, he had acquired an even more complete military education at Turin, Italy, at one of the finest military schools in Europe. To his credit, Lord Cornwallis did not rest on his upper-class status and privileged membership in the British elite like so many other high-ranking officers, taking the initiative to further his military education, including the establishment of close connections with respected Prussian officers and the military-minded German courts during the Seven Years' War. Cornwallis was an elitist and aristocratic Englishman to the core, while Clinton had been born and raised American, when his father had been the longtime royal governor of New York. He was familiar with Americans, unlike Cornwallis, and felt more sympathy for them in general. Cornwallis became the second Earl of Cornwallis, after his father died. To his credit, he was a soldier's soldier to the very end. He disliked the traditional pomp that went with high rank, and his heart lay with the common soldiers who fought and died far from home in a long war of attrition that they were fated to lose. Cornwallis felt that how a general performed on the battlefield was more important than the accumulation of fancy titles, riches, and lofty social standing: something that he repeatedly demonstrated by a courage that often bordered on recklessness on the battlefield, which made him one of the finest and most remarkable British military commanders in America.

And instead of taking mistresses while on campaign, Cornwallis was supremely devoted to his wife, Jemima Tulikens, who hailed from an established military family. He had married for love and had children with Jemima, while remaining devoted to her despite her lower social status. In 1778, he had rushed to England from America to her bedside when he learned of her illness, but Jemima died in less than a month after his arrival. Cornwallis was devastated by the tragic loss, and only returned to America as second-in-command under Clinton to fight a war in a futile attempt to forget about the loss of the greatest love of his life—a personal tragedy that continued to tear at his heart and soul long after her death. Not surprisingly, he never remarried or took a lover to compensate for Jemima's loss, because he never lost his love for her. Clearly, in his personal life, Cornwallis was a man of character. Of course, such a privileged and aristocratic background also made Cornwallis hardly the ideal subordinate of the ever-quarrelsome Clinton, while they "eyed each other like a pair of highly bred British bulldogs" in a dirty alley in east London along the Thames.[87]

However, such was not the case with either Ferguson or Tarleton, who were young men on the rise and which explained in part why they performed so well together in South Carolina. Unlike Cornwallis and Clinton, Tarleton and Ferguson possessed no lofty titles, realizing that they would have to rise on their own merits and achievements in this war.[88] Despite Lord Cornwallis and his favored top lieutenants functioning like a well-oiled machine while fighting in South Carolina and winning one victory after another, the commander possessed a dark prophetic sense about Major Ferguson. Cornwallis received a June letter from Lieutenant Colonel Nisbet Balfour about the ambitious Ferguson, revealing a personal quality of the Scot that troubled him, which was a heightened aggressiveness: "He seems to me to want to carry the war into North Carolina himself at once."[89] Major Ferguson knew that he failed to possess the confidence of his commander now at Charlotte. Unfortunately for him, "Ferguson was not part of the inner circle [of Cornwallis and] took this to heart and was determined to win over Cornwallis through achieving victory."[90] As if drawn by fate itself and determined to demonstrate the validity of his sobriquet of "bulldog," Ferguson was about to find his long-awaited opportunity to reap his much sought-after glory for himself and his well-trained Loyalists at an obscure hilltop just below, or south of, the North Carolina border, Kings Mountain.

Meanwhile, the Overmountain and backcountry men continued their long journey slightly southwest through a beautiful countryside and headed toward Gilbert Town and their eventual fateful meeting with Major Ferguson, after having departed the McDowell farm at Quaker Meadows on the headwaters of the Catawba River. Harmony and close cooperation between Patriot leadership distinguished the lengthy trek from Sycamore Shoals. The Overmountain and backcountry men were closely bonded together by the single goal of destroying Major Ferguson and his command in what they considered a holy war. However, the potential for the sudden rise of problems always existed among the independent-minded members of the enlisted ranks of these frontier units, because of the simple fact that the popular leaders of the various units "controlled their troops only through voluntary agreement on the part of the privates," which helped to make this a most unique, democratic, and unorthodox American army.[91]

Chapter III

Encroaching Showdown at Kings Mountain

The horrors of the guerrilla war in the South—America's first civil war—were second to none. As fate would have it, none other than "Bloody Bill" Cunningham was now serving in Major Ferguson's ranks on Cornwallis's left wing, and he would fight at a remote hilltop in the western South Carolina Piedmont known as Kings Mountain, fearing for his fate if captured.[1] Ironically, the infamous Loyalist partisan leader of some of the most hardened Loyalists of the Saluda River country was destined to face the fire of some Patriots at Kings Mountain whom he would eventually kill. One such victim, Colonel Joseph Hayes of Laurens County, South Carolina, led his South Carolina boys and fought with distinction at Kings Mountain. He would replace Colonel James Williams after he was killed near the backwoods battle's end on October 7, 1780. This situation was one reason that explained why Colonel Hayes was destined to be personally hung by Bloody Bill on November 19, 1781, barely a year after the one-sided victory at Kings Mountain.[2]

Even more, one of Major Ferguson's top lieutenants at Kings Mountain was none other than the capable Lieutenant Colonel Patrick Cunningham of the Little River Regiment, which consisted of around two hundred men from the Saluda River country. The Loyalist Cunningham family was originally from Pennsylvania, then Virginia, before migrating to South Carolina's Saluda River area in the late 1760s. Cunningham was a bold leader who orchestrated the audacious interception of Patriot powder and lead on the way to the Cherokee in the South Carolina government's vain hope of keeping them from waging war against the frontier settlements in the war's beginning.[3]

Somehow, Bloody Bill was destined to escape the Patriots' trap that was so masterfully sprung on Major Ferguson by Colonel Shelby at Kings Mountain, where he was seen killing one American by at least one Patriot, and then slipped away from the entrapment to reach Charles Town by October 23.[4]

Private Jacob Bealer, who fought beside his brother Joseph, revealed that all of Ferguson's command was captured "except those who might have run before [Kings] Mountain had been surrounded."[5] Private William Kerr, who had been born in Pennsylvania in 1764 and was not in the Battle of Kings Mountain, later "assisted in capturing Tories who had been defeated at Kings Mountain."[6]

As fate would have it, Private Samuel Mayes, who had been born in the Ninety-Six District in 1759 and was a veteran of Kings Mountain, "was captured by 'Bloody Bill' Cunningham and held six weeks [and] then held four weeks by Col. Tarleton," before escaping to rejoin the fight.[7] However, Cunningham had previously been captured by a party of Patriots, which included Ensign Robert Kirkpatrick, of Irish descent and from the Camden District, but he had escaped the retribution that he richly deserved.[8] In time, Bloody Bill Cunningham became so notorious that Captain Richard Johnson became famous for having been "in the pursuit of 'Bloody Bill' Cunningham."[9] Meanwhile, the list of Cunningham's victims rose to lofty levels both before and after Kings Mountain, like in the case of ill-fated Private Samuel Miller, who had been born in either Ireland or Virginia. In October 1781, he became separated from his command after having been wounded in a skirmish. He lodged in a Patriot house to recover in a remote location, which was always a risky undertaking. However, Miller "was betrayed and murdered by 'Bloody Bill' Cunningham near Michael Blaine's plantation at Swansea's Ferry," or Swancey's Ferry, in today's Greenwood County, South Carolina.[10] Captured at the fall of Charles Town, Captain Oliver Towles, who had been born in Virginia around 1734, "was killed by Tories under 'Bloody Bill' Cunningham."[11] The backcountry plantation home, known as Walnut Grove, of heroine Kate Barry, who served as a scout and intelligence gatherer for the Patriots, was the scene of still another Bloody Bill atrocity. To this day at the old mansion house located just south of Spartanburg, South Carolina, the "bloodstains on a bedroom floor remains to show where a wounded patriot was slaughtered in his bed by the detested Tory, Bloody Bill Cunningham."[12] In the end and for ample good reason, Bloody Bill Cunningham "was charged with committing scores of wanton murders, including women and children" who were members of unfortunate Patriot families.[13] Still another one of the victims of Cunningham was Captain Sterling Turner, who was killed by Bloody Bill at Lexington, South Carolina.[14] But, of course, plenty of other Loyalists were the cold-hearted killers of Patriots like Captain Thomas Woodward. Born in

Virginia around 1729 and married to Elizabeth Stokes May, Woodward "was killed by Tories during 1779."[15]

To their horror, the settlers west of the mountains had learned the nightmare stories of civil war savagery from Colonel McDowell's refugees from Burke County and from others who had crossed the mountains to escape.[16] For such reasons, the commander of the American army in the South before the arrival of General Gates, General Johannes de Kalb, a large Bavarian who knew about war's horrors from his years of campaigning in Europe, had been shocked by what he saw Americans doing to fellow Americans in South Carolina with a savagery seldom seen. Prophetically, de Kalb, who died a hero's death at the Battle of Camden when in command of Continental troops after so many citizen-soldiers of the militia had fled the field in a shameful rout, wrote to wife Emilie in regard to the harshness of British actions: "They cannot possibly triumph in the end. Their cruelty and inhumanity must sooner or later draw down upon their heads the vengeance of Heaven, and blast a Government which authorizes these outrages."[17]

Because of so many of these British cruelties, a holy vengeance was about to be unleashed upon Major Ferguson and his Loyalists at Kings Mountain. On October 1, eager for a showdown with Major Ferguson and his hated Loyalists, a total of 1,390 Patriot militiamen had departed the broad pasture lands of Quaker Meadows on the Catawba River, after having become invigorated by the much-needed rest on the McDowells' property. They pushed slightly southwest toward Gilbert Town at a good pace for another eighteen miles to a new camp site, where they encamped in the late afternoon near the head of the spring-fed waters of Cane Creek at South Mountain Gap that cut through the South Mountains.[18] In regard to the overall strategic situation, the upcoming strike on Ferguson was immediately benefited by Cornwallis having pushed north from South Carolina to Charlotte with too few troops, which reduced the likelihood of reinforcing Ferguson. Add to that the fact that he had been forced by too many partisan bands to garrison too many strongpoints with regular troops across South Carolina in his rear, which had severely weakened him. Hence, it was supremely important for Ferguson to now raise as many Loyalist troops as possible to the west, upon which the entire Southern Strategy was based. Most of all, Lord Cornwallis's failure to concentrate his invasion force left British and Loyalist forces vulnerable—especially Major Ferguson on the western flank of the main army because of the closeness of the Overmountain settlements to the west and distance from Cornwallis to the east.[19]

Frontier Democracy at Work

Meanwhile, the Patriots' continued movement slightly southwest toward Gilbert Town was swift partly because they were finally out of the most rugged part of the mountains and partly because the terrain became more favorable below Quaker Meadows, which had been fueled by the belief that the hunters were nearing their prey that was thought to be at Gilbert Town just to the south. On another positive note, the trekkers were reinvigorated after resting in the grassy fields of Quaker Meadows, about forty miles northeast of Gilbert Town. There they joined Colonel Cleveland's Wilkes County men, Winston's Surry County volunteers, and Andrew Hampton's Burke County citizen-soldiers before moving farther south to the headwaters of Cane Creek. However, a matter of crucial importance shortly raised its head, and hasty preparations were made by the citizen-soldiers, because Ferguson was believed to be at Gilbert Town only eighteen miles southwest of Quaker Meadows.

Below the highest mountains that they had just crossed after so much effort, the weary men of the task force encamped just above Gilbert Town for the next two nights, October 1 and October 2. But not all was well. Spirits were low, partly because it was feared that Ferguson might have already departed Gilbert Town by that time. Heavy and cold autumnal rains began on the night of October 1. The hunger and weariness in the ranks began to result in "petty disorders" and a lack of discipline among these frontier individualists, who were loudly complaining seemingly about everything in the citizen-soldier tradition. The disgruntlement among the common soldiers had reached a new high as the cold rain continued to pour down from black skies the next day while they were lying low in the same dreary, water-soaked camp above Gilbert Town. This disturbing situation was all but inevitable given the individualistic spirits and nonconformist attitudes of these citizen-soldiers, who had volunteered for this crucial mission at a time when they were still worried about Cherokee attacks on their homes and families. This was an omnipresent fear that grew with each passing day. And it was only by the consent of the average fighter in the ranks, the lowly privates, that frontier leaders retained their authority in the democratic tradition.

Of course, under these circumstances, the tempers of the sojourners had grown considerably shorter because of the arduous trek through the mountains. Indiscipline was one of the longtime weaknesses of employing militiamen on lengthy campaigns. In consequence, it was now left to the chosen Overmountain and backcountry leaders to think wisely and act carefully to quell what might even evolve into a full-fledged mutiny among these free-thinking men of the militia regiments, if not properly handled intelligently and with delicacy. Consequently, it was necessary to hold an ad hoc commanders' conference on the evening of October 2 to address the rise of unruliness. The most immediate solution was to choose a single leader in charge of all of the separate militia commands that were now led by men of the equal rank of colonel, all popular and respected colonels from three different states (actually four, counting Tennessee, which only became a state in 1796), because they were operating far beyond the knowledge and control of General Gates and the Continental Army at their Hillsborough, North Carolina, headquarters. All in all, this was the kind of situation that led to a certain degree of confusion and unrest, especially during a risky campaign far from home.[20]

Clearly, a single high-ranking leader was needed to command the more than a half dozen separate commands and militia leaders for greater discipline in the upcoming battle. Colonel Shelby explained how "little disorders and irregularities" had begun "to prevail among our undisciplined troops."[21] As usual, Colonel Shelby was being diplomatic in commenting about these "little disorders," because he now commanded, like other leaders, "some of the unruliest men in America."[22] For ample good reason and in his usual candid style, Shelby admitted how the unruly behavior of these ever-independent fighting men, whose frontier notions of democracy were notoriously excessive, "created much uneasiness in the commanding officers—the Colonels commanding the regiments."[23]

Colonel Shelby's Wisdom Continues to Rise to the Fore

In Colonel Shelby's words about the ad hoc officers' conference on the evening of October 2 when the sense of anticipation was high now that they were closing in on Ferguson:

> It was resolved to send to Head-Quarters [at Hillsborough] for a general officer to command us; and that, in the mean time, we should

> meet in council every day to determine on the measures to be pursued, and appoint any of our own body to put them in execution. I was not satisfied with this course, as I thought it calculated to produce delay, when expedition and dispatch were all important to us. We were then in sixteen or eighteen miles of Gilbert Town, where we supposed Ferguson to be. I suggested these things to the council [of top officers], and then observed to the officers, that we were all North Carolinians [before Tennessee became a state] except Col. Campbell, who was from Virginia; that I knew him to be a man of good sense, and warmly attached to the cause of his country; that he commanded the largest regiment; and that if they concurred with me, until a general officer [from Hillsborough] should arrive from Head-Quarters, appoint him to command us, and march immediately against the enemy. To this proposition some one or two said 'agreed.' No written minute or record was made of it.[24]

Making a smart decision, Shelby's shrewd maneuver and forward-thinking initiative was wisely calculated to thwart the general expectation that Colonel McDowell—as he assumed partly because he had been active in the field all summer and now commanded the large contingent (nearly double the size of Shelby's Sullivan County militia) of around four hundred backcountry Virginians from Burke County situated on the mountain's eastern slope and had general command of the area where Ferguson was expected to be encountered—would naturally lead the task force. Colonel Shelby, the youngest of the principal frontier leaders at twenty-nine, knew that McDowell was too old at thirty-seven and "too slow," in Shelby's on-target estimation, for leading the command in such a crucial situation. Likewise, Colonel Cleveland, the oldest colonel at forty-two, was also considered too old and less energetic than a younger man, especially because of his rotund physique. Quite simply, as everyone realized, a much younger commander and veteran Indian fighter needed to be unofficially in charge of this vital mission, before Major Ferguson withdrew east to reach the safety of Cornwallis's army or was reinforced by his lordship from Charlotte.[25] Colonel Shelby had calculated correctly in having determined, in his own words, about the key decision not to allow McDowell to lead the expedition, because too much was now at stake to take that risk: "He was a brave and patriotic man, but we considered him too far advanced in life [at thirty-seven], and too inactive, for the command of such an enterprise as we were then engaged in."[26]

Colonel William Campbell, who led citizen-soldiers from Washington County, Virginia, then requested a private moment with Shelby outside the informal conference in which he declared that he wished his name to be withdrawn from taking command of the entire task force and suggested that Shelby be named the overall commander. Shelby was too smart to make this mistake in judgment, which had the potential to cause greater discontent among the men at a time when so much was now on the line. As an outsider, being a Virginian, Campbell's overall leadership of the expedition would reduce the rivalries that existed between mostly North Carolina colonels, including Shelby. But knowing better than to excuse Campbell,

> to this, Shelby correctly replied that he was the youngest Colonel present; and that [Major Joseph] McDowell [Jr., who had taken over his brother's regiment in Charles McDowell's absence] under whom he had served, would resent his elevation to the chief command [partly because] Shelby probably realized that the over-mountain men, at all times unaccustomed to strict military discipline and somewhat prone to insubordination, would not readily accept the leadership in this meteoric campaign of a militia commander conspicuous neither for rare discretion nor for exceptional efficiency. The selection of Campbell [as nominal commander of the task force, but Isaac Shelby was the actual leader in almost every way] was undoubtedly a temporary expedient, a tactful mode of bridging an awkward situation; yet it is clear that these border leaders would never have agreed to Shelby's suggestion that the chief command be given, even temporarily, to Campbell, had they not recognized in him an efficient leader and known him to be a true soldier.[27]

Most important, young Colonel Shelby's keen insights and frontier reasoning won the day by reducing the possibility of the increase of command rivalries, internal dissension in the ranks, and the rise of jealousy among the mostly North Carolina leadership dominated by strong personalities and egos based on considerable past achievements, while gaining the most suitable commander for the task force to ensure the overall success of this far-flung expedition.

McDowell accepted the final decision of who was to take overall command of the expedition as the wisest one under the circumstances. Shelby's wisdom shone brightly since "as originator and prime mover in the expedition, more than any other [Colonel Shelby] was entitled to the chief command."[28]

However, in the democratic tradition, Shelby had led this informal conference on October 2 in which important decisions were now to be made by committee in the crucial days ahead, although Campbell was now the nominal commander. Colonel Campbell, the least experienced of the five colonels, was now commander of the frontier army in name only, ensuring that the best leadership decisions would be made by a committee of colonels in the democratic tradition, but Colonel Shelby was considered the expedition's leader. After all, as Shelby wisely reasoned, this crucial mission east of the mountains was too important to allow a single man to command and potentially make a wrong decision at the crucial time.[29] Indeed, as explained Colonel William Hill of South Carolina: "The Officers of each army then convened together, the proceedings that took place was to give Col Campbell a nominal command over the whole [and] this was in courtesy as he & his men had come the greatest distance & from over the mountains."[30]

In consequence, "William Campbell was commander in name, but Isaac Shelby was the driving force" of the expedition from beginning to end during one of the war's most important missions, which possessed the potential to turn the tide decisively in the Patriots' favor.[31] Now, Colonel Campbell took over nominal command, but "he was regulated and directed by the determinations of the Colonels, who were to meet in council every day" in true frontier style.[32] Meanwhile, Colonel Charles McDowell volunteered to ride to Hillsborough to request General Horatio Gates, officially in command of America's Southern Army, to dispatch a general officer to command the newly formed army of untrained citizen-soldiers. From a location in Tryon County just north of Gilbert Town on October 4, McDowell hastily departed on his mission, leaving his brother Major Joseph McDowell in command of his Burke County, North Carolina, boys.[33] McDowell carried a letter to General Gates signed by Shelby, Sevier, Cleveland, Hampton, Winston, and Campbell:

> Sir, We have now collected at this place about 1500 good men, drawn from the counties of Surry, Wilkes, Burke, Washington and Sullivan Counties in this State, and Washington County in Virginia, and

> expected to be joined in a few days by Col. [Elijah] Clarke of Georgia, and Colonel [James] Williams of South Carolina, with about 1,000 more—As we have at this time called out our Militia without any orders from the Executive of our different States, and with the view of Expelling the Enemy out of this part of the Country, we think that such a body of men worthy of your attention, and would request you to send a General Officer, immediately to take the command of such Troops as may embody in this quarter—Our Troops being all Militia, and but little acquainted with discipline, we could wish him to be a Gentleman of address, and able to keep up a proper discipline, without disgusting the Soldiery—Every assistance in our power, shall be given the Officer you think proper to take the command of us . . . We are in a great want of Ammunition, and hope you will endeavor to have us properly furnished with that Article.[34]

With his hands full when in charge of the new Southern Army of Continentals and militia and with a low opinion of citizen-soldiers after the Camden fiasco that he had narrowly escaped thanks to a fast horse and a lack of nerve, Gates simply ignored the request.[35] But it no longer mattered at all what the hero of the great victory at Saratoga, New York, thought or even did anymore, much like General Washington, the Congress, and the Continental Army, because this frontier army continued to act on its own. What was most important was what militiaman Benjamin Sharp emphasized after Colonel Campbell was appointed by committee to the nominal commander of the expedition: "Within one hour after; we were on our horses and in full pursuit of the enemy."[36]

Dramatic Final Personal Decision of the Men in the Ranks

The next morning, October 4, before beginning the last effort to cover the relatively short distance southwest to Gilbert Town, the respective colonels asked the men of their commands to assemble, because they expected to meet Major Ferguson and his men on the following day and inflict a decisive blow. These citizen-soldiers of the frontier formed no neat or organized line when assembly was called. Instead, they casually formed in a large semicircle around their frontier spokesmen who were leading them they knew not where, while leaning on their trusty long rifles and hanging on every word of their popular leaders. By any measure, it looked like a motley hunting expedition to Kentucky's uncharted wilds, but smart leaders like Shelby fully appreciated the combat prowess of these young men and boys.

In the democratic tradition, Shelby and the colonels spoke to the men. Colonel Benjamin Cleveland, with a loud voice that emitted from the depths of his impressive size, first addressed the troops. He informed the men that a good many of them were certain to die somewhere east of the mountains, where their bodies would lie for eternity far from home. In consequence, they offered anyone with family members, especially those with elderly parents and infants in need of close care or anyone simply not up to the challenge for whatever reason to immediately remove themselves from the ranks and no one would think any less of them as men. Representing Wilkes County, North Carolina, Cleveland emphasized patriotism, stressing how he expected his boys to perform in the upcoming battle in a manner that their families and future generations of Americans would rejoice in forever more.

In addressing his Holston River Valley troops, who looked more like deer hunters and even Native American warriors, in some cases, than soldiers about to alter America's fate, Colonel Shelby emphasized to his Sullivan County men how "You have been informed of the offer. You who desire to decline it, will, when the word is given, march three steps to the rear, and stand, prior to which a few minutes will be granted you for consideration."[37] After a few seconds, Colonel Shelby gave the order to those men who wanted to leave the expedition to step back. At this moment, Shelby was never prouder of his young Overmountain men and boys, including teenagers yet to shave, because no one moved an inch, while leaning contentedly on their long rifles and looking serious. With emotion swelling up inside him, Colonel Shelby spoke with heartfelt words to his citizen-soldiers, who had made their own personal decisions:

> I am heartily glad to see you are men resolved to meet and fight your country's foes. When we encounter the enemy, don't wait for the word of command. Let each one of you be your own officer, and do the very best you can, taking every care you can of yourselves, and availing yourselves of every advantage that chance may throw in your way. If in the woods, shelter yourselves, and give them Indian play; advance from tree to tree, pressing the enemy and killing and disabling all you can. Your officers will shrink from no danger—they will be consistently

> with you, and the moment the enemy give war, be on the alert and strictly obey orders.[38]

Colonel Shelby's words of wisdom revealed the supreme importance of a strict reliance on Indian-fighting skills of the common fighting man, which had been fully demonstrated during the 1776 Cherokee War and other frontier conflicts to preserve the homeland. Colonel Shelby still recalled the tenacious fighting that had defeated the Shawnee and Mingo warriors at Point Pleasant in the Ohio Valley during October 1774. Young Lieutenant Isaac Shelby, in command of father Evan's company, and trusty frontiersmen, like Orderly Sergeant John Sawyers who was his right-hand man at Point Pleasant like during this expedition to Kings Mountain, had played key tactical roles that led to victory.[39]

This ad hoc assembly of the troops bound for Kings Mountain ended when the top officers passed around jugs of corn whisky to their followers as a reward for their do-or-die commitment to destroy Ferguson and his command at any cost. There was now no turning back for anyone, from lowly privates to top officers. The passing around of liquor was most symbolic because everyone instinctively realized that this might well be the last drink of alcohol for many of these young men and boys.[40] Early on the morning of October 4, officers ordered their citizen-soldiers, who were basically light cavalrymen, to once again mount up.

It was time to continue the journey in pursuit of Ferguson, who was still thought to be at Gilbert Town. After exhausted horses had been fed, rubbed down, and perhaps attended to with curry combs to keep them healthy if time allowed, the push of so many revenge-seeking Patriots resumed when the lengthy column of horse soldiers, with only two days of food supplies, was once again on the move.

They proceeded down Cane Creek as it descended to the lower lands to the south and led all the way to Gilbert Town just to the southwest. Colonel Campbell and his men moved at a brisk pace all day along the clear waters of Cane Creek, which had been named for the luxurious canebrakes that grew along its banks because of the soil's richness. All the while, they basked in the relative cool of early autumn now that the hottest part of the North Carolina summer had faded away like a soft summer dream. During the eighteen miles southwest over the rolling, forested hills from Quaker Meadows toward Gilbert Town and following the trickling waters of Cane Creek, the seemingly endless column of fighting men crossed and recrossed Cane Creek a number of times. These cold waters from nearby springs provided refreshment to sweaty men and tired horses. Feelings of not only excitement but also tension were sky-high by this time, which invigorated the men because they believed that they were about to engage in battle. As the ground gradually descended toward Gilbert Town, situated at the foothills of the Blue Ridge, they drew ever closer to the county seat of Tryon County where Ferguson was thought to be located. In consequence, the level of natural anxiety and nervousness, especially among the teenagers in the ranks who were yet to engage in their first fight, unlike their fathers and older brothers who had long battled Native Americans, increased among the fast-moving column of frontier horse soldiers.

The Prey Slips Out of the Net

However, upon reaching Gilbert Town on October 4, they were sorely disappointed because Ferguson and his Loyalists were long gone, leaving hardly a trace of their occupation of the county seat of Tryon County. The wily Scotsman and his command had slipped away somewhere in the backcountry, having seemingly vanished into thin air of the western North Carolina Piedmont. Scouts were hurried out to scour the countryside to ascertain if Ferguson was headed south to Ninety-Six or east to Charlotte and Cornwallis. Colonel Clarke and more than thirty of his diehard Georgia partisans, who were far from home, now joined the main Patriot command.[41]

Colonel Campbell's men gained satisfaction in the mistaken belief that a seemingly fearful Ferguson had fled their approach, but such was not the case. Eager to raise more Loyalist troops and still hoping to nab the troublesome Colonel Clarke and his Georgians, including civilian refugees and family members, on their flight north toward the safety of North Carolina's mountains, Ferguson had made the decision to finally leave Gilbert Town on Wednesday, September 27—the day after the Overmountain and backcountry men had departed Sycamore Shoals in the most grueling expedition of their lives. Ironically, however, Ferguson had pushed south from Gilbert Town and for the Broad River not from fear of the fast-approaching Patriot task force of which he was not aware, but while spreading the clever rumor that he was headed south and all the way to Ninety-Six, which was not the case.

Then, a Loyalist scout brought the first news of the Patriots' approach to Ferguson on September 30, when he was encamped on the Broad River, but this report lacked any specific details or collaborative intelligence for definite verification. Consequently, Ferguson still possessed his doubts because he could not believe that the enemy had reacted so quickly to his menacing threat and in such an overwhelming manner: swift developments thought to have been impossible under the circumstances, causing him to linger at his Broad River encampment for three days in the hope of the arrival of additional Tryon County recruits to swell his ranks, while he prudently penned a letter to Cornwallis requesting reinforcements. Surgeon Uzal Johnson recorded in his journal: "Constant information that the Rebels were collecting in force at Burk Court House, under Colls. Shelby, McDoul, & Cleveland." In the direction of the important western South Carolina forward post of Ninety-Six to the south, the Scotland-born major and his Loyalist command had initially headed southeast from Gilbert Town primarily because he had received a recent letter from Lieutenant Colonel John Harris Cruger. The well-connected Cruger was a member of the leading New York mercantile family for which young Alexander Hamilton, now serving as General Washington's chief of staff, had worked as a clerk for the family's trading firm on the Caribbean island of St. Croix from 1766 to 1768. He had informed Ferguson that Elijah Clarke and his Georgians were retreating in his direction to cross the mountains in an attempt to reach the safety of the Overmountain settlements. Consequently, in "sheer folly" that resulted in a waste of time, an obsessive Ferguson still remained more focused on intercepting and nabbing Georgia's leading partisan commander. Therefore, before being enlightened by Sevier's two deserters about a new frontier army's approach, Major Ferguson had believed that he was the pursuer of Clarke, while arrogantly convinced that his ill-advised threat to the Overmountain men had been heeded. Such a forceful response, which was now forthcoming with speed, by the Overmountain men was still not imagined by Ferguson until it was too late.[42]

Colonel Clarke and his small band of Georgia men, like his teenage son John Clarke and Irish frontiersman Captain Paddy Carr, had become the personal obsession of Ferguson for some time, because of the role that they had played with Colonel Shelby in the victories at Thicketty Fort, Cedar Springs, and Musgrove's Mill, while the major from Scotland was the obsession of Shelby and other leaders of Campbell's command. These dual differing priorities resulted in divergent pursuits along different paths that were shortly destined to finally meet at Kings Mountain, as if drawn together by fate.[43]

Ferguson had only avoided an earlier climactic showdown with his pursuers because he had come to the sensible conclusion that he was situated too far west at Gilbert Town and had lingered too long deep at the foot of the towering Blue Ridge Mountains for his own safety, when the two deserters, Samuel Chambers and James Crawford of Colonel Sevier's Washington County, North Carolina, militia, had informed him that he was now the prey.[44]

Major Ferguson then realized that he faced a serious quandary in purely tactical terms and began to see that he was in danger, while Patriot forces were now on his trail. First, while lingering at this Broad River encampment in Tryon County just south of Gilbert Town, he was still too far west and too far away from Cornwallis at Charlotte. And, of course, he now realized that he needed more men for the upcoming clash of arms that was increasingly inevitable. Consequently, to gain much-needed strength, he had been forced by circumstances beyond his control to remain stationary at this fixed point to gather additional Loyalists and for his furloughed men to return to his command, and especially to await the arrival of reinforcements from Cornwallis.

Ferguson was every inch a fighter and the idea of fleeing rapidly east to Charlotte to rejoin Cornwallis was almost an admission of failure, in his mind. And retiring east toward Charlotte meant that the approaching task force of Colonel Campbell and Colonel Clarke and other partisans would then have a greater opportunity to unite into a more formidable fighting force that possessed the potential to disrupt Cornwallis's entire campaign to invade North Carolina by launching a flank attack.[45] Therefore, as Lieutenant Anthony Allaire described Ferguson's most immediate obsession in his diary on Saturday September 30, "Lay [in camp] at James Step's [plantation] with an expectation of intercepting Col. Clarke on his return to the mountains; but he was prudent enough to take another route."[46]

Clearly, with the onset of October, Ferguson had wasted valuable time in waiting for an imaginary victory that he would win over Clarke that would never be, while the Overmountain and backcountry men ominously drew ever closer. However, having sensed his danger when so far west in unfamiliar and hostile country, Major Ferguson had possessed the good sense to have departed Gilbert Town.

At the Broad River encampment south of Gilbert Town and because of this most recent intelligence from the Overmountain men deserters, Ferguson had wisely, but belatedly, penned his missive dispatched by courier to Cornwallis at Charlotte only around sixty miles to the east, requesting reinforcements to meet the new threat that had seemingly magically appeared out of nowhere. Likewise, the Patriots had wasted no time upon almost immediately having discovered the desertions of the two men from the Washington County regiment and knew that the traitorous Crawford and Chambers were headed for Ferguson's camp to warn him of the approaching danger, which only hastened their pace and sense of urgency.

All in all, Ferguson waited three full days at his Broad River camp just north of the South Carolina line from where he had written to Lord Cornwallis at Charlotte that he planned to move east and "toward any reinforcement that your Lordship can send." Of course, it was a belated message, which was carried by local Loyalist Peter Quinn Abram Collins who then caused suspicions in the countryside and sparked a pursuit of him that resulted in the wasting of more time, when time was already rapidly running out for Major Ferguson and his men. By the time the two Loyalists reached Cornwallis with their messages, it was too late because the Battle of Kings Mountain had already been fought and Major Ferguson was dead and buried on the wooded slope where he had met a cruel fate, like his entire command that had been decimated.

Still Another Serious Miscalculation

Ferguson desperately needed large numbers of loyal Tryon County men to rise up to join him as soon as possible to maximize the number of troops to face his fast-moving pursuers, who he knew were on his trail. Posted on October 1 after he had written it out on a piece of paper on the same day from his encampment at Denard's Ford (which the Patriots would reach on October 4 and after having briefly lost the trail by continuing south toward Ninety-Six before turning east in the right direction) on the Broad River south of Gilbert Town, which he had established the first day of the month after a twelve-mile march through the North Carolina Piedmont, Ferguson's proclamation to men of Tryon County contained the usual bombast for which he was already well known, especially to Colonel Shelby and the Overmountain men, while appealing to the manhood and worst fears of backcountry Loyalists:

> Gentlemen:—Unless you wish to be eat up by an inundation of barbarians . . . who by their shocking cruelties and irregularities, give the best proof of their cowardice and want of discipline; I say, if you

> wish to be pinioned, robbed, and murdered, and see your wives and daughters, in four days, abused by the dregs of mankind—in short, if you wish or deserve to live, and bear the names of men, grasp your arms in a moment, and run to camp. The Back Water men have crossed the mountains: McDowell, Hampton, Shelby, and Cleveland are at their head, so you know what you have to depend upon. If you choose to be degraded forever and ever by a set of mongrels, say so at once, and let your women turn their backs to you, and look out for real men to protect them.[47]

Inflicting another self-administrated wound in his brash style, Major Ferguson continued to make himself enemy number one with this bombastic proclamation, when he should have done everything in his power not to do anything to stir up a hornet's nest, especially while still too far from Cornwallis and the main army. Once again, he had insulted the manhood of the backcountry settlers in general and especially the Scotch-Irish. Quite simply, Major Ferguson had not yet learned his lesson. Because of his own attitudes and words, he had now become nothing less than the number one target of the Patriots from the backcountry and Overmountain region—just like the heathen leader of the ancient Midianites who had threatened to bring fire and sword to the land of the Israelites, before God intervened to chastise him by unleashing the terrible "sword of the Lord and Gideon."[48]

Meanwhile, Ferguson took his time about departing Denard's Ford on the Broad River and moving east and ever closer to Cornwallis in the hope that large numbers of Loyalists would answer his October 1 proclamation. He was also still obsessed with destroying or capturing Clarke and his refugee Georgians. Compounding his mistakes, he failed to move rapidly east, despite knowing he was now the pursued. As mentioned, to throw his pursuers off his trail in the hope that they would continue south toward Ninety-Six, which was a stratagem that only briefly worked, Major Ferguson then abruptly turned east from Denard's Ford on October 1 and marched only a dozen miles down the left bank of the Broad River in the direction of his lordship and Charlotte, but his leisurely pace endangered his own safety. On October 2, he marched only four miles from his Broad River encampment after fording the river, moving at a snail's pace, almost as if he desired to allow the pursuers to catch up with his command. However, the next day before daylight, Ferguson was on the move and journeyed around twenty miles southeast, crossing Sandy Run Creek and then Buffalo Creek, before encamping near William Tate's "pretty plantation," which was located on the Broad River's east bank at the fork of Buffalo Creek and southeast of Gilbert Town. He then remained for two days "out with the rebels," in the words of surgeon Uzal Johnson, a New Jersey native, in the field. He also stayed at his picturesque tented camp at the Loyalist Tate's place on the banks of the Broad River, around ten miles west of Kings Mountain, on October 4 and 5, hoping for the expected swarm of Tryon County men to join his ranks. Here, around fifty miles slightly southwest of Charlotte, the ambitious Scotsman revealed his increasingly muddled thinking with two conflicting letters to Cornwallis: The first indicated how he was seeking a showdown with his pursuers and then his second request shortly thereafter for reinforcements implied less confidence about the outcome of the approaching inevitable battle. However, because of his ego and Scottish sense of pride, a defiant Major Ferguson was still in no great hurry because of his unlimited contempt for his opponent.

On October 5 while encamped on the Broad River at the Tate Plantation, Ferguson finally gained more definite intelligence about the ever-elusive Colonel Elijah Clarke and his partisan command whose exact whereabouts in the remote backcountry were still unknown. But these were ominous developments, because the Scotland-born major learned that these Georgia men—more than thirty Patriots under Major William Candler in Clarke's absence—had bolstered the ranks of the pursuing frontier army, which occurred on October 4, while the trekkers were encamped near Gilbert Town, along with a contingent of South Carolinians from Chester and York counties under Colonels James Williams and Edward Lacey. Major Ferguson now realized that the odds were gradually being stacked up even higher against him with each passing day, while he was still distant from the main army. The Scotland-born major must have been immensely frustrated, if not infuriated, by the news, which verified that he had failed to achieve his goal of capturing Clarke's Georgians, before they linked with his pursuers. In haste because of new developments that were swirling around him, Ferguson was shortly to pen his last, or second, letter to Lord Cornwallis in Charlotte from the Tate Plantation. In this letter, he again asked for assistance and implored in desperation that "something must be done soon." Displaying more prudence, Ferguson then continued farther east and ever-closer to Cornwallis for safety's sake, before it was too late.[49]

In his second-to-last letter to Cornwallis on October 5, an overconfident, if not somewhat delusional, Ferguson outlined his plans that reflected his current state of mind and increasingly urgent desire to secure reinforcements from his lordship: "I am on the march towards you, by a road leading from Cherokee Ford, north of King's Mountain. Three or four hundred good soldiers, part dragoons, would finish this business [because] Something must be done soon. This is their last push in this quarter and they are extremely desolate and awed."[50] On the same day in the afternoon, Thursday, October 5, Dr. Uzal Johnson, the surgeon of the Loyal American Regiment, who was with the baggage train, wrote of the news that greatly alarmed Ferguson: "There was a strong Party near the fording Place watching for us [and for the baggage train to move] a Mile & half to Buffalow [sic] Creek, where we joind Coll. Ferguson & the Detachment."[51]

This sudden turn east of Ferguson from Denard's Ford had fooled the pursuing Patriots. In the words of James Collins, one of the pursuing militiamen: "It has been expected that Ferguson would cross Broad River, high up [on its upper headwaters], and they [the task force] would meet him on his march. But he had turned his course, took a road to the right, and steered more to the east, towards Charlotte."[52]

Ironically, in command of the forward outpost at Ninety-Six to the south and failing to send the requested reinforcements north because of his own manpower weaknesses at this advanced outpost in the western backcountry, the New York blueblood Lieutenant Colonel John Harris Cruger had more initial prophetic foreboding about the seriousness of Ferguson's situation deep in the Carolina western backcountry than the Scottish major himself, who had been partly blinded by a dangerous hubris. Indeed, Cruger's October 3 reply to Ferguson's September 30 letter revealed a higher state of alarm than exhibited by Ferguson at this time because "so considerable [a] force as you understand is coming from the mountains" for the express purpose of vanquishing the cocky Scotsman and his Loyalist command.[53]

Clearly, because of the most recent intelligence, Ferguson continued to be worried about his exposed position situated too far west from the main army. Sounding almost like an ancient Roman centurion battling against a howling tide of Celtic warriors who had so often poured forth from the forested mountains of Scotland, Britain, and Wales, Lieutenant Colonel Cruger also wrote to Ferguson with a sense of growing alarm: "I don't see how you can possibly [stand and defend] the country and its neighborhood that you [are] now in

[and] I flattered myself they [the backcountry Loyalists] would have been equal to the mountain lads, and that no further call for the defensive would have been [made] on this part of the Province. I begin to think our views for the present rather large. We have been led to this, probably, in expecting too much from the militia" of the Carolinas.[54]

Indeed, out of a deep-seated Scottish pride that was partly based on his ancestors' glorious military deeds long ago and his deep personal hatred of the Overmountain men, especially Colonel Shelby, Ferguson simply could not force himself to do what would have been most prudent: ordering a forced march east to reach the safety of Cornwallis's army or to enhance the possibility of reinforcements reaching him in time from Charlotte by moving more rapidly east. But Ferguson thought differently despite the increasing danger and precariousness of his exposed position in unfamiliar country, envisioning a glorious battle in which he and his well-drilled troops would prevail to reveal all of his hard work in creating good fighting men and redeem his diminished reputation in the eyes of Cornwallis and his top lieutenants by achieving his longtime goal "to dispose once for all of this barbarian mountain horde."[55] Ferguson looked on the Overmountain men as the lowest and most uncouth of barbarians like the ancient Romans had long viewed Celtic warriors and peoples. A highly educated aristocrat, Ferguson was a reader of the ancient classics like other members of the British upper class, and the word barbarian had always been used by the ancient Greek writers for anyone who was non-Greek and especially in regard to the Persians, or Asians. To Major Ferguson, it must have seemed to him that he was now in the backcountry wilds and had marched to the end of the earth like a member of Alexander the Great's army that had moved against the Persian Empire and all the way to India so long ago.[56]

After having reached Gilbert Town on October 4 and after discovering that Ferguson had fled south, the Overmountain and backcountry men had rested before continuing south in following the false trail in the belief that the elusive Scotsman was now headed farther south to the safety of Ninety-Six, according to the deliberately planted rumor that initially proved effective in fooling the Patriots. Meanwhile, Patriot morale increased with the arrival of Major William Chronicle, a "young man of great promise," and around twenty of his "South Fork Boys" who hailed from Lincoln County, North Carolina, which was the backcountry region of the South Fork of the Catawba River.[57] At this time, the Patriots were still not sure of Ferguson's exact plans and in what direction he was moving, after having reached Denard's Ford just below Gilbert Town. After Ferguson turned east toward Cornwallis at Charlotte, Patriot scouts had briefly lost the trail in moving along the west bank of the Broad River and then continued in the same direction, thanks partly to the recent rain that eliminated tracks. As mentioned, they had continued to push south in the mistaken belief that Ferguson was headed for Ninety-Six.

Ironically, there might well have been no Battle of Kings Mountain had Major Ferguson not shortly decided to make his last stand on the fateful high ground located just south of Cherokee Ford and the North Carolina border, after having finally decided to depart Tate Plantation before sunrise on October 6. Here, as noted, he had remained for three days wasting valuable time, after having moved indecisively and erratically across the Piedmont during the first three days of October. Hampering Ferguson's march of sixteen miles on October 6, heavy rains drenched the lands of the backcountry, slowing the Loyalist's progress to the east. After crossing the Broad River at Cherokee Ford, Ferguson marched his men off the main Charlotte Road and toward the highest ground that dominated the distant horizon to the south, heavily forested Kings Mountain. The ever-unpredictable Major Ferguson was not going to Charlotte after all, as seemingly everyone expected on both sides.

Timely Enlightenment

Meanwhile, everything suddenly changed for the better for the Patriots, who had been moving in the wrong direction (south toward Ninety-Six) when two South Carolina colonels with lofty reputations unexpectedly rode into camp. Colonel Edward Lacey reached the Patriot camp of no tents, with everyone sleeping on the cold ground in thin blankets along the banks of the Green River at Alexander's Ford, in the early morning hours of Friday, October 6, after a lengthy night ride from Thomas Sumter's partisan command that was camped at Flint Hill just northeast of Gilbert Town. Lacey brought news of Ferguson's proper direction (east) toward Charlotte seemingly to link with Cornwallis or receive reinforcements and not south toward Ninety-Six, as Colonel James Williams had recently led them to believe. Williams had envisioned an attack on the key British forward post, which was vulnerable and there for the taking, in his home area and that of his followers, Ninety-Six.

With time of the essence and the growing fear that the Cherokee might now be attacking the western frontier settlements, the Patriot colonels faced a serious dilemma, because they had to determine fact from fiction by quickly analyzing the latest intelligence, after having sent out scouts to gather information about Ferguson's proper direction. Basically, what they had to cipher was which South Carolina colonel possessed the correct information: Was Ferguson heading south to Ninety-Six as Williams emphasized, or east toward Charlotte as Lacey had maintained with equal vigor? A key decision—one upon which the entire success of the expedition now hinged and perhaps even the outcome of the American Revolution—would have to be wisely made by the Patriot colonels of their respective commands. The ad hoc democratic committee of frontier leaders must now decide which colonel possessed the most accurate intelligence and which one was right about Ferguson's whereabouts deep in the back country.

In the end, this timely information from Lacey, one of Thomas Sumter's top lieutenants, was absolutely crucial and Colonel Shelby and the other leaders made the smart decision to rely on it instead of Colonel Williams's information that Ferguson was still moving south toward Ninety-Six. This situation now meant that the hated Scotsman had to be struck before he escaped entirely or was reinforced by his lordship, fueling a greater sense of urgency. Another officers' conference was called and crucial decisions were made by committee. It was decided by senior frontier officers that the best mounted men would be selected for the next phase, the final one, of the pursuit: to gradually turn east and set out for the Cowpens, South Carolina, situated just south of the North Carolina-South Carolina border and northwest of Kings Mountain, with trailing foot-soldiers following behind the horsemen. Most important, this well-known expanse of pastureland amid the wilderness known as the Cowpens became the next rendezvous site for the acquisition of much-needed additional forces, South Carolina boys in this case, to join the main army.[58]

The Key to Decisive Success—Moving Fast and with Secrecy

In the end, Lieutenant Colonel John Harris Cruger's fears about Ferguson's ultimate fate when on his own in the remote backcountry were well founded. The Scotsman had finally belatedly departed his tented encampment at Denard's Ford on the Broad River, heading east. Most important, the Patriot colonels now realized that a much more rapid pursuit in the form of a forced march was needed to catch Ferguson before it was too late, because of the rumor that Tarleton and his British Legion had been dispatched from Charlotte by

Cornwallis to reinforce him. However, the arduous journey over the mountains had sapped the morale and stamina of both men and horses, after having struggled onward for days throughout the autumn-tinted forests.

Consequently, after the colonels had accepted Colonel Lacey's version of Ferguson's whereabouts, the fittest men and healthiest horses were selected to be part of the "flying column" by the sharp-eyed colonels at Alexander's Ford, which was located on the waters of the Green River on the night of Friday, October 5–6. Around seven hundred of the finest fighting men were chosen as the rapid strike force for the upcoming forced march east to catch Ferguson, with the Cowpens, located just below the North Carolina line and northwest of Kings Mountain, as their first objective. Most of the finest remaining horses of the expeditionary force had "trappings dyed red and yellow and worked with beads like Indian horses," which matched their frontier owners who looked more like Indians than white men.[59]

For some time, horses had been breaking down from the lack of food and exhaustion. Benjamin Sharp described how "after hard marching for some time, we found our progress much retarded by our footmen and weak horses that were not able to sustain the duty."[60] Like the frontier and backcountry colonels, Virginia-born Captain David Vance, of the North Carolina militia from Burke County, had to make some hard decisions. He emphasized that orders were for those citizen-soldiers who were unable to embark upon "a severe march" to immediately "fall back into the foot troops [men without horses who followed in rear of the mounted forces] and give their horses to footmen [and] a number of exchanges were made."[61] With no time to sleep, the entire night was spent in selecting and preparing the task force to catch Ferguson before he escaped or was reinforced. With the dawn of October 6, the task force of the best men and horses rode at a brisk pace southeast for the Cowpens, which they were about to cross on this first Friday of the month.[62] Meanwhile, a new detachment of "footmen and worn horses" was created under Captain William Neil of Virginia. Neil was ordered "to follow as fast as his detachment could bear [and] Thus disencumbered we gained fast upon the enemy."[63]

In Colonel Shelby's words: "Having gained a knowledge of [Ferguson's] design, it was determined in a council of the principal officers to pursue him with all possible dispatch. Accordingly, two nights before the action the officers were engaged all night in selecting the best men, the best horses and the best rifles, and at the dawn of day took Ferguson's trail and pursued him [because]

The mountain men had turned out to catch Ferguson [who was] their object" to be destroyed.[64] Most of all, it was now fully realized that if Lord Cornwallis dispatched reinforcements, especially Tarleton and his crack British Legion, and if they arrived before the Patriots struck a blow, then all would be lost. Therefore, this was now very much a race to catch Ferguson before reinforcements arrived. In the words of Ireland-born Colonel William Hill: "If this battle was not fought before the [expected] reinforcement [Tarleton] came the certain probability was that it never would be fought."[65]

As the Overmountain and backcountry colonels fully realized, nothing was more important in successful warfare from time immemorial than moving swiftly and stealthily to catch an unwary opponent by surprise. The brilliant Prussian war theorist Carl von Clausewitz, who fought against Napoleon Bonaparte, a true military genius, emphasized the supreme importance of the element of surprise, which was the subject of Chapter Nine in his famous work about the art of war, *On War*. In Clausewitz's immortal words, the element of surprise "becomes the means to gain superiority, but because of its psychological effect it should also be considered as an independent element . . . it confuses the enemy and lowers his morale; many examples, great and small, show how this in turn multiplies the results [and] The two factors that produce surprise are secrecy and speed. Both predispose a high degree of energy on the part of the attacker [and] they require great efficiency."[66]

Besides the lethal long rifle, nothing was now more important to the Overmountain men than the quality and condition of their horses. As far back as the Scottish struggles for independence and the Scottish-English border wars, the men of the Celtic clans had especially prized good horses and equestrian skills like the men of Kings Mountain. One reason for the success of the Scottish borderers, or reivers, during their slashing raids into northern England was the reliance on their skilled horsemanship to move swiftly over long distances—the same tactical formula for success of light horsemen of the mounted militiamen that eventually allowed them to surprise Major Ferguson and his Loyalists at Kings Mountain. For a host of reasons in the end, it was the key factors of secrecy and speed of a relatively small, highly mobile task force of experienced fighting men that ultimately doomed Major Patrick Ferguson and his entire command: vital lessons that had been already learned during the 1776 Cherokee campaign, when mounted horsemen of the frontier militia covered long distances to repeatedly vanquish the dismounted Cherokee, which was a New World tactical formula for success against native people stretching back to the days of the Spanish conquistadors who had conquered the mighty Aztec Empire in 1521.[67]

Ironically, Lord Cornwallis, who still waited in Charlotte for word from Ferguson, who commanded his left flank, before he could push north to resume his invasion of North Carolina, had long smartly appreciated the swift effectiveness of "Ban" Tarleton's cavalrymen as the ultimate killing machine, but he never imagined that the Patriots might also utilize speed in the same way to destroy his most isolated command upon which he now depended. Consequently, Ferguson was destined to never receive the last message, an especially ironic one, "I now consider you perfectly safe," sent too late to him by Cornwallis, because he was already dead and his entire command eliminated at Kings Mountain.[68] Clearly, Lord Cornwallis failed to understand the hard-hitting potential and superior mobility capabilities of the frontier's experienced mounted militiamen, while underestimating their combat capabilities, just like Ferguson.

Indeed, what has been most often overlooked as a key to victory at Kings Mountain was that this was actually very much a story about the utilization of the capabilities of cavalry, or mounted militia. For all practical purposes, the bold strike on Ferguson was a mounted raid of experienced horse soldiers who utilized the element of surprise, thanks to their horsemanship and superior mobility.

A traditional raid (not mounted) had long been a regular feature of Indian warfare for centuries when tribes battled each other for a wide variety of reasons, and the second most common and oldest tactic after the ambush, which Native Americans had transformed into time-proven tactical masterpieces. The Overmountain backcountry men had taken the Indian tactic of launching devastating raids, especially preemptive strikes, deep into hostile territory and combined it with skilled horsemanship—Native Americans fought for centuries primarily on foot before the Spanish arrived—to bring the art of the lightning-strike raid to catch the enemy by surprise to a higher level on the frontier, where it had evolved into an even harder-hitting tactic.

Because each frontier farmer on both sides of the mountains had to possess a good horse for daily survival, the forgotten capabilities, especially in moving long distances, of homespun cavalry of the Overmountain and backcountry militia of each county proved invaluable in now bestowing this key tactical asset at the right time and in the right place. As mentioned, these frontier horsemen of the well-organized local militia from both sides of the mountains had played the decisive role in the winning of the 1776 Cherokee War, when they had worked closely together to eliminate the greatest threat to their vulnerable homeland to the west. Contrary to traditional views about the fighting farmers of the backcountry and Overmountain region, they can be more correctly viewed as legitimate light cavalrymen of a formidable nature, but not in the traditional sense because they fought far more effectively dismounted like in the case of Kings Mountain. However, it took a high level of resourceful fighting men and equally resourceful commanders, who were as imaginative, innovative, and inventive as they were daring in their tactical thinking to become masters of the frontier raid and to prevail in the bloody art of Indian warfare.

For generations, almost all books about the story of Kings Mountain have placed emphasis on the fact that the day was won by frontier riflemen using the long rifle, which was indeed the case: a story long embellished to have become part of the mythical frontier. But, of course, without the fine horses and equestrian skills of the Patriots during the rapid descent on Ferguson, there would have been no surprise that ensured the one-sided victory won by the firepower and accuracy of the long rifles: a remarkable tactical success only made possible by the durability, strength, and conditioning of the horses from the beginning. The notable lack of emphasis of generations of historians on the important role played by these natural horsemen should not be surprising. After all, cavalry played an undersized role throughout the American Revolution on both sides, especially in regard to the British. However, in many ways, this war saw the birth of the United States Cavalry, despite the extremely small numbers of horsemen in Washington's Continental Army. But in terms of overall effectiveness, it was not the Continental cavalry of the regular army that truly shone to make any kind of a decisive impact in the war's outcome. Instead, it was the informal cavalry of the mounted infantrymen, or the fighting farmers of the backwoods militia, from both sides of the mountains, on horseback in the South that truly demonstrated how mounted infantry troops should be best utilized to win the key battle in this war for the heart and soul of America: a forgotten legacy of the Kings Mountain showdown.

Cultural and geographical differences also played a part in the final equation of victory when it came to the horse. The fact that England was relatively small (around 50,000 square miles) deemphasized the importance of journeying long distances to minimize the overall importance of the horse: the antithesis of the situation in America where the land seemed endless, especially on the frontier, and where journeying long distances was required. Therefore, settlers on both sides of the mountains needed a good horse to cover long distances in everyday life and survival often depended upon that fact. During this war, the English lacked a large cavalry arm in North America because of an overreliance on infantry; the thousands of miles between England and America made transporting a cavalry regiment's horses across the Atlantic almost an impossibility, and the great expense that involved equipping and arming cavalry units. The overall strategic price paid by England for having *only two* dragoon regiments assigned to America during the entire war was enormous, proving almost incalculable. From the beginning, the many victories won by the British over Washington's Continental Army and other Patriot allies were never followed up by a decisive stroke delivered by cavalry, which was its traditional role, allowing Patriot armies—ironically, quite unlike Irish and Scottish nationalist armies of ill-armed commoners over the centuries—to survive and fight again to ensure a lengthy war of attrition across America's vastness. The British early attempted to compensate for this glaring regular cavalry weakness by raising Provincial volunteer dragoon regiments among the Loyalists in New York and New Jersey, but it was never enough.

However, the key to the outstanding successes of Banastre Tarleton and his elite British Legion, whose Loyalist cavalry had been raised in the North, was due to Tarleton's emphasis on securing the swiftest and fastest horses (confiscated in America, especially in South Carolina) for greater mobility and greatly enhanced war-waging capabilities: the key advantage now held by the men of Kings Mountain, which would allow them to literally run down Ferguson. With no exaggeration but considerable insight, author John Knight concluded in regard to the British army's lack of more cavalry and the crucial importance of swift, hard-hitting tactics and mobility in this war: "It was a scarcity that went some way to losing Britain the war."[69] Likewise, Lord Cornwallis realized as much, writing how, "Without good cavalry we can do nothing in this country."[70] In striking contrast, Leonard Hice, one of Colonel Campbell's Virginia men, proudly described himself and his comrades as "Mounted Riflemen," and now hundreds of these confident fighting men were headed Ferguson's way at a fast pace.[71] Born in Westchester County, New York, just north of New York City, in 1755, Lieutenant Anthony Allaire, one of Ferguson's top officers and of

Huguenot (French Protestant) descent, complimented the mounted backcountry partisans of South Carolina that he and his men had chased in vain: "The jockeys being on horseback easily made off."[72]

Therefore, the importance of Tarleton's Legion of Loyalists in advancing north to guard Cornwallis's right flank near the coast to invade North Carolina on the east while Ferguson's mounted Loyalists pushed north through the backcountry of western North Carolina to guard the army's left flank was crucial for success, while Lord Cornwallis advanced in the center: a three-prong advance over an extremely wide area that was mostly hostile to the invaders. The defeat of Ferguson or Tarleton on either flank had the potential to sabotage the aristocratic lord's entire ambitious and optimistic invasion plan. In the words of a young French officer that were right on target, especially in regard to the war in the South, Lord Cornwallis had "always made the Americans tremble" and this now included the early fall of 1780.[73] But now, the Overmountain and backcountry men were about to make Ferguson and even Lord Cornwallis himself tremble in their leather boots.

Desperate Bid to Thwart Cornwallis's Plan of Destroying Washington's Continental Army

The desperate race of around seven hundred hard-riding militiamen during their march southeast toward the open grasslands of the Cowpens could not have been more important in overall strategic terms, because Ferguson posed no ordinary threat. By early October 1780, the British and Loyalists had emerged triumphant and were easily winning the war in the South, according to the bold strategic plan of conquest of Clinton and Cornwallis. Even though they did not realize it at the time, the fast-moving Overmountain and backcountry men were about to overturn the core foundation of the main strategy for winning the war: Cornwallis's planned march northward into North Carolina, Virginia, and then into Pennsylvania to vanquish Washington's Continental Army, after Clinton pushed south from New York City to catch Washington in a deadly pincer movement.

In moving southeast toward the Cowpens on the rainy morning of October 7 at a rapid pace, this task force of handpicked citizen-soldiers, whose numbers were about to increase, had no idea that they were about to reverse the war's course. In the history of European colonization and especially in the case of the Irish, Welsh, and Scots over the centuries thanks to England's might and utter ruthlessness, never had any colonial people succeeded in a revolt against the mother country. However, the lowly and humble mostly Scotch-Irish of the Overmountain region and the backcountry were about to take a giant step to change the course of history with their long rifles, swift horses, Indian fighting experience, and a good deal of courage. Although they were mostly poor men, the Scotch-Irish—who were the the elite fighters on both sides of the mountains—were most commonly called "pack of beggars," "patriot ruffians," "mongrel race," "white savages," "scum of the Earth," "crackers," "dregs of mankind" (Ferguson's words), and worse by the elitists of both sides. They were held in such contempt by both friends, including in Philadelphia and especially in Charles Town, and foes that no one could imagine that they were about to change not only the course of the American Revolution, but also the military annals of American history at Kings Mountain.[74]

Most of all, these were young men and boys of high character and devout faith whose hearts were filled with love for their people, families, and communities, which were the key motivators on decisive October 7, 1780.

These ordinary men were about to demonstrate that Patriot militia, part-time fighting men who were untrained, and undisciplined citizen-soldiers could prove to be not only highly effective but also quite lethal on the battlefield when pitted against Royal Provincials who had been trained as British regulars.[75] In the words of teenage James Collins about the pursers: "Everyone ate what they could get, and slept in his own blanket, sometimes eating raw turnips, and often resorting to a little parched corn" during the long race to catch Ferguson by surprise.[76]

A Righteous Rage

A righteous rage now dominated the task force of the Overmountain and backcountry men, which helped to propel their push ever faster toward the Cowpens and eventually Kings Mountain. One backcountry Patriot wrote how the memories of all of the foe's past injustices and cruelties at the hands of both the British and Loyalists were never far from their minds when journeying onward to meet Ferguson: The "ill behavior of the enemy made an impression on the minds of the most serious men . . . and raised their courage under the belief that they would be made instruments in the hand of Heaven to punish this enemy for his wickedness and blasphemy."[77] Young James Collins, who served in the ranks of Major William Chronicle's boys from the South Fork of the Catawba River in Lincoln County, perhaps said it best in moral terms: "Our danger began to increase [because] Ferguson was coming on with his boasted marksmen, and seemed to threaten the destruction of the whole country [and] The Tories were flocking to his standard from every quarter, and there appeared very little safety for us, but as God would it a patriotic army sprang up" at the last minute.[78]

Private Burt Moore, who had been born in Halifax County, Virginia, was a savvy frontiersman, having served as a "spy," or scout, in the war against the Cherokee. Like so many other backcountry Patriot families, he had been driven west of the mountains when "Ferguson overran the upcountry" of South Carolina, and now wanted revenge whenever they met the hated major.[79] But it was not just Ferguson who was targeted for elimination in this campaign, but also the behind-the-scenes author of Ferguson's actions. In the angry words of one American soldier written to Lord Cornwallis: "The history of your transactions in Georgia and the Carolinas is a history of cruelty and injustice unparalleled in the annals of a civilized country."[80] Hard-earned experience had come to this band of determined men from the backcountry by way of a good many forgotten skirmishes in the long struggle for possession of the South Carolina backcountry, which included the little-known fights at Cracker's Neck, Juniper Springs, Dean's Swamp, White Bridge, Fish Dam Ford, Black Swamp, Biggin Church, Quinby Bridge, Little Flat Rock Creek, Bull Swamp, Black River, Wappoo Bridge, Edisto Swamp, and other obscure places that few people had ever heard about. Here, in South Carolina, more battles and skirmishes were fought than anywhere else in America, which created savvy and resourceful fighters who were destined to rise to the fore at Kings Mountain.[81]

But for these common men, no memory of any battle lingered stronger and longer in their minds to generate a righteous rage than the slaughter of Colonel Abraham Buford's Virginia Continentals at the Waxhaws, South Carolina, by Tarleton's command on May 29, 1780. Consequently, on decisive October 7, 1780, the official countersign of the Patriot troops when they were finally unleashed on Ferguson's troops was "Buford."[82] However, this righteous rage would not have been so effective without the continued overconfidence and arrogance of British leadership at all levels.

Flowing Grasslands of the Cowpens

The task force of the best seven hundred or so men and horses continued southeastward and finally reached the open and gently rolling lands of the Cowpens in the northwest South Carolina Piedmont after darkness had fallen on the evening of October 6. This timely respite presented the opportunity for a one-hour rest in what was actually a broad natural meadow of tall grass with only a scattering of trees and the chance to dine on some fresh beef from the farm of a Tory. Because of the desperate race to catch Ferguson before it was too late, the brief rest at Cowpens would be the only one before they would finally reach Kings Mountain. The picturesque meadow situated amid a scrub pine wilderness had been long used by generations of frontier farmers for the fattening up of cattle in winter—a frontier pasturing ground for the upcountry—for market before the final drive to Charles Town and the highest bidder. In timely fashion, the weary Patriots were joined by more South Carolinians from Thomas Sumter's command under Colonels William Hill and Edward Lacey. Lacey once had his Tory father bound for fear of his alerting the enemy when about to catch German-born Captain Christian Huck, a Philadelphia lawyer, and his command in York County, South Carolina, by surprise to win a spirited victory on July 12, 1780. They were also joined by Colonel William Graham's North Carolinians under Major William Chronicle and Lieutenant Colonel Frederick Hambright not long after the recent addition of Colonel Elijah Clarke's small band of Georgians under Major William Chandler.

At this time, the Cowpens was owned by a Loyalist named Saunders, who was forced out of bed to provide information and who watched helplessly while his cattle were slaughtered and his fifty-acre cornfield razed in only "about ten minutes," according to Silas McBee, by the hungry Patriots, who would need all their energy and strength for the battle that lay ahead. That same night at Cowpens, Joseph Kerr, an exceptional Patriot spy of Scotch-Irish descent, entered the encampment at the Cowpens. Providing much-needed fresh intelligence, especially in regard to Ferguson's carelessness in posting no sentinels or pickets after having successfully posed as a Loyalist, he reported that he had just scouted out Major Ferguson's encampment at Peter Quinn's farm barely a half-dozen miles from Kings Mountain. Most important, Kerr informed the colonels that Ferguson planned to camp for the night on the remote mountaintop south of Cherokee Ford called Kings Mountain with just under 1,500 Loyalists. Kerr's latest intelligence prompted another hasty commander's call of the Overmountain and backcountry colonels to ascertain the next best course of action. Because Ferguson was now so close to Charlotte and Cornwallis, the audacious colonels, especially Shelby, decided that even more drastic action was needed or the hated Scotsman and his Loyalists would either escape or be reinforced, nevermind the danger of attacking one of his lordship's top lieutenants right under his nose. After having been joined by around 450 South Carolina men under Colonel James Williams, the militia colonels decided to once again cull the ranks of the flying column task force for the finest men and horses in a second selection, which now included the best soldiers and horses from the newly arrived reinforcements, for the last pursuit. Once the swift reorganization was made to secure the best men and most fit horses, they immediately galloped off and headed east around nine o'clock that dark and cloudy night of October 6 without sufficient rest. Prudently, the colonels also ordered their most reliable scouts to gather as much fresh intelligence about Ferguson as possible.

Until they were slowed by downpours of rain, the lengthy Patriot column headed east toward Kings Mountain from Cowpens and parallel to the North Carolina-South Carolina border just to the north. The new flying column now consisted of 910 carefully chosen men and horses for the desperate pursuit. The original task force of seven hundred men that had been selected on the Green River were now bolstered by 210 South Carolina boys under Lacey, Hill, Williams, and Major William Chronicle. Chronicle's small band of South Fork Boys had linked with the main body at the Cowpens. Chronicle's and German-born Lieutenant Colonel Frederick Hambright's men all hailed from Lincoln County, North Carolina. Most symbolic, but entirely by accident, the final flying column that was destined to nab Ferguson at Kings Mountain—located around thirty-three miles east of Cowpens—was now about equally divided between Overmountain men at 440 and backcountry men at around 470, which disproves the enduring myth that it was primarily an Overmountain task force that finally caught Major Ferguson and wiped him out with blazing long rifles before he could escape.[83]

Even more, and what has been often overlooked about the final push east through the South Carolina backcountry from Cowpens on the rainy night of October 6, around eighty men, who Shelby described as "foot-cavalry," without horses, now marched to the rear under Captain Neil, hoping to join their mounted comrades in the upcoming fight of their lives.[84] This made good sense because Kerr had informed the frontier colonels that the Scottish major was going "to the top of Kings Mountain [south of the main road and Cherokee Ford] and remain there a few days in order to give protection to all the 'rebels' who would join Ferguson's standard."[85] Ferguson was going nowhere and now things seemed to be more on the side of the Patriots at a time when every man would be needed.

The arrival of Colonel James Williams and his approximately 450 South Carolina troops at the Cowpens had been a timely addition—an invaluable contribution of vital manpower that has long been minimized by historians—to the fast-moving task force, whose members were weary from the lack of rest throughout the long journey. Williams was a good representative example of the high quality of the South Carolina backcountry contingents that compared favorably to the Overmountain men, whom historians have long excessively focused on in the telling of the Kings Mountain story. By way of his own achievements and those of his mostly forgotten men of the Little River Regiment from the Little River District, Colonel Williams had risen to the fore in the war's darkest days to help orchestrate the surprising victory at Musgrove's Mill, thanks to Colonel Shelby's successful ambush tactics, and then at Kings Mountain—a key role played by him and his South Carolina men that has been largely forgotten in part because he was fatally cut down on October 7 and because of the self-serving actions of political rivals.

In his own words, Virginia-born Williams, thirty-nine, a migrant to the South Carolina backcountry from North Carolina, and once a distinguished member of the First Provincial Congress which had represented the backcountry, explained in a June 1779 letter to his son why he fought with such determination and eventually sacrificed his life, affirming that God was never far from his mind: "I am, by the care of Providence, in the field in defense of my country [because] I am obliged to take the field in defense of my rights and liberties, and that of my children. God only knows that it is not of choice, but of necessity, and from the consideration that I had rather suffer anything than lose my birthright, and that of my children."[86] Like so many South Carolinians, Williams was a devout Presbyterian and a faithful member of the Little River Presbyterian Church, which was revealed in his late September 1779 letter to his wife while fighting for America's liberty, when he solemnly prayed to God "to protect and defend us, in all danger, and through every difficulty; but, my dear, let us, with one heart, call on God for his mercies, and that his goodness may be continued by us, under his blessing, may have the happiness of enjoying each other's society once more."[87]

With his son Daniel, who was a proud member of South Carolina's Little River Regiment, Colonel James Williams now headed east for Kings Mountain. He also had a personal "score to settle with Ferguson."[88] In June 1780, Ferguson and his men had paid a nasty visit to the colonel's home when they occupied the Williams family plantation in the backcountry on Little River, which was a tributary of the Saluda River, Mount Pleasant. Worst of all, they had callously turned his wife and children out of the family home to fend for themselves as best they could to ensure that a rage now burned deep inside the heart of Colonel Williams.[89] But, of course, the seemingly endless crimes of the Loyalists, including troops under Ferguson, fueled the motivations of these citizen-soldiers to an excessive degree. For instance, Scotch-Irish Joseph McJunkin, who served in South Carolina's Little River Regiment, and his sister Jane, who was known for her defiance and hatred of Loyalists, were incensed by the fact that the Loyalists had "taken one of our bravest fellows, John Johnson, Esqr., [and] hanged him without judge or jury."[90]

As mentioned, in the hope that the Loyalists from Tryon County would turn out in large numbers in answering his October 1 proclamation after having departed Denard's Ford on the Broad River, Major Ferguson continued to move east at a leisurely pace and ever-closer to Cornwallis at Charlotte until sighting Kings Mountain looming on the distant horizon to the south, despite knowing that he was being pursued by not only the Overmountain men and backcountry men, but also Colonel Clarke's Georgians and a large body of South Carolinians.[91] The rapid pursuit was closing in on Major Ferguson and his command, because the Patriots possessed the advantage of swift mobility. In contrast to the Scottish major's men, the Patriots made much better time in their wild dash east through the South Carolina backcountry, because they, in the words of James Collins, "had not a single baggage waggon [sic] or any kind of camp equipage" to slow them down, unlike Ferguson's command.[92] The determined pursuers "never halted to refresh ourselves or horses," in the words of militiaman Benjamin Sharp.[93]

Fatal October Mistake: Deciding to Make a Stand on Kings Mountain

Ironically, despite informing Cornwallis on October 5 that he was on the "march towards you by a road leading from Cherokee Ford north of Kings Mountain," Ferguson had then turned south, because he had dismissed out of hand any possibility of joining Cornwallis at Charlotte. Instead, on October 6, he now most of all desired to make a stand, as if tired of being pursued by the citizen-soldiers whom he detested as "mongrels." With the Scottish fighting spirit of his Highlands ancestors rising to the fore, Ferguson now wanted a fight at Kings Mountain, only thirty-five miles southwest of Cornwallis at Charlotte.[94] As penned in his journal, Surgeon Uzal Johnson merely noted how after having "marched sixteen Miles to Kings Hill [we] took up our Ground."[95] However, Major Ferguson's ambition overlooked the unsettling reality and uneasy feeling of some of his wiser followers that "we [are] separated from all the army, acting with the militia."[96]

With rain falling and needing to keep his men dry when south of Cherokee Ford, Ferguson had decided to encamp on the barren eastern spur of Kings Mountain or on "Little Kings Mountain," as Lieutenant Anthony Allaire penned in his diary on October 6. Here, around ten miles south of Cherokee Ford, Ferguson was now positioned on his coveted high ground perch 1,019 feet in height primarily because he was "well informed in the arts of war," in the New York lieutenant's complimentary words. Without consulting Cornwallis or anyone else for that matter, the risk-taking Scotsman had decided to make a defensive stand on high ground on October 6 to fight rather than retreat any farther east as if ashamed of fleeing "mongrels," expecting the arrival of a large number of Loyalists, whom he believed would enthusiastically answer his October 1 call to arms. And Ferguson had belatedly requested Lord Cornwallis on October 3 and 5 to dispatch reinforcements from Charlotte, which was within a day's ride at only around thirty miles to the northeast—requests that were already too late.

As fate would have it and fortunately for the Patriot task force, the hard-hitting Lieutenant Colonel Banastre Tarleton was now still too ill for the vital mission of reinforcing Ferguson, which was then given to Scotsman Major Archibald McArthur of Ferguson's own 71st Regiment of Foot (Scottish Highlanders). This reinforcement was most symbolic, because Ferguson had been first promoted to the rank of major of the Second Battalion, 71st Regiment, which was a Highlands Light Infantry command consisting of tough and well-disciplined Scottish fighting men. McArthur immediately marched southwest with a battalion of this crack regiment of Scotsmen to Arness Ford on the Catawba River, where Cornwallis instructed Ferguson to meet McArthur: an all-important dispatch that was destined to never reach

Major Ferguson, however. Without such vital knowledge, Ferguson had made his fateful decision to make his stand on the high ground that appeared most promising to him. After having sighted the imposing elevation in the distance to the south and then deliberating upon securing the highest ground in the area, Ferguson had turned away from a push toward the Catawba and marched south for Kings Mountain instead of the Catawba Ford for the ordered rendezvous in what was a key missed connection that helped to change the course of history.[97]

Ferguson's complete faith in Lord Cornwallis and the fighting prowess of his men was almost limitless, especially his crack American Volunteers, which consisted of New Jersey and New York Provincials who were trained and disciplined like British regulars. As he had informed Cornwallis in his request on October 5, "3 or 400 good soldiers part dragoons [Tarleton] would finish the business" to ensure a decisive victory in the upcoming clash of arms and perhaps even win the war in the South in his estimation.[98] However, the Scottish major, who still carried the scars from his wound suffered at Brandywine Creek, was much too confident, if not delusional, even at this late date. Therefore, he was guilty of committing a cardinal sin in the warrior's art by forfeiting the initiative and all mobility, especially when the Scotsman knew that he was being pursued by Overmountain and backcountry men. Then, Ferguson shockingly "made little effort to gather fresh information by scouts and roving patrols" to prevent surprise upon which the Patriots depended so much.[99]

In his final letter to Cornwallis on October 5, Ferguson had written:

> I have arrived today at King Mountain and I have taken a post where I do not think I can be forced by a stronger enemy than that against us. I have wrote for the militia assembling under Colonel [Mathew] Floyd [an Irishman who had migrated to the backcountry from Pennsylvania years ago] to join me tomorrow evening [ironically, after the battle had already been fought and] I understand that we have little or no reinforcement to expect from Col. Cruger [at Ninety-Six] or his militia immediately. Good soldiers as reserves behind our riflemen and a few real dragoons [especially Tarleton's men] to second with effect and support the flanks would enable us to act decisively and vigorously . . . if you are pleased to order us forward.[100]

However, Ferguson was not simply guilty of ignorance or hubris, especially in regard to overlooking his command's weaknesses. Even the recent rainy weather had convinced the optimistic major that the pursuit had been significantly slowed by this time and that the Patriots had been forced to stop to keep their powder dry. But Ferguson had badly underestimated the tactical astuteness and smarts of the ever-relentless Shelby and other frontier leaders, not fully realizing that the rains had ensured that no dust clouds would be raised to warn him of the enemy's approach.[101] For a wide variety of reasons, instead of prudently marching northeast for the safety of Charlotte and the main army, Ferguson felt confident in making his audacious defensive stand at Kings Mountain (more of a ridge than a mountain proper and standing only around seventy-five to a hundred feet above the surrounding, relatively level, terrain), located about a mile south of today's North Carolina-South Carolina border. Here, he was about to face his greatest challenge, while itching for a decisive fight instead of marching northeast to Charlotte and safety. Ferguson's bold decision was primarily based on the natural advantages of defending the high ground, especially after having repeatedly requested reinforcements not only from Cruger at Ninety-Six, but also from Cornwallis and the South Carolina backcountry militia under Irishman Matthew Floyd and a backcountry partisan commander named Isham Moore, who was expected to arrive on the evening of October 7. In addition, he had chosen this elevated position because it was located on the main road along which reinforcements from Cornwallis could reach Kings Mountain, if they had been dispatched as he fully expected. And a fine spring of fresh water was located on Kings Mountain near the crest to ensure that he and his Loyalists would have a reliable supply if besieged until the arrival of reinforcements.

In part because this forested hill, covered in virgin hardwoods and some towering pines, in the South Carolina Piedmont reminded him of the picturesque mountains located near his hometown in Scotland, and because he was concerned about the five hundred (some estimates are as low as three hundred) inexperienced North Carolina militia under Colonel Ambrose Mills, who had recently joined him, the major was now standing firm on his lofty perch. He had simply dismissed the most prudent course of action—to continue the push northeast to Charlotte, only thirty-five miles distant—because of the possibilities for success that he saw in making a stand at Kings Mountain. A proud man of ability and a naturally aggressive commander who had great faith in his troops after having diligently trained them, Ferguson wanted to avoid any appearances that he was afraid of his pursuers. Ironically, these Loyalist fighting men, both Royal Provincials—Ferguson's beloved American Volunteers—and Loyalist militia were basically the same as the Patriot militia in tactical terms: light infantry that moved swiftly and traveled lightly with quick-strike capabilities that were vital tactics of the bitter partisan war that raged in the backcountry.

Ferguson, who was clearly guilty of seriously underestimating his opponent, believed that he now possessed the long-awaited chance to finally "finish the business," especially if Cornwallis dispatched Tarleton and his hard-hitting dragoons, the army's supreme killers of the British Legion to his assistance, as requested.[102] However, as fate would have it, both Tarleton (malaria) and Cornwallis (fever) were ill at this time, which also helped ensure that no assistance would be forthcoming to Ferguson, despite the fact that on Ferguson's orders, "I sent express to the [Loyalist] Militia officers [Moore and Floyd] to join us here" on Kings Mountain, wrote Captain Alexander Chesney, who had immigrated from Ireland and joined the Loyalists in 1780, in his diary.[103] In regard to Ferguson's final decision to stand and fight atop this heavily wooded elevation, Lieutenant Colonel Nisbet Balfour was correct when he informed Cornwallis in no uncertain terms, "As to Ferguson, his ideas are so wild and sanguine [that] it would be dangerous to trust him with the conduct of any plan."[104]

Despite his deep concerns about Major Ferguson having been assigned to the vital mission of serving as his left, or western, flank protector, Cornwallis had decided to gamble because so much was now at stake on the "risky, but potentially winning plan to employ Loyalist militia in an independent offensive role" under Ferguson in western North Carolina "to stabilize the security situation to the west sufficiently to allow the British regulars to resume their march into North Carolina" in a bid to win it all.[105] After taking position atop Kings Mountain on October 6 and less than a day's march from Charlotte and safety, Ferguson confidently informed Cornwallis of his bold decision without having consulted anyone, not bothering or even worrying about asking for approval because he was exercising independent command, which he relished: "I do not think I can be forced [off Kings Mountain] by a stronger enemy than that against us."[106] On the same day, the Scottish major, who had failed to realize that he was already well in over his head in this all-important campaign against his archenemy Shelby and other frontier leaders, penned a letter to Major Robert Timpany and bragged in a premature triumphal manner that was badly misplaced, "Here we are Kings of Kings Mountain."[107]

A letter from one Loyalist emphasized the overall tactical situation and his commander's delusional reasoning, because what was offered in defensive terms by "King's Mountain was so pleasing that [Ferguson] concluded to take post there, stoutly affirming that he would be able to destroy or capture any force the Whigs could bring against him."[108] Loyalist Captain Alexander Chesney, who had been born in Ireland before his family settled in South Carolina, observed a key factor that was destined to undo Ferguson's tactical plan: "Kings Mountain from its height would have enabled us to oppose a superior force with advantage, had it not been covered with wood which sheltered the Americans and enabled them to fight in their favorite manner."[109] In the belief that the enemy was still far away in their pursuit, Ferguson believed that he had the time to gain additional recruits, including, of course, the reinforcements from Cornwallis. Ferguson even dispatched around two hundred men of a foraging party into the countryside on the morning of October 7 and sent out patrols to reconnoiter, which reduced and "seriously weakened" an effective fighting force of 1,125 men to less than 950 men. Even more, Ferguson made no defensive preparations because he felt that he possessed sufficient strength after occupying the bald crest at the ridge's highest point on the northeast end of the lengthy oblong ridge that spanned around six hundred yards in a northeastern direction.[110]

Atop Kings Mountain, although he neglected to strengthen his position in any way that would have been the wisest course of action, Ferguson had penned his last message to Cornwallis, which was deliberately exaggerated to ensure a quick response in the form of timely reinforcements: "My Lord: A doubt does not remain with regard to the intelligence I sent your Lordship. They are since joined by Clarke and Sumter—of course are becoming an object of some consequence. Happily their leaders are obliged to feed their followers with such hopes, and to flatter them with accounts of our weakness and fear, that, if necessary, I should hope for success against them myself; but numbers compared, that must be doubtful [but] Three or four hundred good soldiers, part dragoons, would finish the business. *Something must be done soon*. This is their last push in this quarter, etc."[111] However, Ferguson's optimistic vision of winning a sparkling victory with the assistance of Cornwallis's expected reinforcements and the additional flow of new recruits from the North Carolina Piedmont remained dominant in his mind, becoming the most dangerous of illusions while he stood defiantly atop Kings Mountain. He would never live to see the news contained in the October 7 letter (written on the day of the battle) penned to him from Lord Cornwallis: Lieutenant Colonel "Tarleton [and the dragoons of his British Legion under the command of a top lieutenant as Tarleton was still ill] shall pass at some of the upper Fords, and clear the Country; for the present both he and his Corps want a few days rest."[112]

The truth of the strategic reality was even more grim for Ferguson, who had no idea that he had been left on his own and abandoned by Cornwallis and his top lieutenants partly because his appeals were issued too late. And as noted, Tarleton was unable to come to Ferguson's assistance because he was seriously ill with malaria and Cornwallis was sick with a "feverish cold."[113] Moreover, Ferguson received word that Lieutenant Colonel John Harris Cruger at Ninety-Six would be unable to send any reinforcements because of the limited capabilities and weakened state of his command—a serious blow to the major's plan.[114] The lack of reinforcements guaranteed Ferguson's tactical thinking was as ill-fated as it was misplaced, because of his penchant for risk-taking that had been entirely unnecessary. In the words of Colonel William "Billy" Hill, a former South Carolinian born in Belfast in north Ireland on September 13, 1741, and a former South Carolina politician from York County who was married to an Irish woman named Jane McCall:

> notwithstanding Col Ferguson was a brave military character it appeared that he was infatuated & brought to his own ruin by chosing [sic] this spot of ground [Kings Mountain] on which he had to fight under every disadvantage . . . there being a small flat of ground where he had pitched his camp on, the sides of the mountain being very Rocky & steep as well as a great number of fallen & standing trees so that the Americans could attack his camp on all quarters [sides], [and] he trusted [too] much to the bayonets . . . he had trained his men to that purpose & those which he could not furnish with this weapon he had contrived a substitute by getting the Blacksmiths to make long knives to answer this purpose with a tang put in a piece of wood to fit the calibre of the gun & a button to rest on the muzzle of the piece.[115]

In this regard, Major Ferguson had demonstrated his trademark outside-the-box thinking by ensuring that his militiamen possessed homemade bayonets for the launching of bayonet charges, if the detested rebels dared to charge up the hill. But now Ferguson's unorthodox thinking in other regards had come back to haunt the brash Scotsman by putting him into a stationary, sitting-duck position for the fast-approaching Overmountain and backcountry men.[116] By imprudently ignoring his own defensive weaknesses and liabilities, Ferguson still felt that he possessed all the advantages. He believed that he had set a brilliant trap for the oncoming Patriots by taking a commanding defensive position atop Kings Mountain, especially if Cornwallis responded to his request for reinforcements as expected. Throughout the summer of 1780, Ferguson had spent week after week recruiting Loyalists and training his Americans mostly from the South Carolina Piedmont to his exact standards that were exceptionally high. He had long drilled and maneuvered his disciplined troops to the shrill notes of a long silver whistle that was destined to be heard above the roar of the upcoming backcountry battle for possession of the high ground. Major Ferguson was especially proud of his American Volunteers, who were finely honed Provincial regulars in red uniforms. These dedicated Loyalists from New York and New Jersey, northerners who detested Southern "crackers," especially those men west of the mountains, were tough fighting men who Ferguson depended upon to win it all at Kings Mountain.

Consequently, the ever-optimistic Ferguson now envisioned a bloody replay of the easy British victories that had resulted in the slaughter of a good many Patriots of Colonel Buford's command at the Waxhaws and Colonel Thomas Sumter's command at Fishing Creek, especially from the launching of the much-feared British bayonet attack. Even if Tarleton's dragoons of the British Legion failed to arrive in time, Ferguson still believed he possessed a golden opportunity to reap an impressive success because he commanded soldiers well trained in unleashing the bayonet charge and holding the high ground, which was the usual formula for victory. Most of all at Kings Mountain, Ferguson firmly believed that he had created a golden opportunity to prove that his Loyalists could win an important victory entirely on their own, unlike at Camden in mid-August 1780, without the aid of British regulars to verify the wisdom of the British strategic plan of "Americanization"—the Southern Strategy—for winning this lengthy war of attrition. At this time, leading Loyalist troops to victory was now the career shortcut for ambitious officers like Ferguson to gain prestige and higher social status, when they were without independent wealth and social connections of the upper-class elite, by demonstrating their abilities in independent command: winning impressive victories that would place them on the fast track to eventually become generals in the British military establishment. This avenue, which was one now desperately needed by Ferguson, was the quickest way for young officers to advance and escape a dead end of undistinguished careers because of politics, money, and social status, since their rank in commanding Provincial troops was only temporary. Omnipresent rivalries and jealousies among Cornwallis's Machiavellian top lieutenants had played a role in undermining his superior's opinion of Ferguson. So this upcoming fight at Kings Mountain, in Ferguson's mind, was his chance to win Cornwallis's favor.[117]

For such reasons and as if he had already won a victory by gaining the highest ground in the area without a fight, Major Ferguson crowed from atop his remote hilltop in the middle of nowhere that "he was on King's Mountain, that he was the king of that mountain, and God Almighty could not drive him from it."[118] However, as mentioned, the high ground of Kings Mountain presented a host of disadvantages not readily apparent at first glance, especially the wooded and boulder-strewn slopes that provided ideal cover for experienced men who fought Indian-style with great skill. And the rocky ground and narrowness—at some points along this oblong ridge a man standing at the top could be shot from two sides—of the lengthy crest, running northeast, meant that earthen defenses could not be constructed because the Loyalists possessed no entrenching tools. However, Ferguson should have ordered his men to create wooden breastworks from fallen logs and cut timber because the entire mountain was covered in timber except along the narrow crest that connected the two spurs at opposite ends of the lengthy ridge. Ferguson had not ordered defensive works because that would have seemed like he feared the rustics in rebellion, and he was determined to rely on the thorough training of his men with the bayonet. After all, in Ferguson's mind, why order his troops to build a breastwork when victory could be won with the unleashing of a bayonet charge like at Camden, where an entire American army, including a good many Continental troops, had been destroyed? British bayonet attacks had long demonstrated that the Americans, especially militiamen, simply could not stand up to the sweeping bayonet charge of regulars or men trained like the Provincial regulars, especially when they were facing nothing more than "a set of mongrels," as Ferguson was convinced in his hubris.[119]

None of the seventeen British supply, ammunition, and baggage wagons were utilized before the battle by Ferguson for defensive purposes: a laager of wagons encircling the tented British encampment, including Ferguson's headquarters, for protection if they were attacked on all sides. Instead, the wagons were parked according to British regulations near Ferguson's headquarters tent on the ridge's northeastern end at its widest point.[120]

Lord Cornwallis remained stationary at Charlotte less than forty miles away to the northeast and waited to learn of Ferguson's exact situation on his left flank before advancing deeper into North Carolina, because suffering a reversal on his left flank under Ferguson would sabotage his ambitious plans to push north from Charlotte, jeopardizing the entire invasion of North Carolina. He fully realized that "keeping possession of the Back Country is of the utmost importance. Indeed, the success of the war in the Southern District depends totally upon it."[121]

This indisputable strategic reality (ironically long overlooked by modern historians who have mostly focused on Washington's campaigns far to the north, although they were devoid of decisive victories year after year) had been early realized by the "Rice Kings," the wealthy rice planters of Charles Town and the South Carolina lowlands along the east coast. Therefore, the radicals, including the wealthy Rice Kings, had early sought to rally support in the backcountry to join their militant stance against Great Britain, knowing "that without the support of the Back Country, where some two-thirds of the white population lived, revolution in South Carolina was a dead letter": an undeniable reality that was about to be convincingly demonstrated in the upcoming showdown at Kings Mountain.[122] To the astonishment of overconfident British leadership on both sides of the Atlantic, South Carolina had become a "veritable hornet's nest of Rebellion," but Cornwallis was about to learn that a far more dangerous front lay farther to the west.[123]

As revealed in an October 2, 1780, letter that was published in the pages of the *Maryland Gazette* on November 3, Colonel James Williams, from York County, South Carolina, described the forces that were moving toward Major Ferguson in the hope of eliminating their greatest threat:

> I am, at present . . . with 450 horsemen, in pursuit of Colonel Ferguson [and] This moment another of my expresses is arrived from Colonels McDowell and Shelby: they were on this march, near Burk

> courthouse, with 1500 brave mountainmen and col. Cleveland was within 10 miles of them with 800 men, and was to form a junction with them this day [October 2]. I expect to join them to morrow, in pursuit of colonel Ferguson, and under the direction of Heaven, I hope to be able to render your honour a good account of him in a few days.[124]

Ironically, Major Ferguson had made the job of his own destruction by the Patriots much easier by way of his ill-fated decisions and grand illusions. Indeed, "Ferguson's errors were political, strategic, and tactical, which is about as wrong as a soldier can get: he overestimated Tory support and underestimated the patriot resistance in his area of responsibility; he failed to retreat when faced with defeat in detail; he failed to outpost Kings Mountain; failed to fortify it for frontier-style fighting, and failed to see that his position was 'more assailable by the rifle than defensible with the bayonet,'" in the astute words of Henry "Light-Horse Harry" Lee, who was one of Washington's finest cavalrymen and the father of Robert E. Lee of Civil War fame.[125]

A Most Paradoxical and Misplaced Name

As fate would have it, destiny itself was rapidly drawing the backcountry and Overmountain men closer to an obscure mountaintop located just south of the North Carolina line. Paradoxically, the name of this so-called mountain in the remote South Carolina Piedmont had nothing at all to do with King George III or any previous king of England. This property was owned by the King family, who lived at the base of the heavily timbered mountain.[126] This isolated part of the South Carolina backcountry, which was heavily populated by the Scotch-Irish, was diehard Patriot country. Like many of his neighbors from this area, North Carolina-born Private Robert West, who enlisted during the autumn of 1780, had ridden off in pursuit of Bloody Bill Cunningham with his neighbors and was destined to become a future member of the "Swamp Fox" command of Francis Marion, after having left his home "on Kings Creek near Kings Mountain."[127]

Private John Cunningham, of Scotch-Irish descent and a fortunate survivor of Thomas Sumter's disaster at Fishing Creek in August 1780, was not only descending on Kings Mountain with his Piedmont command of volunteers but also nearing his own home situated not far from where the battle was about to erupt. Indeed, Cunningham's home "was so near to this battle his wife-to-be [Ann] could hear the drums when the fight started."[128] Another Patriot, Scotch-Irish Private John McCann, lived near Kings Mountain and called this frontier region in the South Carolina backcountry home.[129] And Private Nathaniel Offutt, who had been born near Three Sisters Ferry, South Carolina, in 1762, had just joined the Overmountain and backcountry men as they neared Kings Mountain and his own home.[130] As fate would have it, Major William Chronicle and Captain John Mattocks, both of whom were fated to be killed at Kings Mountain, had encamped on the open hilltop of Kings Mountain last autumn during a deer hunt. They had joined the task force's encampment during the long journey south. With his usual skill, the popular Major Chronicle commanded the enthusiastic South Fork Boys, who hailed from the rugged backcountry lands in the forks of the Catawba River around today's Lincolnton, North Carolina.[131]

In the foremost ranks leading his Overmountain men onward to a rendezvous with destiny, Colonel Isaac Shelby continued to serve as the main driving force and moral and spiritual leader of the entire expedition, especially in the final push southeast and then east from the Cowpens on October 7. "Born to the Indian struggle," only twenty-nine and destined to be the future first governor of Kentucky in 1792, Shelby was about to earn the reputation of "Old Kings Mountain" that he continued to bask in at age sixty-two when leading young men in still another conflict against the same English foe during the War of 1812.[132] Captain William Davis was another tough fighting man on the frantic push east from Cowpens and closer to the settling of old scores at Kings Mountain. Fortunate to have survived the rout of Sumter's command during the nightmare defeat at Fishing Creek, Davis was a respected elder of the Bethel Presbyterian Church in the York District of South Carolina.[133] As mentioned, the gathering of the mostly Celtic clans had produced a large number of relatives who now served together in companies that more resembled familial units. The family of Private William Henry was well represented in the ranks, including his four sons. Even more, he and his boys were nearing their own home, which was around three miles from Kings Mountain. Fortunately, the father and sons would survive the upcoming struggle for possession of Kings Mountain.[134]

From beginning to end, Major Ferguson failed to understand the very foundation of the considerable fighting prowess of the Overmountain and backcountry fighting men—the familial aspects of these companies and regiments of citizen-soldiers and their devout religious natures and moral convictions that translated into a high fighting spirit and morale that fueled formidable combat qualities and capabilities that actually exceeded his own cherished American Volunteers, who were the elite fighters of his command. Quite simply, these were the most lethal Patriot fighting men in America, as would be revealed in full at Kings Mountain during the "greatest hour" of the Southern militiaman. However, in the eyes of Ferguson and the British who had made monumental errors in judgment on multiple levels, this mysterious backwoods foe whom they knew so little about was nothing more than members, in the words of Colonel George Hanger, "of a heathen race known by the name of Crackers."[135]

Forgotten Black Patriots in the Ranks

Contrary to general assumptions about the men of Kings Mountain and the common stereotype that the Patriots consisted solely of Overmountain men, fundamental truths have been left out of the Kings Mountain story by generations of historians, especially the multicultural and diverse ethnic composition of the men who were now descending rapidly upon Kings Mountain and their elusive prey. Long absent from the traditional narrative, the best example of this unfortunate development of outright negligence, if not a deliberate historical silencing, has been in regard to the forgotten Black Patriots who fought with distinction at Kings Mountain. Despite the lack of documentation but based on overall percentages and the few existing examples, almost certainly more Black Patriots served in the backcountry and county militias than in the Continental Army—an estimated five thousand, mostly in Washington's Army—and more in the ranks of the Southern militia than in the New England militia, where it has been long thought most Blacks served in the ranks as fighting men: a long forgotten distinguished chapter in the annals of American military history that has been silenced for racial reasons in the South, including in South Carolina.

For instance, at least a dozen African American soldiers, the majority of whom were free men, served at Kings Mountain, but most likely even more men of African descent fought on October 7. At least two Blacks fought as slaves and they were later freed by their master, including for their service at Kings Mountain. Among these Black freedom fighters were Ishmael Titus from Rowan County, North Carolina, Essius (or Esaius) Bowman of Captain Joel

Lewis's Virginia company, and Primes (Primus).[136] Titus served as a substitute for his drafted master in the ranks of Captain John Cleveland's company to win his freedom.[137]

Ironically, one free Black who fought in the ranks of Campbell's Virginia Regiment from Washington County, Southwest Virginia, possessed the same name as the most hated opponent. Private Andrew Ferguson was the name of this teenage warrior. He later briefly described his role in the battle that was fought "away down in North Carolina."[138]

Also forgotten has been the fact that large numbers of slaves served in Continental regiments of the South, including South Carolina units and such regular regiments as the 1st North Carolina Continental Regiment and the 2nd North Carolina Continental Regiment (each contained around twenty-nine Black soldiers at one point). These Black fighting men served beside white Southern soldiers in integrated units like the Southern militia from the war's beginning to it's end. Likewise, Blacks served in South Carolina's Continental Regiments as drummers and fifers who led the way during assaults. And at least eight Blacks—fighting men and not musicians—served in the 3rd South Carolina Continental Regiment. Likewise, both slaves and free Black men fought in North Carolina and Virginia Continental regiments and militia units.[139] Austin Dabney, a free Black of mixed race from Georgia, volunteered and served in the command of Colonel Elijah Clarke, the leading partisan of the Peach State, in attempting to hurl the British and Loyalists out of the state. Dabney fought with skill until disabled by wounds.[140]

Private Berry Jeffers, of South Carolina's Richland District, was another Black soldier who fought at Kings Mountain. Like his white comrades, Jeffers was highly motivated and eager to meet the enemy. To even up old scores with the Loyalists, who were also slave owners in the backcountry and low-country just like Patriots, Jeffers had first served as a private in the 3rd South Carolina Continental Regiment, in which at least seven Blacks served, and he then served in a ranger command.[141] However, as noted, not all the African Americans who now served with the Overmountain and backcountry men were free. Broddy was a mulatto slave owned by Colonel William Campbell of Washington County, Virginia. He now served as the personal manservant to the colonel. However, Broddy became a fighting man at Kings Mountain on his own initiative and demonstrated courage.[142] Likewise, Ishmael Titus fought as a slave at Kings Mountain but was later freed for this faithful service to his country. Titus's life had been a true odyssey, having been brought to America "in chains" from Cameroon, located on the Gulf of Guinea.[143]

Forgotten German Patriots

German Patriots were the most forgotten and overlooked ethnic group that fought at Kings Mountain, after Black fighting men. It was not just the Scotch-Irish and other Celts who had migrated to the western frontier, but also the Germans for basically the same reasons, especially freedom of worship (Protestantism and Catholicism) and the love of an independent lifestyle far from abusive government. Both Protestant peoples—more so in regard to the Scotch-Irish than the Germans—of vastly different societies and cultures (one Celtic and one Teutonic) were intensely religious. Migrating south from Pennsylvania, which had attracted the first original German immigrants like the great tide of migrating Scotch-Irish, the Teutonic people had been among the first settlers to push into the wilderness of the backcountry and even west of the mountains, but to a much lesser degree than the Scotch-Irish.[144]

Lieutenant Colonel Frederick Hambright was the top German Patriot leader who served at Kings Mountain. He had been born in Bavaria in 1727 and his family migrated to America in 1738, settling in Pennsylvania like so many other Germans because of the colony's tolerance of people of all faiths. The western frontier continued to beckon to opportunistic Germans and the Hambright family headed south to Virginia around 1755. Then Frederick pushed farther south and west to settle in North Carolina in 1760. He soon became a leader of the local community, despite his German birth, because of the western frontier's egalitarianism where a man's worth depended on his character and marksmanship with a long rifle. Hambright was an early Patriot of note in his community because of his popularity and winning ways. He was elected to the North Carolina Provincial Congress in 1775. Not content to play only a political role in the struggle for liberty, Hambright had early taken the field of strife in defense of his adopted North Carolina homeland. Along with his neighbors, he was also a veteran Indian fighter, serving in the 1776 Cherokee campaign. By 1779, Hambright had gained the rank of lieutenant colonel. One of the oldest leading officers in the task force at fifty-three and speaking with a heavy Bavarian accent, Hambright now commanded around fifty Lincoln County men of the Catawba River country with Colonel William Graham.[145] One of the young citizen-soldiers whom Hambright led onward was his own son, John, who was determined to reap victory like his dynamic lieutenant colonel father.[146]

A number of German-born men filled the enlisted ranks of the task force now rapidly headed for Kings Mountain. Private Devault Keller had been born in Germany in 1749. He had been captured in Charles Town's fall, but escaped the British. He then rejoined his old regiment at Ninety-Six. Private Keller was destined to fall wounded with a bullet in the left arm on October 7, but survived the harrowing ordeal. When he fought at Kings Mountain for his adopted country, Keller "barely understood English," while bravely fighting for the golden promise and dream of America.[147] In overall historical terms, the German name in general has been blackened because the Hessians, who were King George III's hired mercenaries, have overshadowed the key roles played by German Patriots during the American Revolution. For example, the German Fusiliers of Charles Town was one of the finest uniformed units that were part of the defense of Charles Town in 1775. Privates Moses Welt and George Wershing and Sergeant Philip Werner were proud members of the German Fusiliers of Charles Town. German Patriots also served in partisan bands in the backcountry, riding with their Celtic comrades against the Loyalists. Private Nicholas Cobia, who had been born in Charles Town in December 1759, later served under a German captain named Stobel before joining the guerrilla ranks of Francis Marion, the famous "Swamp Fox" of South Carolina.[148]

Private Philip Greever, who was a member of Colonel William Campbell's Virginia militia regiment, was of Huguenot descent, having had ancestors who had migrated to America from the Netherlands, or Holland, and not Germany as was long assumed.[149]

Excellent Overmountain and backcountry fighting men of German heritage were about to make their presence felt at Kings Mountain. The Germans across America were a divided people like so many non-Germans, including, to a lesser degree, the Scotch-Irish. Therefore, at Kings Mountain, deep in the South Carolina Piedmont, this forgotten Teutonic civil war was one in which "German fought German, and more than once a German surrendered to his own family, resident citizens of America."[150]

Chapter IV

A Time for Killing and Revenge, October 7, 1780

In a desperate race that continued unabated across the rain-soaked backcountry where the dense forests of hardwood trees were already colored red and yellow, the Patriot task force of around 910 men continued to move east with good speed toward Kings Mountain. By the time the early autumnal sun peeked over the tree-lined eastern horizon among the gently rolling hills of the South Carolina Piedmont on Saturday, October 7, the pursuit was relentless, which Colonel Shelby knew was the key to success. Early that morning, Colonel John Moffett, a veteran Indian fighter who had been born in the Shenandoah Valley of Virginia in 1741 and a member of the Turkey Creek militia regiment of the South Carolina backcountry of Colonel Edward Lacey's command, prudently dispatched three of his men to Whitaker Mountain to search for a party of Loyalists rumored to be in the area. Private Hugh Allison, who had been born in Pennsylvania in 1746 of Scottish parents and whose brother Robert also served in the Patriot ranks, was one of these scouts. They tracked a large group of Loyalists of around six hundred men. They then followed the tracks of more than a thousand horses that led toward Kings Mountain and Ferguson, giving more proof that the major had sent out the call to the militia. Without thinking twice, the handful of Patriots naturally decided not to engage them and allowed them to proceed.[1]

Ironically, while Colonel Campbell's task force pushed closer to Kings Mountain in a desperate race east to strike Ferguson before he was reinforced by Cornwallis, especially if Tarleton and his hard-hitting British Legion had been dispatched to the southwest, some Patriots were already atop Kings Mountain, but not by their own choosing. Virginia-born Private John Fisher, twenty-four, was one of Ferguson's prisoners. In only a short time, it was Fisher's good fortune to escape during the noise and chaos of the upcoming battle.[2] Likewise, Scotch-Irishman Orderly Sergeant John McCutchen was another one of Ferguson's captives who was now atop Kings Mountain and contemplating an uncertain future.[3] The destiny of still another soldier at the Loyalist encampment on the top of Kings Mountain was about to change. He was a Loyalist named Private John Franklin, who had served in the American ranks in 1777 and 1778. After having joined Ferguson, he was now ready to defend Kings Mountain with his life. However, Franklin was destined to join the other side, including service with the "Swamp Fox," Francis Marion.[4] Some of Ferguson's pursuers were sidetracked by a new threat that had unexpectedly emerged. Private Hugh Knox, of Scotch-Irish descent who had been born in the Chester District of South Carolina, in 1755 and had served against the Cherokee, had three brothers who faithfully served the Patriot cause with their hearts and trusty long rifles. He and his comrades had unexpectedly "met a group of Indians who were in the British Service and chased them across the Broad River."[5]

In Overall Bad Physical Shape After Departing the Cowpens

In the words of Colonel Shelby: "Ferguson [was now] their object, and for the last thirty-six hours they never alighted from their horses but once to refresh at the Cowpens for an hour (where they were joined by Col. Williams of South Carolina, on the evening of the sixth with about four hundred men), although the day of the action was extremely wet that the men could only keep their guns dry by wrapping their bags, blankets, and hunting shirts around the locks [of rifles and muskets], which exposed their bodies to a heavy and incessant rain."[6] Virginia-born Captain William Lenoir, of French heritage, described the men as "almost exhausted by fatigue, hunger, cold and wet, and, for want of sleep," and in overall bad shape after their long ordeal.[7]

After the Patriot task force had reached the Cowpens on the afternoon of October 6, Colonels Edward Lacey and William Hill, who was still recovering from a wound suffered in the fight at Hanging Rock, South Carolina, had joined the task force with around four hundred militiamen from the South Carolina backcountry, which raised the spirits of the pursuers. Fortunately, this timely reinforcement and the brief rest at the Cowpens had fueled even more confidence in the destruction of Ferguson and his command.[8] After having left the Cowpens behind, these men "had had no sleep for many hours and very little rest or refreshment, but every man had energy for a hard battle" that was about to erupt in full fury.[9] With a good deal of understatement, Captain

William Lenoir described how the young men and boys who fought at Kings Mountain "were almost famished" by this time.[10] Armed with "my large old musket," teenage Private Young described how, "I had no shoes and of course fought the battle barefoot."[11]

As weary as the common soldiers in the ranks, Lieutenant Samuel Newell penned that he was "nearly thirty-six hours without any kind of refreshments and marched under an almost constant torrent of rain" that weakened him like other men.[12] From the beginning and as could be expected, the key driving force of the final push to Kings Mountain continued to be Colonel Isaac Shelby. He had endlessly emphasized the urgent necessity to keep moving east as fast as possible. Shelby had played the leading role not only in orchestrating the creation of the frontier army but also in getting it to Kings Mountain in time to catch Ferguson. Consequently, more than nine hundred of the best fighting men and horses continued east as rapidly as possible without a halt or break.[13]

Clearly, Colonel Shelby fully realized the importance of moving as fast as possible until the target was reached and struck with a powerful blow, and he was relentless throughout the chase in imploring everyone onward. Incredibly, the backcountry and Overmountain men had steadily neared the imposing height of Kings Mountain from the north without having been detected. At this time, they knew from the latest intelligence that Ferguson was encamped at the northeastern spur of the long ridge because of the ready availability of a spring that provided good water to his command. After the thirteen-day journey of 330 miles south across the mountains and then southeast and then east, including in nasty early fall weather—an odyssey in itself—the hard-riding Patriots were badly in need of rest by this time. They were about to complete a forced march of thirty-three miles from Cowpens since the night of October 6, riding through a cold drizzle and hard rains. Some Patriots had not eaten a bite of food since having departed Quaker Meadows far to the north, suffering not only from severe hunger but also malnutrition and bodily weakness.

Still another generally overlooked factor also explained the Patriots' utter exhaustion. Before the call to assemble in the most picturesque of settings at Sycamore Shoals, many citizen-soldiers of Colonel Shelby's and Sevier's militia commands had just returned from service east of the mountains and were already in overall bad shape, including severe fatigue and malnutrition even before the race to chase down Ferguson. However, after having returned home west of the mountains in late August, they had forgotten their weariness and need for rest and recuperation by immediately volunteering to answer Shelby's and Sevier's call to gather along the grassy meadow on the Watauga River at Sycamore Shoals on September 25.

After having journeyed across the formidable Blue Ridge Mountains and the dash through the North Carolina and South Carolina Piedmont, these men presented a deplorable sight by this time, especially when compared to Ferguson's American Volunteers in neat scarlet uniforms: red-eyed, stained with sweat, long hair tangled and matted together, newly grown short beards, and boots, shoes, and moccasins tattered or rotting, and hunting shirts and pants grease-stained and dirty.[14] By sunrise on October 7 when they headed toward the rain-swollen Broad River, which was brown with churning waters, at Cherokee Ford, Captain William Lenoir wrote how the mounted "detachment [was] almost exhausted by fatigue, hunger; cold and wet, and for want of sleep."[15] Indeed, in the words of Benjamin Sharp, the fatigue was mind-numbing after riding "all night," since departing the broad grassy meadow of the Cowpens and "cross[ing] Broad river [at Cherokee Ford] by the dawn of day; and although it rained considerably in the morning, we never halted to refresh ourselves or horses."[16]

However, the long rifles of the Overmountain men and a lesser number of the backcountry men were in excellent shape and ready for action, despite the early autumn rain. And, most important, the precious reserves of black powder were dry, which was more important than anything else. However, the pursuers' deplorable condition seemingly did not bode well for the upcoming showdown at Kings Mountain, especially because Ferguson was considered "a man of some genius" and a determined leader.[17] In general, Ferguson was correctly viewed as a fighter with "a brave military character" and "a man of military talents," in the complimentary words of Ireland-born Colonel William Hill.[18] Still embracing his illusion of winning "undying laurels" from the gods of war, Major Ferguson, because of his own Scottish heritage and intimate knowledge of the long-suffering Scottish people and their tortured history, should have known better than to make a defiant stand when a large, mostly Celtic task force—literally a case of "the Campbells were coming" to destroy him—was on the way at breakneck speed. But Ferguson was now relying "too much on the pluck and luck" that had protected him in the past in one battle after another.[19]

The motivations among the pursuers, who also believed that they possessed a special destiny, could not have been higher, because they were closing in on their prey, and they were determined to do whatever was necessary to protect friends, families, and neighbors back home. Colonel John Sevier, whom the boys affectionately knew as "Nolichucky Jack" and "Chucky Jack" and was the "Cherokees' nemesis," was still burdened by a recent personal tragedy. His beloved wife, Sarah Hawkins-Sevier, had died in early 1780 primarily because of the personal demands stemming from the many dangers of a two-front war. At the family cabin in the Watauga River Valley in Washington County, Sarah had just given birth to the couple's tenth child when intelligence arrived about an impending Indian attack. In frantic haste, John and the family loaded up the wagon with a few essential possessions and then raced for the safety of a Nolichucky River fort, where panicked frontier families gathered for protection. However, Sarah was so weakened from the daunting experience of the widespread panic and childbirth that she didn't survive the considerable exertions, dying from exhaustion to the horror and shock of Colonel Sevier.[20]

For such reasons, the Sevier family was well represented in the ranks. In Sevier's Overmountain regiment of Wataugans from Washington County, the Sevier clan was like so many other familial groups that filled the ranks of every county regiment. Private James Sevier proudly emphasized that his father possessed in his regiment of frontiersmen "four brothers besides himself and two sons—myself the youngest, being at that time sixteen years old. There were only seven of our family able to bear arms; they all fought in the battle" of Kings Mountain.[21]

Gaining Even More Timely Intelligence

The prospects of the flying column of more than nine hundred men—including Campbell's Virginians of Washington County who had become lost in the long journey through the night's darkness thanks to a guide's misdirection but had quickly recovered—were reinvigorated and bodies reenergized with the scent of victory hanging in the air. These men realized that they were about to catch the overconfident Major Ferguson and his men napping on an open mountaintop in the South Carolina Piedmont when still too far away from timely support. To confirm their beliefs when successful efforts were made to retrieve the wayward Virginia boys, timely and accurate intelligence was about to be gained from more than one source with the dawn of October 7. Captain William

Lenoir, a veteran Indian fighter whose Huguenot Protestant ancestors had fled Catholic France, described the last phase of the march to Kings Mountain, after having departed the Cowpens:

> March all night (being dark and rainy), and crossed Broad river [at sunrise nearly several miles downriver at Cherokee Ford after the wary colonels, as if once again battling the Cherokee west of the mountains, deciding that crossing at the intended Tate's Crossing by the most direct route risked the possibility of ambush until scout Enoch Gilmer, of Major William Chronicle's South Fork Boys, from the forks of the Catawba River investigated and signaled that all was safe when returned singing the tune 'Barney-Linn' the next morning, where an attack was expected. But not finding the enemy, the [mounted] detachment [now] pursued their march a few miles.[22]

After crossing the high, brown waters of the Broad River at Cherokee Ford, a new crisis situation suddenly developed. A brief halt was called by Sevier, Cleveland, and Campbell, the nominal leader of the task force, and not Shelby, who was the true leader of the expedition, three miles from the ford to rest worn horses, which were hot, sweaty, and weakening. Here, they hastily ate a scanty cold breakfast of whatever little was left of the food in saddlebags and pockets, including scouring a nearby cornfield along the road. The precious uncooked corn kernels were eagerly consumed from the cobs. Meanwhile, the bone-chilling rain continued to pour harder from the dark skies, depressing spirits but not the determination to strike Ferguson as soon as possible. With visibility decreased by the sheets of rain and the fear that their black powder and weapons had become wet, this impromptu halt had been ordered because several leaders believed that it was an absolute necessity. However, this abrupt decision had not been decided upon by committee like past leadership decisions, which was a violation of a golden frontier rule.

Shelby continued to demonstrate that he was the real leader of this expedition when he became angered because his three fellow colonels had called the halt without his consent. But Colonel Shelby knew that he had to be careful not to offend his fellow commanders whom he respected and vice versa. Therefore, in this sensitive and delicate situation, when the three colonels informed Shelby that they had been forced to call a halt, their revered leader firmly snapped in an unmistakable sharp tone but without insulting or berating anyone that if Ferguson escaped or was reinforced before they struck: "I will not stop until night if I follow Ferguson into Cornwallis's line" at Charlotte.[23]

The stunned colonels, who knew that they had been sharply rebuked, said nothing in response to Colonel Shelby's unexpected outburst because the order presented in this diplomatic but unmistakably stern manner was made to guarantee unity and a continued good working relationship among the officer corps, especially with a big battle on the horizon. Without looking at each other and not saying a word after Shelby's sharp words, the colonels then rode away and returned to their commands in silence. Consequently, the vigorous pursuit was continued without a break because Shelby was exactly right and had known that it was absolutely necessary to catch up to Ferguson as soon as possible before he departed or received reinforcements, the very key to achieving decisive victory at this time. Everyone now continued to ride east toward the high ground of Kings Mountain, knowing that they must reach this elevated point before Ferguson wised up and suddenly slipped away forever.[24]

Captain William Lenoir wrote how the journey continued until "they met two men from Col. Ferguson's camp, who gave some account of his situation" on Kings Mountain.[25] Providing more detail than Lenoir's postwar account, Virginia-born Private Silas McBee, a South Carolinian of Scotch-Irish descent not yet fifteen years of age from the Spartanburg district who had been raised in the backwoods along Thicketty Creek and a member of Colonel Thomas Brandon's command of Colonel James Williams's Little River Regiment, described how "at [Solomon] Benson's, a kind of half Whig half Tory as occasion required took two Tories prisoners, and required them at the peril of their lives, to pilot the army to Ferguson's camp. Shelby took one, Cleveland the other."[26]

Major William Chronicle and one of his top lieutenants, Captain John Moffitt, also served as guides for the long column of frontier riders because they had once hunted deer on Kings Mountain during the previous autumn, when the big white-tailed bucks were in rut and hunting for does in heat.[27] Most importantly, Ferguson and Kings Mountain lay only eight miles away to the southeast and the men were becoming increasingly eager and anxious about the impending battle.[28] For fear of their lives because they were threatened by hardened men who were Indian fighters to the core, the two part-time Loyalists willingly presented an abundance of information to their captors. An ad hoc officers' conference was immediately held in the wet leather saddles of their worn horses to discuss this new intelligence. In Lenoir's words:

> Then being revived by the hopes of gaining the desired object, the officers held a short consultation—sitting on their horses—in which it was concluded that said detachment should be formed into four columns; two of the columns should march on each side of the road, as silently as they could, and that they should govern their march by the view of each other; Col. [Joseph] Winston was placed at the head of the left; and Cols. Shelby and Sevier at the heads of the two middle columns.[29]

Acting on the timely and accurate intelligence that they had repeatedly verified by crosschecking the steady flow of the most recent information (the Patriots had already easily won the intelligence war over Ferguson even before the first shot had been fired) from excellent scouts, spies, and interrogated prisoners, local Patriots and Loyalists, Patriot leadership had already demonstrated a great deal of flexibility and adaptability in the field of intelligence. In the past, this uncanny ability of these veteran Indian fighters had been one of the keys to having defeated the resourceful Cherokee in a brutal war. And it was now equally important for the colonels to make the proper decision by believing the Loyalists' words, after they were verified by other intelligence sources. While the rain poured down throughout the chilly morning of October 7 to thoroughly wet the Patriots, who nevertheless managed to keep their black powder dry, the men had long been using whatever they could to protect the firing mechanisms of their rifles and muskets, including wrapping their hunting shirts around the firing locks. However, despite the misery of the early autumn chill, the heavy rain that pounded the lengthy column of weary men was actually a godsend, because no dust clouds were raised for Ferguson and his men to see, even from their high ground perch. Then, almost as if God, as Patriot leaders believed, was playing a role in setting the stage for the upcoming showdown at Kings Mountain, the rain finally stopped suddenly around noon and the long-elusive sun poked through the dark clouds, which the men in the ranks took as a good omen. Then, a cool breeze rose to soothe sweating men and horses.

A string of good news followed with timely intelligence from multiple sources beyond that of scout Enoch Gilmer, brightening spirits along with the improving weather. First, at a log house of a Loyalist along the muddy road located around half a dozen miles east of the Solomon Benson home, the inhabitants informed the mountaineers and backcountry men that Ferguson was close by. A young girl, who was more of a Patriot than the questionable male informants, later followed a handful of Sevier's Washington County men out of the house and told them what they wanted to hear to verify that Ferguson had not fled to Charlotte, when she pointed south to the ridge on the southeastern horizon around three miles away: "He is on that mountain."[30] After everyone mounted up, the rapid pursuit southeast continued down the narrow country road. Meanwhile, the refreshing warmth of the afternoon sun began to dry out their hunting shirts and pants, promising a nice autumn afternoon.

Farther down the muddy road that led south to Kings Mountain, the fast-moving column continued on, but some leaders, including Colonel William Campbell and Major William Chronicle, halted when they spied the horse of scout Enoch Gilmer tied to the gate of a farmhouse. They entered the small country house and enacted a ruse with Enoch, who was sitting at the dinner table and playing the part of a Loyalist with the Loyalist family. The arriving officers pretended that they were now taking him to be hanged, after putting a rope with a noose around Gilmer's neck. Gilmer was promptly taken out of the house to be "hung," and then revealed what he had learned from the two women. Enoch mentioned that one of the Tory women had recently taken live chickens to Ferguson for dinner. Most importantly, Gilmer had learned that Ferguson "was camped on a ridge between two streams where deer hunters [had hunted on] a spur [the eastern one] of King's Mountain."[31]

This new intelligence gained from Gilmer resulted in another hasty commanders' conference among the frontier colonels on horseback, because they now knew of Ferguson's numbers and even the exact site of his encampment. On Colonel Shelby's suggestion, they then "agreed on a very simple plan. They would surround the hill and attack. Since the riflemen would be firing uphill, there would be no danger of men being hit by friendly fire," especially if they attacked simultaneously up all four sides of the mountain to surround their enemy.[32] In true democratic fashion, the colonels knew that they had to inform their men to make sure that everyone was in perfect agreement with the ambitious plan of surrounding Ferguson's entire command. If someone had a better idea, then it would be hastily contemplated and debated if it had merit. Clearly, these veteran leaders respected the wisdom and intelligence of the common soldiers in the ranks, which would have utterly shocked any soldier, especially officers, who wore a red uniform. Of course, the men of the enlisted and non-commissioned officers' ranks readily gave their consent to the very good plan of action that called for an immediate strike. Then, the long column of Patriots continued the pursuit southeast toward Kings Mountain.[33]

Colonel Sevier and his Washington County boys were in the advance heading down the road toward Kings Mountain when they stealthily nabbed a small scout party of Loyalists without firing a shot only a few miles from their target. Since their lives were under threat, the captured Loyalists talked freely and rapidly to reveal all that they knew in the hope of being spared from the Patriots' wrath. They verified what Enoch Gilmer had learned from the Tory women. Once again, Ferguson's lofty position atop Kings Mountain on its northeastern spur was verified to the relief of one and all because of the fear that he would have dashed off to Charlotte by this time, and best of all, the exact location of Ferguson's pickets protecting the approaches to the forested hill.[34] Still leading the way and nearing their long-sought prey, Sevier's mountaineers, who were enough to terrify friend or foe by just their rugged looks alone, then captured, at Lieutenant Colonel Frederick Hambright's smart urging, John Ponder, age fourteen. Young Ponder was a dispatch rider from Ferguson to Lord Cornwallis. The most recent intelligence from the young man, whose brother was a Loyalist fighting man, told the whole story: Ferguson was still holding his ground in the hope of securing reinforcements from the main army at Charlotte to the northeast. Ponder was asked to give a description of Major Ferguson. He responded that Ferguson wore a checked shirt, or duster, which a rider needed on the South's dusty roads during summer and early fall days, over the resplendent scarlet uniform of a British major. Now the Patriots had singled out Ferguson and passed the word about his appearance—something that no one forgot on this day of destiny—throughout the task force of sharp-eyed marksmen. Despite having been in America since around 1738, Lieutenant Colonel Frederick Hambright told his South Fork Boys in his German accent, "Well, poys, when you see dot man mit a pig shirt on over his clothes, you may know who him is, and mark him mit your rifles."[35]

The last intelligence coup on October 7 that enlightened the Patriots came from a fellow lover of liberty within only one mile of Kings Mountain. George Watkins, who was one of Colonel Thomas Brandon's men of the 2nd Spartan Regiment, suddenly appeared, after having been released on parole by Major

Ferguson. Of course, this unexpected development when so near the ultimate target only enhanced the already high level of confidence among the pursuers, because it was clear that Ferguson had no idea that the Patriots were so near or he never would have released Watkins. In addition, Watkins's ill-timed release proved that Ferguson had not been brutalized by this war, because he had not hanged Watkins like so many other British officers might well have ordered. He reconfirmed that Ferguson was still on top of his commanding hilltop as if without a care in the world.[36] Young Private Thomas Young, one of Brandon's militiamen who gamely kept up with the command despite having no shoes but plenty of fighting spirit, described the last intelligence coup: "We came to an open field . . . we met George Watkins, a Whig who had just been paroled by the Enemy. He gave our officers information that we were within half a mile of Ferguson's party on the top of Kings Mountain, & of their position. Orders were immediately given to tie our blankets behind us, pick & prime" our weapons.[37]

Another ad hoc commanders' conference occurred among the carefully calculating colonels while sitting in their well-worn leather saddles, resulting in the final preparations for the descent on Kings Mountain just to the south, when facing its heavily timbered southwestern slope. As if still battling the Cherokee in the western mountains, they decided to wisely instill more discipline for the final approach to Kings Mountain that was absolutely necessary at this point, because not a single mistake of any kind could now be made. New orders were issued to the men—no more talking and immediately prepare weapons for firing. With their final goal so near, there was now no hesitation despite the fact that the men had ridden all night and most of the day all the way from the Cowpens, while Ferguson's men had rested in their tents, eaten their daily rations, and believed that they were on the verge of a great victory when the rain had drenched Kings Mountain. Confidence increased because Shelby fully realized that Ferguson continued to be sloppy and careless about his encampment's security, as if he believed that his pursuers were a hundred miles away and of no consequence whatsoever.

However, no mistakes or misfires could be made now. Consequently, between approximately two and three o'clock in the afternoon of October 7, the 910 mounted Overmountain and backcountry soldiers were quickly formed in two columns with two riders abreast. The steady flow of intelligence could hardly have been more thorough or more accurate, including Ferguson's numbers (1,125 men), exact location of the Loyalist camp on the northeastern spur, the existence of only a relatively small number of Loyalist pickets who had been positioned to sound the alarm and their location, and even the major's dress and appearance. Colonel Campbell took his position at the head of the right column of horsemen to begin the encirclement from the south, while Colonel Shelby took charge of the left column that stretched through the thick woodlands, for the encirclement on the north. Without making a sound, Shelby and Campbell motioned for the two columns of silent mounted men to move forward as one in a case of perfect timing. Fortunately, besides the absence of rising dust clouds, there had been no thunder of hundreds of horses' hooves pounding on the wet and muddy ground until they had splashed through the waters of Ponder's Branch at a fast pace and then past the lower branch of King's Creek, flowing roughly parallel to and north of Kings Mountain, and then galloping forward to its east side.[38]

Colonel Shelby, who might have marveled at the irony of the creek and mountain that had been named after the King family because his father Evan had built the first family home in a place called King's Meadow in the north Holston settlement near the clear-flowing river of the same name, described how during the final approach to Kings Mountain:

> The American line of battle was formed as follows—Colonel Campbell's regiment headed by himself formed the center column to the right. Colonel Shelby's regiment commanded by himself formed the center column on the left. The right wing was composed of Colonel Sevier's regiment, Col. McDowell's regiment, Col. Winston's regiment & commanded by Col. Sevier in front. The left wing was composed of Col. [Benjamin] Cleveland's regiment. Col. [James] Williams' regiment, Colonel [Edward] Lacey's regiment & Colonel [Thomas] Brannum's [Brandon's 2nd Spartan] regiment, & headed in front by Col. Cleveland's regiment, & headed in front by Col. Cleveland himself, in this order the American Army advanced in four lines until it arrived in sight of the Enemy's Camp on Kings Mountain at three o'clock in the afternoon of Saturday the 7th of October, 1780.[39]

These frontier and backcountry leaders were direct representatives of the citizen-soldiers, who they were now leading forward, and "were at the head of troops not through family contacts or wealth but through their actions as men in the communities. These were a people who thought little of talk and demanded actions from their leadership"—a bond of trust and faith that was now about to pay immense dividends.[40]

Now in command of his Chester District [county] from north central South Carolina, which had been named by early Scotch-Irish settlers who had migrated from Chester County, Pennsylvania, comprised of citizen-soldiers from the backcountry including members of the Fishing River Presbyterian Church, Colonel Edward Lacey, who now commanded around a hundred men, was every inch a fighter. Colonel Lacey's life had been an amazing odyssey. He had been born in Shippensburg Township, Pennsylvania, in September 1742, when the area was still an untamed frontier and a dangerous place. Wanderlust had bitten him at age thirteen, when he had decided to run away to join Pennsylvania militiamen during British General Edward Braddock's 1755 ill-fated expedition over the mountains and into the remote vastness of the wild Ohio country in the beginning of the French and Indian War. He had somehow survived the deadly ambush and slaughter of much of the English and American Army by savvy French, Indian, and Canadian frontier fighters. Then, three years later, he had again run away from home to the South Carolina frontier in the Chester District and served as a respected captain during the 1776 Cherokee campaign. Lacey won distinction in backcountry battles, including the elimination of Captain Christian Huck's command on July 12, 1780, after catching the Loyalists by surprise and inflicting severe damage. He now led "the Chester Troops" at Kings Mountain with a combination of pride and skill.[41]

In another account, Colonel Shelby described the overall situation, including the final approach after riding up a branch and ravine nestled between two rock knolls and then the final deployments for action:

> Ferguson, finding he could not elude the rapid pursuit of the mounted mountaineers, had marched to King's Mountain, which he considered a strong post, and which head reached the night previous. The mountain, or ridge, was a quarter of a mile long and so confident was Ferguson in the strength of his position, that he declared, 'the Almighty could not drive him from it' [and] When the patriots came near the mountain they halted, tied all their loose baggage to their saddles, fastened their horses, and left them under charge of a few men,

> and then prepared for an immediate attack. About three o'clock the patriot forces were led to the attack in four columns—Col. Campbell commanded the right centre column, Col. Shelby the left centre, Col. Sevier in the right flank column, and Col. Cleveland the left flank.[42]

It was only Shelby's and Campbell's men of the lower ranks who tied their horses to trees, while leading officers remained mounted.[43]

These frontier and backcountry leaders had been chosen by the men in the ranks not because they were primarily popular as in militias in the east, but mostly because they were hard-nosed fighters of skill: exactly the kind of tough men who were needed to ensure the survival of families and communities on the frontier. Experienced leaders like Colonel John Sevier, who had long demonstrated his military skills by repeatedly vanquishing the Cherokee, "was the idol of the soldiery" of the Overmountain region.[44] Therefore, when about to engage in the most important battle of their lives, it meant a good deal to these citizen-soldiers that officers provided encouragement to inspire their worn men, who had not eaten or rested in the last thirty-six hours.[45] The revered frontier leaders, or "Great Captains" like Shelby and Sevier, had been chosen by these largely Scotch-Irish soldiers in the ancient Celtic clan tradition of Scotland and Ireland. In the end, the final ambitious plan of surrounding and destroying Ferguson had been largely born of a combined influence of the Celtic, frontier, and Indian fighting experiences and tactics, stemming primarily from the irrepressible Colonel Shelby.[46]

These experienced leaders, especially Shelby and Sevier, possessed winning ways and "personal magnetism [that] was contagious [and their] discipline was voluntary," while the men in the ranks respected their common sense, intelligence—a rare combination—and judgment on the battlefield, especially when it came to Indian-style, or irregular, fighting.[47] The Patriots' approach could not have been stealthier because it had been so well thought-out. As mentioned, after having reached a thick belt of woods on the east side of Kings Creek and behind a low ridge just northwest of Kings Mountain, orders had been whispered by Shelby and Campbell and then passed down the line, while the other commands remained mounted to move into their assigned positions farther northeast along the lengthy ridge, to "dismount and tie your horses [to trees and] take off great coats, blankets, etc., to your saddles" before moving on toward the heavily forested mountain.[48] The veteran colonels had then hurriedly conferred to fine-tune their final tactics from the vantage point of the low ridge covered in dense forest. Here, they had orchestrated the final details of completely surrounding the mountain, according to Shelby's detailed plan: The attack would open in unison with all nine separate commands acting as one when a frontier battle cry first echoed from each side of the mountain to verify that each commander and their troops were in their assigned positions and were ready to fight. It was now time for the final approach on foot like when so many of these same leaders and men had defeated the Cherokee in the fall of 1776.

After the force was divided into four separate columns of more than nine hundred men to approach each side of Kings Mountain, Shelby and Campbell and their men advanced stealthily on foot through the woods to get into position to fulfill the dual assignments of Shelby beginning the encirclement on the north just beyond the southwestern spur and Campbell doing the same to the southwest on the edge of the spur itself. Therefore, the frontier team of kindred spirits—Shelby and Campbell—were destined to strike first, while the other troops of the two columns would continue onward northeast along both sides, north and south, of the lengthy ridge, because they had the farthest to go to reach their assigned positions, including to the ridge's northeastern end where the bare summit, covered in the white tents of Ferguson's encampment, rose above the wooded slopes to dominate the open crest.

At this time, Ferguson's mind was still dominated by a host of delusions that were about to be shattered forever. He was now waiting for the reinforcements from Charlotte that would never come and reach him in time, after having reduced his force to less than 950 men (less than the generally assumed 982 soldiers) when he had dispatched the two-hundred-man foraging party early on October 7 in still another foolish decision that could not have been more ill-timed and detrimental to his chances for success. The major's messengers, who wore civilian clothing to look just like Patriots and never wore a bright red uniform because of the roving bands of partisans who would have riddled such inviting targets with a hail of bullets, had either been captured or fatally delayed. In consequence, while he was dreaming of yet achieving a great victory, Ferguson now "sat on the mountain waiting while an army of mountain men" were about to strike.[49]

Feeling secure like Ferguson, Captain Alexander Chesney, a member of the 1776 Cherokee campaign and a Patriot before deciding to defect to the

British after Charles Town's fall in May 1780, penned how the entire command had encamped atop Kings Mountain "with a view of approaching Lord Cornwallis's army and receiving support."[50] And now the pursuers had reached Kings Mountain in time only because of Colonel Shelby's determination in initiating, organizing, orchestrating, and leading the expedition to destroy Ferguson. Looking stern and grim, the determination of the young Sullivan County colonel from the Holston River country was best represented by his recent words spoken while on the move east: "I will not stop [even] if I follow Ferguson into Cornwallis' lines."[51]

Meanwhile, Captain Chesney, now acting as Ferguson's adjutant, had just inspected the pickets stationed at the wooded base of Kings Mountain and about halfway up the slope of the southwestern spur of the ridge. He was about to report to Ferguson at the headquarters tent on the northeastern end of the ridge of Kings Mountain that all was in order. However, Chesney would not have a chance to present his oral report to Ferguson. Here, at the summit of the northeastern spur, Ferguson was faithfully attended in numerous ways, including in bed at night by two Southern women of loose morals and youthful good looks according to legend—Virginia Sal and Virginia Paul. Officially, they were cooks and laundresses working at headquarters for the major and his staff officers to disguise their bedtime activities with the major in the tradition of British officers enjoying attractive, buxom Loyalist women who accompanied their lovers during active campaigning.[52]

Even to the last moment, Ferguson continued to be a victim of unrealistic views. First and foremost, Ferguson had repeatedly tempted fate like an addicted gambler when he had brashly boasted to Sir Henry Clinton how the highly disciplined British had already significantly "gain'd that superiority in the woods over the Rebels which they once claimed!" Of course, this imagined development in a delusional mind was entirely premature and about to be proved utterly false at Kings Mountain.[53] Usually in a conventional battle, occupying the high ground practically always equated to victory for a strong, well-armed force of disciplined soldiers. However, Major Ferguson was about to learn the hard way that the upcoming showdown for possession of Kings Mountain was destined to be anything but a conventional battle. Covered with fallen logs and boulders, the heavily wooded, boulder-studded slopes and steepness of Kings Mountain were about to prove the ideal setting for fighting Indian style for more than nine hundred Patriots. Even more, the extremely narrow ridgeline running along the open oblong crest and the barren top of the spur at the ridge's northeastern end—an open, grassy plateau—provided no cover and left little room for either deployment or maneuver once the battle erupted, limiting Ferguson's tactical options and overall chances for success. And the lack of cover along the open crest guaranteed heavy losses for Loyalists deploying upon and moving along the ridge where Tory soldiers would be silhouetted against the skyline to present excellent targets, and their dense ranks in tight alignment, as prescribed by British army regulations, could be easily cut to pieces by expert riflemen firing from behind trees and boulders on the slopes on all sides of the ridge: essentially a deadly turkey shoot for the expert marksmen.[54] The Patriot colonels told their eager men "to kill every Tory in sight."[55]

By this time, such orders were unnecessary because the hatred of the Loyalists was high among virtually every man in this task force. In a rare letter written by Andrew Creswell, of the Virginia backcountry and part of Colonel William Campbell's command of around two hundred Washington County troops, he described the Loyalists who defended Kings Mountain as a "dirty crew" of men and believed in his heart of hearts that "God [should] eternally damn the Tories to Hell's Fires."[56] Hatred and contempt also manifested themselves on the other side because Ferguson and his Loyalists viewed the rustic Patriots, especially the Overmountain men, as nothing more than criminals. Lieutenant Anthony Allaire, for instance, described the surrendered Patriots of Charles Town in May 1780 as "poor Rebel dogs," while having rejoiced at the sight of how the British victors "leveled the thirteen stripes with the dust."[57] Today was a time of vengeance for the loss of Charles Town, which had paved the way for South Carolina's conquest and other humiliating defeats across South Carolina, especially at the Waxhaws on May 29, 1780.

To fully understand the overall strategic importance of the upcoming battle, Charles Town's fall—barely four months before—was a low point for Patriot fortunes in overall strategic and political terms, after the loss of not only Georgia, but also South Carolina. Historian Thomas Fleming described how "both North and South Carolina now seemed prostrate [and] There was no patriot army in either state strong enough to resist the thousands of British regulars. Georgia had been conquered [and] There were rumors that America's allies, France and Spain, were tired of the war and ready to call a peace conference."[58] A distraught New England congressman penned how "it is agreed on all hands the whole state of So. Carolina hath submitted to the British Government as well as Georgia [and] I shall not be surprised to hear N. Carolina hath followed their example"—exactly what Lord Cornwallis had planned.[59]

Appropriately, Colonel Shelby and His Holston River Country Soldiers Strike First

Colonel Shelby, especially confident after coming off his recent victories at Thicketty Fort, Cedar Springs, and Musgrove's Mill, now focused on the next tactical challenge of extreme importance: the elimination of the small party of pickets, who had been assigned to sound the alarm at any approach of Patriots, as quickly and silently as possible, before the alarm could be given.

Colonel Shelby, the most experienced Indian fighting commander, was the ideal man for this important job of wiping out the pickets before they could shout a warning or fire a shot. Even more, Shelby's key mission of striking first to eliminate Ferguson's foremost pickets was also symbolic for a number of reasons. First, Shelby had already played a leading role in winning the three recent victories in 1780, which had garnered the Patriots' crucial initiative and momentum that had set the stage for the sudden descent upon Kings Mountain. Most important, he had developed the winning tactical formula of catching the enemy by surprise with swift movements like in his victories at Thicketty Fort and Musgrove's Mill.[60]

On Shelby's orders, his men of his entire Sullivan County militia regiment had already taken off their hats to make themselves less conspicuous, and this was now especially the case of his small detail of chosen men. Like other members of Shelby's regiment, these chosen few frontiersmen had also bound their long, matted hair by donning handkerchiefs around their heads to guarantee a more inconspicuous advance up the heavily wooded mountainside in the bid to dispose of Ferguson's pickets, whom the recently captured Loyalists said were situated on the road at Kings Mountain's base. After having left their horses less than a mile behind at a safe hidden place not far from Kings Creek just north of Kings Mountain, behind a low timbered ridge to muffle sounds and ensure concealment, Shelby and his best men, with their long rifles freshly primed with new charges of black powder, carefully sneaked in silence through the fall woodlands and ever closer to the mountain's base and the exact location of the pickets. Advancing ahead of the column, these professional killers, who knew how to use the tomahawk and hunting knife, including for scalping victims, with a silent lethalness stemming from years of battling the Cherokee, remained perfectly quiet while easing through the tall timber and underbrush.

Then, Colonel Shelby, who was beginning to understand how this fight had distinctive numerous commonalities with the bloody showdown with Shawnee and Mingo warriors at Point Pleasant in the autumn of 1774, first spied the handful of Ferguson's pickets near the road. These Loyalist pickets—Carolina militiamen rather than Provincial regulars—were anything but prepared or wary.

The carpet of crisp autumn leaves covering the forest's floor were still soaking wet because the sun had not dried them under the dark shadows of the forest's canopy, ensuring that they made no sound when stepped on by Shelby's small advance party. Even more, the gentle rustling of the leaves of the trees from the slight, cool breeze of early autumn also muffled all sound.

Significantly, Shelby knew of the size and location of Ferguson's picket force—only a few men who were not vigilant on this carefree autumn afternoon when it seemed that no danger existed for many miles around—which had been posted at the mountain's base. Of course, this vital advance knowledge gained from the two deserters of Ferguson's command and the American prisoner who had been released by Major Ferguson made Shelby's mission considerably easier, bestowing added confidence for the tricky job of silencing the pickets before they issued a warning.

Fortunately for the eventual outcome, Major Ferguson had made his first mistake by not having stationed a large force at the mountain's base nor erecting some slight defenses—at least some piled up logs and brush like Colonel Shelby had smartly ordered at Musgrove's Mill when about to meet the advancing enemy in large numbers—and perhaps using musket butts and bayonets to create a small earthen defensive point, because the soil was softer and less rocky at the mountain's base as opposed to its top along the rocky crest. However, these prudent defensive measures were inconceivable to Major Ferguson's overconfident mind, especially since he had primarily trained his men to fight offensively.

Revealing the extent of his conventional military thinking, Ferguson had positioned his most advanced picket's guard of only a few men at the road leading to the mountain, as if he expected that the Patriots would march down the road in a neat formation like a conventional military force of British regulars.

But, of course, these men were Indian fighters who never advanced toward an enemy position down an open road or through an open field, especially after harvest time. For Ferguson to be successful today, the very first thing that he needed to avoid was a fight in the dense woodlands covering the mountain's slopes: a situation that ensured the supremacy of Indian-style fighting, of which Shelby's Overmountain men and the backcountry soldiers were masters. Most of all, Ferguson now needed level and relatively open terrain—the antithesis of the rugged, heavily timbered slopes of Kings Mountain—where the bayonet charge and refined discipline of his well-trained men could prevail like on the field of Camden, if the backwoods "mongrels" dared to attack him on his high ground perch.

Private Benjamin Sharp, who had been born in Lancaster County, Pennsylvania, in 1762 and was a member of Colonel Campbell's Washington County militia, described the situation that had bestowed the key advantages to Shelby for a successful mission of eliminating the pickets: "In the [early] afternoon [of October 7 we] fell in with three men who informed us that they were just from the British camp, that they were posted on the top of King's Mountain, and that there was a picket-guard on the road not far ahead of us. These men were detained lest they should find means to inform the enemy of our approach, and colonel Shelby, with a select party, undertook to surprise and take the picket; this he accomplished without firing a gun or giving the least alarm, and it was hailed by the army as a good omen."[61]

What cannot be denied was the fact that the men of Kings Mountain, especially the Scotch-Irish Presbyterians who were the majority, were a superstitious lot and the immortal words of the Old Testament remained paramount in their hearts and minds, especially in regard to delivering a righteous retribution. If the majority of the men indeed viewed the easy taking of Ferguson's pickets, thanks to the dense woodlands that provided limited vision and the well-honed skills of Colonel Shelby and his hand-picked Overmountain boys, without a sound as "a good omen," then they also viewed it as God's favor.[62] In Shelby's contemptuous words in regard to the final showdown against "Ferguson and his crew" of traitors: "The day was wet, and that Providence who always rules and governs all things for the best, so ordered it that we were close around them before we were discovered."[63] Indeed, Shelby and his Holston River Valley men could now approach Ferguson's hilltop position with much greater ease, while possessing the honor of having struck the first blow at Kings Mountain, after capturing the pickets, cutting their throats with their sharp hunting knives, or tomahawking them to death with swift blows to the temple to guarantee that the victims made no sound. This striking of the first blow with quick, stealthy precision that left dead pickets was most appropriate and symbolic because of Colonel Shelby's dominant role in this far-flung expedition.[64]

However, it was much more than God's favor and timely informants with accurate intelligence that had come to Shelby's aid in silently eliminating Ferguson's pickets. As noted, Ensign Robert Campbell described how one of the keys to Shelby's surprise of Ferguson's pickets was the fact that "the forenoon of the day was wet, but they were fortunate enough to come on him [Ferguson] undiscovered, and took his pickets [who evidently assumed that no threat existed because of the rainy weather], they not having it in their power to give an alarm. They were formed in such order as to attack the enemy on all sides."[65]

Consequently, Shelby's swift and smooth elimination of Ferguson's pickets eventually allowed the Overmountain and backcountry men to successfully perform the tactical maneuver that Ferguson never expected, partly because it was a standard tactical feature of Indian warfare: the eventual complete surrounding of Kings Mountain, while retaining the vital element of surprise, which was a rather remarkable tactical achievement.[66] After the quiet elimination of the Loyalist pickets, Colonel Shelby explained the tactical formula for success to ensure the surrounding of Kings Mountain, because after the Patriots had come "to the foot of the mountain, the right centre and right flank columns deployed to the right [south], and the left centre and left flank columns to the left [north], and thus [eventually] surrounding the mountain they marched up [and were just about] commencing the action on all sides."[67] To surround the oblong mountain in its entirety according to Shelby's bold plan, and make sure that Ferguson was trapped with no escape from his high ground perch that dominated the surrounding area, each colonel led his separate command toward their assigned positions.[68]

Sons of Erin and Other Celtic Warriors Forward

Not only first- and second-generation Scotch-Irish filled the ranks, but also a good many fighting men of the Presbyterian faith who had been born in north Ireland. By this time, Captain James Dysart, who had been born in Ireland around 1744 and came to America at age seventeen to settle in Washington

County, was ready for action. Leading a company of Virginia boys of Campbell's county regiment, the patriotic Irishman from an ancient Celtic clan of Horne Head Castle, Emerald Isle, carried his trusty firearm and a unique frontier powder horn that had been fashioned by two horns joined together by a wooden band.[69] Not an officer, although he now carried his prized handmade sword with the distinctive curve of a horseman's weapon, John Rhea also moved forward with his mostly Scotch-Irish comrades in the ranks of Campbell's Washington County militia command. He hailed from the Emerald Isle like so many others whose Irish brogues were distinctive. He had been born around 1753 and then moved to the Virginia frontier in 1778, after having first settled in Pennsylvania and then Maryland, before heading farther south for greener pastures.[70]

Just from South Carolina alone, a good many other Irishmen advanced in the surging ranks, such as William Adams, who had been born on the Emerald Isle in 1733. Likewise pushing forward through the hardwood trees of the forest, William Armstrong had been born in Ireland on August 14, 1765. He lived in the South Carolina backcountry in the Fairfield District and was a seasoned veteran who was often in the forefront of battle, including one in which four bullets had pierced his uniform coat in close calls with death.[71] Born in Ireland in 1763, John Patterson of the South Carolina backcountry was also determined to vanquish Major Ferguson and his Loyalist command at any cost.[72] John Scott, who had been born among the green rolling hills of County Antrim, Ulster Province, in March in either 1754 or 1755, represented the Fairfield District, South Carolina, at Kings Mountain like a good many other sons of Erin from this heavily Irish district in the backcountry.[73] Now advancing with firearm in hand, James Steen had also been born in County Antrim, Ireland, but in 1724. He fought not only at Kings Mountain but also later at the Battle of Cowpens on January 17, 1781 like a good many other Scotch-Irish men. In the future, a cruel fate followed this Irishman, because he "was stabbed to death while attempting to arrest a Tory in Rowan County," North Carolina.[74]

James Hawthorn was another excellent Irish soldier from South Carolina. He had been born in County Armagh, Ulster Province, north Ireland, around 1750. Hawthorn's life had been a true frontier odyssey. In 1762 while living on the South Carolina frontier, he and his mother and two sisters had been captured by Native American raiders. As if seeking revenge, he then served in the 1776 Cherokee campaign to strike back at his former tormentors, leaving his blacksmith's tools aside to pick up a musket and go to war. He now appropriately served in the ranks of north Ireland-born Colonel William Hill, who led his contingent of South Carolinians onward in the dark forest, when "there was very little military subordination," in his own words.[75]

In addition, Edward Martin, who had been born in Ireland and lived in the Fairfield District of the South Carolina backcountry, also advanced on Kings Mountain with the determination to do or die.[76] Likewise, David Morrow, who had been born on the Emerald Isle on February 28, 1761, was about to engage in the largest battle of his life, like so many of his Scotch-Irish comrades, including men who would never survive October 7.[77] Another South Carolina citizen-soldier, William White, who had been born in Ireland in 1753, was also shortly to enter the upcoming fray at this obscure hilltop in the South Carolina Piedmont.[78] Born in Pennsylvania and of Scotch-Irish descent, the Porter boys, James and William, also surged forward with the conviction to do whatever was required to save the South Carolina homeland. Major James Porter was destined to fall wounded on the hot afternoon of October 7 in battling for possession of Kings Mountain.[79]

However, far more Irishmen served in the Virginia, North Carolina, South Carolina, and Georgia militia commands, and most of these sons of Erin remain unknown to this day, because of the lack of documentation and incomplete records that often failed to list place of birth. And, of course, the sons of large numbers—almost certainly the majority of those who fought at Kings Mountain—of Irish immigrants born in America were listed as having been born in Virginia, Maryland, Pennsylvania, and the Carolinas without any hint of Irish antecedents. For instance, Samuel Morrow Jr. had been born in the port of Baltimore, Maryland, in March 1760 of Irish immigrant parents, who moved to the Camden District (today's Chester County), South Carolina, when he was five years old. He fought under Colonel Edward Lacey and with the Chester County men at Kings Mountain.[80] In a true brother's war, they were about to face a good many Scotch-Irish Loyalists of the North Carolina and South Carolina militia from the backcountry and a small command of soldiers under Irish immigrant Captain David Larimer to reveal another aspect of the forgotten civil war among the Scotch-Irish and Irish in the South.[81] No one seemed to notice on the Loyalist side that the men who Ferguson held in such absolute contempt—those who he called "barbarians," "mongrels," and the "Back Water men"—were very much like most of the backcountry Loyalists who he commanded and trained except in regard to political beliefs and the uncontrollable dynamics of complex wartime situations that had determined their choosing of sides.[82]

Arthur Patterson, the "old Irishman," was the newest Celtic-Gaelic addition to this unorthodox frontier army of mostly Scotch-Irish, who were his own countrymen from across the sea and the green hills of Ulster Province, north Ireland. Despite his advanced years, he now surged forward with his old musket not only because of his considerable hatred of the British, but also because Ferguson's men had taken captive his two sons and a relative, William, Thomas, and Arthur Jr. They were now held atop Kings Mountain and risked being hanged for their beliefs. As fate would have it, at a time when his "old Irish blood" was up to do his best against his people's most ancient foe, Arthur Patterson was about to lose his life, while his two sons were destined to escape their captors when confusion reigned supreme in the Loyalist encampment during the attack. Symbolically, when Arthur Patterson was killed in the upcoming engagement, his son Thomas was fighting in Patriot ranks, after escaping and having picked up a musket from a wounded soldier and joining the fight with typical Irish fighting spirit.[83]

However, of course it was not only Celtic soldiers from the Green Isle like John Brown, who had been born in County Derry, Ulster Province, north Ireland, who were advancing in the ranks with loaded muskets and long rifles. Many soldiers of another Celtic nation, Wales, could be found mixed in with the mostly Scotch-Irish soldiers. Not only Colonel Shelby and his brothers, but also men like William Meredith were of Welsh heritage and the inheritors of the nationalist and revolutionary tradition of famed Welsh leader Owain Glyndwr. Meredith was the backcountry neighbor of Colonel Benjamin Cleveland and he now served with other Wilkes County fighting men.[84] And Major Micajah Lewis, Captain Joel Lewis, and Lieutenant James M. Lewis of the Wilkes and Surry County troops of Cleveland's regiment were also of Welsh heritage and all three brothers were destined to fall wounded in the upcoming clash of arms.[85] A veteran of the French and Indian War and Indian campaigns like quite a few other Celts in the ranks, Samuel Martin had been born in Ireland in 1732. He was married to an Irish lass named Margaret McCurdy.[86]

A good many Scottish soldiers, some who had been born in Scotland and others the descendants of Scottish immigrants, also served in the ranks. These Celts never forgot that England had ruthlessly conquered Scotland in the most brutal manner and ruled with an iron hand for centuries, while destroying the nationalist dreams of an independent Celtic nation with the distinctive traditions and value systems of a unique culture. For instance, James Johnston, who had served in the 1776 Cherokee campaign, had been born in Scotland around 1742, and his father had settled in the area of Lincoln County, North Carolina. Born in New Jersey, David Witherspoon was now serving as an officer in Cleveland's Wilkes County Regiment while his young brother, John, was now a private at Kings Mountain: a most symbolic role because their esteemed relative Dr. John Witherspoon had been a signer of the Declaration of Independence.[87]

In addition, numerous Celtic clans were distinguished by father-son fighting teams at Kings Mountain. Joshua Nichols served beside his father, who commanded the militia company of citizen-soldiers from Rowan County, North Carolina.[88] The volunteer company of Ireland-born Captain James Dysart, who still recalled the beauty of his native County Donegal, Ulster Province, north Ireland, at the height of springtime after having migrated to America as a teenager, led the advance of Campbell's Virginia regiment of mostly Scotch-Irish fighting men toward the westernmost and southwestern end of the lengthy ridge, which reached its highest point on the southwest. Dysart was about to receive a serious wound in the "left hand, which crippled him for life."[89]

Colonel Elijah Clarke's Georgia soldiers, more than thirty good fighting men, were the most forgotten (after Black soldiers of course) contingent at Kings Mountain in part because they represented the smallest command from any state. These veteran partisans hailed from Elbert (northeastern part of the state) and Columbia (the east central part of the state around Augusta) Counties, and were now under the leadership of Major William Candler in Clarke's absence. An excellent leader who was popular with his troops, Candler had been born in Belfast, Ulster Province, north Ireland, in April 1735. He had migrated from the Emerald Isle to America as a child with his family. He married Elizabeth Anthony in 1760 and then moved to the Georgia frontier to start a new life. Here, he became a deputy surveyor in 1771. Son Henry Candler now rode by his father's side in another familial fighting team, who were fully committed to the cause of liberty and served with distinction at Kings Mountain. It was most appropriate that the capable Candler commanded the Georgians, which included mostly Scotch-Irish and Ireland-born men. A great killer of Loyalists and the Achilles-like Celtic warrior among the Georgians, Patrick "Paddy" Carr had been born in County Derry, Ulster Province, north Ireland. He was the most lethal Celtic Patriot from the Peach State at Kings Mountain on this day of destiny.

Other Ireland-born and Scotch-Irish soldiers from Georgia filled the ranks, including Indian fighter Isaac Connor, who had been born in Virginia; Ebenzer Fain, born in Pennsylvania and who was about to fall with a nasty leg wound; Virginia-born Vardry McBee; Josiah McCloskey, who had been born in South Carolina; William McKinney; William McMaster, who migrated with his family to America from north Ireland at age thirteen; John Patterson, who was born in January 1763 in Ireland and was an experienced Indian fighter; and a good many others.[90] Non-Irish soldiers, especially Captain William Hammett who had two brothers killed at the Battle of Kettle Creek, Georgia, on February 14, 1779, which was a backcountry Patriot victory, led their mostly Scotch-Irish and Irish command from Columbia and Elbert counties, Georgia, forward. At least one father-son fighting team served that afternoon to proudly represent Georgia, Charles Hammond and son Abner.[91]

Caught Completely by Surprise!

Fortunately for the Patriots, in an incredible omission that revealed an astounding degree of negligence for a top leader in the British Army, Ferguson had never "seriously prepared for an active defense of the ridgeline" and no efforts were made by the Scottish major and his top lieutenants "to prepare defenses, conduct training, or perform rehearsal actions; instead, Loyalist actions in the hours leading to the battle seemed focused more on housekeeping details."[92] This was most ironic because the stakes could not have been higher for both sides. Quite simply, "if the Loyalists under Ferguson couldn't whip backwoods militia, it would be a fateful day for Britain and the whole philosophy of getting the Americans to do the fighting" to win this war.[93]

Indeed, on this Saturday in early autumn when cooking fires were lit for the early afternoon meal and a cool autumn breeze gently rustled through the brightly colored leaves of the trees, more than nine hundred of Ferguson's men at their tented encampment were perfectly at ease, as if it was a lazy Sunday afternoon of British occupation at Ninety-Six in the South Carolina Piedmont or at the Atlantic port of Georgetown, just north of Charles Town. Basking in the October sunshine that had first appeared in midafternoon after the recent rains had finally passed and rolled east toward the coast, the Loyalists on the high ground were resting, cleaning weapons and gear, and engaging in routine camp duties and chores. They felt completely secure after having only taken their lofty position on the previous day, October 6. No one, not even Loyalist scouts and spies, had any idea that hundreds of their archenemies were nearly to the foot of Kings Mountain.

Like Captain Alexander Chesney, second-in-command Captain Abraham De Peyster, who officially commanded the Provincial Regulars (Loyal American Volunteers), had just checked on the status of his pickets at the mountain's base. Neither officer had ascertained any problems or any sign of a threat. De Peyster's top lieutenant was Captain Samuel Ryerson, born in New Jersey in 1752 and the descendant of Dutch immigrants (Ryerse in Holland) who had migrated to New York in the mid-1600s. Captain De Peyster officially commanded the elite "backbone" of Ferguson's task force, the tough and disciplined Provincial Regulars. Third in command, Ryerson had old scores to settle with the rebels. He had been persecuted for his beliefs before joining the Loyalist ranks, and his New Jersey lands and property were confiscated in 1779.

In the quiet, serene encampment atop the northeastern spur, Major Ferguson and his top officers were engaged in conducting routine military matters while awaiting the arrival of Lord Cornwallis's reinforcements, preferably Tarleton and his hard-hitting British Legion of Americans, that were sure to come. Ferguson possessed great faith in the commanders of the Loyalist regiments, especially his crack Provincial regulars, and believed in them totally. Ferguson's command was also known as Provincial Rangers, whom he had raised in the North and trained with paternalistic care. He especially prized his best fighting men of a force of around 140 Provincial Regulars from New York and New Jersey. These well-trained men of Ferguson's own prized regiment were known by various names, especially the Loyal American Volunteers, the Loyal American Regiment, or just the American Volunteers, which had been organized by Ferguson in New York in late 1776 and early 1777.

These young men and boys of the American Volunteers were crack soldiers and they looked the part, wearing the bright red uniforms of the British regulars, whom they had been trained to emulate to Ferguson's exacting standards. On October 7, Ferguson would repeatedly employ his finest men as his reliable Grenadier Guard, or hard-hitting shock troops, in the upcoming battle, because they had been well-honed and disciplined for the unleashing of the British Army's most effective tactic, the bayonet charge. They served as the sturdy foundation around which Ferguson had formed his militia regiments, and they gave him supreme confidence for successfully defending Kings Mountain.

Ferguson was also relying on the Loyalist militia commands of six regiments from South Carolina and North Carolina. Without the usual contempt or hatred, Colonel Arthur Campbell described them as "upland Tories, mostly riflemen" of the backcountry. Since the summer, the South Carolina militiamen had been trained and disciplined like regular British soldiers. Ferguson now commanded Colonel Ambrose Mills and around five hundred of his North Carolina boys of the Spartan Regiment (eight companies) from Tryon County who had only recently joined his command; Colonel Daniel Plummer of the Fair Forest Regiment (eight companies of militia) of around two hundred men from the Ninety-Six region of the western South Carolina backcountry; Major Patrick Cunningham, who led the Little River Regiment (eight companies) of around two hundred soldiers and which also hailed from the South Carolina Piedmont; Richard King's Long Cane Regiment (four companies now attached to Colonel Plummer's regiment) of around a hundred men; the Dutch Fork Regiment (two companies attached to Colonel John Cotton Sr.'s regiment and two companies attached to Major Cunningham's regiment) of around a hundred Loyalists; and Colonel John Cotton Sr.'s Stevens, or Stephen's, Creek Regiment (eight companies) of around two hundred Tories.

After Colonel Mills's Tryon County command, the most militiamen of Ferguson's command served in Colonel Daniel Plummer's Fair Forest Regiment and Lieutenant Colonel Zacharias Gibbs's Spartan Regiment (around a hundred men in each regiment, although Gibbs, a Virginian who had settled on Fair Forest Creek, South Carolina, not long before the war's beginning, was not present in the battle), which were from South Carolina's northwestern region. However, at Kings Mountain, Ferguson possessed contingents of primarily six of the seven that he had formed at Ninety-Six, South Carolina.

Unlike the American Provincials, who wore red uniforms with different colored trim on the sleeves and along the row of uniform coat buttons that distinguished them from British regulars, yet ironically like the Patriots of the county militia regiments, these Loyalist commands consisted of short-term militiamen. In addition, these militiamen consisted of two distinct classes of soldiers. The first class was young and mostly unmarried men, who were under the obligation of serving for six months each year, of the militia regiments that Ferguson had raised from the backcountry area of western South Carolina around Ninety-Six during the summer. By this time, these Loyalist militiamen had been training heavily in the bayonet charge and volley firing in the tradition of the British regulars. The least trained and less experienced men were the most recent arrivals—the raw North Carolina militia from Tryon County, North Carolina. Ferguson had armed these men with the available Brown Bess muskets that he carried in large numbers in his support wagons for arming newly arriving Loyalists.

Major Ferguson most of all counted on his around 140 elite Provincial Rangers, the crack American Volunteers in their smart scarlet uniforms with long-tailed coats and armed with the long or short land pattern Brown Bess musket of .75 caliber. What united these men, both the Provincials from New York and New Jersey and the South Carolina and North Carolina militiamen, was a severe underestimation of the so-called "Backwater" (a contemptible British term for the Overmountain citizen-soldiers) men. As mentioned, the Scottish major was so confident of success on the morning of October 7 that he had ordered a two-hundred-man foraging party to scour the countryside for supplies to make for plentiful dining on the mountaintop by suppertime, while waiting for Cornwallis's reinforcements. After all, in his own words, Ferguson was now only threatened by the "dregs of mankind" from remote regions west of the mountains that were still unknown and not even located on British and colonial maps.[94]

Some of Ferguson's Loyalists from the Carolina backcountry were still motivated by ancient hatred against the Patriot elite planter class and wealthy aristocrats of the East Coast. Other Loyalists were convinced that their future and rights lay with the British government, while other Tories were more cynical and wanted to profit from the confiscation of rebel lands and personal property, including slaves, for their faithful service to the Crown.[95] Lieutenant Anthony Allaire had bragged about a past success of Ferguson's best troops in his diary, describing how in a March 1780 skirmish "the bayonet was introduced so effectually that a Capt. Mills, and sixteen privates of the Rebels could not exist any longer."[96] Meanwhile, as always when battling Native Americans, British, and Loyalists, Colonel Shelby and other leaders and the men in the ranks had placed their trust in God, a righteous cause that they believed in, and the deadly long rifle: "It appears that under the auspices of the same Divine Power that so advantageously conducted the right hand column of the Whigs to the battle of King's Mountain, from that period good fortune seemed to preponderate in every direction in favor of the common cause of liberty," in the words of Captain William Lenoir.[97]

Ironically, the Loyalists atop Kings Mountain would have possessed even more contempt, if that was possible, for the Overmountain men and rebels in general had they known some unique details about the citizen-soldiers, who were now headed directly toward them with vengeance in their eyes and the determination to do God's will in a bloody, but righteous, manner. First, not a single Continental uniform could be found among the more than nine hundred citizen-soldiers. After all, these men had volunteered and formed the most egalitarian army in America on incredibly short notice "without any orders from the Executive" from four states, if the future state of Tennessee was counted, and who were "but little acquainted with discipline" of any kind, which made them the antithesis of Ferguson's well-trained Provincial regulars, who always went by the regulation book.[98]

Major Ferguson was about to be surprised by 910 Overmountain and backcountry men: Shelby and his 120 Overmountain men; Sevier and his 120 Overmountain men; Campbell and his 200 Virginia fighters; McDowell and his 90 North Carolina boys from Burke County; Cleveland and 100 of his Wilkes County, North Carolina, volunteers; Winston and his 60 men from Surry County, North Carolina; Hill and Lacey and their 100 men and Colonel Williams and his 60 men who all hailed from York and Chester Counties, South Carolina; Lieutenant Colonel Frederick Hambright and Colonel William Graham's 50 Lincoln County, North Carolina, men of a "composite force" that also included Major Chronicle's 20 "South Fork Boys" from Lincoln County, North Carolina; and around 30 Georgians from Elbert and Columbia Counties under Major William Candler, of Colonel Elijah Clarke's partisan command.[99]

However, despite Shelby and his men having effectively silenced the pickets without a shot fired that would have warned Ferguson of the danger, problems shortly developed to slow the ambitious tactical plan that was based on attacking in unison all around the mountain. On the south, Major Joseph Winston's Surry County regiment headed toward the wrong hill to block Ferguson's line of retreat, while Colonel Benjamin Cleveland's backcountry men from Wilkes County on the north encountered a low-lying and swampy area, thanks to the recent rains, on the ridge's northern face. And Colonel Sevier's Washington County, North Carolina, men were slow in moving up to gain their assigned position just to the southwest of Shelby's jumping off place to begin the assault on Shelby's right and closer to the southwestern spur.[100]

At least one, but certainly more volunteers from the surrounding area had recently joined the ranks during the attack. As mentioned, Ireland-born Arthur Patterson, seventy-two, was one such volunteer. He was mad as hell and desperately wanted his fair share of revenge for what Ferguson's men had done to his sons, young Thomas and William, on the morning of October 7. He had sent the boys out early in the morning to hunt for some stray cattle that had wandered off in the woods in the King's Creek area just north of Kings Mountain. The sons were captured by a patrol of Loyalist militia and initially tied to trees to prevent them from alerting any lurking Patriot force before being taken to the top of Kings Mountain by their captors. Around noon when his sons failed to return home, Patterson had snatched his rifle from above the fireplace and gone in search of them. Instead of finding William and Thomas Patterson, Arthur stumbled into the Patriots moving into position to attack and joined them to become the oldest fighting man on either side at Kings Mountain.[101] Eager to strike a blow upon the hated Ferguson at the head of his Lincoln County citizen-soldiers, Lieutenant Colonel Frederick Hambright carried a horseman's saber manufactured in Europe. Ironically, he should not have been in command of the South Fork Boys from the Catawba River country, except for the unexpected change in command structure because of Colonel William Graham's recent departure from the column when nearing Kings Mountain. Graham had requested permission from Colonel Campbell to depart because he had just learned of his wife's serious illness with colic only sixteen miles away.

Colonel Campbell, who was not the kind of man who tolerated anything less than a diehard commitment to the sacred cause of liberty, would have none of it. He emphasized that Colonel Graham needed to stay with his men when about to engage in the upcoming battle that would be the largest and most important one of their lives, because if they prevailed then the victory would be "as good as a dose of medicine" to completely revive Graham's wife. However, Graham continued to insist on departing the command, which only raised Campbell's well-known temper. Then, Graham asked the younger and more sympathetic Major William Chronicle for permission to leave, and the major concluded, "It is woman's business [so] let him go." Then, Graham requested a protective escort through the countryside because of the many Loyalists in the area and picked David Dickey. However, in no uncertain terms, the independent-minded Dickey strongly objected to the decision, saying that "he would rather be shot on the spot." However, Dickey finally relented and he and Colonel Graham departed the column in a hurry.[102]

The unexpected loss of Colonel Graham, who departed on the eve of combat cast some doubts on his courage among his Lincoln County men. To compensate for the sudden loss, Major Chronicle yelled to his men: "Come on, my South Fork boys" and moved forward.[103] But the most serious initial tactical problem for Shelby's plan developed from the failure of Major Joseph Winston and his Surry County men to initially fulfill their mission of securing a nearby hill on the north to cut off Ferguson's line of retreat to the main road to completely close the trap on the brash Scotsman and forever crush his soaring ambitions. Without maps, unfamiliar with the lay of the heavily forested land, and unable to see far because most autumnal leaves were still on the trees, they secured the wrong hill in the blinding forest.[104]

In overall strategic terms, this was an important hill adjacent to Kings Mountain to secure, as Colonel Shelby fully realized. At this time, Ferguson was still concerned that Thomas Sumter's South Carolina partisans would join the Overmountain and backcountry men to create an even more formidable fighting force. As he penned to his friend Major Robert Timpany, 3rd Battalion, New Jersey Volunteers, on October 6, when under the considerable threat of the "barbarians" in his contemptuous designation of some of America's finest citizen-soldiers: "Here we are Kings of Kings Mountain [and] although there is indeed another throne [like Kings Mountain] or ridge [Brushy Ridge, which was much smaller than the Kings Mountain ridge] opposite us where Genl. Sumpter's [sic] and your humble servant may . . . reign [in a face off] in day Light."[105]

In this letter, Major Ferguson remained confident of success throughout the day before his death: "We are inferior in number but [not] as to quality."[106] However, he was sufficiently realistic to understand the inferiority of "our young [North Carolina] Militia [from Tryon County under Colonel Ambrose Mills because of the] over match" with the veteran Overmountain men.[107] Indeed, the major possessed ample reason for concern because of the inexperience of the North Carolina militiamen from the backcountry, who fought for their own welfare and that of their families like their fellow Patriot Americans. In addition, these rural Loyalists from the backcountry overturned today's common stereotypes that the Loyalists were primarily conservative upper-class elites from the cities and along the east coast. Josiah Brandon provides an example of one of the backcountry Loyalists in the ranks. The teenager had departed his home in Burke County, North Carolina, and joined Ferguson only three weeks before the dramatic October 7, 1780, showdown, despite having previously served as a Patriot. He did so at the considerable urgings of his father, who was a Loyalist officer. Like so many young men of the North Carolina militia, Brandon lacked combat experience, which was about to suddenly change at Kings Mountain.[108]

A victim of fate that revealed the central tragedy of the Loyalist experience in the Carolinas, John Franklin was another inexperienced fighting man, who was destined to serve for less than two weeks before his capture at Kings Mountain. He explained with honest candor how and why he had suddenly found himself on Kings Mountain in the Loyalists' ranks, after returning home to North Carolina in September 1780: "The country [was] in a fearful and desperate situation [as] The Tories and Whigs were furiously contending together and scarcely any man could be found at home. I did not know what to do, or which party to join [but Major Ferguson] was then with a large British force . . . in Burke County North Carolina . . . and I amongst many others of the peoples who took protection under him as a British Subject and was immediately marched by him with the rest of his force to Kings Mountain," where he would be taken prisoner.[109]

When about to close in on Ferguson's command on foot after having tied horses to trees like his comrades, Private James Collins, fifteen, never forgot how "the sky was overcast with clouds, and at times a light mist of rain was falling; our provisions were scanty, and hungry men [now felt] his situation; the last stake was up and the severity of the game must be played; everything was at stake—life, liberty, property, and even the fate of wife, children and friends seemed to depend on the issue: death or victory was the only way to escape suffering."[110] Then, with the fighting about to erupt in full fury across Kings Mountain, the last general order was whispered down the lengthy lines of backcountry and Overmountain men, who had their loaded firearms at the ready: "Every man go into battle firmly resolving *to fight till he dies.*"[111] About to engage in his first battle, an anxious and nervous Private Collins had "come to this conclusion: never to retreat alone, shoot without an object; or lay down my gun until the last extremity; for, I thought, a gun, though empty, might keep an enemy at bay."[112]

Looming before them was the heavily wooded slopes and imposing height of Kings Mountain, which was not really a mountain, but more of a lengthy ridge with a spur, or plateau, situated at each end. This rocky elevation in an oblong shape rose high above the dense hardwood forest at the hill's base like a beacon that could be seen for miles around. Kings Mountain was actually only part of a lengthy range of hills that stretched around sixteen miles north to south, extending south from North Carolina into the Piedmont of northwestern South Carolina. Along its barren and open crest that had been cleared of trees and underbrush, the top of Kings Mountain spanned around six hundred yards in length in a northeast direction. The width of the open crest is less at around sixty yards at its southwestern end, or spur, while it is widest at around 120 yards at its northeastern end, or spur, where Ferguson had established his tented encampment in regular British Army style and had positioned his seventeen baggage, supply, and ammunition wagons. The narrowest part of the crest was located at its southwestern spur, or plateau, at about only seventy feet wide. The wooded slopes and the narrowness of most of the ridge's length made it all but indefensible for Ferguson's men if a swarm of attackers were surging up both slopes to catch any defenders in a deadly crossfire.[113]

Indeed, the ridge, or "plateau[,] upon which Ferguson was encamped was the top of an eminence about six hundred yards long and about two hundred and fifty from one base across to the other; and its shape was that of an Indian paddle, varying from one hundred and twenty yards at the blade to sixty yards at the handle in width. Outcropping boulders upon the outer edge of the plateau afforded some slight shelter for Ferguson's force; but . . . Ferguson had made no abatis to protect his camp from the attack to which it was so vulnerable from the cover of the timber surrounding it on all sides."[114] Colonel Shelby wrote how Ferguson and his men "had taken post [atop the mountain] with the confidence that no force could rout them; the mountain was high, and exceedingly steep, so that their situation gave them greatly the advantage; indeed, it was almost equal to storming a battery."[115] In his first big battle like a good many other citizen-soldiers, Private Thomas Young was somewhat unnerved by the daunting challenge posed by Kings Mountain: "Major Ferguson had taken a very strong position upon the summit of the mountain, and it appeared like an impossibility to dislodge him, but we had come there to do it, and we were determined, one and all, to do it, or die trying."[116] However, in truth, "Ferguson and the fate of his corps were quite hazardously perched in a precarious uncertainty" at that crucial moment.[117]

Meanwhile, Captain Alexander Chesney, a fine Celtic officer of Colonel Daniel Plummer's Fair Forest Regiment of militia from the South Carolina backcountry, had ridden back up the hill to Ferguson's tented headquarters. He was about to present the report that the pickets were in position and in good shape, after his recent inspection just before they had been cut down by Shelby and his scouts. However, the dashing captain from near the small town of Ballymena, County Antrim, Ireland, never had a chance to even dismount and inform Major Ferguson of the situation, because Colonel Isaac Shelby and his boys had already arrived in full force and were about to strike.[118] At this time, hundreds of revenge-seeking Patriots were moving forward with the determination to settle old scores with Ferguson and, in the words of one officer of Colonel Williams's Little River Regiment from the South Carolina backcountry, "the faithless & treacherous Tories [who had been] Killing the rebels as they called the friends of America—burning, plundering, & distressing women & children."[119]

Chapter V

Shelby's Overmountain Men Fired upon While Moving up the Slope Among the Tall Trees

It was a only matter of time that the Patriots would be discovered, especially after Shelby's advance was briefly slowed by the rain-swollen creek in a wooded draw, which contained a spring and the headwaters of more than one stream, located at the northwestern foot of the ridge just northeast of the southwestern spur covered in dense timber.[1] Fortunately, the one and "only Patriot unit on the north side of the mountain (leading the Left, or north, Division) moving at good speed and unimpeded was Shelby's column" to outdistance its sister units.[2]

Nevertheless, despite the marshy ground, Shelby's North Carolina men of the Sullivan County militia benefited from an overall easier initial approach on the north compared to the other commands, and the early afternoon shadows assisted in masking their stealthy approach from the west by providing shade, guaranteeing that they would be the first to strike more by happenstance than by deliberate tactical design, since the slope was more rugged in the Virginian's sector at the ridge's western and southwestern end.[3] Concerned about friendly fire like he had suffered a couple times in the past, Colonel Shelby had already ordered his men to remove their hats and coats for a more stealthy approach and to reduce the chances of self-inflicted losses in the confusion of battle once it erupted along the wooded slope: a wise precaution not taken by any other regimental commanders on that afternoon.[4] The closeness of the unleashing of Campbell's and Sullivan's attacks was emphasized by a typically modest Shelby when he wrote how "Washington [Campbell] and Sullivan [Shelby] regiments began the attack on the front and left flank."[5]

In the words of Captain Chesney, who was now about to be stunned by fast-paced developments like everyone else in Ferguson's command, about the totality of the surprise: "So rapid was the attack that I was in the act of dismounting to report [to Ferguson] that all was quiet and the pickets [were] on the alert when we heard their firing about a half mile off."[6] In his journal, surgeon Uzal Johnson wrote how suddenly "we were alarmed [as] the Enemy were directly upon us."[7]

Indeed, not long after three o'clock in the afternoon, Loyalists from atop Kings Mountain spied movement on the north slope below. They suddenly opened fire on Shelby's men, who were advancing through the trees, after having first seen a glint of sunlight reflecting off the metal of a long rifle or some other item among the approaching Sullivan County men, because no dust betrayed the approach or maneuvers since the ground was wet. Word of the enemy's approach was immediately relayed to a very much surprised Major Ferguson, who flew into action. Buckling on his prized saber and rushing out of his headquarters tent on the encampment's east side, Ferguson shouted for the long roll to be beaten. While young drummer boys frantically beat their drums with all their might, the major hurriedly formed his troops for action in "columns of companies" and then "columns of regiments formations" in preparation for unleashing bayonet charges at the first sight of the attackers, while issuing tactical instructions by blowing his long silver whistle, which could be heard echoing over the heavily forested mountain. The major's blasts from his silver whistle commanded his men to maneuver and position themselves in short order as long practiced at Ninety-Six throughout the past summer for just such a key showdown with the hated rebels. Leading Loyalist officers, who responded splendidly to having been caught by surprise by getting their men quickly into formation, remained mounted on their war horses, like leading Patriot officers, to direct the course of the battle.

With the opening of the action with the sudden and completely unexpected appearance of Colonel Shelby's men just below the southwestern spur, the major from Scotland ordered forth his crack fighting men—the shock troops who were his pride and joy—of his Provincial regular battalion (American Volunteers) southwest along the open crest on the double to meet Shelby's threat, which appeared within a quarter mile of Ferguson's encampment. Ferguson was easily recognizable to one and all today: mounted on his fine war horse at the forefront of the action and his lengthy formation of troops, blowing his silver whistle and carrying his saber in his left hand because of his old Brandywine wound from September 11, 1777. Continuing his account that revealed when and how they were detected after Shelby's quiet capture of the pickets on the main road leading to Kings Mountain, Benjamin Sharp described how "we then moved on, and as we approached the mountain, the roll of the British drum informed us that we had something to do."[8] Captain Chesney and other Loyalist officers likewise were busy in carrying out Ferguson's directions as quickly as possible. As Chesney penned in his diary: "I immediately paraded the men and posted the officers."[9] Dr. Johnson of the American Volunteers described the quick reaction from the surprise: "We were alarmed, & got under Arms ready for action."[10] At this time with so much at stake, Major Ferguson had finally "come to a moment of destiny far from his native Scotland and far from English gunmakers who were still turning out the 'Brown Bess'" instead of his innovative fast-firing rifle (the so-called Ferguson Rifle) as fate would have it.[11]

Because of the more favorable terrain compared to Colonel Campbell's sector, his own woodsmen skills, and fewer natural obstacles, Colonel Shelby and his men had moved faster to become the first to reach the base of Kings Mountain and the first to begin to cautiously push up the timbered slope just northeast of the spur to the southwest, since he knew that the other commands were not yet in place to launch what he had envisioned as a simultaneous attack of Patriots surrounding the mountain. Indeed, significantly and contrary to the views of some historians, it was Shelby's men who were the first to receive not only fire on the early afternoon of October 7, but also "a hot fire" because they had attacked first—the same explosion of gunfire of a volley evidently from a picket outpost located along the north slope, but also very likely unleashed from a Loyalist company deployed along the crest. This fire erupted from Ferguson's men after Shelby and his men had moved forward up the slope about one-third of the way to the southwestern spur. It was this first Loyalist fire that sparked Shelby to open the attack up the slope and through the trees, since he now had no choice because Ferguson was about to order his American Volunteers southwest down the ridge's open crest and toward him with fixed bayonets.

However, because they had the shortest distance to travel compared to Shelby's men, Campbell's Virginians had been the first troops to arrive at their assigned attack position on the highest ground of the ridge before the western and southwestern end of the southeastern spur, but this did not mean that they attacked first as assumed by generations of historians. This tactical situation developed because the Virginians faced the most steep and rugged part of the ridge—the most formidable ascent of any part of the entire ridge—unlike the Sullivan County troops to the northeast. In Campbell's case, he still faced advanced pickets, ensuring that Shelby's advance faced opposition, which was not the case in regard to the Virginians, because the Overmountain men had moved faster over easier terrain. And Shelby struck closer to Ferguson's encampment than Campbell, who faced the southeastern spur, to ensure that the first Loyalist response was directed at the Sullivan County men. However, without considering the exact terrain, historians have long assumed that Campbell struck first primarily because he was the nominal commander, which was not the case.

Based largely on inadequate and conflicting sources, Lyman Draper only speculated that it was Campbell and not Shelby who struck first, assuming that "evidently" Shelby was fired upon when moving in position instead of attacking up the slope. Even Campbell wrote how "Col. Shelby's regiment and mine began the attack" at about the same time, but with Shelby actually striking first shortly before Campbell attacked. In fact, Campbell only ordered his attack up the slope when he heard so much firing in Shelby's sector, because Colonel Shelby had already begun the attack.

Indeed, knowing that there was not a minute to lose after having been fired upon by guards and hearing the long roll of Ferguson's drums sounded on the mountaintop, Shelby had been the first to lead the assault up the slope. Shelby made a bold decision to attack on his own because he was fired upon first and no time could be wasted. Instead of waiting for all nine commands to reach their assigned positions when every second was precious, Shelby demonstrated tactical flexibility and adaptability in this situation. As if still battling the Cherokee in the western mountains or in the Ohio country's woodlands at Point Pleasant in October 1774 and knowing the importance of not allowing the enemy any additional time to recover from their initial surprise, he initiated the attack up through the trees before the rest of the commands had reached their assigned positions, except Colonel Campbell's Virginians: an overly ambitious tactical plan which would take considerable time (fifteen to twenty minutes) and effort because of rough terrain, swampy ground, and a rain-swollen stream combined with the greater distance for those units assigned to surrounding the ridge and the northeastern spur. Because no other Patriots had fired or raised shouts, Shelby had correctly realized that the other commands were not yet in position and that he needed to buy time, even if it meant drawing attention to himself and engaging alone, which he succeeded in accomplishing.

In a stealthy manner like during Indian warfare, Shelby's men continued to advance up the timbered slope in a loose, almost informal, grouping—no line or formation whatsoever like the British and Loyalists—that consisted of "buddy teams" (while one man fired from behind a tree, the other was ready to fire while his comrade reloaded to prevent an attacker from charging forward to exploit the fact that one soldier now possessed an unloaded weapon and needed protection, which was an old, hard-earned lesson learned from Indian fighting), which moved steadily from tree to tree up the northern slope northeast of Campbell.

Prudently, even after having been fired upon, Shelby refused to allow his more trigger-happy men, who fairly lusted to kill Loyalists at the first opportunity, to open fire at the assault's beginning, because targets—the American Volunteers on the crest after Ferguson had dispatched them southwest—were still not clear in the thick woodlands covering the steep northwestern slope and still too far away, knowing the supreme importance of not wasting any ammunition on this day of destiny. Shelby, therefore, prudently directed his men to "press on to our places, and then your fire will not be lost."[12] However, Colonel Shelby's orders to his followers not to return fire not only surprised the eager fighters from the Holston River Valley, but also caused some discontent among the overeager Sullivan County frontiersmen. Some "Sons of the Mountains" declared within Colonel Shelby's hearing: "It would never do to be shot down without returning the fire."[13] All the while, Shelby "went right onward and upward like a man who had but one thing to do, and but one thought—to do it."[14]

As the expedition's inspirational and most forceful leader on all scores, it was most symbolic that Shelby, while mounted like other principal Patriot leaders, was leading the day's first attack up the steep slope from just northeast of the ridge's southwestern end. After all, the young colonel, only in his twenties, had already played such an early key role in leading the way with a new aggressiveness east of the mountains during the past summer because he almost instinctively, like Lord Cornwallis, understood how this brutal conflict was going to be won in the backcountry.[15] However, in overall tactical terms, Shelby's early attack across generally more open and less rugged terrain left him and his Sullivan County Overmountain men more vulnerable to Captain De Peyster's forthcoming counterattack of the American Volunteers, after they had been ordered southwest down the crest by Ferguson.[16]

Colonel Shelby, consequently, was now even more determined to continue to fuel the momentum of this bitter struggle for possession of the backcountry, sensing that the most remarkable of victories was in the making if and when all of the commands would finally gain their assigned positions to completely surround the mountain. In the attack up the slope covered in heavy timber, Colonel Shelby was characteristically leading the way as usual, encouraging and cheering everyone onward through the tall hardwood trees and toward the open crest.[17] Like when battling Native Americans, Shelby repeatedly warned his frontiersmen to make every shot count and "never shoot until you see an enemy and never see an enemy without bringing him down."[18] Fifteen-year-old James Collins, who already knew that a split second often separated life from death in this fight, described a prudent and wise tactic learned from years of Indian fighting: "We were soon in motion, every man throwing four or five [lead] balls in his mouth to prevent thirst, also to be in readiness to reload quick."[19]

Incomparable Captain John Sawyers

Advancing up the slope with his long rifle at the ready, Captain John Sawyers was one of Shelby's most experienced and reliable men. He now led a company of Overmountain boys and might well have been one of the handpicked men who had played a part in eliminating Ferguson's foremost pickets in stealthy fashion. In his mid-thirties and an experienced Indian fighter since his teenage years as early as 1761, Sawyers was a fast-thinking tactical innovator on the battlefield. He had played a key role under young Lieutenant Isaac Shelby, who had taken over command of the Virginia volunteer company of his father, Captain Evan Shelby Sr., at the hard-fought Battle of Point Pleasant on October 10, 1774. At that time in the Ohio country, Isaac and John had worked together in masterful fashion as a close-knit team to turn the tide of battle in a critical situation, when the Shawnee and Mingo warriors were on the verge of winning.

An Indian-fighting son of hopeful immigrants to America, Captain Sawyers was a good example of the superior combat capabilities and resourcefulness of the average Overmountain fighting man: experienced Indian fighter, tactically astute and innovative, a natural inspirational leader, highly motivated, and an expert marksman with the long rifle. And now, appropriately, the highly capable tactical team of Shelby and Sawyers was once again together on another October afternoon a half dozen years after the Virginian's victory over the Shawnee and Mingo warriors in the Ohio country at Point Pleasant. John Sawyers had been born in 1747 in Augusta County, Virginia, in the Shenandoah

Valley to James Sawyers and Rachel Ball-Sawyers. He married pretty Rebecca Crawford in his beloved valley of striking beauty on January 30, 1776. At this time, Sawyers was the proud father of a new infant, Mary Sawyers, who had been born the previous October. During the advance up Kings Mountain and through the trees, Captain Sawyers looked every inch a true Celtic warrior of old. He stood six feet tall at more than two hundred pounds. Lengthy red whiskers, which had now merged in a short red beard since he had not shaved since departing Sycamore Shoals, was a familiar characteristic of the fighting men of the Sawyers clan for generations. Sawyers personified the fighting spirit and heightened combat capabilities of this unique kind of fighting man from west of the mountains, where he had left behind an enduring physical legacy named after him for the safety of his family and local people, Sawyer's Fort.[20]

All the while during the campaign in the South Carolina Piedmont and even at this moment, these hardened fighting men like Captain Sawyers were burdened with the fear that even now the ever-vengeful Cherokee, who had plenty of old scores to settle because of the hard-hitting expeditions that had destroyed their villages in 1776, were now attacking the settlements and isolated log cabins to take advantage of their absence. Even now, they feared the massacre of their wives and children. If so, then not only would these soldiers lose their families but also their homes, which were situated on lonely hilltops and isolated sections along the crystal-clear rivers and creeks, that they had hacked out of the wilderness. Then, after returning home if they survived the Battle of Kings Mountain after faithfully performing their duty for God and country, the Overmountain men might well find only the charred remains of the bodies of loved ones, who had been scalped and mutilated, and burned-down log cabins in war-torn valleys. If fortunate, then kindly neighbors might have buried dead family members in a nearby grassy meadow by the charred remains of their log homes, overgrown by weeds and vines by the time these citizen-soldiers returned from Kings Mountain.

Here Come Those Yelling Boys!

While advancing relentlessly up the slope after having received an initial Loyalist volley that was ineffective but had alerted Ferguson to the location of the threat on the timbered slope, Shelby finally felt that it was time to hold nothing back. Knowing that the time was exactly right and hoping to terrify the enemy perched on the high ground as much as possible, especially any young soldiers without battle experience, Colonel Shelby ordered his Overmountain men from the Holston River country to unleash their famous war cries from the frontier—a regular "frontier whoop, half-animal, half-Indian" yell that served notice to the Loyalists that they were now in serious trouble.[21] Most of all, the frontier colonel inspired his followers by ordering them to "shout like hell and fight like devils!"[22]

Meanwhile, Williams, Lacey, and then the Lincoln County command of Chronicle-Hambright, from west to east or left to right, continued moving northeastward through the trees and clinging underbrush at the mountain's base. In silence, they followed the ridge's base on the north to extend the battle line in attempting to surround Ferguson on the north at the northeastern spur, while encountering more difficult terrain and swampy ground than either Shelby or Campbell. Meanwhile, Cleveland's Wilkes County men on the north to Shelby's left also had been slowed in crossing a small stream at the mountain's base.

What erupted like thunder from the throats of Shelby's attackers was a high-pitched war cry that was very close to a Cherokee war cry that uplifted Patriot spirits and confidence. The frontiersmen's battle-cry was shrill like that of the Native Americans, but slightly hoarser, although not by much. But it had the same psychological effect of helping to demoralize the enemy, who now knew that a good many attackers were coming straight at them. A master of psychological warfare, Shelby fully understood the psychological advantage of the unleashing of these fierce war cries that reverberated through the tall trees to echo over Kings Mountain. He had recently demonstrated a winning brand of psychological warfare at Thicketty Fort, bluffing in masterful fashion to gain the fort's surrender without the loss of a single man. This surprising success in the South Carolina backcountry had additionally endeared him to his roughhewn Overmountain followers, especially the teenagers in the ranks, who looked upon Shelby like a father figure.

Whenever he and his hardy Overmountain men had met a war party or descended upon a mountain village in a wild charge during the 1776 Cherokee campaign, Shelby relied on the same spine-tingling war cries of his attackers to unnerve the enemy. Ironically, in these wilderness battles and skirmishes that had no name, Shelby and his men had almost always charged downhill while screaming their lungs out, because most Cherokee villages were situated along clear mountain streams and rivers that ran through deep valleys, where the Native Americans farmed the rich bottomlands, mostly raising corn crops. Consequently, like at Musgrove's Mill when he had brilliantly transformed a seemingly no-win situation for the Patriots into a clever ambush to prevail in the end, Colonel Shelby was now in the unfamiliar situation of attacking straight uphill, when the enemy held the supreme advantage of the high ground.

Atop the crest of the hill peering down the steep slope through the trees, the five hundred or so rookie North Carolina boys of the Loyalist militia from Tryon County under Colonel Ambrose Mills must have thought that they were now under the attack of a large number of Native American warriors because of the unearthly war cry of Shelby's men. But the veterans in Ferguson's command knew better because they had already heard these same high-pitched yells of Shelby's attackers at Musgrove's Mill. Becoming more nervous by the echo of the piercing war cries cascading over the mountain like an Indian death song, some rookie North Carolina militiamen, who were not Indian fighters like Shelby's hardened frontier warriors, must have wondered if they would be scalped alive or tortured by the unknown number of attackers, who had somehow surprised the entire command, even Major Ferguson himself. Surely, only Native American warriors could have caught the entire command of good fighting men so completely by surprise and raised such a shrill war cry that had broken the calm stillness of Kings Mountain.

Captain Abraham De Peyster, an experienced professional soldier of Dutch descent from New York City where he had been born in 1753 as the privileged son of a rich member of the New York gentry class, knew the shocking meaning of this eerie, high-pitched sound erupting from the throats of Colonel Shelby's attackers from the west side of the Blue Ridge mountains, which no British leader or soldier had ever seen before. Barely able to speak in his astonishment, De Peyster could only manage a few words to enlighten an equally stunned Major Ferguson: "Things are ominous. These are the yelling boys!"[23]

He also informed the astonished Scottish major how "Those are the same yelling devils I fought at Musgrove Mill."[24] But it did not matter to Ferguson, who was ready to fight his conventional battle like Cornwallis at Camden, in which the British bayonet of cold steel would sweep all before it. He knew that American fighting men, from militia to Continentals, could not stand up to the bayonet charge from disciplined and well-trained troops, especially his crack American Volunteers, who he had ordered southwest along the open ridge to confront Shelby's attackers, when the first firing had suddenly broken out.[25]

Colonel Shelby described the early price paid by Ferguson for his strict adherence to conventional tactics: "Ferguson's men were drawn up in close column on the summit, and thus presented fair marks for the mountaineers, who approached them under the cover of the trees."[26] When Shelby's men finally opened fire, Captain Alexander Chesney presented a fine target like all the Loyalist officers, especially those leading the American Volunteers, who were mounted and riding back and forth along the open crest beside their neat formations to lead the way. As the Irishman from Ulster Province in a resplendent red uniform penned in his diary: "During this short interval [of the Provincial regulars forming for action] I received a wound which however did not prevent me from doing my duty; and going towards my horse I found he had been killed by the first discharge."[27]

Of course, in the end, the task of ultimately vanquishing Major Ferguson and his entire command was infinitely easier when the Patriots were eventually able to complete their planned encirclement because the Scotsman had concentrated his troops on the barren top of Kings Mountain instead of having ordered breastworks created at the mountain's base or even along the slope to early thwart the attackers. Ensign Robert Campbell described the tactical coup that eventually sealed Ferguson's fate: the eventual positioning of all troops "to attack the enemy on all sides [with] The Washington [County, North Carolina, today's east Tennessee] and Sullivan [County, North Carolina, today's east Tennessee] regiments were formed in the front and on the right flank; the North and South Carolina troops under Cols. [James] Williams, [John] Sevier, [Benjamin] Cleveland, [Edward] Lacey, and [Thomas] Brandon on the left."[28]

Because of these nine separate commands that had been ordered to attack each side and both ends of the main ridge, all assaults this afternoon were destined to be disjointed because of ill-timing. In the process of surrounding Ferguson and due to variations in the terrain, including ravines, streams, and marshy areas, the various commands would eventually reach their assigned positions at different times in order to surround the mountain in the most ill-coordinated of attacks: ironically, contrary to a traditional battle, a tactical situation that would actually work to the Patriots' benefit in the end. Indeed, the initial attacks up Kings Mountain were not coordinated or in unison, because the nine separate commands would all eventually reach their respective launch positions and begin their assaults at different times, but within a relatively short period of only around fifteen or twenty minutes from beginning to end.[29]

Shelby and his volunteers had to pay a price for attacking not only first and on their own but also across more relatively open ground—woodlands largely devoid of underbrush—before the other eight commands could launch their assaults up the wooded slopes. Colonel William Campbell described how "Col. Shelby's regiment sustained the whole fire of the enemy for about ten minutes, while the other troops were forming [to the east and northeast] around the height upon which the enemy was posted."[30] Just as Shelby's citizen-soldiers had early displayed their fighting spirit with the unleashing of the Cherokee-like war cries when surging up the slope, so Ferguson and his boys answered with a fiery spirit of their own in their determination to hold the hill at all costs: The shrill sounds of Ferguson's silver whistle ordered his best troops into action, after pushing southwest across the open crest to reach a high ground position before Shelby. These men consisted of around 140 Provincial Rangers—the major's own regiment—mostly from New York, the New Jersey Volunteers, the King's Loyal American Regiment, a contingent of the Prince of Wales Royal American Volunteers, and a small detachment of the Queen's Rangers, who had been among the first troops to enter a conquered Philadelphia in September 1777, in green uniforms (originally, the British government planned to clothe all Loyalists in green uniforms in the war's early days). Ferguson ordered these Provincial regulars to fire a massed volley from the commanding crest and then to charge, with Captain De Peyster leading the way, down the northern slope and through the towering hardwood trees. Ferguson was determined to demonstrate the quality of his "pet" men whom he had long trained, believing that they would be more than a match for the Overmountain men, who he was convinced could not withstand a bayonet charge.

Like when battling the Native Americans of the forests, Shelby and his boys stubbornly fell back after Ferguson had ordered his crack American Volunteers to unleash their tactical ace in the hole: the combination of a volley fired from the high ground almost immediately followed by a bayonet charge down the slope. All the while, Shelby's men adhered to their ever-flexible and innovative battle plan, which called for every man to fight Indian-style behind the good cover provided by trees and logs to minimize the impact and momentum of the bayonet charge. Prudently and as planned while continuing to load and fire as fast as possible, Shelby's mountaineers slowly moved down the slope before the bayonet charge of the approximately 140 American Volunteers. All the while, Shelby's boys fired from tree to tree to cut down charging fellow Americans now wearing red coats during America's first civil war.

Clearly, in demonstrating tactical flexibility and agility, Colonel Shelby's smart tactics of falling back according to the prearranged plan saved lives and allowed the men time to catch their breath in the afternoon heat and reload while succeeding in negating the overall effectiveness of the repeated bayonet charges, because each subsequent attack would be less effective due to losses and exhaustion among the Loyalists, transforming what Ferguson thought was his winning tactic into a largely useless one that cost lives in both the charge and then the slow withdrawal back up the steep slope to regain the strategic crest, when the weary redcoats were shot from behind by a scorching fire of expert riflemen: a most advantageous tactical scenario that Shelby exploited to the fullest. However, the elite American Volunteers inflicted their own fair share of damage in return. In the end, Shelby's men were hard hit by the series of sweeping counterattacks that were destined to continue after Campbell shortly—just after Shelby—launched his assault up the slope on the southwestern spur. Indeed, "in one of these charges, Shelby's column was considerably broken; he rode back and rallied his men, and when the enemy retired to the summit, he pressed on his men" and surged up the slope with wild shouts.[31] Captain Moses Shelby, the colonel's brother and the man who had taken the crucial message in person to the stubborn Colonel William Campbell to solicit his support on this expedition, was felled by two bullets this afternoon, while leading his company from the front, but he survived to tell the tale like brother Major Evan Shelby Jr.[32] In his journal, Surgeon Uzal Johnson described this early phase of combat in Shelby's sector: "They advanced up the Hill pretty rapidly, as soon as they got the Brow of the Hill the Amn. Vols. Charged them with success and drove them down the Hill."[33]

Forgotten Early Turning Point

Colonel Shelby had chosen the right time to issue new orders to ensure the end of the first withdrawal down the slope: "Now, boys, quickly reload your rifles and give them another hell of fire." Shelby's frontiersmen had then hurriedly reloaded to blast away from trees, boulders, and fallen logs, after the redcoats, fellow Americans, unleashed a volley as trained by Ferguson at the farther penetration point of their charge down the slope, before slowly retiring with discipline back up the slope, presenting easy targets to backwoods marksmen. Even more, the loose formation of Shelby's men in buddy teams over a wide area of the timbered slope meant that the farther the Loyalists attacked down the hill, then the longer their assault formation could be hit by deadly enfilade fires that simultaneously raked by both flank fires to cut down more men. Some of Shelby's citizen-soldiers armed with muskets, rather than long rifles, had loaded their weapons with "buck & ball" to unleash shotgun-like blasts of a lead ball with three smaller lead balls, or buckshot, to inflict widespread damage to Loyalist bodies. Then, after showing little fear in the face of the Loyalists' sixteen-inch bayonets that were less ominous than Cherokee tomahawks and scalping knives, Shelby and his boys charged back up the slope with spirit and their trademark war cries, surging through the trees with abandon.[34]

That the fighting men from the Holston River country had rallied and counterattacked so quickly on orders barked out by Colonel Shelby, whose mounted presence was seen by one and all, after having been initially repulsed, was no small accomplishment in overall tactical terms. After all, the key to winning this battle lay in all of the Patriot commands surrounding the mountain at the same time without any of the nine separate units being permanently repulsed and knocked out of the fight to deny Ferguson, who benefited from interior lines and possessed the ability to swiftly maneuver his well-trained troops for the possibility of defeating each isolated command whenever the newest threat emerged. In consequence, Patriot success on that afternoon lay in closely coordinating and synchronizing their attacks as much as possible, but surprisingly positive results resulted from these staggered attacks because Ferguson would not be able to permanently eliminate any attacking command before he had to hurriedly face the next threat. Most of all, "Shelby's front-line leadership was critical in rallying and returning his men to the fight after the Provincial bayonets charges."[35] Surgeon Johnson of New Jersey described the tactical dilemma in regard to the first attack downhill by the American Volunteers who "drove them [Shelby] down the Hill, but were not able to pursue [at length], our Number being so small, we then retreated in order to [re] gain the [crest] & prevent their getting possession of it."[36]

This wise stratagem of an early withdrawal as ordered by Shelby was all part of a plan based on the advantages of falling back and then counterattacking when Ferguson's attackers withdrew back to the summit. Indeed, one Patriot officer explained the flexible and wise tactical plan based on common sense and Indian fighting tactics and the certainty that Ferguson would rely on the bayonet charge with his well-trained men: "stand your ground as long as you can. When you can do no better, get behind trees and retreat; but I beg you not to run quite off. If we are repulsed, let us make a point of returning and renewing the fight."[37]

Most important, and even before gaining the strategic crest, Colonel Shelby's inspired leadership and well-honed tactical skill repeatedly shone brightly along the wooded slope in rallying his men all three times his command was driven down the slope by both the Provincial regulars, under Captain Abraham De Peyster, and the Loyalist militia, who had "previously whittled down the handles of their butcher knives so they could be inserted to the muzzles of their rifles."[38] Some historians have claimed that only the Provincial regulars counterattacked with Captain De Peyster leading the way, but at some point either the North Carolina militia, South Carolina militia, or both joined in the counterattacks of their better-trained comrades, after exhaustion and losses had taken their toll among the crack American Volunteers. But Ferguson's acute tactical dilemma, which was truly vexing, was quite simple: how to beat back each of the suddenly emerging threats in different sectors and on both sides of the ridge, simultaneously? In Colonel Shelby's words: "When the enemy retired to the summit, he pressed on his men and reached the summit while Ferguson was directing a charge against Cleveland" to the northeast, after the Wilkes County men would finally ease into position far to Shelby's left to the northeast to strike a blow.[39]

From beginning to end, Major Ferguson was relying far less on the Loyalist militia from the Carolinas to reap decisive victory than the splendidly trained New York and New Jersey troops of his own regiment, the American Volunteers. These redcoats were experts in the bayonet charge, which explained why Shelby's men would be repeatedly driven down the slope. In his diary, perhaps Lieutenant Anthony Allaire, who called this fight the struggle for "Little King's Mountain," said it best about the fighting spirit of these Loyalist Americans, because "the American Volunteers would have defied all Washington's Army."[40]

Colonel William Campbell's Virginians Attack up the Slope

Because he took immediate action upon hearing the first firing in Shelby's sector slightly to the northeast, Colonel William Campbell was destined to unleash his attack not long after Shelby advanced up the timbered slope. With a loose formation wrapped around the wooded base of the westernmost spur on the west and southwest, the Virginians faced the southwestern spur, which was the highest point of the approximately six-hundred-yard ridge along the crest at 1,020 feet. More so than Shelby's men to the northeast, they had been slowed during their approach: the overall tactical situation which had allowed for Shelby to strike first on the ridge's northern side almost directly opposite Campbell because the terrain in the Virginian's sector was "the most craggy, rough, steep and difficult part" of Kings Mountain.[41]

Hearing the unleashing of the first Loyalist volley that poured down the slope at Shelby's Holston River Valley soldiers to echo over Kings Mountain, Colonel William "Bill" Campbell had instantly jumped into action with his trademark enthusiasm. Here, at the western and southwestern edge of the ridge, he instinctively knew that the time had come, when Shelby had suddenly opened the action. Campbell possessed a reputation of being "too rash" in battle when his fighting blood was up. Like his ancestors from the Scottish Highlands before they had migrated south to Ulster Province, north Ireland, and now carrying an expertly made dirk with a six-and-a-half-inch blade in a silver sheath like a true Scottish warrior from the Highland clans of long ago, Colonel Campbell immediately threw off his uniform coat on this hot day, because it was time to go to work. As his Virginians realized, he was simply getting down to the business of fighting and moving up the southwestern and western slope of the extreme southwestern end of Kings Mountain, because this was indeed the case of "the Campbells were coming."[42]

Feisty Colonel Campbell could not have been more motivated in leading the attack on the southwestern and western side of Kings Mountain. In the war's beginning, he had been a primary author of an inspirational message from the Washington County, Virginia, Patriots which had emphasized how "we declare that we are deliberately and resolutely determined never to surrender them [personal rights] to any power upon earth but at the expense of our lives."[43] And now Campbell was possessed by the same determination to destroy Ferguson and his entire command. To additionally unnerve the Loyalists, he ordered his mostly Scotch-Irish men from the Holston River country to "raise the Indian halloo" during the "rush up the mountain," in the words of Pennsylvania-born James Davison, who fought beside brothers John and Joseph Davison in Campbell's command.[44]

As noted, a good many experienced Indian fighters served in Campbell's ranks, such as Benjamin White. White was a former Continental soldier who had also served under Washington at the showdown at Princeton, New Jersey, in early January 1777 and other battles far to the north. Like Shelby and the White family clan, including his father, White had battled the Shawnee and Mingo at the Battle of Point Pleasant in October 1774.[45] In the words of one historian, these experienced fighting men "under Campbell, were a peculiar people . . . almost to a man, Presbyterians [and] quite tenacious of their religious and civil liberties, as handed down from father to son from their Scotch-Irish ancestors."[46]

One of Colonel Campbell's father-son fighting teams was the Scotch-Irish McCulloch clan, which hailed from the southwest Virginia backcountry of Washington County. An experienced Indian fighter, John McCulloch was destined to see his father Lieutenant Thomas McCulloch mortally wounded on that bloody afternoon.[47] The Bowen boys of southwest Virginia were another example of an experienced familial fighting team in Campbell's ranks. Lieutenant Reece Tate "Rees" Bowen, born in the Shenandoah Valley in 1750 and who died at Kings Mountain, was a veteran of the fight at Point Pleasant with brothers Arthur, William, Charles, and John Bowen.[48]

Meanwhile, Major Joseph McDowell's Burke County and Major Joseph Winston's Surry County men, from left to right, or west to east, who had advanced in Campbell's column, continued northeast, while mounted on the ridge's southern side, toward their assigned positions near the ridge's southern base to Campbell's right in an early phase of establishing the anaconda-like ring around Ferguson to choke the life out of his command. Major Joseph Winston had been originally assigned to take possession of the hill located just north of Kings Mountain to block Ferguson's escape route to the road leading northeast to Charlotte. After completing that mission and leaving some good men on that strategic hill as reliable guardians, Winston had then led his troops south around the northeastern spur toward their assigned position on the south and all the way to the southern end of the northeasternmost summit of the ridge.

In a lengthy, loose concave line that extended through the forest along the slopes, Campbell's Washington County Virginians lapped around the southwestern and western end of the spur to cover a wide front, which diffused his overall strength, unlike Shelby's more concentrated command. During the approach through the towering trees to the southwest and west of the ridge's southwestern spur, the resourceful Campbell then developed an innovative tactic on the fly, because Ferguson's Provincial battalion was facing Shelby's men to the northeast. Because he confronted Ferguson's pickets of a fairly sizeable guard located about halfway down the steep slope to protect the strategic southwestern spur, which was Ferguson's left flank, Campbell hoped to negate this defensive position without having to attack the formidable high ground position that would cost too many lives. Significantly, while Shelby battled the American Volunteers northeast of the Virginians on the ridge's northern side, this tactical situation and respite allowed Campbell an opportunity to unleash a new tactic, because the regular Provincials had not yet reached the southwestern spur because they now confronted the Sullivan County men under Shelby.

Thinking tactically outside the box as if battling the Cherokee, Colonel Campbell ordered a special detail of dependable men to ride to the crest and across the spur to outflank the enemy's advance guard and their defensive position, then return to the advancing lines along the slope. Captain Andrew Colvill, one of the finest officers of the Virginia Regiment from Washington County, brothers Major Micajah Lewis and Captain Joel Lewis who were of Welsh heritage and proud of it, and their band of followers galloped up the slope and "right on the spur of the Mountain," in the words of Lieutenant Samuel Newell, to drive off the advance guard of Loyalists. Here, the first Loyalists were shot down in this sector southwest of Shelby, while Lieutenant Newell was wounded, Lieutenant Robert Edmondson Sr. and "the [Virginia] ensign [Ensign John Beattie] was" killed. In the past, historians have confused this attack of Campbell's small party on the main guard on the southwestern spur as the first eruption of the battle proper, which was not the case because Shelby had already struck first and engaged first the pickets and then the American Volunteers dispatched by Ferguson.

While dashing across the open summit of the southwestern spur, experienced members of Colvill's Southwest Virginia company overwhelmed a lone Loyalist picket. In the advance in his sector, Philip Greever, who had been born on November 2, 1745, of Netherlands Huguenot ancestry and who carried a Pennsylvania long rifle with a curly or striped maple stock, shot down one picket who was about to fire back at the long-haired interlopers advancing through the trees. Greever described how he was in the forefront and "ran up the mountain, when I saw a Tory behind a tree who I shot at" in Campbell's sector.[49]

With a sense of accomplishment stemming from this early tactical success, Private Joseph Starns described how "a man named Philip Giever [sic] . . . shot a man who came out from the British guard into the woods. This made the enemy's guard retreat [northeast along the open crest and toward the American Volunteers who were facing Shelby's men to the northeast, while leaving fallen men behind them] to the main body—we advanced toward them before they could form and gave them a fire."[50] This hot skirmish that raged briefly across the southwestern spur alerted Ferguson to the fact that he was under attack from both sides of the ridge—Shelby on the northern side of the ridge and then Campbell on the southwestern and western end of the ridge. To Major Ferguson and Captain De Peyster, Shelby's attack at this point seemed more serious because he struck first and closer to the Loyalist encampment and the major's headquarters.[51]

Like other Patriot commands, family members, including father-son fighting teams, filled Campbell's ranks of mostly Scotch-Irish men from Washington County in the most familial major battle of the American Revolution. As mentioned, Charles Bowen served in the company commanded by his brother, Captain Reece Bowen, who was killed in the struggle for possession of Ferguson's mountaintop.[52] Ensign Matthew Kincannon advanced up the slope with his brothers, Andrew, a tall, gangly pioneer from the Shenandoah Valley and an early gunsmith and blacksmith who had made the first horseshoe in the remote Kentucky settlements, and James. The Kincannon boys proudly represented their Scotch-Irish family from the hills of southwest Virginia that reminded them of Ulster Province, Ireland, far away. Andrew Kincannon took over company command when Ireland-born Captain James Dysart fell wounded during the hot exchanges of gunfire erupting in the escalating struggle for possession of the high ground.[53]

Meanwhile, Campbell's men of Washington County continued to advance up the slope with determination, but with no bayonets fixed to rifles like all Patriot citizen-soldiers at Kings Mountain. Confusing some historians into incorrectly thinking that the Virginians attacked first, a scattered fire whistled over the Virginians when unleashed by either the advanced guard or the newly arriving American Volunteers atop the crest, after they pushed Shelby's boys down the slope and then moved southwest up toward the highest point of Kings Mountain to confront Campbell's men, who had suddenly emerged as the next threat. Ensign Henry Dickenson described how "we were up the mountain pretty rapidly, within view of the enemy, when they fired a few guns at us at long range" from the open crest.[54]

The Edmondson Boys of a Hard-Fighting Scotch-Irish Clan

Now serving as respected officers in Campbell's Virginia command were the Presbyterian members of the Edmondson family, including Robert Edmondson Sr., who had participated in the 1776 Cherokee campaign and had served on Colonel Evan Shelby Sr.'s Chickamauga campaign in today's northeast Georgia during 1779. Robert Edmondson Jr. (his son), and Robert Edmondson (who were "near kinsmen") were among the eight total Edmondsons who served at Kings Mountain. Robert Sr. would shortly be killed while the younger Edmondson, a capable lieutenant, was wounded. The hot firefight that had suddenly erupted atop the southwestern spur quickly sputtered to an end as quickly as it began. The Loyalist guardians of the southwestern spur had retired to the crest, after having fatally cut down two of Campbell's attackers, including Edmondson Sr.[55]

Captain Andrew Colvill's surprise sortie across the spur, which was open on the top, caused grief to surge through Campbell's regiment. "Watching helplessly below [the clash that cost the lives of Ensign John Beattie and Lieutenant Robert Edmondson, Sr.] were Beattie's two brothers and the two sons [including Lieutenant Robert Edmondson Jr.] of Robert Edmondson, Sr. [and now with] tearful eyes and vengeful hearts, brothers, sons, and friends of the fallen Patriots all rushed headlong" up the slope.[56] Captain William Edmondson, who had served with Colonel Campbell in the Cherokee War, and both men had founded the town of Abingdon, Virginia, was destined to be shot in the head and killed along the slope.[57] In total, eight Edmondson boys served in the ranks of Campbell's Virginia command, demonstrating the Scotch-Irish love of liberty and the resolve of this hard-fighting clan: three killed and another wounded member of the Edmondson family.[58]

The Fighting Intensifies

Ferguson's foremost troops withdrew northeast along the crest toward where Shelby was fighting, soon reaching the point near where the American Volunteers had been engaging Shelby's men, whom they had just driven down the slope. Ferguson's best fighting men were now prudently repositioned by the Scottish major on the crest to face Campbell's escalating threat to the southwest, after Shelby's boys had been repulsed: an ideal high ground position from which to charge southwest along the crest to regain the mountain's highest point and push Campbell's interlopers down the slope to regain and preserve Ferguson's left flank.[59]

Atop the summit, meanwhile, Major Ferguson was disturbed to hear the ever-increasing volume of gunfire. The crescendo of shots and the rising chorus of war cries revealed that a large number of attackers was surging up the ridge's southwestern end, not long after Shelby's boys had been pushed down the slope by the redcoats' bayonet charge. By this time, the counterattacking American Volunteers had returned back to the summit of the western spur after attacking Shelby. Consequently, they were ready to face Campbell's attack after pushing southwest toward the mountain's highest point. At this point, Ferguson and his officers utilized the advantage of interior lines to swiftly maneuver their troops to face multiple threats posed by Shelby and Campbell. The American fighting men of his elite regiment of well-trained Royal Provincials were now in an ideal position and ready for the next challenge, which came from Campbell's attack to the southwest. In this sense, Campbell's element of surprise and the impetuousness of the initial attack had been largely negated by the firefight with the spur's pickets and especially because Ferguson's crack troops had already been shifted southwest along the crest after meeting Shelby's threat.[60] An animated Colonel Campbell, with waving sword after having taken off his uniform coat in a hurry once he heard Shelby's fight to the northeast, continued to lead the way up the steep southwestern slope of the ridge and through the virgin timber, while shouting encouragement to inspire his followers: "Here they are boys! Shout like hell and fight like devils!"[61] Virginia's Private Peter Starns, who advanced beside brothers Nicholas and Joseph, never forgot how Colonel Campbell "ordered us to raise a loud scream and rush up the mountain."[62]

Campbell's southwest Virginia men continued surging up the slope with wild shouts while confident in the knowledge that Shelby was attacking on the ridge's other side on the north and other commands were moving swiftly through the woods and into their attack positions on both sides of the ridge to entirely surround Kings Mountain. Then, at some point along the timbered slope below the ridge's open crest, the advancing Virginians suddenly encountered a small group of Loyalists, evidently the survivors of the advance guard of pickets who had lingered in place in a secondary defensive position just before the arrival of the American Volunteers, after having withdrawn northeast along the crest until they reached a rocky outcropping to Shelby's right. Colonel Campbell hurriedly ordered a detachment of men under the reliable Captain Andrew Colville up the slope to outflank the defensive position poised on the high ground. However, the flanking maneuver was not successful due to Loyalist fire not only from the defenders of the small rocky outcropping (one of many along the slope) but also from the fire of the American Volunteers, under Captain De Peyster, aligned atop the crest.[63]

Major Ferguson had positioned the troops of his crack regiment, the American Volunteers, between Shelby and Campbell and along the open ground of the southwestern summit—the ridge's highest point—of the spur, and they had often hurled Shelby's men down the timbered slope. With his troops formed "in platoons," wrote Virginia militiaman James Crow, Major Ferguson directed volleys fired upon Campbell's steadily encroaching Virginians, who were moving from tree to tree and boulder to boulder, while screaming like banshees to match the frontier howls of Shelby's Overmountain boys to the northeast. These sweeping volleys, which were "particularly heavy," noted Ensign Henry Dickenson of the American Volunteers, were effective in causing a considerable amount of death and confusion, including a degree of demoralization among Campbell's hard-hit men who had been swept with a hot fire. For instance, young Private Joseph Starns, from southwest Virginia, described the "tremendous fire" that poured down the slope because Ferguson was now relying on massed firepower, or volley firing, from his crack troops, as they had been long trained, to soften up the Virginians, before he ordered the bayonet charge of his New York and New Jersey troops when Campbell's men advanced even closer to become more vulnerable.

Then, with the howling Virginians surging through the trees only "thirty yards of them," in James Crow's words, and taking full advantage of favorable terrain of his high ground perch of the southwestern spur, the aggressive major from Scotland ordered the American Volunteers to break the cordon that was attempting to surround Kings Mountain by charging down the wooded slope with fixed bayonets in a bid to repeat their tactical success recently achieved against Shelby's attackers just to the northeast. At this time, Campbell's Virginia men were especially vulnerable because they had just unleashed their first fire and their muskets were unloaded when the hard-charging attackers in scarlet uniforms poured down the slope with flashing bayonets. Therefore, the tactically astute and flexible Ferguson, demonstrating correct instincts in the heat of battle, had chosen exactly the right time to launch a sweeping attack downhill with his finest troops.

Courageous Loyalist officers led the way on their horses during the headlong charge down the slope against the Virginians, while Major Ferguson, who was also atop his war horse, orchestrated the tactical offensive in the most aggressive manner possible from the smoke-lined crest. Some of Ferguson's officers, such as Lieutenant Anthony Allaire of the Provincial regulars, rode down the slope and through the tall trees, while waving their swords and shouting encouragement to his bayonet-wielding Americans who were now in a life-or-death struggle. Loyalist officers, with the advantage of height and speed when mounted on their muscular chargers, easily ran down numbers of Campbell's Virginia men, cutting them down with a flurry of swinging sabers in the manner of Tarleton's British Legion dragoons at the Waxhaws. The close-quarter combat was especially vicious among the trees and underbrush along the rocky southwestern slope of the spur, because no-quarter warfare became a standard feature of both sides in Campbell's sector like it had been in Shelby's.

While charging down the slope and through the timber on "an elegant horse," Lieutenant Anthony Allaire caught up with one tall, but slow-moving, Virginia captain. He then killed the unlucky officer "with one blow of my sword."[64] In the lieutenant's words: "When our detachment charged, for the first time [upon Campbell's men], it fell to my lot to put a Rebel Captain to death, which I did effectively with one blow . . . the fellow was at least six foot high, but I had rather the advantage, as I was mounted . . . and he [was] on foot."[65] Lieutenant Robert Edmonson Jr. was also cut down when fighting to avenge his fallen father. In the words of John Craig, a member of Captain David Beattie's company of southwest Virginians: "For my part, I only retreated about eighty yards when I was called to by my Lt. Robt. Edminston [sic], who told me he was wounded in the arm. We covered ourselves behind a tree, while I took his handkerchief and bound up his arm."[66] Private Joseph Starns, who fought besides his brothers Peter and Nicholas in the ranks, described why the charge of Ferguson's best troops was so effective, because after unleashing a volley from the crest and "before we could load again the British formed and charged on us" with fixed bayonets to scatter the hard-hit Virginians.[67]

Armed with a homemade saber forged by a local blacksmith and desiring revenge for the fall of Edmondson Sr., Captain William Edmondson, who was one of the eight Edmondson boys of Campbell's command, "dashed forward into the hottest part of the battle, and there received the charge of De Peyster's [Provincial] Rangers, discharging his gun, then clubbed it and knocked the rifle out of the grasp of one of the Britons. Seizing him by the neck, he made him his prisoner, and brought him to the foot of the hill. Returning again up the mountain, he bravely fell fighting in front of his company, near his beloved Colonel."[68] Indeed, with the knowledge that "several of his family killed and wounded, Edmondson rushed crazily into the Provincial regulars, shooting, clubbing, and slicing his way through their ranks. He then resorted to his fists, beating and clawing at them. In the midst of his rage, he clutched one of the Redcoats by the neck and dragged him down the mountain, while tearing at his throat and beating him senseless. When Edmondson finished his foe, he charged back to the summit where he returned to the fray. At some point in the ensuing melee, Edmondson's adversaries shot him and he fell mortally wounded."[69]

Private Leonard Hice described how he was

> dreadfully wounded, I received two bullets in my left arm and it was broken. We were fighting in the woods and with the assistance of my commander [Captain James Dysart] who would push my bullets [down the barrel of his Long Rifle with a long wooden ramrod], I shot 3 rounds before I was shot down. I then received a bullet through my left leg. The fourth bullet I received in my right knee which shattered the bone by my right thigh and brought me to the ground. When on the ground I received a bullet in my breast and was bourne of the ground [by comrades and] The way that I fought after my arm was broken was to rest my rifle against a tree and take sight and generally take the man I aimed at fell whether my bullet brought the enemy down or not I cannot say for many were as good marksmen as I.[70]

According to a well-laid tactical plan originally formulated by Shelby that now applied to this southwestern sector that had become the center of the storm, Campbell's hard-hit Virginians began to retire down the slope. "Our guns being rifles," in James Crow's words, without bayonets, the Virginians were forced back by the counterattack, but more rapidly than Shelby's men. During the swirl of close quarter combat, desperate Virginians, when cornered by enemy bayonets, swung tomahawks and slashed with long hunting knives because there were relatively few sabers among Patriot officers, unlike Ferguson's officers. Some of Campbell's backcountry men swung musket-butts like clubs to split Loyalist heads like late November pumpkins lying in the fields after the first frost. Fellow Americans fought each other among the trees and boulders even with their fists in the hand-to-hand struggle, even trying to strangle one another along the body-strewn slope.[71] With considerable understatement, Private Starns described the success of the Loyalist counterattack that far exceeded their previous gains in Shelby's sector, because they "charged on us and we retreated across a little hollow and loaded" long rifles and muskets.[72]

Indeed, Campbell's command had been exceptionally hard hit by the combination of heavy volleys and the sweeping bayonet charge of the American Volunteers, who might have been joined by units of the South Carolina or North Carolina militia down the slope, and a good portion—in fact, a shocking portion—of the Virginia command of around two hundred men had been routed to a degree that was destined not to be seen by any other Patriot command that afternoon. Because of the counterattack's shock power and the heavy losses that had been inflicted, including from the flurries of jabbing bayonets by Ferguson's men, the confusion and panic was so great that many stunned Virginians had become unnerved. These panicked Virginians fled all the way across the wooded saddle to the safety of Brushy Ridge and down a nearby draw, before they eventually would be rallied by Campbell and other officers.[73] Colonel Shelby was shocked by the extent of the stunning setback that had not occurred to such an extent when his command had been attacked, because Campbell's "retreat was so rapid that there was great danger of it becoming a rout."[74]

Shelby knew exactly what he was talking about, because he and Captain John Sawyers played a key role in assisting the stemming of the panic among the hard-hit Virginians at its peak, when Colonel Campbell and his fellow officers lost control of their Washington County regiment: a most serious tactical setback that required the real leader of the entire task force to leave his Sullivan County regiment and come to deal with the escalating crisis.[75] Although understated, Shelby's words about the overall effectiveness of the American Volunteers, and perhaps also the Carolina militiamen who might have joined their fierce counterattack since they also possessed bayonets, in their greatest success of the day were no exaggeration when he suggested a rout. However, Colonel Shelby was being diplomatic because it was a disgraceful rout. Quite simply, the Virginians had been swept off the field. Even Lieutenant Samuel Newell, who was "attached" to Captain Andrew Colvill's company, Campbell's regiment, described the rout without accusing the Virginians of cowardice: "When they were charged with the bayonet, they had broke and retreated farther than was necessary, having run across the intervening valley, to the top of the next rise, where I met them [and] Colonel Campbell and Major Edmondson . . . calling on them to halt, used every possible effort and with the assistance of others who halted" and slowly began to rally and organize.[76]

To be fair, when their muskets were unloaded after firing at the Provincial regular attackers, Campbell's Virginians had been extremely hard hit by the bayonet charge, while mounted Loyalist officers slashed with sabers to inflict ghastly wounds to hapless Virginians on foot. One of the foremost Loyalist officers who had perfected the art of killing rebels that bloody afternoon was the infamous Bloody Bill Cunningham. Private Andrew Ferguson, the free Black fighting man serving in Campbell's ranks, never forgot seeing "Bill Cunningham kill an American in two hundred yards of us—he was on horseback and then rode off" toward the crest, when the command retired back up the slope.[77]

However, despite the panic and high losses, Campbell's men were actually fortunate, because the Provincial regulars possessed relatively few men in the counterattacking ranks that surged downhill because of steadily mounting losses, including from the fighting in Shelby's sector to the northeast, as well as exhaustion on a hot afternoon. Surgeon Johnson described in his diary how gains could not be properly exploited because of "our Number being so small."[78]

Had the number of Provincial regulars been higher, since they were Ferguson's best troops, then Campbell's Virginia regiment might well have been swept completely off the field and knocked entirely out of the battle with disastrous consequences for Shelby's overall plan of surrounding the mountain, because the tough Provincial regulars would have retained possession of the southwestern spur or Ferguson's left flank—the key to successfully holding the ridge at its highest point. That would have negated the later successful tactics of the Patriots attacking northeast along the open crest to gain the momentum that eventually overran the ridge's northeastern spur, when united with other attackers to the northeast.

Campbell's Virginians Gamely Rally at Last

After the widespread panic that had caused many Virginians to flee wildly all the way to Brushy Ridge in the day's most serious Patriot setback, Colonel Campbell's panicked Virginia boys finally began to rally near the base of the ridge and points beyond, including on heavily wooded Brushy Ridge. Rallying the Virginia troops was not easy and considerable time was wasted, which meant that the Provincial regulars could return northeast to focus on Shelby's resurgent threat. Rallying such a large number of panicked Virginians was only possible primarily because of the efforts of Colonel Campbell, Colonel Shelby, and Major William Edmondson, who all frantically pleaded with the men to not only reform, but also to return to once again advance up the slope, as if they had not been defeated.[79]

Looking not unlike his Scottish Highland warrior ancestors, the red-haired and blue-eyed Colonel Campbell had frantically attempted in vain to bring order to the chaos, while waving his Scottish claymore sword and repeatedly shouting above the din, "Halt! Return my brave fellows, and you will drive the enemy immediately."[80] As in Shelby's sector, this was a key moment and a turning point. Indeed, much had "depended upon successfully rallying the Virginia men when first driven down the mountain. Had they have become demoralized as did the [Virginia militia] troops at Gates's defeat near Camden [then] they would have brought disgrace and disaster" at Kings Mountain.[81] Even more, had "Campbell's main force been repelled or defeated, the battle might have ended right there."[82]

Private Peter Starns long remembered Campbell's inspirational role and that of other fine officers, especially Colonel Shelby, in not only rallying but also leading their rallied men back up the timbered slope, including "the exertions of our young Lt. [William] Russell [Jr.] who seemed to be entirely fearless and rushed on calling on us to follow" up the mountain.[83] The renewed fighting spirit of Campbell's resurgent men perhaps can best be seen in the case of wounded Lieutenant Robert Edmondson. He was determined to continue to fight despite his recent wound and hastily bandaged arm. In preparation for the second assault up the southwestern slope, he encouraged his friend, John Craig of Scotch-Irish descent, with a few inspiring words that demonstrated his feisty fighting spirit: "Come, let us at it again."[84] Related to John Craig, Captain Robert Craig, an old Indian fighter who had commanded a company during the 1776 Cherokee campaign, also rose to the challenge in rallying the troops after fellow officers were shot down.[85]

However, in truth and as long assumed, it was not so much Campbell and his officers who had succeeded in turning the tide on their own after the shameful rout of the Virginia regiment. In fact, it was the continued offensive efforts of Colonel Shelby and his men who had finally gained control of the situation in Campbell's sector on their right on the western side spur, unlike on the southwestern sector, which was too far south an intermixture of troops of the two commands. But here, where Shelby's right overlapped Campbell's left and contrary to the traditional interpretations about the battle, "Campbell's men had been saved by their [Overmountain] friends and neighbors led by Isaac Shelby," by taking pressure off the Virginians at exactly the right time by their repeated attacks up the slope.[86] As mentioned, by this time the American Volunteers had been ordered back up the slope by a blast of Ferguson's silver whistle to regain the open crest to once again confront Shelby's resurgent attackers, who were pouring up the slope and through the trees a second time with fierce screams. Echoing over the crest, Ferguson's shrill whistle blast directives were especially effective in quickly maneuvering and shifting his Provincial regulars to successfully meet two distinct threats on two fronts on opposite sides of the ridge, as if this tactical maneuvering by whistle notes had been expressly created for this climactic showdown on Kings Mountain.

After returning to the base of the mountain, with Colonel Campbell leading the way, the Virginians again surged up the slope with their chorus of shrill battle-cries that echoed through the tall trees and drifting smoke of battle. The firefight increased with the American Volunteers defending the ridge to meet Shelby's intensified pressure higher up the ridge to the northeast. By this time and as noted, Ferguson was already in serious trouble in facing multiple threats simultaneously on both sides of the narrow ridge, because he was basically playing a tactical game of whack-a-mole that he could never win, especially when completely encircled, which was now only a matter of time. For instance, the opportunity for Campbell, who took advantage to successfully counterattack up the slope a second time, only existed because the American Volunteers had turned again to face Shelby and once again charged down the slope northeast of Campbell: the exact tactical situation that had also earlier presented Shelby's golden opportunity to once again advance back up the slope after the Virginians were pushed far down the slope and well beyond, because the enemy had been pulled in different directions.

Indeed, a fundamental secret to their success that afternoon, Shelby's and Campbell's forces on each side—north and south, respectively—of the lengthy ridge possessed flexibility and resiliency to gamely rebound after each setback relatively quickly. However, this was far more the case of Shelby's Overmountain men rather than Campbell's Virginians. In overall terms, Shelby's command was in better fighting shape because of the preplanned withdrawal to minimize the impact of the bayonet charge and lessen casualties. Thanks to Shelby's efforts in the battle's opening phase, no section of the trap of surrounding the mountain was permanently knocked out of the enclosing circle, before they rebounded to swarm back up the slope with reloaded muskets and even more determination to capture Kings Mountain. In addition, Carolina militiamen, whose numbers were greater than the American Volunteers who spearheaded each counterattack, with their homemade bayonets had also attacked down the slope with the Provincial regulars leading the way, especially later when losses began to mount for Ferguson's finest Loyalist troops.[87]

The determined men of the American Volunteers were able to concentrate longer on the task of attempting to drive Campbell's men off the mountain because it was before the other Patriot units, except Shelby of course, had reached their assigned positions to surround the mountain. In total, consequently, Campbell's troops were hurled three times down the slope by bayonet charges that gradually eroded the enemy's strength and energy in what had become a battle of attrition precisely because they were too successful, in a striking paradox. Indeed, these tactical successes were their undoing in the end. However, Campbell's losses—the highest of any command that afternoon—should actually have been much higher and Loyalist Drury Mathis knew exactly why. In his own words, Mathis explained how "his Loyalist friends were very generally over-shooting the Americans" in unleashing disciplined volleys that swept downhill and through the trees.[88] During the third charge of the American Volunteers down the timbered slope covered in rocks and boulders, Mathis was hit and fell to the ground in Colonel Shelby's sector. And "as the mountaineers passed over him, he would play possum; but he could plainly observe their faces and eyes; and to him those bold, brave riflemen appeared like so many devils from the infernal regions, so full of excitement were they as they darted like enraged lions up the mountain. He said they were the most powerful looking men he ever beheld; not overburdened with fat, but tall, raw-boned, and sinewy, with long, matted hair—such men as were never before seen in the Carolinas."[89]

The cumulative effect of three successive bayonet charges by Ferguson's best troops ensured that Campbell lost the most men of any command. Indeed, the considerable difference between how Shelby's Overmountain men reacted with greater resilience to the repeated bayonet attacks compared to the Virginians was primarily due to the Holston River Valley colonel's superior leadership and the fact that his citizen-soldiers were hardy mountaineers who were magnificent fighting men. All in all, it had been a close call in Campbell's sector. Like other officers who had viewed the disaster at the western and southwestern end of the ridge, Colonel Shelby had feared that Campbell's initial full-fledged retreat might eliminate them entirely as a viable fighting force that afternoon.[90] But in the end, it had been Colonel Shelby and his command on the right that came to the timely rescue of the hard-hit Virginians.[91]

During the multiple charges up and down the wooded slope, New York's Captain Abraham De Peyster played a leading role in inspiring his men to greater exertions. He had gained recognition as the leading and most talented officer in the New York Volunteers and had emerged as Ferguson's top lieutenant and second-in-command on October 7. In leading his men in one counterattack after another on horseback, De Peyster defied death and was fortunate to have survived the close-range fighting. Because De Peyster led from the front, the life of this fine officer of Dutch heritage "was saved by a doubloon in his vest pocket . . . [that] stopped a rifle ball, though the coin was bent by its force."[92] But Captain De Peyster's daring role in leading the way was in vain. In Colonel Shelby's words: "They repelled us three times with bayonet charges, but being determined to conquer or die, we came up a fourth time."[93]

Thanks to Shelby's continued heavy pressure and punishing fire on the Loyalists defending the southwestern spur and the Virginians' renewed advance, Joseph Starns described how the Virginians for the third and final time "advanced on them and kept up such a constant fire they never made us retreat again but we stood still advancing on them till the end of the battle."[94] His brother Peter never forgot the inspirational efforts of Colonel Campbell in encouraging his men up the slope for the final time: "I distinctly remember . . . Colonel Campbell amongst the men on foot in his shirt sleeves, his collar open, and loudly giving orders to his men to advance . . . the amber of his chew of tobacco running down his cheeks [while] We advanced on upon the hill driving the enemy to the edge of it."[95]

A Virginian described the punishment administered to the Loyalists that resulted in a turning point around the embattled westernmost spur, writing how "the enemy fell so fast [that these losses] obliged them to retreat to the top of the Mountain."[96] Indeed, despite having been hard hit by successive bayonet charges that had poured down the slope in their respective sectors, Shelby's and Campbell's men were on the move once again and now advancing together, while on the verge of finally overrunning the embattled southwestern spur and gaining the strategic crest, which was a crucial tactical development because Colonel John Sevier, advancing between Shelby and Campbell, was about to strike on Campbell's left and to Shelby's right with his Overmountain men from the Nolichucky River country.

In a classic paradox, the success of the slashing Loyalist counterattacks actually worked to the Patriots' advantage in an unforeseen way in the end: the bayonet charges downhill broke up the original loose formations of the attackers and left nothing but small knots of expert fighting teams, which were mutually supporting and protecting the exposed flanks of their comrades in the adjacent command while advancing up the slope, which diffused the overall impact of the counterattacks: a highly individualistic means of waging war to create a "swarming" effect, which was how Native Americans, especially the Cherokee, had long waged their brand of warfare, and for which Ferguson had no effective answer. But in the end, this sheer determination of the average fighting man in the ranks would ultimately ensure the capture of the southwestern end of the ridge by a mixture of Campbell's Virginians, whose left was united with the right of Shelby's Sullivan County men. Working as a team, Shelby and Campbell were now focused on capturing the strategic spur in tandem, which meant turning Ferguson's left flank. To the endless frustration of Major Ferguson and his hard-fighting followers, it had proven utterly impossible to simultaneously concentrate on any one group of attackers surging up the wooded slope, when they were striking at once. Capturing the southwestern spur would mean the eventual fulfillment of the first phase of Shelby's plan that called for first turning Ferguson's left flank and then surrounding the mountain on every side.[97]

All the while and most important, the strength and hence the overall effectiveness of the counterattacking Provincial regulars and Carolina militiamen, who were worn and sweat-covered, continued to be gradually reduced by a bloody attrition, while each charge became less effective, resulting in an insidious and gradual deterioration of combat capabilities. Ferguson's successful counterthrusts, therefore, had only reaped minor tactical successes that backfired in the end, because they were steadily leading to a larger tactical defeat, while the Patriots continued to advance after each new setback as if nothing had happened.

Quite simply, by "the end of the third series of bayonet attacks [against Shelby and Campbell], the Provincials had reached their culmination point, and were no longer capable of offensive action."[98] However, this premature evaluation of the capabilities of Ferguson's elite troops was an exaggeration of the actual situation because the American Volunteers, who were spearheading the counterattacks of the Carolina militiamen down the slope, possessed the strength and spirit for unleashing one last powerful counterattack when Sevier's Watauga men suddenly appeared to Shelby's right to fill the gap between the Holston River countrymen and Campbell's Virginians.[99]

The paradoxical truth of the bayonet charge being so effective as to wear down Ferguson's crack Volunteers assisted in wrecking Loyalist morale and spirits as well as their strength. Even more discouraging for the hard-fighting Loyalists, who were trapped in Ferguson's follies, was the fact that "the moment the Britons turned their backs, the [Patriot] Americans [repeatedly] shot them from behind every tree . . . and laid them prostate."[100] In addition, Colonel Campbell's Virginians, like Shelby's Overmountain boys, were emboldened because "the men learned not to dread the bayonets as at first," wrote Lieutenant Samuel Newell, becoming more confident and aggressive.[101] Even more, Major Ferguson had made a tactical error by ordering his counterattacks to stop just short of what might have been a complete success in the decisive elimination of entire units, especially in the case of Campbell's reeling command, taking them out of the fight instead of more thoroughly routing them by a longer pursuit so that they would be unable to recover. The repeated abrupt and premature calling back of his attackers just short of a truly decisive victory was caused by the major's ever-growing concern about his ability to maintain a permanent grip on the strategic crest, because he faced different attacks from multiple directions at the same time. In the words of a thoroughly frustrated Captain De Peyster: "Unfortunately, Major Ferguson made a signal [by whistle] for us to retreat, being afraid that the enemy would get possession of the height on the other side" of the ridge.[102]

So far, this had been entirely Shelby's and Campbell's fight in the struggle for possession of the southwestern spur, which was the battlefield's highest ground, and they battled with intensity for at least ten minutes, likely longer, on their own before the other commands on both sides of the ridge reached their assigned positions from which to launch their own attacks.[103] Thomas Maxwell, one of Shelby's men, revealed as much when he wrote how "Campbell's and Shelby's men were fighting against the British regulars commanded in person by Ferguson, for some time before Cleveland and Sevier's men got into action."[104] This was the narrow window of opportunity in which Major Ferguson might well have won the Battle of Kings Mountain, if his gains and advantages had been properly exploited by him. But that golden opportunity slipped away forever in the fog of war.

The Assault of Colonel John Sevier and His Nolichucky Overmountain Men

Because Colonel Sevier had initially taken a fire support position behind Shelby on the northern to northwestern edge of the southwestern spur, and slightly farther northwest, he attacked with his Washington County, North Carolina, men later than Shelby and Campbell. At last, therefore, Sevier's Overmountain men belatedly moved forward to Shelby's right and nearly opposite Campbell, who was fighting mostly on the southern side of the embattled spur. In addition, Sevier's right extended far enough south to interlap with Campbell's left to the southeast, which ensured an intermixture of the two units. Along with troops of Shelby's, Sevier and most of his Washington County men were positioned between Campbell, on his left, and Shelby, on his right, to plug the existing gap between the two commands.

Like Colonels Shelby and Campbell, Colonel John Sevier was mounted to inspire his approximately 120 Wataugans during the push up the slope in a determined bid to finally gain the strategic crest, where thick waves of whitish battle smoke drifted up through the oak, maple, and hickory trees like a heavy morning fog. To Sevier, who was known as "Nolichucky Jack" to the common soldiers, this was much more than simply a battle for possession of an obscure hilltop in the northwestern South Carolina backcountry. Indeed, as so many Patriots fully realized, this escalating fight along the timbered slopes was all about America's destiny in regard to its western-looking horizons and ambitions. With clarity, Sevier had long ago envisioned the exciting possibilities of leading the way for a new group of pioneers west all the way to the Mississippi River more than a thousand miles away and to its bottoms in the Illinois country of the Mississippi River Valley: an intoxicating expansionist vision that would be stopped prematurely in its tracks by Great

Britain if this war east of the mountains for the heart and soul of America was lost. The forgotten story of Kings Mountain was that it was western people's conflict, which was all about the seemingly limitless future settlement of rich and luxurious lands farther west to the Mississippi and even beyond, where a bright destiny and endless possibilities lay awaiting these frontiersmen, if they won this battle.[105]

Although Sevier's Overmountain boys from the Nolichucky River country only belatedly joined the attack to Shelby's right—on the southwestern and western edge of the summit—the additional attackers made a timely arrival. Shelby's men from the Holston River settlement had first attacked just northeast of Sevier. However, some of Shelby's and Sevier's citizen-soldiers on the right came to the aid of Campbell's hard-pressed troops on the left during the attack in the smoke-filled woodlands around the western part of the southwestern spur, providing timely assistance that helped fuel the Virginians' final bid to gain the strategic summit. In overall tactical terms, Sevier's advancing men from Washington County added extra strength and momentum to Campbell's attack on his left to the south and southeast and to Shelby's attack of Sullivan County soldiers to the northeast on his right, especially after partly merging with these two units.

Colonel Sevier possessed a good many excellent frontiersmen from the Nolichucky River country, including expert Indian fighters who had gained invaluable experience during the 1776 Cherokee campaign and other frontier actions. Second in command of Sevier's Washington County regiment, Virginia-born (October 1750) Major Jonathan Tipton also possessed experience in battling the Cherokee. Captain James Cozby was another such experienced fighting man, whose skills served him well at Kings Mountain. He now carried a homemade cavalry saber, distinguished by a curved blade forged by a local blacksmith. Colonel Sevier was also ably assisted by his Virginia-born brother, Captain Valentine Sevier Jr., another savvy and highly skilled Indian fighter who had served with distinction as a sergeant at the Battle of Point Pleasant in October 1774. He had also excelled at Colonel Shelby's victory at Musgrove's Mill, where he had commanded Watauga and Nolichucky men armed with blazing long rifles, which were used with deadly effect to ensure a surprising victory over the Loyalists.

Swarming up the slope not far from Captain Cozby, John Waddell, who had been born in Philadelphia in 1765 and lived with his family in the

Watauga settlement, advanced with his trusty long rifle in hand. Only fifteen and carrying a powder horn with the date of 1774 that he had carved into it, Waddell was only one of the many teenagers in the surging ranks of Sevier's Overmountain command.

Meanwhile, a desperate Major Ferguson focused his crack American Volunteers and his Loyalist militia on hurling Sevier's newly arrived attackers down the slope during the final lull after Campbell and Shelby had been pushed back for the last time. Additional Carolina militiamen, wearing hunting attire, now attacked to the rear of the crack Provincial regulars in a bid to deliver a double "to cripple Sevier's division" with an overpowering bayonet charge.

However, for the first time all day, the Overmountain Patriots of Sevier's command from Washington County, North Carolina, stubbornly held their ground on the slope in the face of the hard-hitting bayonet attack, which was the seventh one (three had been launched against Shelby and three against Campbell), while riddling the Provincial regulars' ranks, which had been depleted by this time, with well-placed shots. Quite simply, Ferguson's seventh bayonet charge failed to push Sevier's men aside unlike in Shelby's and Campbell's sectors. By this time and fortunately for Sevier, the offensive capabilities of the American Volunteers were severely diminished, because they had been expended in half a dozen assaults against Shelby's and Campbell's attackers. Thus, a defiant Colonel Sevier did not order his men rearward to better absorb the intended knockout blow of the attack down the slope like Shelby and Campbell: a contradiction of Colonel Shelby's orders to give way to offensive efforts to save lives and black powder to negate the most successful British tactic.

Assisting Sevier's Overmountain men in standing firm against the counterattack of the American Volunteers and Carolina militiamen, Shelby's Sullivan County volunteers to the northeast raked the right flank of the Loyalists' formation, inflicting damage and hastening their retreat south back up the slope to again regain the crest: a tactical development that was needed for the Provincial regulars to once again face Shelby's and Campbell's resurgent attackers, who sought to gain the open strategic crest from both sides, instead of Sevier. All in all, this new bolder tactic of standing firm immediately paid dividends to Sevier and his Washington County boys, resulting in the taking of more Loyalist lives to additionally reduce the combat capabilities of the Provincial regulars, and the Carolina militiamen to a lesser degree, by maintaining an effective hot fire from behind trees and boulders. Most important, Sevier's defiant stance succeeded in driving a stake through the heart of the immense pride and *esprit de corps*, which had only recently been sky-high, of Ferguson's elite fighting men, while allowing Shelby's and Campbell's to advance ever closer to the ridge's southwestern spur and the strategic crest during the brief respite in their respective sectors.

Then, a jubilant Colonel Sevier, who could not have been prouder of his rough-hewn Overmountain men, ordered everyone up the rocky, timbered slope in a determined bid to gain the open ground of the strategic crest, after the punished Provincial regulars, whose losses had grown even more severe by this time, had retired up to their commanding high ground perch. But it had not been easy or without cost. At one point, Sevier had been forced to exert greater efforts to rally and inspire his independent-minded citizen-soldiers, who had become more tentative at one point because they had made the mistake of believing false rumors shouted by the Tories that Tarleton and his professional killers—fellow Americans all—of the British Legion of mounted dragoons had arrived to reinforce Ferguson: the greatest Patriot fear and concern on that day.

However, the inevitable price for Colonel Sevier's success had to be paid in full, while Campbell and Shelby were mounting increased pressure on the dwindling number of defenders of the open crest, especially along the embattled southwestern spur. In the Watauga colonel's case, this success came at a deep personal price. Colonel Sevier's brother, Captain Robert Sevier, fell with an ugly wound to the stomach. Joseph Sevier, a younger brother of the colonel, carried the wounded captain to the spring near the hill's base that provided Robert with some much-needed relief. But as a sad fate would have it, Colonel Sevier's brother was fated to die in severe pain in the coming days.

In a joyful moment, the majority of Sevier's Washington County men were finally in the process of linking up with Shelby's and Campbell's men in a final united push to gain the crest by converging on the southwestern spur. Now, of course, the most pressing tactical objective at this point was to gain the strategic crest by all three commands—basically the all-important turning of Ferguson's left flank by first overrunning and capturing the strategic southwestern spur—which was absolutely necessary for them to then push northeastward along the open crest of the thin ridge that led to Ferguson's encampment at the ridge's opposite end at the northeastern spur. By this time, Shelby's, Campbell's, and Sevier's steadily advancing ranks had become disorganized and intermingled after the first two commands had already faced three counterattacks down the hill apiece. In consequence, some of Sevier's men—like Shelby's troops even before Sevier's arrival—on the right had shifted to the southeast to assist the left of Campbell's hard-hit Virginia command on the west, which suffered more than Shelby's Sullivan County regiment. In the previous uncoordinated and piecemeal attacks Ferguson could focus on Shelby and Campbell separately because their attacks were divided and coming from opposite sides of the ridge, but this was no longer possible after Sevier's contingent had bolstered the Sullivan and Washington County boys to create more of a united front.

But now these three resurgent commands—two Overmountain units and one backcountry militia—were coming together as one in the overall united effort to capture the strategic spur and turn Ferguson's left flank, which was vital for the eventual surrounding of the mountain on all sides farther to the northeast—the key to decisive victory. All nine commands were either moving up the slopes or still getting into their assigned attack positions. All the while, the attackers from Shelby's, Campbell's, and Sevier's commands continued to unleash their piercing war cries that cascaded over the hilltop. At this point, the defenders of the strategic crest and spur were both the American Volunteers and the Carolina militiamen, who now realized that they were fighting for their lives in attempting to retain possession of the open ridgetop at all costs.[106] All in all, the North Carolina militiamen fought splendidly, having "twice repulsed a Body that attacked their Line," wrote Surgeon Uzal Johnson with pride in what these hard-fighting Americans accomplished.[107] All the while, however, Colonel Shelby was feeling increasingly confident of success because the "slaughter of the enemy was great."[108]

John Crockett, the father of David, or "Davy," Crockett, the future famed Tennessee frontiersmen and congressman who was born on the Nolichucky River and was killed at the Alamo on March 6, 1836, was one of Colonel Sevier's men. He was a typical Scotch-Irish fighting man, whose father, David, had migrated to America from Ulster Province, north Ireland. He possessed experience as a member of the Lincoln County, North Carolina, militia, which had been early gained when he had lived in the Catawba River country before crossing the mountains to the Overmountain settlements and serving in the Washington County militia under Colonel "Nolichucky Jack" Sevier.[109]

Chapter VI

Colonel Shelby Gains the Strategic Crest at Last and Capturing the Southwestern Spur

With Major Ferguson now primarily focused on Sevier's troops, Colonel Shelby now had the golden tactical opportunity, after having been repulsed three times, to finally gain the strategic crest, while Campbell's and Sevier's combined troops continued to apply heavy pressure to the southwest of the Sullivan County men near the spur. Shelby, Campbell, and Sevier continued the time-consuming process of turning Ferguson's left flank at the southwestern spur, because the Scottish major had no choice but to order his men to retire northeast along the open crest and toward his encampment to avoid having his forces divided and cut off in attempting to defend the southwestern spur.

Colonel Shelby now basked in a sense of hard-earned success when he and his men were the first to gain a permanent toehold on the open strategic crest on Ferguson's left, or western, flank. Shelby's gaining of the strategic crest resulted in two key tactical developments that turned the tide of this escalating battle: forcing the last defenders of the spur to retire northeast along the open ridgetop to avoid getting cut off and then forcing them to retire northeast along the narrow ridge, while ensuring that the strategic southwestern spur fell to mostly Campbell's men, but also Sevier's boys and the right of Shelby's command. The fog of war and the intermixing of commands caused confusion, including the mistaken belief of participants—later embraced by historians—that it was Campbell and not Shelby who first gained the crest. But in truth, the frontiersmen of Shelby's right first gained the crest of the summit of the southwestern spur, which allowed Campbell's advancing troops, who had encountered more rugged, steep terrain on the west and southwest of the spur, to shortly also gain the crest and then for Sevier to reach the crest: the vital uniting of commands on the strategic crest and the open ridgetop that resulted in the capture of the southwestern spur and the turning of Ferguson's left flank, which then allowed for the united drive of the victors northeast up the crest and toward Ferguson's encampment.

With the mounted Shelby leading the way, the Holston River country boys served as the fast-shooting vanguard in the drive northeast along the open crest, while driving the Loyalists before them, after having been the first to gain the strategic crest.[1] In the words of Private Thomas Maxell, one of Colonel Shelby's boys, about the key meeting of Campbell's and Shelby's men, which was closely followed by Sevier's arrival, on the vital crest, "Capt. [Moses] Shelby's company . . . was repulsed as often as twice [like the rest of Shelby's regiment] by the British regulars; were rallied, and renewed the fight, driving the enemy to the top of the mountain, where we were joined by Col. Campbell's main body" of troops.[2]

By this time, Shelby's, Campbell's, and Sevier's men, now intermingled as one, had become the conquerors of the southwestern spur and this portion of the lengthy ridge by relying on "swarming tactics," which had effectively turned Ferguson's left flank. In consequence and as one, they now pushed northeastward toward Ferguson's center in a steamrolling advance that was downhill because of the slope's descent from the ridge's high point, after having buckled his line. Major Ferguson was now in serious trouble because his left flank had been successfully turned and his finest troops, the crack Provincial regulars who were completely exhausted by this time, were being gradually pushed northeast down the sloping open crest of the narrow ridge, which was surrounded by thick forest along the steep slopes, toward the main encampment on the higher northeastern spur.[3] While Ferguson's troops, especially the Provincial regulars, had gradually lost strength, stamina, and fighting spirit with each of the seven attacks down the slope and during the struggle to hold the strategic crest, the Patriots had steadily gained strength, momentum, and the all-important initiative that would not be relinquished.

In the words of Colonel Shelby: "The battle here became furious and bloody [and] In the succession of repulses and attackers, and in giving succor to the points hardest pressed, much disorder took place in our flanks; the men of my column, of Campbell's column, and a great part of Sevier's, were mingled together in the confusion of battle [but] We gained the [western] summit of the mountain and drove [the enemy] along the top of it" toward the eastern end of the ridge.[4] Elation among the attackers grew with the Loyalists reeling and on the run. Their resolution was reflected in the stirring battle cry which revealed an unbeatable fighting spirit: "To fight till he dies!"[5] Even more, the Patriots were "in a singularly foul mood [because in] this area not so far to the west of where Tarleton had operated, they had heard a great deal about [the infamous] 'Tarleton's Quarter,'" and now their "idea of warfare was as ruthless as that of their forest opponents."[6]

A Sense of Mounting Loyalist Frustration

Most important and as noted by the wise employment of highly effective "swarming" tactics, hundreds of experienced Indian fighters had successfully turned Ferguson's left, or western, flank in the process of surrounding the entire mountain to trap his command. Worst of all for the overall defensive effort, it was becoming unclear to Major Ferguson what he should do in tactical terms because the counterattacks by his finest troops had proved ineffective. He was increasingly unable to ascertain when and where to strike because the attackers were advancing in small groups of men from multiple directions using the "swarming" effect that could not be effectively countered by any single tactic. Mounted on a fine warhorse, a frustrated Captain Alexander Chesney, as Surgeon Uzal Johnson penned in his journal, ascertained the no-win tactical situation of the repeated futile bayonet charges down the slopes. Although the "mountaineers [were] flying [down the slope] whenever there was danger of being charged with the bayonet, [they returned] again as soon as the British detachments had faced about to repel another of their parties."[7]

Meanwhile, other Loyalist officers felt the same deepening sense of frustration because the courage and bayonet charges by the Provincial regulars and Carolina militiamen were simply not enough to prevail even when successful. Colonel William Hill, a diehard Patriot who had been born in Ireland, explained the most exasperating of tactical situations and vexing of realities for Ferguson and his hard-fighting men, who were truly in a tactical dilemma of immense proportions: "The ground was so rough . . . that they [not even the elite American Volunteers] were not able to overtake the americans to injure them [during their counterattacks and then] when they had went a certain distance they had orders to retreat to their camp" at the northwest end of the long ridge.[8] Captain Chesney, every inch a fighter, penned in his journal how even topography and natural cover had conspired together against Ferguson's seemingly correct tactical beliefs and decisions, dooming his desperate defense of the heights that had seemed to be impregnable: "Kings Mountain from its height would have enabled us to oppose a superior force with advantage had it not been covered with wood which sheltered the Americans and enabled them to fight in their favorite manner . . . from behind trees and other cover."[9]

As these seasoned frontiersmen, hunters, and Indian fighters realized, they possessed still another key advantage in attacking up the wooded, rocky slopes and then parallel on both sides of the long ridge that led northeast toward Ferguson's encampment. When occupying a high-ground position and firing downhill, the Loyalists had the common tendency of overshooting their targets, sending bullets whistling over the attackers' heads. Therefore, as every experienced frontiersman realized, one had to aim a bit lower with his weapon when sighting on his target to score a direct hit. Of course, the Loyalists possessed few, if any, Overmountain men in their ranks, and British training, as had been long instilled by Ferguson, ignored the sharpshooter's art of aiming the Brown Bess musket and hitting targets with any degree of accuracy, because of the traditional concept of firing massed volleys from tight formations as prescribed by British Army regulations.

In the words of James Collins, fifteen, who had been born in Lincoln County, North Carolina, on November 22, 1764: "Their great elevation above us proved their ruin; they overshot us altogether, scarce touching a man, except those on horseback, while every rifle from below seemd [sic] to have the desired effect."[10] Indeed, these Holy Bible-reading and God-fearing Patriots of humble origins and meager means from both sides of the mountains were convinced that they were now fighting as "instruments in the hand of Heaven to punish the enemy for his wickedness" and evil ways of waging war against both soldiers and civilians.[11] All the while, the attackers continued to wisely utilize trees, rocks, and boulders for good cover during the push northeast, benefiting from this central hallmark of Indian warfare: "The insect-like swarming effect of the small units ascending the hill effectively negated Ferguson's conventional tactics."[12]

However, the difficult terrain—ravines, steepness of terrain, and the trees and rocks—and the loss of officers and men only slightly slowed the Patriots' advance northeast toward the ridge's opposite end and the northeastern spur, because they now possessed the momentum. One notable disadvantage for the attackers was the differences in caliber of the long rifles from .36 caliber to .48 caliber, which guaranteed that there was no standard issue of ammunition, especially since no quartermaster department existed in this frontier army, and there was no chance of securing rounds from the cartridge-boxes of fallen Loyalists since they only used .75 caliber balls. The different calibers of so many weapons, especially the long rifles among the Overmountain men and a lesser number of backcountry fighters, ensured that extra rounds could not be shared. When a Patriot was killed or wounded, therefore, he most often could not pass his bullets on to an able-bodied fighter: a serious liability during the attack compared to the Loyalists who possessed the advantage of having the same caliber weapon—the .75 caliber Brown Bess, which allowed for the sharing of rounds.[13] And, at this time, the mountain was still not yet completely surrounded by attackers, which would still take more time when time was especially precious, ensuring that the battle so far had been largely centered on the stern task of overrunning the southwestern summit, the highest point of Kings Mountain.

Colonel James Williams's South Carolinians Attack

Meanwhile, around 3:45 p.m., Colonel James Williams, who was the respected leader of the Little River District Regiment of Militia, or the Little River Regiment, from the South Carolina backcountry, attacked with his ad hoc South Carolina and extremely small Georgia battalion to Shelby's left to the northeast. Williams's mostly South Carolina attackers, which included Colonel Elijah Clarke's more than thirty Georgia boys under Major William Candler, were separated from Shelby's North Carolina boys on their right by a ravine, or draw, where a small spring trickled down the heavily wooded slope.

The fiery backcountry colonel, James Williams, had won his rank of brigadier general in the South Carolina militia for his inspiring leadership and skills demonstrated in the sparkling victory at Musgrove's Mill, and his 450 South Carolina boys, including his two teenage sons, Daniel and Joseph, of the 2nd Spartan Regiment, now surged up the slope and through the trees laced with whitish battle-smoke, while charging the northern crest at roughly the midway point of the lengthy ridge between the two spurs at opposite ends of Kings Mountain. Leading by example, Williams led the way up the slope with a waving saber and shouts of encouragement to his South Carolinians, after his command had been initially slowed by the rain-swollen stream and swampy ground in the northwestern sector in the time-consuming movement to encircle the ridge on the north.

Colonel Thomas Brandon, an inspirational Scotch-Irish leader, led his 2nd Spartan Regiment of backcountry men who had been assigned to Williams's command. Born in Pennsylvania in 1741 and having migrated to South Carolina around 1754, Colonel Brandon yelled for his militiamen to unleash the "Indian halloo" during the wild charge up the timbered ridge. Brandon's companies were led by experienced officers with mostly Scotch-Irish names: Captains William Young; Gabriel Brown, who was fated to be killed the following month in November 1780 in another fight; Hugh Means; Benjamin Jolley, who was destined to fight at Cowpens in January 1781, which would result in the destruction of Tarleton's British Legion; John Thompson; John Putnam; John Mapp; and Daniel Duffy, who had first served as a private in the heady days of 1776 when the war was young and more idealistic.

These veteran backcountry men of Brandon's 2nd Spartan Regiment were in the thick of the fight amid the boulder-strewn woodlands along the steep slope. Serving together in buddy teams, Private William Sharp, a member of Captain Jolley's company, was busily loading his weapon behind a log for cover when he was horrified to see Lieutenant William "Bill" Giles, another one of Jolley's men, fall to the ground and lie motionless, while bleeding from a head wound that appeared fatal. Enraged by the sight of a friend's death, Sharp fought even more frantically to avenge Giles's apparent death. Then, all of a sudden, a blood-streaked Lieutenant Giles, who still felt personally responsible for leading his men up the slope, dashed ahead as if suddenly risen from the dead, after having only been stunned by the ugly head wound. Now with the familial-like fighting team once again united, Sharp and Giles continued to wage their own private war against the detested Loyalists, while loading and firing as rapidly as possible in pushing up the wooded slope: a classic case of sheer determination that was seen everywhere that afternoon.

Advancing in the ranks of Captain Benjamin Jolley's company of the 2nd Spartan Regiment, Private Thomas Young, who was facing his own Loyalist relatives that afternoon, described how:

> Ben Hollingsworth [who had been born around 1755 and was married to Phebe Posey] and I took right up the side of the mountain, and fought our way from tree to tree [on] our way to the summit [and] I stood behind one tree, and fired until the bark was nearly all knocked off, and my eyes pretty well filled with it. One fellow shaved me pretty

> close, for his bullet took a piece of my gun-stock. Hollingsworth said, 'It won't do here; we shall be killed.' Some of the bark fell in my eyes, & we got into another place where we could stoop & be safe until we had loaded. I then [rose up] and fired with effect.[14]

In the process of loading and firing, Young, a mere feisty teenager whose mother was Colonel Thomas Brandon's sister and who was destined to earn the elevated rank of major, was utterly consumed with his bloody mission of killing Loyalists as fast as possible, because this had become a very personal war and sacred duty for him. His brother John Young, age twenty and a member of the Fair Forest Regiment of militia from the South Carolina backcountry, had been killed in June 1780 by a surprise attack of "Bloody Bill" Cunningham. Consequently, the young man had sworn "that I would never rest until I avenged his death." In fulfilling his sacred oath, Thomas Young proceeded ahead of his comrades surging through the trees while firing, rapidly advancing up the slope until he was too far ahead of Brandon's men and all alone. Private Young then found himself in a precarious position, after having advanced too far up the slope on his own, while firing from tree to tree and moving uphill in a reckless manner. Indeed, "before I was aware of it, I found myself apparently between my own regiment and the enemy, as I judged, from seeing the paper which the whigs wore in their hats and the pine knots [twigs] the tories wore in theirs."[15] In his own words about the escalating struggle in the blinding woodlands full of drifting layers of smoke:

> I got lost from Hollingsworth, & got between the two parties. I heard our regiment [Colonel Brandon's 2nd Spartan] halloo, & looked around & saw our men, about a dozen of them shook hands with me. A little fellow of the name of Cherry [Nicholas Cherry, an older and more experienced man who served as Colonel Brandon's quartermaster] gave me a sound scolding for my conduct, & told me to stick to him, or I would be killed. I did stay with him for some time.[16]

Private Thomas Young never forgot how "in the beginning of the attack [Colonel Williams] charged by me full speed [and] toward the summit a ball struck his horse under the jaw when he commenced stamping as if he were a nest of yellow jackets."[17] At this time, Williams burned with a desire for revenge because Ferguson and his men had occupied his beautiful Mount Pleasant Plantation on the Little River in the South Carolina backcountry and forced his wife and children out of their own home because of their patriarch's service to his country.[18] As Colonel Williams had prophetically penned in a July 4, 1780—the fourth anniversary of the Declaration of Independence—letter to his wife of an awful truth and grim reality that would be fulfilled in full at Kings Mountain: "I expect we will shortly meet the Tories, when they must give an account of their late conduct."[19] And the deeply religious and supremely dedicated Williams, who was fated to be mortally wounded on that bloody afternoon, meant every word of it.[20]

Fortunately, Colonel Williams's South Carolina backcountry men suffered relatively few casualties along the steep slope, after taking heavy volley fire from the Loyalists that swept down from the crest and sailed too high. To escape the hot fire streaming down from the open crest, Williams's citizen-soldiers prudently took cover behind trees and boulders to blast away with enthusiasm. Here, throughout most of the battle until the end, the South Carolinians and Georgians fired at Loyalists now silhouetted on the open crest, where the bright, sunlit skyline revealed excellent targets to Williams's sharpshooting men, who rapidly fired from the deep shadows under the canopy of tall timber to score numerous direct hits.[21]

During the attack up the slope, Virginia-born Major Samuel Hammond, a hardened Indian fighter and veteran of the all-day fight along the Ohio River at Point Pleasant in October 1774 and Shelby's sparkling victory at Musgrove's Mill, rose to the fore with inspired leadership that motivated the men of Williams's South Carolina regiment to keep moving up the slope with determination and firing all the while. At one point, he and a small group of frontiersmen surged ahead and fought completely through the Loyalist line, almost certainly Carolina militiamen at this point, on the high ground along the open crest, which left them vulnerable because most of his command still remained farther down the slope. Hammond sensibly ordered his men to retire back downhill through the trees to escape certain annihilation, but the Loyalists attempted to ease behind his small advance party of exposed men and cut them off from Williams's command. Therefore, another sharp fight at extremely close-range erupted on the timbered and rocky slope, when Hammond and his band succeeded "in cutting their way back" downhill, after another flurry of hand-to-hand combat in the shadowy woodlands.[22]

Advancing with Colonel Williams's South Carolina command were the most forgotten mostly Scotch-Irish men of Kings Mountain—a small group of Georgians, Colonel Elijah Clarke's boys, now under the command of Major William Candler. Although born of English parents, even Candler possessed distinctive Irish roots. He had been born in the port of Belfast, Ulster Province, in north Ireland in 1738 and then the Candler family had migrated to Virginia to start a new life when he was a "mere child."[23] Meanwhile, Colonel Williams continued to lead the way up the slope, encouraging everyone onward with flashing saber and inspiring words. This holy warrior, who loved his Holy Bible as much as the cause of liberty, wanted vengeance that afternoon, vowing to his South Carolina men: "I will kill Ferguson or die in the attempt."[24]

Gradually Applying Even More Pressure

About midpoint on the mountain's south side and northeast of Colonel Campbell's, Shelby's, and Sevier's commands that were intermingled and united by this time in surging northeast along the ridge, Major Joseph McDowell Jr. and Major Joseph Winston, from left to right, or west to east, surged up the wooded slope from the south, while the men of Lacey's and Cleveland's commands, west to east or left to right, struck from the north and headed toward the northwestern edge of the open summit of the easternmost spur upon which Ferguson's encampment was perched.[25] The officers gave relatively few orders because this most of all was a common soldier's fight. Indeed, like no other Revolutionary War battle, this was a true soldier's battle where the Indian fighting skills of the common man were allowed to rise to the fore from beginning to end. And the overall battle plan devised by Shelby could not have been more simplistic and basic to fit the combat capabilities of his men, although it was extremely ambitious. As hardened veterans of numerous battles with Native Americans and Loyalists, these fighting men already knew how to fight, and they did not have to be told what to do and when to do it. In consequence, the common soldiers simply went about their work in businesslike fashion and with methodical determination. For example, Thomas Young described how the orders were simply at "the firing of the first gun for every man to raise a whoop, rush forward, and fight his way as best he could."[26] Ireland-born Colonel William Hill summarized how in the fight for possession of a barren crest of such strategic importance, "there was very little military subordination as all that was required or expected was that every Officer & man should ascend the mountain so as to surround the enemy on all quarters."[27]

Major Joseph McDowell Jr. and His Burke County Men Surge up the Slope

Around a hundred Burke County, North Carolina, men of Major Joseph McDowell Jr., who was the brother of Colonel Charles McDowell, surged up the slope on the south to Colonel Campbell's right and to the left of Major Joseph Winston and his Surry County men, once they arrived from the north after having moved in a wide loop to the south, and struck about midway along the ridge's sprawling length. By this time, Campbell's Virginia troops were advancing on McDowell's left, but McDowell's left was intermixed with the Virginians' right in the forest covering the slope during the attack up the hill.

Like so many other attackers this afternoon, McDowell's Burke County boys had plenty of old scores to settle with Ferguson, who had forced them out of their homeland and caused them to retreat west across the mountains to link with the Overmountain men, after the recent skirmishes at Cane Creek and at Allen's farm on Muddy Creek in Burke County north of Gilbert Town.[28] In consequence, these North Carolina boys were highly motivated and especially eager to strike a blow for God and country. For instance, John Duckworth surged up the slope with a lead bullet still in his body that he had received in the victory over Major John Moore's Loyalists at Ramsour's Mill on June 20, 1780, near today's Lincolnton in Lincoln County, North Carolina. At this time, in Duckworth's words, "My wound had not got well and I fought with a [ball] in my shoulder of considerable length."[29]

Like most fighting men at Kings Mountain, the McDowell clan was Scotch-Irish to the core. In fact, the colonel's father, Joseph Sr., had been born in Ireland in 1715. A weaver by trade, he had migrated to America with wife Margaret O'Neil, settling in Pennsylvania, where so many Scotch-Irish and Irish had found a peaceful home in their pursuit of religious freedom. The restless McDowell family had then migrated south to the Shenandoah Valley of Virginia before heading farther south to the fertile Catawba River Valley in North Carolina before 1760. Because he owned the sprawling expanse of Quaker Meadows and to separate him from his cousin of the same name, Major Joseph McDowell Jr., the major's nickname was "Quaker Meadow" McDowell. Likewise, his cousin was known as "Pleasant Grove" McDowell.

Colonel Joseph McDowell Jr.'s son, Captain Joseph McDowell, of Pleasant Garden, also proudly served in the ranks. A typical frontier family of Celtic descent, the McDowell clan were experienced Indian fighters from the frontier who had long battled for survival in a harsh land, having defended their homeland by taking the war to the Cherokee with a vengeance and thorough destructiveness.[30]

In McDowell's ranks, Sergeant John Dysart was a typical Scotch-Irish fighting man of the frontier like Thomas Kennedy. Born on Christmas Day, 1749 and married to Mary Martha Patton-Dysart since April 4, 1773, he had gained invaluable experience during the 1776 Cherokee campaign. Although he was destined to survive this bloody battle in today's York County, South Carolina, like the fight at Cane Creek, fate was not kind to Sergeant Dysart. Not only his father, James, but also his brother William would be killed at the Battle of Cowan's Ford in a bid to thwart the British crossing of the Catawba River in February 1781.[31]

Colonel Edward Lacey's and Colonel Benjamin Cleveland's Commands, from West to East, Assault the Northeastern Edge of the Easternmost Summit

Then, on the left of Colonel Williams, whose South Carolina troops of the Little River Regiment continued up the slope in the northwest sector, Colonel Edward Lacey's South Carolina command from today's Chester County surged up the the left, or northeast, slope with wild screams that told Ferguson of still another threat—this time much closer to his tented encampment—that the Patriots possessed enough men to surround the mountain and his entire command. Leading the Chester boys, who were mostly Scotch-Irish fighters, Colonel Lacey was a fine officer, having raised the Turkey Creek volunteer company in the war's beginning.[32] As with the men of other commands, these citizen-soldiers adhered to the directive "to give them Indian play," while pushing south up the timbered slope just below Ferguson's encampment situated to the northeast: the winning frontier tactic, which was well-honed by this time, that had thoroughly defeated the Cherokee in 1776.[33]

Then, when the battle had been roaring for nearly half an hour and with Shelby, Campbell, and Sevier now fully engaged and united to the southwest, Lacey's South Carolina troops from the Chester District pushed south toward the crest, while Colonel Benjamin Cleveland to the northeast and his Wilkes

County boys were belatedly about to enter the fray on Lacey's left, because he "had the greatest [distance] to go," in the words of Benjamin Sharp, who served in Shelby's Sullivan County regiment.[34] Joseph Phillips, of Surry County, North Carolina, explained how the Wilkes County men of Cleveland's command had tried extremely hard to make up for lost time, after having finally gained their assigned position to launch their assault much later than expected: "Cleveland's regiment rushed rapidly [northeast] along the road under a heavy fire [from the crest] and succeeded in gaining the position assigned" to launch the attack.[35] Therefore, Cleveland "did not occupy his position in the line till late in the engagement."[36]

A tough, hard-nosed veteran of the French and Indian War and an old Indian fighter who had departed Virginia to settle in 1769 in the picturesque North Carolina foothills of the Blue Ridge along the clear waters of spring-fed Roaring River, a tributary of the Yadkin, Colonel Benjamin Cleveland was a tough fighter and a natural leader. He finally gained his designated position with his self-styled and hard-fighting Bulldogs from Wilkes County on the north to Colonel Lacey's left and facing the high portion of the crest on the northeastern edge of the summit, where Ferguson's white tents stood in neat rows according to precise British regulations. Cleveland was also destined to attack to the right of Major William Chronicle and his Lincoln County men once they reached their position facing the northeastern spur. After crossing the spring-fed creek at the mountain's northeastern base where they were fired upon by Loyalists, most likely either the North Carolina or South Carolina militiamen lining the crest, Cleveland was now in his element, despite having earlier played a diplomatic and political role as a Wilkes County representative in the North Carolina Senate. While sitting atop his prized warhorse named Roebuck just before the attack, he had presented his Wilkes County militiamen with his final instructions, ensuring greater tactical flexibility and adaptability that paid dividends against a better-trained opponent:

> My brave fellow, we have beaten the Tories and we can do it again [and] If they had the spirit of men, they would join with their fellow-citizens in supporting the independence of their country. When you are engaged, you are not to wait for the word of command from me. I will show you, by my example, how to fight; I can undertake no more. Every man must consider himself an officer and act from

> his own judgment. Fire as quick as you can, and stand your ground as long as you can. When you can do no better, get behind trees or retreat; but I beg you not to run quite off. If we are repulsed, let us make a point of returning and renewing the fight; perhaps we may have better luck in the second attempt than in the first.[7]

However, Colonel Cleveland's delay in finally reaching his assigned position ensured that Colonels Shelby and Campbell had been fighting "for some considerable time before Cleveland's command could render [them] any aid," because Colonel "Cleveland's command [had been] compelled to ride along the foot of the mountain, three or four hundred yards [northeast] before they dismounted and pressed up towards the enemy."[38] Nevertheless, in Benjamin Sharp's words that revealed how the Wilkes County boys were making up for lost time after an exhausting effort just to reach their assigned position, Colonel Cleveland's "regiment came up in gallant style."[39] With waving sword and shouting at the top of his lungs, the Virginia-born oldest colonel among the attackers at age forty-two was "a big man, often good natured, but reckless [and also] hot tempered."[40] Despite weighing more than three hundred pounds, he was agile and eager to fight in no small part because of his burning hatred of Loyalists, who he viewed as the epitome of evil. With considerable enthusiasm, therefore, he led his men, who were known locally as "Cleveland's Devils," of the Wilkes County Regiment up the slope, yelling, "Yonder is your enemy, and the enemy of mankind!"[41] As brutal as he was deadly effective, the rotund colonel's personal "war philosophy [toward Loyalists] was 'to give them hell'" and hang them to "get them out of their misery."[42]

Also born in Virginia, John Cleveland, the teenage son of Colonel Cleveland, was not far from his father's side during the surge up the slope. He was already a veteran, after serving "very young as a private," before gaining a lieutenant's rank and leading his company with skill.[43] John Cleveland had survived the disaster at Fishing Creek, where Colonel Thomas Sumter's command had been cut to pieces and scattered by Tarleton and his hard-charging British Legion dragoons. Young Lieutenant John Cleveland now led his men with a determination to succeed at all costs. He was respected and beloved by his men, who knew him affectionately as "Devil John" because of his reckless bravery in battle that was exhibited in full at Kings Mountain.[44] Colonel Cleveland's men never forgot their leader's earlier words that continued to inspire them: "Now is the time for every man of you to do his country a priceless service—such as shall lead your children to exult in the fact that their fathers were the conquerors of Ferguson."[45] Before long, the Wilkes County boys encountered a Tory picket on the slope, following him up ever-higher toward the summit when he ran for his life.[46]

But this time, the North and South Carolina Loyalists on the crest of the northeastern summit were ready to receive the Wilkes County attackers, having been alerted to their dire situation by the firing just to the southwest by Loyalists who had earlier blasted away at Cleveland's men when they were moving the long distance through the woods to gain their assigned position. To meet Cleveland's threat from the north near the southwest edge of the northeastern spur and close to the tented encampment, Ferguson was forced to draw his troops farther northeastward along the ridge's open crest, which allowed Shelby's, Campbell's, Sevier's, and Williams's attackers to the southwest to gain more ground along the crest. As in other sectors, Ferguson whistled the notes of instructions with his silver instrument for his well-trained men to realign to meet the new threat on the ridge's north side posed by Cleveland, who had been assigned to fill the open space on Lacey's left. Atop the open crest, Ferguson's troops not far from and just southwest of their main encampment unleashed a disciplined volley that caused damage among the attackers.

Cleveland's horse was hit twice by the hot fire that sent a hail of bullets ripping through the trees and knocking bark off tree trunks, which dismounted the hulky colonel. Undaunted and carrying his favorite sword, Colonel Cleveland immediately reentered the intensifying fray and gamely proceeded uphill at the head of his Wilkes County boys. In the words of Benjamin Sharp: "The Colonel, himself, coming by the very spot I occupied, at which time his horse had received two wounds, and he was obliged to dismount. Although fat and unwieldy, he advanced on foot with signal bravery; but was soon remounted by one of his officers, who brought him another horse."[47]

Likewise, Colonel Lacey's horse was shot from under him while leading his Chester County boys up the slope, but he continued on foot. During the swirling combat that raged across the wooded slope in Cleveland's embattled sector, the three Virginia-born Lewis brothers of Celtic heritage (the family's ancestors hailed from Wales like the family of Colonel Shelby and his brothers), Major Micajah Lewis, Captain Joel Lewis, and Lieutenant James Lewis, were cut down with six separate wounds in total.[48] Thankfully, however, all three of the Lewis brothers were destined to survive their wounds "much to their mother's delight" and everlasting joy.[49] Other men of Cleveland's command were lying in bloody clumps across the slope, including John Field. During the hand-to-hand combat, he had been "stabbed three times, twice in the legs and once in the left breast," but survived to tell the tale of too many close calls to count.[50] At the head of their citizen-soldiers, Captain Minor Smith and Lieutenant Samuel Johnson were also cut down in Cleveland's charging ranks.[51]

Close calls were too plentiful to count during the intensifying conflict. Of course, mounted officers on both sides were the easiest targets. While leading his South Carolina troops, Colonel Lacey's horse was shot out from under him as in the case of Colonel Cleveland.[52] Even more, a bullet whizzed through Lacey's hat to cut through his hair and burn the top of his head, but no blood was shed to fulfill a prophecy of a woman in Charles Town who had told the young man many years before that he would become a mighty warrior who would never shed blood in battle.[53]

Major Joseph Winston's North Carolinians of Surry County Strike the South End of Ferguson's Encampment

Major Joseph Winston, who had battled Native Americans since age seventeen, had a difficult time on October 7 even before getting his sixty Surry County men into action because their special assignment that afternoon had called for riding a considerable distance from the ridge's north side to the south side, roughly south of Cleveland on the ridge's opposite side in "a big right hook" movement. All had seemingly started out well enough, until he was ordered by Colonel Shelby to take possession of a nearby hill on the north to cut off Ferguson's line of retreat and the direct route to the road that led to Charlotte to complete the trap. Therefore, Winston and his men had originally moved in advance ahead of Campbell's column before the first shot had been fired with the mission of riding in a wide arc, before moving into a position to attack from the south on the northeastern summit. However, Winston had become disoriented in the thick woodlands, still in summer-like growth despite the autumnal colors, and secured the incorrect hill, which was part of today's appropriately named Brushy Ridge, as he shortly discovered. After learning of his mistake, Major Winston had then ordered his backcountry men from Surry County and the Yadkin River country forward in a wild dash through the dense South Carolina woods to gain their assigned attack position on the southeast side of the main northeastern spur upon which Ferguson's encampment was positioned, after leaving behind a detachment to guard the correct hill on the north to block Ferguson's retreat to the main road: a crucial mission that ensured Ferguson's doom.[54] Winston, who had been born in 1746 and began fighting for liberty in 1775, led the way up the slope below the tented encampment that dominated the open ground of the spur. Major Winston's Surry County boys, who were advancing between Major McDowell to the southwest and Major Chronicle to the northwest on the east side of the northeastern spur, charged up the slope while aiming at the southern end of Ferguson's encampment that dominated the summit of the commanding spur on the ridge's northeastern end.

In this sector, Captain William Lenoir was in the very "forefront of the hottest" part of the fighting, leading the way up the slope with abandon.[55] Because of his reckless behavior that inspired the Surry County men of Winston's command onward, while unleashing their war cries that echoed through the woodlands, the daring Lenoir "received two wounds from bullets, one in his side and the other in his arm and a third bullet passed through his [long] hair above where it was tied" in a queue that ran down his back in the frontier style of the day.[56]

Major William Chronicle's and Lieutenant Colonel Frederick Hambright's Attack East of the Easternmost Summit

At around three thirty on what had become a warmer afternoon on the northeastern spur's east and north side while encountering the most rugged, steep, and rocky terrain of any attackers, Major William Chronicle's fifty or so men from Lincoln County, North Carolina, belatedly joined the attack—the last to do so around fifteen to twenty minutes or more after Shelby first struck because of the long distance necessary to gain their assigned position. Chronicle's citizen-soldiers attacked on Cleveland's left to the north and on Winston's right to the south facing the northern and eastern slope of the easternmost spur. Like elsewhere along the slopes, the terrain in Cleveland's sector was heavily wooded, covered in fallen logs and large rocks to impede the attack, presenting the most difficulties of the day except in Campbell's case. Most important, all of the Patriot commands were now in position and in action, fighting and advancing up the slopes surrounding Kings Mountain or already atop the crest like to the west, where Shelby's, Campbell's, and Sevier's commands continued to be united in attacking northeast along the crest and toward Ferguson's encampment, while steadily gaining even more momentum.

The Patriot offensive up the slope at the easternmost spur's high point, just east of Ferguson's tented encampment atop the barren summit, began ominously. While Chronicle and Hambright, whose troops mostly faced the eastern side of the northeastern summit but also the northern side, charged both south and west up the slope, Cleveland attacked south and Winston attacked north just southwest of the spur: a sweeping general advance up the slope and toward the ridge's high point on the northeastern spur. The last-arriving troops ensured that the closing of the circle around Ferguson and his entire command was complete, after much effort. Private Robert Henry, sixteen, and one of the South Fork Boys, moved into action when "Enoch Gilmer called on Hugh Erwin, Adam Barry and myself to follow him close to the foot of the hill."[57] They had hardly begun their assault in pushing up the eastern slopes of the easternmost spur when disaster struck at the head of the attackers. Now having been moved northeast by Ferguson to protect the main encampment, a formation of the North Carolina or South Carolina militia, or both, immediately unleashed an effective first volley that swept down the slope. This blistering fire that exploded from the closed ranks of the Carolina militiamen, who were better shots than the Provincial regulars who never benefited from target practice or having been raised on the Western frontier, raked Chronicle's ranks that now included the Lincoln County, North Carolina, militia regiment, which had been relinquished to the major by Colonel Graham's sudden departure.[58]

Leading the way for his South Fork Boys of Lincoln County and hardly having advanced from the ridge's heavily wooded base, Major William "Billy" Chronicle, twenty-five, who hailed from the south fork of the Catawba like his men, was exposed at the head of his troops. He had just yelled to his men to "face to the hill." At this time, Chronicle did not realize that the Loyalists, who were ready to protect their tented encampment atop the summit at the ridge's far northeastern end, had forsaken the tactics of bayonet charges to now rely on concentrated volley firing down the slope: a tactical adjustment made by the flexible Ferguson after he learned of the futility of bayonet charges down the mountain, forcing him to compensate by now depending on the excellent marksmanship of the Carolina boys from the backcountry, which was a wise decision. The nearly aligned ranks of the Carolina Loyalist militiamen defended the commanding top of the northern side of the easternmost spur upon which Ferguson's headquarters—the largest tent in the encampment—stood. The young Patriot major of outstanding promise was instantly killed by a shot in the head: a severe loss for the Lincoln County Regiment because Chronicle was an experienced, popular leader, admired almost as much as the South Fork Boys revered Lieutenant Colonel Frederick Hambright, despite his thick German accent and old-world Teutonic ways.[59]

In a rare account, teenage Private Robert Henry described the moment when Major Chronicle was killed at the beginning of their attack: "Major Chronicle [advanced] about ten steps before us . . . then Chronicle having a military [trihorn or tricorn] hat, but had let [the sides] down to shelter the rain from him, and had it not yet up, clapped his hand to it in front, and raised it up, and cried, 'Face to the hill' [but] The words were scarcely uttered, when a ball struck him and he dropped; and in a second after a [lead] ball struck Wm. Rabb, about six feet from Chronicle, and he dropped" like a stone.[60] William Rabb, one of the South Fork Boys, was a boyhood friend of Major Chronicle.[61]

At age fifty-three and blessed with ample Indian fighting experience, Lieutenant Colonel Frederick Hambright immediately dashed to the front on his charger. With a waving sword, he led the Lincoln County citizen-soldiers toward the smoke-lined summit and through the timber, while a hot fire streamed down the slope with bullets banging off rocks and cutting leaves from the trees. The seriousness of the overall tactical situation when advancing directly toward Ferguson's encampment, where the defense effort had stiffened in defending the summit of the northeastern spur, was also made clear when Private William Rabb fell dead only around six feet away from Lieutenant Colonel Hambright, not long after Chronicle was fatally cut down.[62] Rising to the occasion, the "great-hearted" Hambright bravely led by example, demonstrating inspired leadership in a crisis situation with Chronicle's early fall. Ironically, Hambright had just deferred his seniority to command the Lincoln County Regiment to the more experienced, but younger, Major Chronicle, only to now suddenly find himself in charge. Hambright, now "sorely wounded [by a bullet through his thigh], his boot over-flowing with blood and his hat riddled with three bullet holes, declined to dis-mount, but pressed gallantly forward, exclaiming in his 'Pennsylvania Dutch': 'Huzza, my prave boys, fight on a few minutes more, and te pattle will be over!'"[63]

When Frederick Hambright's South Fork Boys implored him to ride back down the slope to seek medical care before he bled to death on the body-strewn hillside, the feisty "Dutch commander" said: "No poys, I will stay as long as I can sit up."[64] Charging through the trees on the far east and north of the easternmost spur, Chronicle's and Hambright's Lincoln County soldiers could see the neat formation of Loyalists, including the scarlet uniforms of the Provincial regulars, positioned on the open crest against the skyline before their tented encampment, because their outlines were silhouetted on the high ground against the skyline. In fact, in looking south and also west, some advanced attackers in this embattled sector might already have been able to see the tops of some of the white tents located on the far eastern side of the encampment on the open ground of the northeastern spur's summit.

Like previous attacks of the other eight commands, Hambright's and Chronicle's boys surged over the rugged terrain of the mountain's northern and eastern side around the easternmost spur, while rapidly firing from tree to tree in true Indian style. Then, in a repeat of what Shelby and Campbell had originally faced multiple times in attempting to reach the strategic crest on the ridge's other end, the hard-hitting American Volunteers, who were supported by Carolina militia and led by the brave Captain Abraham De Peyster, poured down the slope to drive them back down the hill. Remarkably, this was the eighth counterattack (three had hit Shelby, three had struck Campbell, and one had hit Sevier) that once again revealed the characteristic up-and-down pattern of intense combat and Loyalist courage. Desperation was now especially high among the defenders because of the urgent need to protect Ferguson's headquarters, sprawling tented encampment, and supply train of seventeen wagons.

Major Chronicle's Lincoln County men, including brothers Captains John and Charles Mattocks before John was killed in the attack, faced some of the day's toughest opposition, especially Captain Abraham De Peyster's attack with the bayonet. Once again, the Loyalists were repulsed like the previous seven times, when Major Ferguson blew his long whistle of instructions for his men to return back to the top of the mountain. However, Patriot losses were lighter than expected because the volleys sweeping down the slope continued to be mostly off target—except in the case of Chronicle's sector when the major had been early killed and other casualties were inflicted with the first volley—because the Loyalists, who had been trained by the book by Ferguson, still had not sufficiently adjusted their aim in the tricky business of firing downhill, when the concept of massed volley firing without aiming dominated the thinking of generations of British leaders, including the Scottish major. Fifteen-year-old Private James Collins, from Lincoln County, one of the South Fork Boys under Chronicle, felt extremely fortunate that the enemy's fire in his sector sailed too high after the initial accurate volley, writing how "the shot of the enemy soon began to pass over us like hail; the first shock was quickly over; and . . . I was soon in a profuse sweat. My lot happened to be in the centre [on the north], where the severest part of the battle was fought [and in] climb[ing] the hill . . . were fiercely charged upon and forced to fall back to our first position; we tried a second time, but met the same fate; the fight then seemed to become more furious. Their leader, Ferguson, came in full view, within rifle shot as if to encourage his men, who by this time were falling very fast but he soon disappeared" to other threatened sectors to blunt the howling attackers, who were now on all sides after having surrounded the mountain.[65]

Indeed, despite the loss of their revered major, the young men and boys from Lincoln County had first stood their ground to meet the "shock of the charge" of the American Volunteers and "a number of their men were shot down or transfixed" by bayonets, while "reserving their fire until the charging column was only a few feet away [and] poured in a deadly fire" before retiring down the slope as planned not once but twice.[66] Virginia-born Captain David Vance, of Scotch-Irish descent, described how Ferguson "ordered his regulars . . . to charge bayonets on Major Chronicle's South Fork Boys. The regulars, having discharged their muskets at a short distance with effect, in turn the Fork Boys discharged their rifles with fatal effect, and retreated, keeping before the points of the bayonets about 20 feet, until they loaded again, when they discharged their rifles, each man dropping his man. This was [harsh] treatment British courage could not stand."[67]

Caught in the swirl of the vicious combat, Private Robert "Bob" Henry described battling Indian-style among the trees and boulders, writing how "we advanced up the hill close to the Tory lines; There was a log across a hollow [where] I stood my stand by, and stepping one step back, I was safe from the British fire. I there remained firing until the British charged bayonets. When they made the charge, they first fired their guns, at which fire it is suppose they killed Capt. [John] Mattocks and J. Boyd, wounded Wm. Gilmer and John Chittim [and] the Fork boys fired and did considerable execution" to the attackers under Captain De Peyster.[68] Henry, only fifteen and one of Chronicle's (now Lieutenant Colonel Frederick Hambright's) South Fork Boys from Lincoln County, was charged by one Loyalist with a leveled bayonet extended to inflict maximum damage. In Henry's words, when in the act of hurriedly attempting to fire in sheer desperation:

> In the act of cocking my gun when his bayonet was running along the barrel of my gun, and gave me a thrust through my hand and into my thigh; my antagonist and myself both fell. The [South] Fork boys retreated and loaded their guns. I was lying under the smoke and it appeared that some of them were not more than a gun[']s length in front of the bayonets, and the farthest could not have been more than twenty feet in front when they discharged their rifles. It was said that everyone dropped a man. The British then retreated in great haste and were pursued by the [South] Fork boys.[69]

After having been bayonetted through the hand and thigh, young Robert Henry had managed to shoot and kill his attacker when they tumbled down together among the virgin timber and rocks lining the slope. However, the weight of the dead Tory pinned the diminutive Henry, who was not yet fully grown and could not move under the Loyalist's weight, to the ground. Fortunately, the Loyalists did not prevail in the sector at that time to finish Henry off with jabbing bayonets while he lay helpless on the rocky slope. Instead, a comrade, William Caldwell, found the trapped teenager and pulled the dead Loyalist off him and then "had to kick Henry repeatedly to loosen the bayonet."[70] In Henry's words: "Wm. Caldwell saw my condition and pulled the bayonet out of my thigh, but it hung to my hand; he gave my hand a kick and went on. The thrust gave me much pain, but the pulling of it was much more severe."[71] Robert Henry was surprised to only then ascertain what deadly work his final shot into the Loyalist had caused, because "the load [of buck and ball] must have passed through his bladder and cut a main artery, as he bled profusely."[72]

Also certainly related to Private Robert Henry, Virginia-born William Henry, who was married to Scotch-Irish Isabella McKeown and lived only three miles from Kings Mountain, entered the battle with four of his sons.[73] The early loss of Major Chronicle north of the easternmost spur was a significant psychological blow to his militia command and reduced its overall combat capabilities. The Lincoln County command, consequently, was the only unit on this bloody afternoon that failed to gain the strategic summit. Fortunately, none of the other eight commands, or divisions, lost their commanders until one near the end of the battle, Colonel James Williams: another key reason for the remarkable Patriot success that afternoon.[74]

Gradually Tightening the Tactical Noose Around Ferguson

After much effort, Colonel Shelby's ambitious strategic plan of surrounding Ferguson was finally complete, when all nine commands were fully engaged in their respective positions. Joseph Phillips, in Cleveland's Wilkes County regiment, described how "our forces around the mountain formed an oblong square" that followed the topography of the lengthy ridge in the process of surrounding Ferguson's entire command, whose position along the crest was gradually shrinking according to Shelby's plan.[75] All in all, the systematic surrounding of the Loyalist command had been only a matter of time after the turning of Ferguson's left flank, because the repeated Loyalist counterattacks, at least eight and perhaps more, off the high ground had been repulsed in every sector and every Patriot command and their leaders had never given up and just kept coming up the slope with wild yells and weapons blazing. Indeed, not long after three thirty, the Patriot commands surrounding Kings Mountain were on the move on every side of the crest and steadily gaining ground. Elation among the Patriot troops was soaring, while the elements of the Loyalist North and South Carolina militiamen and the highly touted American Volunteers were gradually pushed ever-farther northeastward—first down the highest part of the ridge on the southwest across gently sloping ground and then when the ridge's crest began to rise toward the strategic northeastern spur—under the heavy pressure, heading toward the tents and covered wagons positioned atop the northeastern summit of the spur.

Indeed, the onrushing Overmountain and backcountry men continued to scream their Indian war cries, while "continuously firing upward [both in first surging up the slope and then in gaining the crest and continuing the attack northeast along the open ridge], found easy marks for their aim in the clearly delineated outlines of their adversaries; and felt the exultation which animates the hunter who has tracked to his lair and entrapped wild game at bay."[76] Inspiring his Washington County, Virginia, citizen-soldiers, Colonel Campbell continued to lead the way in the very forefront of his troops, while surging northeastward along the top of the open ridge and parallel to it (in the woodlands and mostly on the ridge's south side) with Shelby's and Sevier's Overmountain men. In the words of Benjamin Sharp who never forgot his commander's inspirational example: "During the heat of the action, I saw Colonel Campbell . . . ride backwards and forward in the advance of our lines, in the space between us and the enemy, with his sword in hand," while yelling "Boys, remember your liberty!"[77]

Colonel Shelby described the all-important early uniting of his Sullivan County men and the Washington County boys under Sevier to the southwest in a key moment that promised decisive victory, which had fueled the push northeastward: "Col. Sevier reached the summit about the same time with Shelby [and] They united and drove back the enemy [while] Cleveland's and Campbell's columns were still pressing forward, and firing as they came in" to apply even heavier pressure.[78] Shelby's and Campbell's men continued to be considerably mixed by this time, while steadily advancing northeast along the ridge with everyone loading and firing on the run while steadily closing in on Ferguson's encampment. After his horse had been shot, Colonel Campbell was still leading the way at a considerable distance before his Virginia attackers in an audacious manner, endangering himself not only from the enemy's fire, but also from that of his own men and those of Shelby's and Sevier's soldiers, who were blasting away as fast as possible. An animated Campbell, who was enjoying his finest hour, continued to turn and shout encouragement to his men during the push toward the northwestern edge of the smoke-shrouded summit, sensing that a great victory was drawing closer: "Boys, remember your liberty! Come on! Come on! My brave fellows; another gun [fire]—another gun [fire] will do it! Damn them, we must have them out of this!"[79]

Ironically, Colonel Campbell's loud shouts of "liberty" to his Virginians certainly rang hollow to his mulatto slave, Broddy. In his shirt sleeves and in common dress much like the white soldiers who accepted him as an equal on the battlefield and in the fields where they worked side-by-side, Broddy had been ordered by Campbell to tend to his black horse, Bald Face, while the animated colonel led the way. However, Broddy's curiosity got the best of him like his desire to kill a Loyalist. He rode forward not only to see the fighting for himself but also to engage in it. He perhaps saw fellow Blacks, except that they were free men and fought for that cherished freedom at a time when England dominated the world's lucrative slave trade, fighting in the ranks like Private Andrew Ferguson of Campbell's command.[80] Battling for America and risking his life, Broddy actively took part in the battle at some point and fought beside the white soldiers after Colonel Campbell gave his rifle "to his servant man," in the words of Captain James Keys of the Virginia Regiment, just before the fight had erupted in full fury.[81]

Destined to be wounded three times on this bloody afternoon during the showdown in the South Carolina Piedmont, Leonard Hice of Captain James Dysart's company of Campbell's regiment represented the tenacity that ultimately spelled victory on this decisive afternoon: "I shot 16 rounds [and] the way that I fought after my arm was broken was to rest my rifle against a tree and take sight."[82] A Virginia veteran of the hard-fought Battle of Point Pleasant in October 1774 like his brother Captain William Bowen who was now sick, Lieutenant Reece Bowen commanded a company of Virginia boys. At age forty and an experienced woodsman and scout for Colonel Campbell's Washington County militia regiment in which his son Private John Bowen also served that bloody afternoon, Reece revealed a diehard resolve that could not be broken. He now commanded his company of Virginia citizen-soldiers with skill and inspired leadership, encouraging everyone onward. Unlike his more methodically advancing comrades dodging from tree to tree, Reece Bowen boldly charged up the slope like a man possessed without showing caution or taking any cover. When his friends and neighbors of southwest Virginia called for him to be more careful, Bowen responded, "Take to a tree—no! Never shall it be said that I sought safety by hiding my person, or dodging from a Briton or Tory who opposed men on the field."[83]

However, Lieutenant Bowen had underestimated his opponent, as if assuming they were typical Britons armed with the notoriously inaccurate Brown Bess musket, which was certainly not the case. He failed to realize that he faced skilled marksmen, especially among the Carolina Loyalists, who hailed from the backcountry and were far better shots than the Shawnee warriors at Point Pleasant. Not long after the lieutenant had brazenly informed his comrades of his undying contempt for the enemy, he was struck in the chest by a well-aimed shot and was killed.[84] Reece Bowen was destined to be buried on Kings Mountain, where he fell to rise no more and still lies to this day in an unmarked grave at some unknown location.[85] Leading his company, Captain William Lenoir, who lived in the fertile valley of the Upper Yadkin River, which rose in the Blue Ridge and flowed deep into the wilderness of the North Carolina backcountry, a hardened veteran of the 1776 Cherokee campaign, and who suffered two wounds that afternoon, described how "I noticed one particular instance of bravery. On hearing a man within six feet behind me fall, I look around, and at this instant another soldier jumped at him saying, 'Give me your shot-bag, old fellow!' his own ammunition being exhausted. The gallant patriot gave him, with his dying hand, his ammunition."[86]

The confusion and chaos of battle along the wooded slopes and open crest in the Patriots' determined and frantic drive northeastward was intense. The limited visibility under the high canopy of tall trees half-hidden by dense battle smoke caused close calls among fellow attackers since the antagonists looked much the same, both physically and in regard to civilian attire, as the Loyalist militiamen, who wore tricorn hats like the American Volunteers. When Private Charles Bowen, the thirty-one-year-old brother of Lieutenant Reece Bowen and a member of Captain William Edmondson's company under Colonel Campbell's command, which continued to advance northeast along the crest, heard that Reece had been killed, he flew into a panic. He began frantically searching the body-covered slope for Reece in the hope that he might only have been wounded. He feared the worst when he found his dying captain, William Edmondson, who had been shot in the head by a sharp-eyed Loyalist marksman. Bowen scoured a wide area but without success, moving ever northeastward along and parallel to the crest. Instead of finding his brother, Bowen found himself near the northwestern edge of the smoke-wreathed summit and harm's way, because he was now a good distance before Colonel Cleveland's attackers ascending toward the northeastern summit and only around twenty paces from Ferguson's men. On foot, Colonel Cleveland therefore thought that Bowen was a Loyalist militiaman, after he called for the countersign of "Buford" (the chosen revenge-laden name in reference to the Waxhaws disaster at the hands of Tarleton) and received no response. Bowen, who had temporarily forgotten the countersign, now became an inviting target at close range. Fortunately, however, Cleveland's long rifle misfired, which might well have saved Bowen's life in the smoky confusion. A perplexed Bowen then thought the colonel, who wore no insignia as an officer, was a hated Loyalist, rushed him, and grabbed him by the collar. When about to tomahawk Cleveland with one savage blow, a soldier named Buchanan, of Scotch-Irish descent, thought quickly, grabbing Bowen's extended arm in the nick of time, because he just happened to know both men on sight. Suddenly remembering the countersign after his close call, Bowen then shouted, "Buford!" Colonel Cleveland and Private Charles Bowen then hugged each other in the midst of a raging battle, thanking God for their mutual deliverance. After all, they had "narrowly and unwittingly been restrained from sacrificing each other" in the thick woodlands filled in layers of choking battle smoke that resulted in numerous hand-to-hand encounters of a bloody nature.[87]

Lieutenant Samuel Johnson, one of Cleveland's tough Bulldogs from Wilkes County, displayed his bulldog tenacity like Private Leonard Hice and the Bowen brothers in the swirl of intense combat. In charging up the slope and exchanging fire with sharp-eyed Carolina Loyalist marksmen and leading his men onward, Johnson's leather hunting shirt, or frock, was pierced by multiple bullets without touching the skin. No doubt Lieutenant Johnson now believed that he had a charmed life after having survived these close calls, unlike a number of nearby comrades. However, fate had a different outcome in store for the North Carolina lieutenant. Johnson, a savvy veteran of the 1776 Cherokee campaign, was shortly felled by a bullet in the stomach. Ignoring the pain and bleeding both internally and externally, Lieutenant Johnson still possessed the fighting spirit to encourage the men onward up the slope waving his hand, while yelling, "Huzza, boys!"[88]

All the while during the raging battle that left Kings Mountain wreathed in thick white clouds of drifting smoke, the shrill sounds of Ferguson's silver whistle could be heard echoing at various defensive points along the open crest and then especially on the northeastern summit, where he was destined to make his final stand. The various signal commands blown from Ferguson's silver whistle (actually he possessed two whistles, one long and the other one shorter) had allowed his men to maneuver, shift positions, and counterattack more swiftly to meet multiple threats over an extensive area, especially on both sides of the strategic crest unlike shouted commands that could not be heard for long distances amid the noisy confusion, shouting soldiers, and loud crackle of gunfire.[89] Meanwhile, the onrushing tide of Shelby's, Campbell's, and Sevier's men continued northeast along the crest and through the woods adjacent and on both sides of the open crest and ever closer to the summit of the northeastern spur situation on higher ground. Most important, they were finally joined by the newly arriving troops of Williams, Lacey, and Cleveland who emerged from the wooded slopes on the north to gain the strategic crest: a vital union that additionally fueled momentum and timely concentration of strength that only increased the feeling of confidence, while all but dooming Ferguson and his surrounded command, which was in the process of being cornered on the northeastern summit.[90]

Indeed, Kings Mountain was completely surrounded by seemingly endless numbers of howling and fast-firing Patriots on the move all around the northeastern spur: The center to the North-East was occupied by Cleveland with his Bulldogs, Hambright with his South Fork Boys, from the Catawba . . . and Winston with his Surry Riflemen; to the South were the divisions under Joseph McDowell . . . who was in touch with Winston, Sevier, and Campbell; while the South Carolinians under Lacey, who was in touch with Cleveland [on the left to the east], the Rowan [County, North Carolina] levies under Williams" during the attack.[91] To his credit, Major Ferguson provided inspirational leadership for the dwindling numbers of defenders, who had been hit hard by the accurate fire pouring from the blazing long rifles, and they were paying with their lives for his bold decision to hold tight to his prized hill in the middle of nowhere. The Scottish major was seen "rapidly dashing from one side to the other, oblivious to all danger [and] Wherever the shrill note of his silver whistle sounded, there the fighting was hottest and the British resistance deadliest" on the hill of death.[92]

Ireland-born Colonel William Hill described the fundamental flaws of Major Ferguson's tactical reasoning and ill-fated choice of tactics: "Ferguson was a brave military character [but] it appeared that he was infatuated & brought to his own ruin by choosing this spot of ground on which he had to fight under every disadvantage as it will appear from the following revelation—there being a small flat of ground [on the summit of the northeastern spur] where he had pitched his camp on, the sides of the mountain being very Rocky & steep as well as a great number of fallen and standing trees so that the Americans could attack his camp on all quarters, and their shot went over the Americans without effect, his infatuation would more fully appear when it is known that he trusted much to the bayonet."[93] Colonel Hill's astute tactical views were in agreement with those of Colonel Shelby. In Shelby's words: "Ferguson did all that an officer could do under the circumstances . . . But his position, which he thought impregnable against any force the patriots could raise, was really a disadvantage to him. The summit was bare, whilst the sides of the mountain were covered with trees."[94]

Major Ferguson had made a host of basic tactical mistakes from the beginning which made his defense of the high ground a losing proposition. Having been caught by surprise and never imagining that he could possibly be overpowered by the detested "barbarians," he had failed to laager his tented encampment before the battle with his seventeen wagons in a circle for protection. He fought the battle conventionally, as if he were facing untrained and inexperienced Southern militiamen on the open field of Camden. Consequently, he was most astounded that his bayonet attacks by his finest troops had brought no decisive results, while resulting in an unsustainable amount of losses and the loss of morale.[95] Such fundamental tactical errors were now compounded by the fact that the Loyalists' supply of ammunition was rapidly diminishing, thanks to inaccurate volley firing—the British Army's emphasis on the importance of volume of fire over accuracy to soften the enemy up for the bayonet charge—according to regulations and seemingly endless training of his Loyalists by the diligent Scotsman. And most of all, because Kings Mountain was now surrounded and under the onslaught of nine Patriot commands that were performing together like clockwork, Ferguson's troops lacked a central point or concentration—a vital center of gravity—to attack in order to inflict a decisive blow because the attackers were now coming fast from every direction and were swarming seemingly everywhere like angry bees.

Merely counterattacking to drive the howling attackers back down the slope at isolated points along a lengthy line had been nothing more than mere pinpricks: a tactical dilemma that ensured Ferguson had early lost the initiative and control of the battle, which was now swirling with a will of its own and reaching new heights of ferocity. Ironically, the unleashing of Patriot attacks in a staggered manner at different times and at different points along the ridge (of course, not part of Shelby's original battle plan), especially on both sides, had made it impossible for Ferguson to inflict a decisive blow. He simply faced too many threats from too many different directions that kept continuing to create a truly impossible tactical situation for Ferguson, whose offensive efforts had been insidiously sabotaged and diffused by the Patriots.[96] In the words of Captain Abraham De Peyster to Cornwallis regarding the disastrous situation that ensured that Ferguson's defeat was only a matter of time: "Their numbers allowed them to surround our post and ours was sufficient to form only a single line on top of the hill."[97]

All the while, the raging battle steadily grew in intensity as the Patriots of nine commands poured from every point of the mountain to apply heavy, unrelenting pressure that continued to increase, while the hapless Ferguson and his command were completely surrounded. The bitter engagement intensified and become bloodier, resulting in greater confusion in the heavy timber.

Even identifying the enemy continued to be a problem as the battle progressed in the smoky confusion, which caused additional chaos. Consequently, the Patriots had pinned pieces of white paper on their hats and wore white handkerchiefs as scarves around their heads for identification purposes, but this was not enough. Meanwhile, the Loyalists, except the American Volunteers and the detachments of other Provincial units, were dressed much like their opponents in frontier and backcountry homespun, because they were members of the same class and sometimes from the same neighborhood. In consequence, the Tories of the North and South Carolina militia had placed pine twigs—this was mostly pine country—in their tricorn hats for identification purposes. However, the lack of such necessary identification and the failure to make visual distinctions among many soldiers on both sides often resulted in tragedies, when Patriots killed and wounded fellow Patriots in the confusion of close-quarter fighting.[98]

With these ad hoc identifiers, the ugliest realities among opposing family members were played out in full on the timbered slopes of Kings Mountain. Indeed, hard-fighting "relatives turned their back on wounded kin whose scrape of paper or pine twig did not match their own."[99] America's first civil war should also have been called the brother's war, and this fact was repeatedly witnessed in grim fashion during the brutal slugfest on Kings Mountain. For instance, Colonel Shelby viewed the ultimate horror of a family tragedy when two brothers from opposing sides sighted their weapons on each other and simultaneously pulled their triggers. Each man then tumbled over dead from a direct hit without ever knowing that he had killed his own brother.[100]

Revealing the desperation of this conflict, the fighting spirit failed to diminish even among wounded Patriots. As mentioned, Colonel Shelby's younger brother, Moses, went down with a wound early in the fight. However, he gamely continued the spirited tradition of this hard-fighting Welsh clan. Exhibiting the Shelby family's feisty fighting spirit after he had been assisted down the slope to a small creek at the foot of the mountain with a nasty thigh wound, Moses Shelby was still full of spunk. He sat with his back to a tree with his flintlock, or long rifle, that was most likely a Deckard weapon of choice, at the ready, just in case Ferguson's men advanced down the slope with fixed bayonets. When he spied one Patriot returning from the fight too frequently for a drink at the creek and drinking too slowly during lengthy periods of rest, clearly a ruse to not perform his soldiery duties, an angry Moses yelled a stern warning to the faint-hearted soldier that "he would shoot him himself if he came again" for water.[101]

As the attackers neared the high ground of the northeastern spur and Ferguson's encampment, a new round of close quarter—often no quarter among the trees and thick underbrush—swirled near the embattled summit, because the Loyalists had continued to be forced into smaller and more compact formations from the relentless pressure that had no end and as the result of high losses. In Colonel Cleveland's Wilkes County ranks at the northeastern edge of the spur's summit, Lieutenant Charles Gordon charged up the slope to overrun a Loyalist position among the trees. He overpowered one Loyalist officer, disarmed him in a hurry, and then began to drag him downhill by his long hair like a Viking raider dragging off an English or Irish maiden during a raid in the Middle Ages. But Gordon's prized prisoner suddenly pulled his flintlock pistol, a .62 caliber smoothbore weapon, from his leather belt and fired a shot into the lieutenant's arm. An enraged Gordon then hacked the defiant Loyalist with his sword held by his one good arm until he killed his fellow American.[102]

Drawing to a Bloody Climax on the Northeastern Summit

For all practical purposes, the Battle of Kings Mountain had been determined in the very beginning because of the high quality of Patriot leadership, Major Ferguson's long list of errors and miscalculations, and especially after the turning of his left flank on the southwest. And now Shelby's straggling tactical noose, as had been agreed upon by all the colonels, was being slowly tightened on all sides of the mountain with each passing minute, ensuring that the end of Ferguson and his command was drawing nearer with each yard gained by the attackers in surging ever closer to the summit of the easternmost spur. Indeed, the beginning of the end of the entire Loyalist command had actually come when they began to retire northeast along the open crest toward their tented encampment after losing possession of the crucial high ground of the strategic southwestern spur: effectively, the critical systematic turning of Ferguson's left flank. All the while, Private Thomas Young continued to blast away "with effect" and enthusiasm beside his comrades of the 2nd Spartan Regiment during the relentless drive that pushed the Loyalists closer to their tented encampment on the open ground: the second highest on Kings Mountain.[103]

An Overmountain fighting man named Bailie Peyton perhaps said it best in regard to the battle's fast-approaching climax, when "the mountain appeared volcanic; there flashed along its summit, and around its base, and up its sides, one long sulphurous blaze. The shouts of the mountaineers, the peals of hundreds of rifles and muskets, the loud commands and encouraging words of the respective officers, with every now and then the shrill screech of Ferguson's silver whistle high above the din and confusion of the battle, intermingled with the groans of the wounded in every part of the line, combined to convey the idea of another pandemonium."[104] As mentioned, Colonel Shelby, with drawn saber and leading the way as usual, rode boldly into the thickest part of the fight to lead his troops toward the northeastern summit and the decisive victory that he could already clearly envision. Loyalist officers slashed at the conspicuous leader with sabers and enlisted men jabbed at him with steel bayonets meant to pin Patriots to the ground in death agonies, but Shelby was somehow unharmed.[105]

With their commands intermixed, the onrushing troops of Colonels Shelby, Campbell, and Sevier continued to advance northeastward and along the gradually rising ground of the narrow, open ridge leading to the high northeastern spur, while loading and firing on the run along the ridge's considerable length to draw closer to the summit in the ridge's northeastern corner topped with white tents on the largest and widest stretch of open ground on Kings Mountain. Here, as noted, Ferguson's tented encampment and supply, ammunition, and baggage wagons were not yet aligned in a defensive position, which would only come later when it was too late.

During a close-range firefight, the Loyalists, not only Provincial regulars but also Carolina militiamen, continued to steadily give ground under the relentless onslaught, while retreating up the gradually rising ground toward their main camp and leaving their dead and wounded behind them along the open crest now carpeted with broken bodies and shattered dreams. Meanwhile, other Patriot units, beginning with Colonel Williams (originally positioned on Shelby's left to the northeast) on the north and Major McDowell (originally on Campbell's right to the northeast) on the south and on both sides of the ridge, also gained the strategic crest and then joined the advance of Shelby's Holston River country men, Campbell's backcountry Virginians, and Sevier's Overmountain Wataugans: an ever-increasing amount of heavy pressure with no letup that continued to force the hard-hit Loyalists to retreat northeast up higher ground where they hoped safety could be found, while Ferguson's men were caught in multiple deadly cross fires.[106] In consequence, the spirits among the attackers skyrocketed even higher, because they sensed that the most dramatic of victories was about to be won. Each time the Loyalists turned after briefly making defensive stands and were then shortly forced to retreat farther to the northeast, the sense of elation among the attackers increased with the knowledge that they were definitely winning the hardest-fought battle of their lives and one that would make history.

Desperate Loyalist Defensive Stand at a Rocky Ledge Undone by Shelby's Timely Flanking Movement

Numerous small rocky outcroppings along the slope and near the top of the lengthy ridge were the best natural defensive positions for the reeling Loyalists to take cover, offering ideal places to make defensive stands. Consequently, the "outcropping boulders upon the outer edge of the plateau afforded" good protection on the northeast that helped to briefly stabilize the defensive effort, providing shelter for Ferguson's hard-hit men at various points. However, the rocky outcropping located on the ascending ground of the ridge's southern slope just before Ferguson's encampment before the summit's southwestern edge stood as the most formidable of these rocky obstacles to the fast-moving onslaught of Shelby's, Campbell's, Williams's, McDowell's, and Sevier's attackers surging northeast.

Because Campbell's onrushing Virginia troops were mostly pouring up the southern slope, this ledge on the southern slope posed a formidable challenge. This strong natural position of the Loyalists in an increasingly desperate situation was described as a rocky ledge, which provided ideal cover for the most determined defensive stand during the latter stages of the battle.[107] This "ledge of rock skirts the summit of the mountain on the south side [and] formed a natural breastwork for the enemy, behind which they could lie with their heads only exposed, and leisurely take aim at our troops [mostly Campbell's men since he commanded the largest number of troops on the southern slope] on that side."[108]

Virginia-born Ensign Robert Campbell, twenty-five, described how the Loyalists were formed "on top of the mountain, behind a chain of rocks that appeared impregnable, and had their wagons [which were finally utilized by Ferguson out of desperation] drawn up on the flank across the end of the mountain, by which they made a strong breastwork," which served as an emergency last-ditch defense when the surging tide of Patriots were pouring northeast along the ridge and toward the tented encampment.[109] As revealed by Silas McBee, a member of Colonel Williams's South Carolina command, this was the last place—the "rocky ramparts" of the Loyalists—before the imposing summit of the northeastern spur on its southern side. Here, the desperate defenders concentrated to make a defensive stand from an excellent natural position—the last of the rocky ledges or outcroppings on the southwestern side of the summit before the tented encampment.[110] In McBee's words: "Some of the Tories at the West end of the summit [the southwestern edge of the spur on the southern slope before Ferguson's encampment] were secured among some table or bench rocks."[111]

In this case, McBee choose an improper word in using *secured*, because it was here that the Loyalists made their most determined defensive stand that was destined to last an estimated twenty minutes: about one-third of the time of the entire Battle of Kings Mountain, but this time period might have been exaggerated.[112] Daunted by the sight of the formidable defensive position that stood mainly before Colonel Campbell's Virginians on the southern slope before the northeast spur, Ensign Robert Campbell described this "chain of rocks that appeared impregnable" at first sight.[113] Because of the defender's tenacity for an extended period at the rocky ledge, these especially lethal Loyalists at this point were almost certainly a part of a contingent of the thirty-five crack Loyalists who fired rifles instead of muskets. They already had been smartly utilized by Ferguson as sharpshooters throughout the afternoon to keep the attackers at bay and shoot Patriot officers off their horses. Since they were formidable fighting men and expert shots, almost certainly these Loyalists had been ordered by Ferguson to hold this rocky position that provided a natural breastwork in a last desperate defense of his encampment.

Overturning the pervasive myth that only the Patriots possessed sharp-eyed marksmen, these expert Loyalists were under the command of Ireland-born Captain David Larmier, who hailed from Cuffeytown Creek, South Carolina. He had been previously ordered by Ferguson to bolster the defense of the exposed right flank to protect the encampment on the east. These Tory marksmen under this unsung and forgotten Irishman had joined Ferguson only two months before. Captain Larmier had won the major's confidence, and he and his men now gave an extremely "good account of themselves."[114] Partly verifying as much, another rare account has revealed that these especially stubborn Loyalist defenders of the rocky position were commanded by a "Tory

Captain and a party under him [who] stoutly" defended their craggy perch with tenacity.[115] This "Tory Captain" was almost certainly Larmier, who was an exceptional officer and a determined fighter in the Celtic tradition like most of the men he opposed.[116]

As the attackers learned the hard way, the accuracy of the Loyalist marksmen at this key defensive point should not have been surprising because "many of the Tory militiamen from North Carolina were as skilled frontiersmen as their Patriot enemies."[117] For instance, Jonas Bedford was a French and Indian War veteran who served in the Loyalists' ranks, and he possessed ample warfighting skills. Like his fellow Americans on the other side, Bedford fought with skill at Kings Mountain, and he battled in part to save Loyalists who "were Condemned by the Americans to Death."[118] Clearly, a number of Ferguson's tactical decisions, especially the earlier deployment of sharpshooters from beginning to end at various threatened points to bolster his defense of the high ground, were wise and well conceived, especially this defensive stand at the rocky ledge before the northeastern summit of the spur. By this time, Campbell's, Shelby's, Sevier's, Williams's, and McDowell's troops had already overwhelmed more than two-thirds of the lengthy ridge in having pursued northeast a long distance along the open crest and on both heavily wooded sides of it. Almost certainly, it had been the increasingly desperate Major Ferguson who had ordered members of the North and South Carolina Loyalist militia to take cover with the Irishman's marksmen behind the rocky ledge that lay on the southern slope on the southwestern side of the spur before his tented encampment. In addition, he was now relying on the crack American Volunteers to act as a strategic reserve—another wise decision—in protecting the encampment on the high ground under serious threat from all sides since these New York and New Jersey troops were better trained, disciplined, and equipped than the Loyalist militia from the Carolinas.[119]

The Patriots' thorough utilization of Indian-style fighting skills continued to pay immense dividends throughout this bloody afternoon, including even now in the desperate effort to overwhelm the final natural obstacle before Ferguson's encampment. At this point, Major Ferguson's best defensive position was this rocky ledge, which was held by an especially determined band of Loyalists. These veterans, consisting of some of the finest marksmen in Ferguson's command, rapidly blasted away from the excellent cover of the rocky ledge, which presented a most formidable challenge to the attackers during their surge northeast. Indeed, the swarming tide of onrushing Patriots had seemed unstoppable until encountering this defensive stand, which halted them in their tracks. In the understated words of Ensign Robert Campbell, who had migrated to the Holston River country in 1771 and was a veteran of numerous Indian campaigns, about the tenacious defensive stand of the sharp-shooting Loyalists behind the rocky ledge: "The enemy annoyed our troops very much from their advantageous position."[120]

In the traditional histories of the Battle of Kings Mountain, the focus has always been on the superior quality of Patriot marksmanship, while overlooking the fact that the backcountry and frontier Loyalist militiamen, including Captain Larimer's sharpshooters who have been almost entirely forgotten and have long been absent from books about the battle, consisted of excellent marksmen: ironically, frontier fighting men for the king who were well schooled in pioneering and wilderness experiences like the attackers. In consequence, these backcountry Loyalists were expert shots, especially when armed with the fast-loading and fast-firing Ferguson rifle, which now might have been the case, especially when positioned in their seemingly impregnable defensive position at the rocky ledge. After all, these North and South Carolina backcountry men of the Tory militia had early learned to fire a weapon with accuracy to not only put food on the table, but also in regard to surviving the perils of Indian warfare. No one more than Major Ferguson had early appreciated the excellent qualities of the backcountry Loyalist militiamen, who were "very fit for rough & irregular war, being all excellent woodsmen, unerring shots."[121]

Indeed, these expert Loyalist marksmen blasted away with great accuracy, resting muskets atop the rocks and ledge to steady their aim. All the while, additional Patriots were cut down by their blazing fire, effectively halting the charge of Shelby's, Sevier's, Campbell's, Williams's, and McDowell's men, who were now forced to hurriedly take cover behind trees and rocks, stopping their relentless push northeast up the crest that steadily ascended toward the summit. As usual, Colonel Shelby rose to the occasion. For the first time that afternoon, the attackers' momentum fueled by their sweeping success in pouring north-east had been blunted by the formidable defensive position and the defenders' accuracy for a lengthy period of time. A master in the art of wilderness warfare and Indian fighting, Shelby hurriedly developed a new set of tactics on the fly. In overall terms, the fast-thinking frontier colonel, who had mastered all of the tactical tricks after years of battling numerous tribes of Native Americans, including in their own home country, knew exactly what to do, after he had intently surveyed the Loyalists' rocky position.

After all, almost exactly six years to the day in another beautiful October and in another crisis situation when battling Indian-style, Shelby had likewise risen to the fore to overcome a comparable tactical obstacle at the Battle of Point Pleasant on October 10, 1774. Here, in the deep autumnal forests at the intersection of the Ohio and Kanawha Rivers and when a young lieutenant in his father Evan's company, which he had then commanded because Evan Shelby Sr. had taken a higher command because of escalating casualties, Isaac Shelby had played a key role during the turning point of the day-long battle. At this time, the Virginians' advance had been effectively thwarted by a log and underbrush breastwork (ironically, exactly what Major Ferguson should have created in the beginning to defend his encampment) constructed by the Shawnee and Mingo warriors atop a commanding ridge. At that time, Shelby and his company of Virginia frontiersmen had outflanked the strong Shawnee position, firing down on the warriors behind their lower defensive position from a higher ridgetop that they had gained after a frantic climb to reach a commanding perch to minimize the damage as soon as possible and turn the tide of battle.[122]

In much the same way, the ever-energetic Colonel Shelby now went to work with his usual tactical insights, after hurriedly devising a plan to outflank the strong Loyalist position at the rocky ledge in a bid to eliminate the most "destructive fire [that] was kept up from those rocks."[123] John Sawyers, who was now one of Shelby's best captains, had been a key player in Shelby's flanking movement through the woods that had resulted in winning the day—perhaps the hardest-fought battle of the Indian Wars up until that point—at Point Pleasant, when he had risen to the fore as the orderly sergeant of Evan Shelby Sr.'s command of frontiersmen.[124]

In a hurry, Colonel Shelby now rode over to the colonel's brother, Ensign Robert Campbell, to present him with the key assignment of outflanking the rocky ledge during a crisis situation. Because Shelby's Overmountain men were advancing northeast parallel to the ridge on the north and Campbell's Virginia men were attacking northeast mostly on the ridge's south side, the rocky defensive position of the stubborn Loyalists was in Campbell's area. Shelby needed to eliminate the defenders of this rocky perch near the crest as soon as possible to spare his men from a punishing flank fire, which would have riddled the command's right flank on the south, or nearest the crest. Significantly, Shelby continued to play the role of overall commander, while Colonel William Campbell was merely the nominal leader of this small task force that had been handed by fate one of the most important missions of the American Revolution.

Therefore, Colonel Shelby dispatched Ensign Campbell with a small party of expert marksmen—around forty sharpshooters of not only the best Virginia marksmen but also some expert snipers of his own Overmountain command, like Joseph Culbertson—through the thick woods to the right to outflank the rocky ledge defenders from the south. He also led the way to show the Virginia ensign exactly where to strike the blow for successfully outflanking the rocky ledge. Ensign Campbell's flanking party of Virginians and some chosen Overmountain men advancing alone through the smoky woodlands caused one nervous citizen-soldier to ask Colonel Shelby, "What! Are you taking us there to be marks for the enemy?" which was quickly answered by a more confident comrade, "No, to make marks of the enemy." Meanwhile, the small party of marksmen kept moving downhill through the trees to their right, or south, for more than forty paces of the rocky ledge to finally gain a secluded position on the enemy's left flank to the south down the slope, while the busy Loyalists were occupied in firing away at attackers before them in a hot firefight.

To his shock, Ensign Campbell and his forty men now discovered:

> that our men were repulsed on the other [north] side of the mountain, he gave orders to advance, and post themselves opposite to the rocks, and near to the enemy, and then returned to assist in bringing up the men in order, who had been charged with the bayonet. These orders were punctually obeyed, and they kept up such a galling fire as to compel Ferguson to order a company of [provincial] regulars [under Ensign John McGinnis] to face them, with a view to cover his men that were posted behind the rocks. At this time a considerable fire was drawn to this [south] side of the mountain by the repulse of those on the other [north], and the Loyalists not being permitted to leave their posts. This scene was not of long duration, for it was the brave Virginia volunteers, and those under Col. Shelby, on their attempting rapidly to ascend the mountain, that were charged with the bayonet. They obstinately stood until some of them were thrust through the body, and having nothing but their rifles by which to defend themselves, they were forced to retreat [but] They were soon rallied by their gallant

> commanders, Campbell, Shelby, and other brave officers, and by a constant and well-directed fire of their rifles, drove them back in their turn, strewing the face of the mountain with their assailants, and kept advancing until they drove them from some of their posts.[125]

However, before outflanking the rocky ledge, Ensign Campbell had been nearly killed. From a spur within only forty paces of the enemy's left flank behind the rocks, Campbell and his forty marksmen had utilized their "advantageous position for directing a constant and effectual fire upon the backs of a body of Ferguson's troops which lay guarded in front by the ledge of rocks."[126] These troops were Provincial Rangers under Ensign John McGinnis, who had been dispatched by Ferguson. At such a close range, the first volley of massed firepower fired by the American Rangers had resulted in quite a few close calls. Ensign Campbell had been nearly killed when Ensign McGinnis ordered his first volley unleashed by his American Volunteers because the eruption of fire caught him by surprise. Campbell had "expected to be shot through by several bullets at once," when he saw that the volley was about to be fired from the crest because he was caught out in the open. However, the hail of bullets had soared too high, tearing through the trees, dropping bark, autumnal leaves, and wooden splinters down upon him like rain. Ensign Campbell had then taken careful "aim at the shoulders of McGinnis." Campbell's aim was true, and McGinnis was cut down with a mortal wound.[127] Ensign McGinnis's attack had then shortly pushed Campbell's Virginia men back a short distance, before Campbell's citizen-soldiers then abruptly turned to riddle the attacking American Volunteers with their own hail of bullets to force the Loyalists to retreat. Then, Ensign Campbell led his men back to their advantageous position on the spur to rake the Loyalists behind the rocks from the rear in compliance with Colonel Shelby's original tactical design.[128]

Meanwhile, the resurgent troops before the rocky ledge continued to blast away, and the defenders were hit by a frontal and rear fire from Ensign Campbell's sharpshooters. Silas McBee, only fifteen and having been raised at Thicketty Ford deep in the South Carolina backcountry, described the bitter struggle for possession of the last rocky ledge. Here, the fighting raged with the stubborn Loyalists, who continued to be solidly positioned behind "some table or bench rocks [and] Whenever one popped up his head, a ball from some unerring rifle of the mountaineers pierced through" his head.[129] This was no exaggeration in regard to the lethality of the Patriot fire because "upwards of twenty were [later] found dead after the battle among the rocks, their heads being thus pierced with bullets."[130]

Indeed, at long last after around twenty minutes of intense combat at close range, many Loyalists, including almost certainly the Irish immigrant Captain Larimer who fell seriously wounded from a shot likely fired by Josiah Culbertson of Colonel Shelby's Sullivan County command, had been cut down. This, combined with Shelby's timely flanking movement and the fire of Ensign Campbell's marksmen, who had by now "resumed their galling fire [at close range] upon the back of Ferguson's men," proved decisive. They finally forced the stubborn Tories from the rocky ledge in a hasty retreat northeastward along the open ridgetop and toward the higher ground of the northeastern summit and their encampment.[131] Now, the troops of Shelby, Campbell (who was fighting "in his shirt sleeves"), Sevier, McDowell, and Williams and other attackers continued onward with high-pitched screams after having hurled the Tory sharpshooters from the rocks, pushing northeast up the crest toward the ridge's highest point, where the white tents of Ferguson's encampment glistened in the sun just ahead. At this time, the open crest of Kings Mountain "was covered with flam and smoke and seemed to thunder" like a true Patriot storm that was rapidly descending upon the ridge's northeastern corner and the increasingly desperate Major Patrick Ferguson.[132]

Colonel James Williams, who had belatedly joined the attack northeastward after having reached the crest to Shelby's left, had sworn a deep "vow that he would silence the whistle of Ferguson, whose shrill, clarion notes rang out above the din of battle, and [had repeatedly] brought the wavering Red Coats to the charge" down the wooded slopes.[133] To exploit the added advantage after the advance resumed once the rocky ledge defenders were routed from their rocky perch, Colonel Shelby then ordered Ensign Robert Campbell and his small party of marksmen "to form on a spur of the mountain front [on the crest's north side], and retired. I there kept up a fire on the enemy until they retired [northeast] to their main body" closer to their encampment, wrote Ensign Campbell.[134]

Meanwhile, after the attack was once again resumed northeast toward Ferguson's encampment, Captain John Sawyers once again rose to the fore in confronting the next challenge, when Campbell's Virginia attackers pursued the withdrawing Loyalists too quickly and without caution, as if sensing that decisive victory had already been won after the rout of the rocky ledge defenders, which was certainly not the case. A Loyalist volley at close range suddenly erupted after Ferguson had ordered the ranks realigned and a defensive stand made to protect the threatened western edge of his encampment. This blistering fire caught the Virginians at close range and by surprise, causing heavy losses. All the while, the tactically astute Captain Sawyers watched the Virginia boys getting cut to pieces, but realized that he had an opportunity. Displaying tactical ability as he had learned from having long battled Native Americans, especially at Point Pleasant, Sawyers ordered his company of Sullivan County boys of Shelby's regiment to charge, when only twenty-five paces from the Loyalists who had unloaded muskets in their hands, having just unleashed their volley. When the men of nearby companies saw Sawyers's bold charge to catch the enemy by surprise, they too attacked to spark a general offensive effort in this embattled sector: a most timely and long-forgotten turning point that forced the Loyalists even closer to Ferguson's tented encampment atop the summit.[135]

Relatives on Opposing Sides Met in Mortal Combat in America's First Civil War

The greatest tragedies of all continued to be played out in full by the accidental meeting of relatives on opposite sides, because familial roots and connections were so deeply intertwined in the backcountry: At least seventy-four sets of brothers and twenty-nine sets of fathers and sons fought on the Patriot side alone, but probably even more due to the incompleteness of records and the lack of accurate documentation. Hailing from Tryon County, North Carolina, four of the five Goforth brothers—two Patriots and three Loyalists—were killed, including John and Preston Goforth who were among the attackers.[136] And four Logan brothers of a Scotch-Irish family from Lincoln County, North Carolina, fought each other at Kings Mountain: Joseph, a Baptist preacher, and William Logan on the Patriot side faced John and Thomas Logan, who were members of Ferguson's command. William Logan was killed by a bullet that tore through a hollow chestnut tree that he was hurriedly loading his weapon behind in preparation for the next shot, while Thomas Logan went down with a badly broken thigh in the hail of lead.[137]

Because of the final rush on all four sides of the northeastern spur while Major Ferguson's heavily pressured lines continued to constrict under scorching fires that rapidly dropped defenders, it was now inevitable that even more relatives on opposing sides met face-to-face in close combat situations. For instance, Private Thomas Young of Colonel Brandon's 2nd Spartan South Carolina Regiment described how "just after we had reached the top of the hill, Matthew [McCrary, who was a Loyalist of Scotch-Irish descent] saw me," and then the two cousins embraced with emotion, after "Matt" tossed down his flintlock musket for fear "he might shoot a member of his family." Teenage Private Young thought differently and continued to fight, after angrily shouting at Matthew "to fight or get out of his way."[138]

Described as "a brave youth of nineteen," Private William Twitty, a stepson of Colonel William Graham, who had suddenly appeared to everyone's surprise and entered the battle to lead his Lincoln County, North Carolina, militia after having earlier excused himself from the impending battle because of urgent affairs at home, proved to be a deadly fighter among the timbered slope. A hero of the defense of Graham's Fort on Buffalo Creek in the backcountry during the past summer and one of the South Fork Boys, Twitty had just witnessed the death of one of his friends. Unknown to the North Carolinians, the Loyalists atop the open crest at this point were North Carolina Loyalists. He concealed himself behind a tree and hunted the man who had killed his friend, whose puff of white smoke from his musket had betrayed the Loyalist's presence behind an ancient tree. Twitty then aimed his rifle at the tree's edge where he had seen the smoke and patiently waited, while maintaining a steady aim and praying for just one single opportunity for the sharpshooter to poke his head from behind cover. Shortly, the Loyalist's head appeared from behind the tree and Private Twitty killed his man with a quick, well-aimed shot. He only later discovered that his victim was none other than an esteemed Lincoln County neighbor who had been instantly killed by Twitty's small-caliber bullet that neatly passed through his head.[139]

Witnessing the horrors of this civil war that exceeded the nightmare of Indian fighting, especially when it came to family members now at each other's throats, Colonel Shelby never forgot how "two [opposing] brothers, expert riflemen, were seen to present [weapons] at each other, to fire and fall at the same instant."[140] During the heat of combat, one Patriot brother noticed a fire coming from a hole that had been bored through a hollow chestnut tree—a natural camouflaged firing position that proved most effective for cutting down attackers. The Patriot, consequently, repeatedly fired at the hole at a frantic pace for several minutes, knowing that a sharpshooting Tory, who was an excellent shot, stood on the other side. After the battle, he investigated the targeted position and then found his dead brother on the other side of the hole.[141] This shocking realization at the sight of the blood-streaked body of his brother caused the grief-stricken soldier to become "almost deranged in consequence."[142]

When Captain James Withrow was asked by his seriously wounded brother-in-law, a Tory by the name of Branson, for help when lying near the summit among the bodies of his comrades, the stern-faced officer from the backcountry retorted with angry contempt: "Look to your friends for help!"[143] Captain John Mattocks, who was one of the South Fork Boys, which included his brother Captain Charles Mattocks of a hard-fighting clan in which the backcountry men were "uncommonly stout," met his Maker at Kings Mountain while battling against the hated Loyalists, which included his brother Edward Mattocks. Edward Mattocks fell with a severe wound, which provided the bloody tonic that "cured [him] of his Toryism."[144] Another close brother team of fighters encountered their own family tragedy on the bullet-swept slopes of Kings Mountain. Born at Carr's Creek, Rockbridge County, Virginia, in 1744, of Irish immigrant parents, Captain David Beattie, a fine veteran officer with Indian fighting experience, served with his brothers John and William in the ranks. In search of a better life, the Beattie family had moved to the unruly and dangerous frontier of Washington County, Virginia, in 1772. As a sad fate would have it—leaving a widow, a cousin named Mary, and three grieving children back home—John Beattie received his death stroke on the mountain that continued to rapidly consume and end the lives of many young men and boys on both sides.[145]

Chapter VII

Bitter Struggle at the Mountain's Northeastern Summit, Loyalist Discipline Breaks Down

Meanwhile, the bulk of Cleveland's Wilkes County attackers finally gained the northwestern, northern, and northeastern edge of the plateau at the ridge's far northeastern end to link with Shelby's, Campbell's, Sevier's, McDowell's, Williams's and other attackers, who continued to advance along the ascending open crest and the adjacent woodlands toward Ferguson's camp to the northeast: the gradual fulfillment of Colonel Shelby's ambitious plan of sealing the fate of the hated Major Ferguson and his entire command by surrounding and trapping them on the mountain's northeastern corner.[1] Despite being handicapped by limited knowledge because of the lack of visibility in the woodlands, Joseph Phillips, who was one of Colonel Cleveland's boys from Wilkes County, described the tactical vise that was rapidly closing on the last section of high ground of the summit atop the spur, after the "British and Tories were driven [northeast] along the top of the mountain and then finding Sevier's [and Williams's] command coming up the north-western slope in their rear and Cleveland's on their right flank" to tighten the arms of the tactical trap around Ferguson's entire command like an anaconda.[2]

Even more, Benjamin Sharp, who hailed from the Holston River country and had first joined the fight at age fourteen in the war's beginning, and other attackers saw that Cleveland's attack caught the Loyalists in the right flank and Sevier's and Williams's men blasted away into their rear, while Campbell and Shelby still confronted the Loyalists along the open crest during their steady push northeast up the increasingly higher ground, which "threw the British and Tories into complete disorder, and Ferguson [now began to see] that all was lost," especially the collapse of the rocky ledge defensive stand.[3]

Although belated, the arrival on the northeastern, northern, and northwestern edge of the summit by Colonel Cleveland's fast-firing men, who blasted away with long rifles and smoothbore flintlock muskets loaded with deadly "buck and ball," was also decisive. Perhaps Benjamin Sharp said it best of the timely arrival of Colonel Cleveland and his North Carolina men: "After some time the British turned the weight of their fire [on the foremost attackers along the open crest to the southwest on the lower ground] and perhaps would have succeeded in breaking our lines, but [the commands under Shelby and Sevier and Campbell's Virginians and other troops] were instantly supported by Colonel Cleveland's regiment" from Wilkes County.[4]

Indeed, this was a key tactical development that not only eliminated the Loyalists' last slim avenue of escape but also added to the already heavy concentration of Patriot firepower that now poured from every direction to decimate the Loyalists, including flank fires and cross fires, while the attackers steadily closed the pincer arms of the tactical trap to completely surround Major Ferguson's command in a death grip. This trap had closed ever tighter when Patriot "troops on the right having gained the summit of the eminence, obliged the enemy to retreat along the top of the ridge to where Col. Cleveland commanded, and were there stopped by his brave men."[5]

The final cost of cornering the hard-hit Loyalists on the summit at the ridge's northeastern end had been high. In Campbell's sector alone, Major William Edmondson described the difficult and bloody process of steadily pushing the hard-fighting Loyalists toward their camp, up the ascending ground while hurling aside successive Loyalist defensive stands, including at the final rocky ledge: "They were again driven back a small distance, and rallied a second [time], and then a third time."[6] Serving with Captain Andrew Colvill's company of Campbell's command of backcountry Virginians and describing the hardest fighting in pushing northeastward, Lieutenant Samuel Newell wrote how the Virginians received "two partial checks" in the form of tenacious Loyalist defensive stands, including by the North Carolina militia and also by the Tory sharpshooters at the rocky ledge that stood before the western edge of the easternmost spur.[7] Colonel William Campbell wrote on October 20, 1780, how his Virginians "drove them [northeast] along the summit, nearly to the other end [of the ridge], where Col. Cleveland with his country men were" reaching the spur's smoke-shrouded summit to increase the strength and soaring morale of the attackers.[8] This "last charge" of Colonel Campbell's Virginians, who were intermixed with mostly Shelby's and Sevier's men, was "the longest and warmest that I witnessed," wrote Lieutenant Newell.[9] By that time, the ammunition of the North Carolina militia was nearly "exhausted [and] they were obliged to give way," as Surgeon Uzal Johnson penned in his journal after the lengthy struggle.[10]

All the while, additional Patriots continued to reach the open crest and then turned to attack northeast along the ridge's crest and the wooded ground on either side of the exceptionally narrow ridgetop that ascended toward the summit, while unleashing flank fires that inflicted severe damage on the Loyalists, especially the North Carolina Loyalists whose ammunition was running dangerously low by that time. In the words of Arthur Campbell, who described the battle's turning point: "The enemy was crowded, making their retreat to the other end [and eventually] were driven into a huddle by meeting the fire of Col. Williams' division, they received a heavy fire" that dropped more Loyalists with lethal shots that could not miss their easy targets.[11]

Colonel Williams's South Carolina soldiers raked the dense formations of North Carolina and South Carolina Loyalists deployed along the open crest to present lucrative targets, forcing them ever farther northeast up the open crest toward the summit of the eastern spur.[12] Elated officers at the head of the Patriots' onslaught across the open crest that surged northeastward continued to encourage everyone onward with shouts of "Hurrah my brave fellows! Advance!"[13] Not long after the last stand defenders at the rocky ledge had been pushed aside when decimated by Ensign Robert Campbell's flank fire, discipline collapsed when the neat formations of the Loyalists broke under the heavy cross fires that steadily escalated in volume because larger numbers of Patriots continued to arrive on the broad firing line with the surrounded Loyalists on the crest trapped in a vise that continued to close. In the words of James Crow of Campbell's Virginia command: "Our fire now became very warm, and in a few minutes they broke and retreated [northeast] towards their tents."[14] Dr. Uzal Johnson described the falling dominoes that resulted in the turning of the tide that caused the collapse of discipline when the "North Carolina [militiamen who had exhausted their ammunition] having quit their line, it hove the others into confusion and the Enemy (whose Numbers enabled them to completely surround us) encouraged by the confusion of our Militia rushed on" with wild shouts, while firing on the run.[15]

In a letter, Andrew Creswell, who was one of Campbell's Virginia attackers, described the rout and chase of the defeated foe who was fleeing northeast up the open crest toward the relative safety of their encampment on the double, writing how after "I discharged my gun [and] I waited for nobody" in chasing after the routed Loyalists.[16] The North Carolina Loyalist militia had fallen back not only because they had expended most of their ammunition, but also the mounting fear that their attackers would give them no quarter and the relentless pressure and hot fire from every side that drove them rearward like cattle and without order toward their tented encampment.[17] With the Loyalists on the run, additional Patriots, especially Colonel Cleveland's belated attackers from Wilkes County, continued to steadily reach the summit of the edge of the high plateau. A desperate Ferguson formed his hard-hit troops in a rectangle alignment, or hollow square, along the high ground of the open summit before his tented encampment and facing the woods, now full of fast-firing Patriots, on every side to confront the onrushing attackers, who were coming at them with wild screams while loading and firing on the run. Here, Ferguson ordered his men, who had been hastily assembled in formation, to unleash volleys as they had been trained, once again proving largely ineffective against "swarming tactics" of men rapidly firing from behind trees and logs and wasting even more of the ever-decreasing amounts of precious ammunition.

Forgotten Struggle Around the Wagons

One of the battle's greatest ironies was not unlike the tragedy that befell British troops during the Anglo-Zulu War at the Battle of Isandlwana in Zululand, when the attacking Zulu warriors on January 22, 1879, achieved an astounding victory by destroying their interloping foe nearly to the last man. What resulted was one of the greatest disasters (more than 1,300 men of the British Army were killed) in British history, largely because the encampment's defenders ran out of ammunition and had not corralled their wagons on the open ground of the summit. A comparable disaster occurred at Kings Mountain when first the North Carolina and then the South Carolina Loyalists began to run out of ammunition because of Ferguson's overreliance on unleashing massed firepower in regular volley while firing in formation from the high ground. In the confusion of battle and never believing that his men would not prevail with the unleashing of repeated bayonet charges, the Scottish major had neglected to order details of men to bring up extra reserves of ammunition that now filled some supply wagons, along with 1,200 new Brown Bess muskets. This considerable cache of thousands of paper cartridges wrapped around lead balls and black powder charges now lay only a short distance away in most of the seventeen covered wagons of Ferguson's supply train positioned next to the tented encampment—in part, the reason why the ammunition wagons had not been earlier circled to protect the encampment for fear that they might explode from Patriot rifle-fire.

An abatis of felled timber—green wood was needed to prevent it from catching fire—built around the encampment atop the open plateau would have immeasurably assisted in the last defense of the high ground. However, Ferguson had arrogantly rejected such a wise defensive precaution, despite the easy access and availability of the surrounding woodlands from which an impregnable abatis could have been easily created in short order to keep the howling tide of attackers at bay, especially at the highest part of the ridge on the opposite spur nearly six hundred yards to the southwest: a situation that had partly led to the turning of Ferguson's left flank, which all of the Loyalist counterattacks and volley firing had been unable to prevent.[18] But because of the extent of the crisis situation and having been pushed farther northeastward until they had nearly reached the western edge of their tented encampment, the desperate Loyalists belatedly attempted to create an ad hoc defense at the wagons on the western edge of the plateau when the attackers were practically atop them, just west of the neat rows of white tents: a classic case of too little, too late.[19]

In the words of John Craig when he reached the ridge's northeastern summit with the rest of Campbell's Virginia men: "They had formed something like a hollow square out of their wagons [which] presented the appearance of a temporary breastwork."[20] Ensign Robert Campbell, who was encouraging his Virginia boys onward toward the open summit, wrote how Major Ferguson and his men "had their wagons drawn up on their flank across the end of the mountain, by which they made a strong breast-work."[21] Ensign Henry Dickenson never forgot the dramatic sequence of events that had resulted in the turning point when the Loyalists on the crest "broke and retreated upon the Mountain where they halted again a few minutes but on our advancing and firing, they continued their retreat to the wagons and halted behind them, which were on the summit of the Mountain."[22]

Major Ferguson had one last tactical trick up his sleeve in his defense of the line of wagons, after realizing that this defense was going to be a losing proposition. The wagons aligned to protect the west end of the encampment could be easily outflanked since the Loyalists were surrounded, and there were not enough wagons to create a wider circle for all of his men. Here, Ferguson developed a two-tier defense in depth with a formation of Provincial regulars and Carolina militiamen aligned before the wagons facing west to protect the camp's western end. If this hastily established defensive line broke, then the American Volunteers and other defenders could fall back only a short distance and fight under or beside the row of wagons. Ferguson possessed a clever plan for the staggered defense of the wagons on the summit's western edge. He had ordered his defenders on the west before the wagons to reserve their fire until the attackers drew close: deliberately baiting them to advance closer and with greater confidence. He then ordered a close-range volley to be fired. At this time, the Patriots, who noticed the diminishing amount of return fire, especially massed volleys, were now taking relatively few losses, assuming that the Loyalists were almost entirely out of ammunition, which was the case with the North and South Carolina militiamen. In truth, however, Ferguson had ordered his men with rounds, principally the crack American Volunteers, to now rely on a "reserved fire" tactic by holding their fire for a longer time than usual to fool the Patriots and only again opening fire when the attackers were practically atop them to deliver an especially punishing blow.

Thus, the Patriot attack of weary and thirsty men on an increasingly hot day was haphazard and disorganized in a rush toward the disciplined Loyalist formation protecting the wagons on the west side of the encampment—a distinct advantage for the Loyalists that could be exploited in full because the Provincial regulars, after their last volley, could now reload more quickly with the Brown Bess than the long rifle and faster than the attackers could cover the distance between them and the Loyalist formation. Patriot Captain John Sawyers clearly saw how the disorganized mass of attackers would lose their desperate race to reach the Loyalist line before Ferguson ordered another volley to be delivered. Consequently, Captain Sawyers had prudently ordered his company not to join the wild attack. While the frontier captain, one of the best and most experienced officers in Shelby's regiment and one of the colonel's top lieutenants, had saved the lives of his men, Sawyers watched the unfolding tragic drama with regret. The disorganized charge with everyone racing forward in a reckless manner had been just what Major Ferguson had expected. Therefore, "near the place of the wagons, brought many of our men level with the British and their reserved fire, which was then discharged in its horizontal direction, did fatal execution in our ranks at that place" just before the line of wagons.[23]

However, ignoring their most recent losses, the Patriots demonstrated their resilient qualities by once again launching a new attack. By that time, the day's total losses and increasing panic among the Loyalists, with ammunition completely out, were so great and the pursuing Patriots were so close behind them that not even the newly created line of wagons, for a defense facing west toward the open crest, served as an effective defensive position. Virginian Henry Dickenson, of Campbell's Virginia regiment, described the encirclement: "We soon drove them down to the end of the mountain, where I suppose they were met by the troops [Cleveland's Wilkes County men] sent around to that quarter."[24] According to one account, Moses Shelby was one of the attackers in the forefront and he and some other men "leaped upon the wagons of the enemy's breastworks," but he shortly fell wounded.[25]

All the while, Colonel Cleveland's attackers continued to strike from the northwestern, north, and northeastern edges of the embattled summit, fueling greater momentum that forced the Loyalists deeper into their encampment.[26] Meanwhile, additional Patriots, who were yelling and firing like crazy, continued to gain the crest and the northeastern summit, while unnerving additional Loyalists who seemed about to be crushed by the onslaught from all sides. The determined push of onrushing Overmountain and backcountry attackers, who looked "like so many devils from the infernal regions," in the view of one astounded Loyalist, continued to be too much for the five hundred untrained North Carolina militiamen who had recently joined Ferguson.[27] The combination of inexperience and the lack of ammunition had ensured the complete undoing and rout of the North Carolinians in the face of the relentless "swarming tactics" of the elated Patriots, who could now sense the kill, and the hard-hit Loyalist militiamen, who were running low on ammunition, fled to their tented encampment.[28] The pressure increased on the reeling Loyalists after Colonel Cleveland's Wilkes County gained the crest and added their fire to that of Shelby's, Campbell's, Sevier's, McDowell's, Williams's, and Lacey's men. All the while, consequently, the volume of Patriot fire increased to reach a deafening din, while Loyalist fire steadily decreased from spiraling losses and low ammunition.[29]

At this point, the contest was the "last desperate grapple [with both sides] within thirty or forty yards of each other; and was the most hotly contested part" of the action.[30] Robert Campbell described the murderous volume of fire unleashed upon the Loyalists, who were now only concerned about self-preservation and surviving the brutal battle, "a constant and well-directed fire of their rifles, drove them back" to where there was no escape, the encampment.[31] The sight of the Carolina Loyalists retreating rapidly into their tented encampment fueled the Patriots' hunter and killer instincts. Therefore, hatred of the enemy reached an even higher level, with everyone loading and firing ever faster while charging onward on the smoke-wreathed summit. While waving his saber to encourage his Lincoln County boys onward, David Dickey of Colonel Graham's command, now led by Lieutenant Colonel Hambright after Major William Chronicle had been killed, expressed the representative mood of around nine hundred enraged Patriots on the verge of winning one of the most dramatic victories of the American Revolution, screaming "Damn the Tories!"[32]

Even the most steadfast Loyalists, the Provincial regulars upon whom the Patriots had specifically concentrated their fire because of their bright red coats rather than the civilian-dressed Loyalists of the Carolina militiamen, began to waver after the large number (originally around five hundred men in total) of raw North Carolina boys, exhausted and with no rounds remaining in leather cartridge boxes, continued to flee before the attacking and screaming swarm of "shirtmen" and entered their encampment in a jumbled mass of panicked men. The shock among the Loyalists, now staring at defeat or worse when they had only recently believed that they could not fail, was extreme, because of how quickly seemingly everything had turned against them, despite their best efforts. In a letter to his father, Evan Shelby Sr., Colonel Shelby described the overall evolution of the climactic battle: "They had taken post at that place with the confidence that no force could rout them; the mountain was high, and exceedingly steep, so that their situation gave them greatly the advantage; indeed, it was almost equal to storming a battery. In most cases, we could not see them until we were within twenty yards of them. They repelled us three times with charged bayonets; but being determined to conquer or die, we came up a fourth time, and fairly got possession of the top of the mountain," and then ascended upon the northeastern spur with abandon.[33]

Like at the Battle of Point Pleasant on another hot October day, Shelby won another extremely hard-fought battle largely because of his decision to "give them Indian play."[34] Loyalist Samuel Williams described the panic that spread like wildfire: "Numbers being without ammunition gave way, which naturally threw the rest of the militia [first the North Carolinians and then the

South Carolinians] into confusion."[35] Private James Collins, only fifteen and hailing from Lincoln County, wrote how the attackers on "the left and right had gained the top of the [ridge and] the enemy were completely hemmed in on all sides, and no chance of escaping."[36]

After having put up a good fight until their ammunition was exhausted, the panicked North Carolina militiamen had already disrupted the disciplined ranks of the American Volunteers, who were aligned in a neat formation, in their wild flight. In the words of one: "Tho the officers cut some of them down [with their swords], they intermixed themselves with our detachment, and broke us in such a manner that we could no longer act" in an organized and disciplined manner.[37] In a letter, Private Andrew Creswell, a member of Captain Andrew Colvill's Virginia company of Colonel Campbell's regiment, described how "I ran [northeast and up the open crest toward the summit] without a halt" all the way to the enemy's encampment like everyone else in the glow of victory.[38] Inspirational leaders, including noncommissioned officers, led the way like Lieutenant Samuel Newell. Henry Dickenson, one of Campbell's Virginia boys, never forgot the sight of Samuel "Newell, a little before we got to the wagons, on horse-back, his thigh very bloody from the wound he had received, encouraging the men to advance," and he continued leading the way to the defensive line of wagons.[39]

In a letter to Cornwallis, Captain Abraham De Peyster described the sequence of the disastrous rout that sealed Ferguson's doom: "The left on seeing us broke gave way, got all in a crowd on the Hill"—the open plateau at the ridge's northeastern end.[40] The undisciplined and untrained North Carolina militiamen from Tryon County had been the first to break and fled in panic, causing confusion among the Provincial regulars and South Carolina militiamen, all of whom were terribly exposed to accurate fire from every direction on the open ground of the tented encampment, where they concentrated for the final time at about mid-point of the rows of white canvas tents that offered no protection from the hail of bullets fired from the long rifles. Indeed, with a surging tide of fierce-looking and screaming homespun attackers pouring in from all sides and rushing through rising clouds of whitish smoke, while loading and firing rapidly, the hard-hit Loyalists, falling to multiple fires from four directions, huddled together in their camp in a milling crowd of desperate, fearful men, who had lost discipline under cross fires and flank fires.[41]

Knowing only too well that the end was finally near, unlike the hard-fighting major from Scotland and demonstrating considerable good sense, one of Ferguson's mistresses, Virginia Paul, who had already seen a random shot earlier snuff out the life of Virginia Sal, prudently deserted him and his doomed command. She smartly fled the embattled high ground, dashing away from the ill-fated encampment surrounded by howling Patriots on horseback. A Patriot officer on the wooded slope detained her and then learned about Major Ferguson's appearance and his exact location and even the fact that his large headquarters tent was located at the camp's eastern end.[42]

Playing his last high card, Ferguson relied upon his best commander, Captain Abraham De Peyster, and his finest troops, the surviving King's American Volunteers, or Provincial Rangers, to somehow reverse the tide. He ordered another massed volley to be fired at the interlopers who were overrunning the northeastern summit with wild screams and maintaining a heavy fire. In the words of Thomas Young: "We now had the Enemy huddled up on the top of the Mountain; they wheeled to fire a platoon [volley that whistled] over us, some of our men ran back, but I was too much fatigued to run. They fired, but without effect."[43] Still defiantly refusing to surrender while seemingly countless attackers continued to descend upon his command trapped on the northeastern summit, Ferguson then ordered a final counterattack from the crack Provincial regulars. But it was already too late. Ensign Robert Campbell described Ferguson's desperation in attempting to bolster the few scattered pockets of resistance, which were all under intense pressure and at the point of completely collapsing, on the summit: "Ferguson being heavily pressed on all sides, [had earlier] ordered Captain [De Peyster] to reinforce some of the extreme posts [on the ever-shrinking perimeter] with a full company of British regulars [and] He marched, but to his astonishment when he arrived at the place of destination, he had almost no men, being exposed in that short distance to the constant fire of their rifles."[44]

James Crow, who was one of Campbell's feisty fighters, described the dramatic sequence of events in his sector, evidently on the south slope at the summit's southwestern edge, near the end of this desperate fight for survival in regard to the surrounded Loyalists, whose desperation had reached a new high: "They tried to form before they got to their tents, but only a few formed."[45] Watching in shock, Major Ferguson could hardly believe the sight of the thorough decimation of his command in short order by the hail of fire from the deadly long rifles. He then turned to Lieutenant John Taylor, who commanded Ferguson's only force of cavalry of around twenty horsemen. But it was already too late to do anything. Ensign Robert Campbell described the tragedy of a swift decimation when Ferguson "then ordered his cavalry to mount, but to no purpose [because] As quick as they were mounted they were taken down by some bold marksmen," who did not fail to hit their targets.[46] Meanwhile, larger numbers of Patriots continued to compress the reeling Loyalists "into an indefensible hollow [or lower saddle] on the northeast section of the spur," where they were raked by fire from both above and below and seemingly from every possible direction and angle.[47] At that time, the attackers knew that the end of Major Ferguson and his command was near, while steadily closing in "for the kill."[48]

Major Ferguson's ignominious end was about to conclude the distinguished career of one of Cornwallis's top lieutenants that was destined to send shockwaves across America. Then, in the words of Silas McBee, not long after "Cleveland and Williams appeared on the northwest side, and gave one or two fires . . . the [white] flag was hoisted after which, even, some fired" both by deliberate design and accidentally because of an unawareness of surrender attempts in the noise, confusion, and smoky haze or not knowing of the meaning of the white flag or not caring in the least.[49] At that time, emotions were running exceptionally high and adrenaline was flowing through the veins of the disorganized throng of attackers, who were thoroughly convinced that the Loyalists were nothing less than "the enemy of mankind!"[50] Meanwhile, after all offensive and defensive efforts had failed with a greater loss of lives, the surviving mass of Loyalists then fled even farther east through the tented encampment that offered no place for a defensive stand and toward Ferguson's headquarters at the camp's eastern edge. At last, Major Ferguson and other desperate officers hurriedly formed their available men just beyond, or east of, their tents near the eastern end of the summit. James Crow described how "after passing their tents [in flight eastward] around sixty yards, they formed and fired a few rounds [and] Here they found themselves surrounded" and without hope of any kind.[51]

Major Ferguson's Last Charge

To quell the desperate appeals, including from his most respected officers, to surrender and white handkerchiefs hoisted without his authority or consent, an enraged Ferguson was forced to take even more drastic action. Despite zero chance for success, Ferguson was determined to fight to the bitter end at whatever cost, including his own life if necessary. Demonstrating their diehard resolve, Major Ferguson and fellow officers rode along his increasingly shrinking formations of desperate Loyalists to cut down with sabers several raised white flags, including handkerchiefs tied to the tops of Brown Bess muskets that had suddenly appeared among his defeated men. As if feeling that he was invincible, Ferguson had pressed his luck by remaining in the forefront and on the firing line all afternoon, after already having two horses shot from under him while riding along the open crest to inspire his men. With the day's most severe crisis at hand, the Scottish major, who could not have been more desperate, now saw only one solution to his most daunting challenge and dilemma: leading a final bayonet charge down the timbered slope north of the body-littered summit, where resistance appeared the most thin in a final bid to reach the main road to Charlotte.[52] To the very end, Major Ferguson remained true to his word, because he had loudly boasted how "I will never surrender to such a damned banditti as the mountain men."[53] Therefore, when Captain Abraham De Peyster first suggested to Ferguson that it was time to capitulate, Ferguson rejected the proposal out of hand with an air of angry contempt and disgust. All in all, Ferguson's "efforts on the battle-field seem[ed] like a mad rush against fate; for his position was indefensible against the peculiar tactics of the frontiersmen [while] the line was drawn tighter and tighter around the trapped and frantically struggling army. . . . The game was caught and bagged," because no hope remained for Ferguson and his surrounded men.[54]

Indeed, after Captain De Peyster's last failed counterattack with the best remaining troops and in the words of Ensign Campbell, Major Ferguson, who was mounted on a white charger, "then ordered his cavalry [relatively few men under Lieutenant John Taylor] to mount, but to no purpose. As quick as they were mounted, they were taken down by some bold marksmen. Being driven to desperation by such a scene of misfortune, Major Ferguson endeavored to make his escape, and with two colonels [Vezey Husbands and Daniel Plummer, who were also fated to be shortly shot 'out of their saddles'], mounted his horse, and charged on that part of the line which was defended by a party who had been ordered round the mountain by Colonel Shelby, it appearing too weak to resist," but such was not the case.[55]

In Captain Abraham De Peyster's words in a letter to Cornwallis, after "the left [on the west] broke [and] gave way, got in a crown on the Hill [and] nothing now offered but to make a breech through the enemy" if possible.[56] In absolute desperation and refusing to concede defeat or any thought of surrender, Major Ferguson prepared to make his final charge to push his way down the slope north of the spur's summit with half a dozen officers, including Colonel Husbands and Colonel Plummer. Of course, Ferguson's desperate attempt to break through the Patriots' anaconda-like encirclement, which was ever-tightening and squeezing the life out of the surrounded Loyalist command, was as doomed as it was suicidal. To "wrest victory from defeat," in Captain De Peyster's words, the increasingly infuriated major had also gathered a dozen or so faithful infantrymen, evidently mostly of his own regiment of Provincial regulars, for his final effort.

With a last blast of his silver whistle, which had already echoed over Kings Mountain for nearly an hour and "with great spirit and audacity," Ferguson kicked with his boots and dug his spurs into the flanks of his white war horse. In a final desperate act, he led his last charge down the northern slope in a "forlorn hope." Surgeon Uzal Johnson described in his journal how "Ferguson gave the Word to charge again, and he then rushed in amongst the Rebels with about half a Dozen Men," in a final offensive effort to break through and escape the trap.

The Scotsman raced down the timbered slope with only a handful of devoted followers in a last-ditch attempt to fight his way out of the fatal entrapment and escape the humiliating prospect of surrendering to the hated Overmountain men, especially his nemesis and personal enemy, Colonel Shelby. However, by that time, far too many excellent marksmen, especially Sevier's Overmountain men, were ready and waiting with loaded long rifles in hand, after Shelby had ordered these Washington County, North Carolina, expert shots to guard against an attempt by Ferguson to gain the main road to Charlotte. This situation guaranteed that Ferguson's last charge was nothing more than an ill-fated bid to reverse the hands of fate, after a long list of misjudgments, tactical mistakes, and miscalculations at a time when he had believed that he was on the verge of achieving a great victory. These various factors had all combined to lead to his most desperate moment, which ensured that Ferguson was about to meet his Maker.

One of Sevier's powder-stained men, who was catching his breath with his back to a tree for protection while wounded in several places and ignoring the pain, was perhaps the first man on the wooded slope to spy Ferguson's desperate attempt with only around half a dozen men to break through the surrounding ring of howling attackers. Ferguson rode north down the wooded slope toward where the Overmountain men of Sevier's command, including Robert Young and John Kusick from Washington County, were located, armed with deadly long rifles. A wounded citizen-soldier, John Gilleland, who was a surveyor from the small frontier community of Jonesborough in Washington County, North Carolina (today's east Tennessee), somehow possessed the strength to attempt to raise his long, heavy rifle to shoot Ferguson. The Scottish major, who was on his finest warhorse now galloping downhill at a rapid rate of speed, was wearing a long, checkered duster that everyone had been looking for thanks to prior intelligence. However, upon slowly squeezing the trigger, Gilleland's musket only snapped without firing when his flint failed to ignite the black powder charge, after having carefully sighted his long rifle on the fast-moving Scotsman. He then yelled to Private Robert Young, "There's Ferguson, shoot him!" Young immediately drew a bead and aimed down the length of his .40 caliber long rifle on Major Ferguson like he was nothing more than a fast-moving white-tailed buck bounding through the trees and said, "I'll try and see what Sweet Lips [named for his Overmountain wife Mary Douglas-Young] can do."[57]

Ferguson's past suddenly came back to haunt him, because his right arm had been shattered by a bullet at the Battle of Brandywine, Pennsylvania, in June 1777, and his saber in his left hand provided an additional clue to his identity. Therefore, when "accompanied by a few chosen officers, he headed straight into a hail of bullet fire, ignoring several wounds, slashing left-handed with his sword. Every soldier in the army had been given directions how to recognize [based on prior intelligence, including most recently from Virginia Paul who escaped off the hilltop and informed the Patriots how to identify] Ferguson—the left-handed sword, a check[er]ed shirt [blue and white checkered duster] over his [red] uniform [of a 71st Regiment of Foot Scottish Highland officer and] One soldier estimated as many as fifty rifles were leveled" at him during his ride down the timbered northern slope.[58]

Indeed, in the words of teenage Silas McBee, who was raised along Thicketty Creek deep in the South Carolina backcountry: "The troops had been cautioned to pick Ferguson off, they being told he used his sword in his left hand, his right having been rendered nearly useless from a wound received [at Brandywine but] I did not need the caution—I knew him, having often seen him, and I aimed a shot at him."[59] However, by the time that Private Robert Young raised trusty Sweet Lips and aimed down its long length of more than sixty inches and slowly squeezed the trigger, dozens of other men had also sighted on Ferguson and likewise fired almost at the same time. Riddled in the hail of bullets, Major Ferguson tumbled from the saddle with multiple wounds.[60] Ferguson was hit with "at least six well-aimed and close range shot [and] One of the largest caliber rounds was driven into his face, several other entered his torso, and his limbs were bloodied."[61] Major Ferguson's death warrant—his infamous October 1 threat issued less than a week before—that sealed his tragic fate had been when he had boldly denounced and mocked the Overmountain men as nothing more than "the dregs of mankind" and "a set of mongrels." These words now resulted in the flow of the aristocratic Scottish major's blue blood down the steep, wooded northern slope, ending his grandiose dreams and ambitions for all time.[62]

Along with the well-placed bullets from other sharp-eyed marksmen who had fired simultaneously, Private Robert Young's shot seemed to have been the fatal one to drop Ferguson, whose booted foot and spurs caught in one of the iron stirrups and dragged him across the leaf-covered forest floor like a rag doll. But no one really knows who was responsible for the Scottish major's death. A general rejoicing erupted among the Overmountain and backcountry men at the sight of the major's terrified horse dragging Ferguson's body, now bloody and lifeless, down the wooded slope just below the northeastern summit of the ridge of death.[63] Private James Collins described how "seven rifle balls passed through his body, both his arms were broken, and his hat and clothing were literally shot to pieces."[64] A free Black soldier named Essius (or Esaius) Bowman, who served as a member of Captain Joel Lewis's company of Virginians in Campbell's Washington County regiment, "claimed to have killed Ferguson," although he has not been heralded or acknowledged by historians largely because of his color.[65]

Colonel Shelby wrote how desperate Major Ferguson "attempted, a little before the close of the action, to make his escape on horseback, but was intercepted by a few riflemen . . . and fell dead when forcing his way" down the slope.[66] Many Patriots saw Ferguson's last charge in a less than heroic light. In the opinion of common soldier Benjamin Sharp, who viewed the major's last frantic efforts as a deliberate suicide because of his refusal to endure the humiliation of surrender: "Ferguson seeing that all was lost determined not to survive the disgrace, he broke his sword, and spurred his horse into the thickest of our ranks, and fell covered with wounds."[67] Captain De Peyster paid a sad, but appropriate tribute to the fallen Ferguson by writing how "his silver whistle, with which he was accustomed to give his orders was heard no more."[68]

Colonel John Sevier's Overmountain men had cut down more than Major Ferguson. They also killed Colonel Vesey Husbands and riddled the body of Colonel Daniel Plummer, who commanded the Fair Forest Regiment of South Carolina backcountry men. Plummer was so "horribly wounded" that he was "left for dead" where he fell, but miraculously recovered from his terrible injuries.[69] In a letter to his family that provided a sad requiem that had now become a cruel reality, a reflective Ferguson had written philosophically how the "length of our lives is not at our own command," as had been demonstrated in full at Kings Mountain.[70]

No Mercy and Slaughter atop Kings Mountain

With Major Ferguson killed in a hail of small-caliber bullets from long rifles and his riddled body lying in the autumn-colored woodlands along the northern slope, Captain Abraham De Peyster, who was now in command by right of seniority, rose to the challenge. He immediately ordered his remaining North Carolina and South Carolina militiamen to attack in a desperate bid to break through the encirclement. However, the immediate "cry throughout the Militia was," in the Loyalist surgeon Johnson's words, "We are out of ammunition, this being our unhappy condition . . . and the militia [was now in the] utmost disorder, it was thought most expedient to send out a [white] flag to save a few brave men that had survived the heat of action."[71]

The finely uniformed captain, who had been fortunate in having survived leading so many counterattacks with the American Volunteers, finally did what Ferguson should have done earlier to save lives. De Peyster, who was only concerned about doing whatever was necessary to save what was left of "the little army," described the deplorable situation: "The British were about to be slaughtered to no purpose like 'ducks in a coop.'"[72] From New York, Captain De Peyster described the closing drama when the Loyalists were clumped together:

> all in a crowd on the hill and tho every officer used his endeavors to rally the men, as nothing now offered but to make a breach through the enemy; I am sorry to say was not able to get a man to follow them. The

> chief part being without ammunition . . . while the other officers were doing their best amongst the crowd to collect more to follow them . . . Major Ferguson was killed before he advanced 20 yards. Ensign [John] McGinnes [McGinnis of Lieutenant Colonel Isaac Allen's Third Battalion, New Jersey Volunteers] was also killed . . . which rendered the militia he commanded almost useless [and] finding it impossible to rally the militia, I thought proper to surrender as the only means of saving the lives of some brave men still left [alive].[73]

Given this disastrous situation, the aristocratic New York captain wrote how he "ordered a white flag to be raised, in token of surrender, but the bearer was instantly shot down [but] He soon had another raised and called out for quarter."[74] As fate would have it, a good many Loyalists died in the period between the sending out of the first flag and then the second flag, which had taken some time in the chaos and noise. Captain Alexander Chesney described how we "sent out a flag of truce [a white handkerchief carried by an officer on horseback], but as the Americans resumed their fire afterwards ours was also renewed under the supposition they would give no quarter; and a dreadful havoc took place until the flag was sent out a second time, then the work of destruction ceased" at last.[75] But in fact, three different white flags were destined to be ordered forth before the firing entirely stopped on Kings Mountain during a lengthy period that ensured the loss of more Loyalist lives.[76]

In the words of Ensign Robert Campbell who described the confusion of the process of surrender: "As soon as Captain [De Peyster, who was still mounted] observed that [Ferguson] was killed, he raised a [white] flag and called for quarters. It was soon taken out of his hand by one of the [Patriot] officers [almost certainly Shelby] on horseback, and raised so high that it could be seen by our line, and [in time] the firing immediately ceased. The Loyalists, at the time of their surrender, were driven into a crowd, and being completely surrounded, they could not have made any resistance."[77]

This was a bloody afternoon of no mercy for Loyalists even when they attempted to surrender. In a representative example, Charles Bowen, who was "half-crazed" because he had heard of the death of his brother Lieutenant Reece Bowen, who had been born in Maryland and had fought against the Shawnee and Mingo warriors at Point Pleasant in the Ohio country in 1774, saw the first white flag raised, but it made no difference to him whatsoever. Serving in his brother's William Bowen's company like Reece, Charles described how he "slipped behind a tree, cocked his guns, and shot the first man who hoisted the [white] flag among the enemy and immediately turned his back to the tree to reload."[78]

Other attackers, especially North Carolinian Patriots during this brutal civil war among old friends and neighbors, were incensed because the men of "the North Carolina militia had twice repulsed a Body that attacked the Line," before running out of ammunition.[79] The terrified Loyalists were now huddled amid a slight hollow atop the embattled summit. All the while, individual Loyalists continued to wave white handkerchiefs in attempting to surrender in the shallow hollow where the tented encampment was located, but many frontiersmen either did not know the meaning or couldn't care less while continuing to fire with frantic energy into the milling crowd of defeated men. Therefore, exhausted in battling a relentless foe, low on ammunition, and with their fighting spirit having vanished like their fatal dreams of reaping glory, a good many Loyalists cried for "Quarters! Quarters!" in a desperate attempt to surrender and save their lives. However, in the deafening noise, the drifting layers of smoke, and the heightened confusion, other more determined Loyalists continued to rapidly load and fire partly because they could not see the white tokens of submission that had been raised, while some men also feared what might happen to them if they surrendered. Likewise, the Patriots maintained a steady fire at close range because increasing numbers of men were just now reaching the summit and automatically opened fire at the first sight of Loyalists without knowing what was happening.

Acting on instinct mixed with quick calculation in the most confusing of situations, a mounted Colonel Shelby, who was in front as usual, saw what was happening. "At the close of the action, when the British were loudly calling for quarters, but uncertain if they would be granted, I saw the intrepid Shelby rush his horse" practically in the Loyalists' midst.[80] The leader of the Sullivan County men dashed to within only "fifteen paces," in the words of Benjamin Sharp, "of their lines and commanded them to lay down their arms, and [that] they should have quarters."[81] Now practically surrounded by Loyalists, including those diehard men who especially hated Patriots, Colonel Shelby, who was naturally concerned about his life because many Tories continued to fire and fight back, frantically shouted, "Damn you! If you want quarters, throw down your arms!"[82] Indeed, at great risk to his life in the confusion of the Loyalists simultaneously fighting and surrendering, Shelby rode across the summit to ensure their surrender. At this time, "Shelby was the first man who spoke to them—was the first man among them, and the fire on the opposite side of the mountain did not cease, as they did not know of the surrender, under Shelby, who was actually among the British," took control of the chaotic situation.[83] Sharp summarized how Colonel Shelby's bold actions, when fully exposed while mounted on his war horse, were viewed in more than one way in this chaotic situation when men on both sides continued to be shot down: "Some would call this an imprudent act, but it showed the daring bravery of the man" from west of the mountains.[84] Colonel Shelby, covered in sweat and black powder stains, looked like the devil incarnate to the dazed Loyalists, while galloping back and forth across the summit. A close blast from a Tory musket had just "burnt off your hair, for it was much burnt on one side," in Colonel John Sevier's words to Isaac Shelby when they finally met on the summit.[85] Not only Shelby but also Sevier rode among their men to get them to cease firing, which won the admiration of Joseph Graham and other amazed Patriots, who were impressed by the timely leadership that revealed considerable courage.[86]

In his "shirt sleeves and his Collar open," in the words of James Davison, that made him look more like "a sturdy farmer" than a high-ranking officer, Colonel Campbell was also on the summit but on foot unlike Shelby and Sevier, who remained mounted for all to see.[87] Meanwhile, a good many Patriots felt most fortunate, because they had numerous close calls—bullets had pierced their clothing, cut through their hair, and banged off equipment and flintlocks during the last full hour of close-range combat. Private Thomas Young, who lived to tell the tale, described how a "bullet took a piece of my gun-stock" off.[88]

Surprise Volley from the Rear and Colonel James Williams's Fatal Wounding

Major Ferguson's approximately two hundred-man foraging party suddenly returned to Kings Mountain, after having hurried to assist their comrades before it was too late. Upon catching sight of the advancing Patriots in Colonel James Williams's sector on the summit's northwestern side and not knowing anything about the surrender on the northeastern plateau, members of this large foraging party of several companies of either the North Carolina or South Carolina militiamen unleashed a single volley. The hail of bullets raked the rear of Williams's command, catching everyone by surprise. The lead balls fired at the hard-fighting colonel, who was more visible than his followers because he was mounted, of South Carolina's Little River Regiment, which had been formed in the Little River District during early 1775, struck home. Colonel Williams was hit in multiple places. He was mortally wounded at the same time as Loyalists were still attempting to surrender.

In severe pain and trusting in God, Colonel Williams realized that the end was near, declaring to his followers, "I'm a gone man." Some of Colonel Campbell's Virginians who saw Williams fall from his horse assumed that the so-called surrendering Loyalists had taken advantage of the hard-won established peace to kill top Patriot commanders in a desperate bid to reverse the tide of battle. Naturally, given this pervasive view of Loyalist treachery, Campbell's Virginia soldiers became incensed by Colonel Williams's mortal wounding. After all, this seemed like just another act of Tory insidiousness. Especially angry was Colonel Campbell, the nominal commander of the expedition, who once again lost his legendary temper and flew into a rage. Not knowing the source of the Loyalist fire that had mortally wounded Colonel Williams, the Virginia colonel threatened the prisoners with death if any additional firing erupted to cut down Patriots, especially top officers. Lusting for revenge, Colonel Campbell then yelled for the nearest troops—Colonels Williams's "maddened followers" of the Little River Regiment and Hambright's South Fork Boys—to immediately open fire once again on the bunched-up Loyalists, who stood like "a herd of deer in a corral." Campbell also gave the order to open fire because he believed that the Tory foragers were the advanced elements of Tarleton's arriving British Legion dispatched by Lord Cornwallis, especially the much-feared dragoons in green coats. But the general opinion, especially in Campbell's mind, among the Patriots at the time was that the trapped Loyalists now planned to kill Patriot leaders in preparation for an escape attempt. In consequence, a large number of Patriots opened a heavy close-range fire, and the Loyalists, some armed and others unarmed, began to fall like leaves on a windy autumn morning.

The opening of this point-blank fire cut down dozens of Loyalists in record time until nearly a hundred of them had fallen to the ground to rise no more. The slaughter of mostly unarmed men shocked the distraught Colonel Shelby to the core, because he believed that he had already forced a legitimate surrender that had been mutually agreed upon. Lieutenant Joseph Hughes, who was an excellent officer of Colonel Thomas Brandon's Spartan Regiment from the South Carolina backcountry of today's Chester County, recalled how the enraged Patriots were out of control by that time and "we killed near a hundred of them" and many enraged citizen-soldiers wanted to kill "the whole of them." Now Shelby feared that the battle would resume with renewed fury when he saw Loyalists picking up their Brown Bess muskets and then renewing their fire "under the supposition that they would not give quarters," wrote Captain Chesney. Fearing a terrible retribution, the Tories expected the worst because of the endless revenge-seeking actions of both sides in this war. Many vengeful Overmountain and backcountry men only desired to satisfy their heightened bloodlust when an excessive amount of adrenaline was flowing, allowing their strong feelings to dictate that they continued to rapidly load and fire and murder more hapless Loyalists. All the while, they shouted, "Give them Buford's play" (repayment for the slaughter of Patriots at the Waxhaws by "Bloody Ban" Tarleton) and "Tarleton's quarter" in memory of past killings of so many helpless Continental and militia soldiers who had thrown down their weapons and attempted in vain to surrender.

Indeed, these Loyalists were commonly seen not only as vile traitors but also criminals guilty of long abusing Patriots and their families, and Major Ferguson was viewed as the greatest criminal of all. In this sense, murdering Loyalists was nothing more than the harsh frontier and Old Testament justice of "an eye for an eye." Knowing as much, therefore, some of the most diehard Loyalists continued to fire in part because they feared the worst, while angry Patriots likewise blasted away to reap a terrible vengeance. Andrew Evins, twenty-one, a fine soldier who had served under Captain William Edmondson before their revered leader was killed, and his comrades, who had seen the shooting down of the Edmondson boys, continued to fire into the milling throng of surrendered Loyalists. Colonel Campbell ran up to him, knocked up his rifle barrel, and screamed, "Evins, for God's sake, don't shoot. It is murder to kill them now, for they have raised the white flag." However, this slaughter that had broken out during the process of surrendering was now completely out of control, because firing continued to pour from the weapons of many Patriots, including those men who had just reached the easternmost summit and simply opened fire on natural instinct, when they saw Loyalists clumped together in the open without knowing that the process of surrender was underway.

A shocked Captain De Peyster, who was mounted atop a fine gray horse, had just handed over his sword and white flag, or handkerchief in this case, to

Maryland-born Major Evan Shelby Jr., the colonel's brother. The handsome major, a savvy veteran of the 1776 Cherokee campaign, who had been one of the first Patriots to reach the summit, gallantly presented the New Yorker's sword to Colonel Campbell because he was the expedition's nominal commander. Other Loyalist officers asked, "Where is your General?" since no one was wearing a uniform, and some powder-streaked privates with long hair finally pointed to Campbell. Colonel Campbell had just remarked, "I am happy to see you Sir," which De Peyster, with his Dutch temper rising, responded to by saying that he swore to God that he was not happy to see him in this humiliating situation. Sickened by the slaughter of his helpless men, who were dying before his eyes, De Peyster then gave Campbell a stern rebuke: "It was damned unfair! Damned unfair!" An angry Colonel Campbell, who was in no mood to be insulted by anyone, especially Ferguson's top lieutenant, at this point after an hour of intense combat in which he had lost many good men and friends, ordered the captain and other Loyalist officers to immediately dismount to save them from Patriot fire.

Caught in a true dilemma not of his own making and for once unable to come to a quick solution to the most serious and chaotic of situations on a battlefield, Colonel Shelby turned in perplexed astonishment to Virginia-born Captain John Sawyers. As noted, the Virginia-born Sawyers was Shelby's right-hand man ever since the Indian campaign that had ended with the bloody victory at Point Pleasant in October 1774. The captain had explored the Holston River country in 1768 and served in the 1776 Cherokee campaign and in the Chickamauga Campaign in 1779. Most memorable of all was the fact that Sawyers, when an orderly sergeant under Shelby, had played a stirring role at Point Pleasant with young Isaac Shelby a half dozen Octobers ago and had likewise made an impressive contribution to the winning of decisive victory on October 7 like against the Shawnee and Mingo warriors on the Ohio River. Befuddled by the chaos and mindless killings, a frustrated and thoroughly vexed Colonel Shelby asked, "Good God! What can we do in this confusion?" The commonsense Captain Sawyers, who had led his Overmountain company of Sullivan County men with a blend of daring and exceptional skill that day, then provided the ultimate solution—incredibly simple but highly effective under the circumstances that seemed to have no solution—for Shelby by responding, "We can order the prisoners from their arms." A suddenly relieved Shelby, who had lost control of the situation for the first time, then responded, "Yes, that can be done." The young colonel, who had been the architect of the remarkable success, then shouted for the hundreds of captives to sit down and then be immediately marched away under a heavy escort off the summit and out of harm's way.[89]

Colonel Shelby's frantic actions, with the timely help of Captain Sawyers who continued to serve as a key problem-solver, were decisive in defusing the dangerous situation, because the murderous fire unleashed by the Patriots, including those men who continued to arrive on the summit and had no idea that a surrender was taking place, "did not cease [until Shelby] ordered them to sit down [and only then] The American fire instantly ceased" at long last.[90] By that time, Colonel Campbell's frantic efforts also paid dividends that helped to defuse the emotion-driven situation when hatred had darkened hearts. In the words of William Moore about the dynamic Campbell, who wore "a handkerchief tied about his head [and] At the close of the action—when I was just shot down, having my thigh broken—I saw him waving his sword downward, and calling to his men to cease firing, that the enemy had surrendered. He was still in his shirt sleeves. I had just been shot down by having my thigh broken and [was] flat on the ground."[91]

Joseph Sevier, the promising young son of Colonel Sevier, was one of the last Patriots who continued to load and fire as fast as possible at the confused mass of Loyalists because of an inner rage from having earlier heard incorrectly that his father had been killed when it was actually Captain Robert Sevier, the colonel's brother, who had been mortally wounded. Consequently, Joseph Sevier continued "firing upon the huddled Tories until admonished to cease, when he excitedly cried out, with the tears chasing each other down his cheeks—'The Damned rascals have killed my father, and I'll keep loading and shooting till I kill every son of a bitch of them.'"[92] Meanwhile, Private Thomas Young was on his own personal mission after he had "heard the cry that Colonel Williams was shot. I ran to his assistance, for I loved him as a father, he had ever been so kind to me, almost always carrying a [hoe] cake in his pocket for me and his little son, Joseph. They carried him into a [British] tent, and sprinkled some water in his face. As he revived, his first words were, 'For God's sake boys, don't give up the hill!' I left him in the arms of his son Daniel and returned to the field to avenge his fall."[93]

Young Joseph Sevier only now finally stopped his personal war of revenge when Colonel Sevier, who was very much alive and well, rode up and the mere youth then realized his mistake. Private Young very likely had pulled the last trigger in the bloody slugfest.[94]

In the end, with his abundant frontier leadership abilities and skills once again rising to the fore, Colonel Shelby had saved the day by restoring order in a most timely manner amid the utter confusion of both Americans and Loyalists to ensure that all firing finally stopped. Shelby was still mounted and covered in sweat and powder stains, looking more like a dirt-stained tobacco or corn farmer from the backcountry than the architect of one of the war's most masterful victories. Colonel Shelby described what happened upon meeting Colonel Sevier on the smoke-covered summit of the northeastern spur: "I was almost the first—and, I believe, the very first—officer that you met at the surrender of the enemy. Your first words to me at the surrender were—'By God, they have burst off your hair' . . . my hair on the left side was very much scorched—this happened just before the surrender, when both parties were almost promiscuously mingled together."[95]

As noted, even Private Thomas Young had ceased firing with abandon like a madman, after having left the dying Colonel Williams with "his [oldest] son [who was still a teenager], Daniel [captain in the Little River Regiment that later fought at Cowpens in January 1781], and returned to the field to avenge his fall."[96] When the dying colonel from the South Carolina backcountry heard the firing diminishing significantly, he had asked a tearful Young, now holding him tightly in his arms, which side had won the day and received the thankful reply that relieved his pain and anguish, "We have." Then, Colonel Williams, the inspirational Presbyterian warrior who was perfectly at peace with his Maker and faithful member of the Little River Presbyterian Church, responded by saying, "Well, now I die satisfied."[97] A man of vengeance in following the harsh words of his revered Old Testament of the Holy Bible, the devout colonel of the Little River Regiment might have been equally satisfied if he had known how his fall had resulted in the Patriots opening up a scorching fire that had fatally cut down an estimated one hundred Loyalists like the "Sword of the Lord" slaying the Philistines of southern Canaan in a "dreadful havoc," including "many of the Tory wounded [who] were hurried to oblivion."[98]

Most important, a more complete victory could hardly have been achieved in the relatively short period of time of barely one hour. In the words of Jacob Bealer, an Overmountain soldier who fought beside his brother Joseph, about the efficient thoroughness of one of the most sparkling successes during the eight years of the American Revolution: Like his comrades, he now basked in "the death of Ferguson and the total defeat [that resulted in the] capture of his Army except those who might have run before the Mountain had been surrounded."[99]

Chapter VIII

Storm over Kings Mountain Comes to an End

At last "the battle closed not far from sundown," wrote Benjamin Sharp. The curtain finally fell on the bloody drama that had been played out in gory fashion on the natural stage of Kings Mountain, but only after the Loyalists were completely at the mercy of the victors and surrender remained the only recourse.[1] In Ensign Robert Campbell's words describing the tactical situation that had resulted in the bitter end for the Loyalists: "The Loyalists, at the time of their surrender, were driven into a crowd, and being closely surrounded, they could not have made any further resistance."[2] Finally, after what seemed like an eternity, the killing finally ended, primarily due to the frantic efforts of Colonel Shelby. To his everlasting credit, the desperate attempts of the Patriots' foremost frontier leader to stop the firing and force the surrender were crucial in ending what had become a massacre. Demonstrating sterling leadership qualities in the most confusing of battlefield situations, Shelby made sure that the surrender was respected by riding along the summit among the still angry Patriots, who continued to lust for revenge, while his "commanding presence helped compel the vengeful Whig riflemen to grant quarter to the desperate Loyalists," after they had already thrown down their weapons.[3]

Symbolically, the battle actually ended when Major Evan Shelby Jr. took the final submission of surrender, a white handkerchief, in an unofficial ceremony on the body-strewn summit, after the first two Loyalist flag bearers had been shot down.[4] However, in truth, the bitter fight at Kings Mountain had only concluded this bloody afternoon because of the encroaching darkness and the brutal reality that "the slaughter [had] continued, until the Americans were weary of killing."[5] A good many Loyalists had been killed unnecessarily during the long minutes of confusion in what was nothing less than a massacre.[6]

Three Mighty Cheers for Liberty

After hugging, shaking hands, and backslapping, the homespun victors, covered in sweat and black powder stains, unleashed a spontaneous cheer that echoed across Kings Mountain and through the autumnal woodlands now wreathed in sulfurous smoke.[7] An ecstatic Colonel Campbell directed his men from Washington County, Virginia, to give three hearty cheers, or huzzahs, for liberty, while the sullen Loyalists looked on in a mixture of dismay and disgust, as if not believing what had happened in barely an hour's time.[8] However, dozens of victors were far too pained and disabled with ghastly wounds and torn limbs and bodies to even think about cheering, although some tried their best because the feeling of victory was overwhelming. Lieutenant Samuel Newell was one of these men. In his own words about his suffering and the high cost of liberty that had been paid in full at Kings Mountain: "I had lost, by my wound, as much blood, perhaps as any one could and retain life; and my wound was then Extremely painful. As soon as [they] began to ground their arms [in surrender], and the danger over I turned my horse and moved to on top of the ridge, where it took four men to take me off, and lay me down by a fire."[9]

Perhaps no one was happier that this grueling battle had ended than teenage Private Thomas Young. He had fought barefoot all that October afternoon and had suffered severely in consequence. Young could now rest his weary feet, which were "much lacerated and bleeding."[10] Nevertheless, Young and his comrades were jubilant, savoring the astonishing victory that no one had expected or could hardly imagine possible under any circumstances, because Major Ferguson and his entire formidable task force were no more. With a great deal of delight and after a terrible retribution had been reaped on this autumn afternoon in the South Carolina Piedmont, William Snodgrass penned with unconcealed delight how Major "Ferguson himself was [now well] beyond surrendering."[11]

Grisly Evidence of Slaughter

In his diary, Lieutenant Anthony Allaire was sickened by the fact that "our poor little detachment" of Provincial Rangers "were all killed and wounded but twenty" men in red coats: symbolically, Major Ferguson's prized unit of elite fighting men from New York and New Jersey had basically gone down fighting with their esteemed Scottish major, who was no more.[12] Captain De Peyster also lamented how "we had only Seventy American Volunteers (fifty of whom got killed and wounded) . . . Two hundred and twenty five Militiamen were killed and seventy-two wounded."[13] All in all, even the Indian-fighting "hardened frontiersmen were sickened by [the] bloodiness" of the brief but incredibly intense battle for possession of an obscure mountaintop in northwest South Carolina.[14] Surgeon Uzal Johnson, of the American Volunteers, penned in his journal how "the engagement lasted an Hour and five Minutes, we were then reduced to the Necessity of Yielding to far Superior Numbers, we had only Seventy Amn. Vols. (fifty of whom got killed & wounded, among the killd was Coll. Ferguson, and Ensign McGinnis of Coll. Allen's Corps, among the wounded was Capt. Ryerse) and eight hundred Militiamen engaged, two hundred and twenty five Militiamen were killed, & seventy two Wounded."[15]

It was not only the burning desire of the Patriots for bloody vengeance that cost so many Loyalist lives before their bloodlust was finally satisfied. James Crow, one of Campbell's Virginia boys, explained in regard to the backwoods soldiers who were only schooled in the ways of frontier fighting and fundamental Old Testament truths, while knowing nothing about the conventional ways of war: "Our young men did not know the meaning of the [white] flag."[16] Partly because of this reason, more than 225 Loyalists now lay dead on the gory slopes and open crest, which spanned around six hundred yards, and at least another 123 men lay wounded, while 716 Loyalists became prisoners, which represented the thorough elimination of Ferguson's entire command. In the end, very few men escaped Colonel Shelby's masterful tactical entrapment and the wrath of his expert fighting men. Shelby wrote that 375 Loyalists had been killed and wounded. The Loyalist officer corps had been cut to pieces in the desperate attempt to fight off the swarming Patriots who seemed to be everywhere and just kept coming through the trees and along the open crest with weapons blazing. Colonel Daniel Plummer, who commanded the approximately two hundred men of the Fair Forest Regiment, and Lieutenant Thomas Cunningham of the Little River Regiment were wounded, while numerous Loyalist captains and lieutenants lay dead, mostly on the high ground along the open crest that they had defended with their lives. Only twenty-eight Patriots were killed and sixty-two wounded, which was a surprisingly light cost for attackers of a formidable high ground position in a highly unusual loss ratio equation that, of course, can be mostly explained by a thorough reliance on Indian-style fighting skills and the excellent cover provided by the woodlands and boulders along the slopes.

Behind the last ledge of rocks on the ridge before Ferguson's encampment and just south of the northeastern summit from where the Loyalists' desperate last stand had been outflanked, at least twenty Tories lay dead with small-caliber holes in their heads: a grim testament to the deadly fire of the long rifles that Shelby had directed to be turned against these tough and tenacious defenders, including his outflanking movement that had paid high dividends in a key situation. Quite simply, Major Ferguson's command had been thoroughly annihilated, which was a symbolic payback at the hands of a good many angry young men and boys, whose countersign on this decisive afternoon had been "Buford!" the doomed Virginia colonel who had commanded at the Waxhaws disaster and had seen his command slaughtered by a flurry of Tarleton's slashing sabers.[17] The scene on the southern slope near the open crest was especially gory where the most tenacious defensive stands had been made by the Loyalists from behind the "table or bench of rocks" before the northeastern summit, because the boulders and rocks were splattered with the spray of Tory blood and brains, where a hail of bullets from a good many long rifles had shattered so many Loyalist heads. In Silas McBee's words: "Upwards to twenty were found dead after the battle among the rocks, their heads being thus pierced with bullets."[18]

However, Major Ferguson was correct in his high estimation of the overall quality of his men, especially his Provincial regulars, who had fought extremely well before the survivors were forced to surrender out of urgent necessity, because the Patriots had especially concentrated their wrath on shooting down the crack fighting men in red uniforms, which they knew was one of the keys to decisive victory. During the past summer, Major Ferguson had complimented his men, both the American Volunteers and the Carolina militiamen, informing Lord Cornwallis that "he can depend upon [them] for doing their duty and fighting well."[19] In a rare tribute from the gifted Overmountain leader, Colonel Shelby also wrote how the Loyalists "fought bravely" in this battle that was furiously waged for the heart and soul of America.[20]

Triumphant Patriot officers now carried Loyalist swords that had been surrendered to the victors in the chaos that had consumed the gory summit. Now in command after Ferguson's fall, Captain Abraham De Peyster of the American Volunteers had first presented his fine hunting sword with an ebony grip, a blued steel blade of nearly thirty inches, and a wolf's head pommel of silver, which had been most certainly made in Europe, to Major Evan Shelby

Jr. in a token of submission. In a magnificent gesture, Major Shelby then gave the saber to Colonel Campbell because he was in nominal command. Loyalist swords had been handed over even while the firing had continued by late-arriving attackers who had continued to gain the smoke-wreathed summit without initially knowing anything about the surrender or simply not caring.[21] Lieutenant Andrew Kincannon, of Scotch-Irish descent, accepted the saber of Captain Samuel Ryerson, of Dutch heritage from New Jersey and third in command of the Loyalist task force.[22]

Meanwhile, Patriot officers gained other swords from the hands of surrendering Loyalists either in the red uniforms of the American Volunteers or in the backcountry homespun of the Loyalist militia from rural North and South Carolina. The British Army had equipped American Loyalist officers with sabers like in their regular regiments. Captain William Lenoir, who had been raised near the small community of Tarboro, North Carolina, in the backcountry, accepted a fine sword with each side of its steel blade engraved with Latin mottos: "Sheath me not without honor" and "Draw me not without cause."[23]

However, even the traditionally smooth process of surrendering swords had been problematic during the confusion on the summit, because firing had continued, there was no time for traditional surrender ceremonies, and there was a lack of rank insignia among the victors. Ironically, even after his men had first pointed him out to surrendering Loyalist officers that he was in (nominal) command, Colonel Campbell initially had difficulty in conveying the proper impression to status-conscious British officers that he was actually in command of the entire task force, because of his homespun attire in shirtsleeves, open collar, and common man looks. In consequence, they had displayed an initial reluctance to hand over their sabers to a man who looked more like a backcountry corn and wheat farmer than a dynamic leader of some of the fiercest fighters in America.[24] In the end, either Colonel Sevier or Cleveland took possession of Major Ferguson's sword, which had been broken at the hilt by a direct hit by a bullet or resulting from the hard fall from his horse. Regardless, Ferguson's sword truly belonged to Colonel Shelby, the architect of an amazing victory, because he had contributed more than anyone else to the remarkable campaign from beginning to end.[25]

In a joyous letter to his father, a thankful Shelby, who duly praised God for the incredible victory, described how "Providence who always rules and governs all things for the best, so ordered it that we are around them before we were discovered, and formed in such position, so as to fire on them nearly about the same time, though they heard us in time to form and stood ready. The battle continued warm for an hour; the enemy finding themselves embarrassed on all sides, surrendered themselves as prisoners to us at discretion."[26] For ample good reason, because of the dominance of the Scotch-Irish in the ranks, the vanquished Loyalists were fully justified to declare a well-justified curse with a great deal of understandable bitterness: "Damn you, Irish."[27] But Colonel Shelby said it best without exaggeration, writing, "A more total defeat was not practicable."[28] In the end, Major Patrick Ferguson had indeed met his Waterloo at Kings Mountain, ending a long and distinguished career in record time of barely an hour in which his entire command was neatly eliminated. Captain De Peyster concluded in regard to Ferguson's folly of having decided to stand firm atop his cherished mountain in the South Carolina Piedmont: "Ferguson set an inordinate value on the position which he had selected, which, however, strong against a regular attack, was not defensible against the attacks which were about to be directed upon it . . . he had grievously . . . erred as to the intrinsic availability of King's Mountain as a military position [and] its bald, rocky summit merely served . . . for the immolation of the victims."[29]

The Tragic Cost of Victory at Kings Mountain

A captured Loyalist officer, who naturally desired to disguise the miserable defeat as much as possible, felt not only a sense of satisfaction but also great pride in his men, who had fought exceptionally well in their one-sided defeat: "I must confess I was pleased . . . to see their loss superior to ours [and] although they got the better of us, damn 'em, we made them pay for it . . . we deserved success, although it was not in our power to command it."[30] However, these words were no exaggeration because most Patriot losses came not from the volley firing of the well-trained Provincial regulars, but from the sharpshooting skills of the large number of North and South Carolina militiamen, who were "as good marksmen as our own."[31]

After the short battle, the burial of the dead by Loyalist prisoners began early on the following morning, Sunday, October 8—an appropriate time on the Sabbath to attend to a Christian duty for these Holy Bible-reading and devout fighting men, who were true holy warriors. As could be expected, a total of twenty-eight Patriots were buried with greater care than the Loyalists, but, in truth, the dead of both sides were given hasty and inadequate burials partly because of the utter exhausted state of the victors. In addition, decent burials were almost impossible because of the thin and rocky soil of the rugged mountain in the Piedmont. Most of the Loyalist wounded were left where they had fallen along the slopes and the open crest to make out the best that they could under the most deplorable circumstances.

The bodies of 225 out of the 925 Loyalists in the climactic battle were hastily buried in a shoddy manner that revealed the extreme bitterness of this savage war that was waged between fellow Americans who ironically were actually more alike than different, except in regard to politics and uncontrollable circumstances. Roughly one-third of the Patriot casualties were suffered by Colonel Campbell's southwest Virginia command from Washington County: a significant loss that revealed how, of all the county regiments, it was the Virginians who had been the largest number of attackers that afternoon, who had first advanced up the steepest slope of the highest part of the mountain and then received several counterattacks before attacking northeast along the entire distance of around six hundred yards along the ridge's length from its southwestern corner to the northeastern end. Indeed, the enemy's three bayonet attacks directed against Colonel Campbell's men and the openness of the crest in the assault northeastward ensured heavier casualties among the hard-charging Virginians than other troops.

The most bitter memories of Loyalist rampages, murders, rapes of young country girls, and burning down of houses, including even churches in South Carolina, surfaced vividly in Patriot minds to ensure that the dead Loyalists were given the most inadequate of burials by the overseeing members of the burial detachment. Many Loyalist bodies were simply dumped into ravines and covered with logs, fall leaves, and rocks since the ad hoc burial party possessed no shovels and the ground was rocky and the topsoil was thin. Even moreso and as noted, time was precious because of the fear of Lieutenant Colonel Banastre Tarleton's possible arrival if he had been dispatched by Lord Cornwallis from Charlotte. For a variety of reasons, therefore, the burials of both Tories and Patriots were "badly done," admitted Private James Collins with surprising honesty. Already, rumors were swirling that Lord Cornwallis had dispatched reinforcements to Major Ferguson's assistance and that the Cherokee were about to once again attack the Overmountain settlements that were now far away west of the Blue Ridge Mountains.[32]

Total Patriot losses revealed how the excellent cover of rugged terrain, rocks, boulders, and woodlands had minimized losses, despite having repeatedly attacked up the high ground—the opposite of the usual situation in which the attackers in battle suffered high losses in such a tactical and geographic situation. Of the 910 Patriots engaged in the battle, twenty-eight were killed and sixty-two were wounded, but almost certainly more according to some sources, which was a loss of less than 10 percent compared to a 44 percent loss suffered by Ferguson's command.[33] Ferguson's loss in killed, wounded, and captured was a staggering total of 1,016 men.[34] Sickened by the killing, Colonel William Campbell lamented how "I have lost several of my brave friends, whose death I much lament. Maj. [William Edmondson] will give you [Colonel Arthur Campbell] their names, though I must myself mention Capt. [William] Edmondson, his two brothers [Andrew and Robert Edmondson, Jr.], and Lieut. [Reece] Bowen. My regiment has suffered more than any other in the action."[35] Lieutenant Samuel Newell described the high cost among the officer corps of Campbell's Virginia regiment from the southwestern hills that they loved and defended with their lives: "Killed were Captain William Edmondson, Lieutenant Commandant Reece Bowen, Lieutenant Robert Edmondson Jr., Lieutenant Wm. Blackburn, and Lieutenant Thomas McCulloch, died with his wound, and Ensigns John Beatty and Nathaniel Dryden."[36] Like Colonel Campbell, Lieutenant Newell lamented the Virginia Regiment's high loss, writing how "not more than one-half of our regiment, that is two hundred [men], were in the battle—the rest being left behind [in advancing on foot]. Thirty-five of the killed and wounded were of our regiment, thirteen of whom were commissioned officers."[37]

Private James Collins was thankful for the remarkable victory, which reflected the representative mood of the victors, who felt blessed: "As God would have it, there had but few of our men been slain—fifteen or sixteen—but of that number some of our bravest men; Colonels Williams and Hambright, with Major Chronicle, and some other distinguished men, had fallen. These were buried in the flag ground under the hill, near where the battle commenced."[38] On October 7 and early the next day, the Patriot wounded were treated by home remedies, including tree moss and other native plants found in the forest because wilderness life had long taught these frontiersmen how to treat injuries, including what had been learned from Native Americans. The wounded men received good care from their comrades, who were often relatives, including fathers and sons. Most important, they received professional care from Loyalist Surgeon Uzal Johnson, who wrote how "I [was] employed to dress [Patriots] in preference to their own Surgeon" with much less education and experience. The highly capable Johnson was now the only surviving British physician, after two others had been killed in the fighting partly because their red uniforms had made them ideal targets. Johnson had practiced medicine in New Jersey before the war. Along with one Patriot country physician of less ability but no less devotion in helping to relieve the suffering soldiers, Johnson treated the men of both sides for a wide variety of injuries. Many Patriots had suffered bayonet wounds from the repeated attacks down the slopes.[39]

Quite a few citizen-soldiers far from home were beyond saving, however. Married to a woman named Agness and having survived the disaster at Fishing Creek, South Carolina, on August 18, 1780, David Duff, of Scotch-Irish descent, had been killed while battling for possession of the strategic crest.[40]

In regard to some of the typical casualties among the South Carolina men, Virginia-born James Coiel was wounded with a broken leg; William Griffis had been hit by a bullet in the right shoulder and a bayonet had been plunged through his leg, but he survived to fight another day, while his two brothers were fated to be killed at the Battle of Eutaw Springs on September 8, 1781; German-born Devault Keller had been hit in the left arm by a bullet; David Kerr, born in Virginia and of Scotch-Irish heritage, was wounded in the ribs and arm; Robert Miller, of the Chester District (today's Chester County, South Carolina), was "severely wounded" but survived; Virginia-born Benjamin Neighbors was wounded twice but he also survived to become a Baptist minister, as if to compensate for the killing and surreal horrors of Kings Mountain; Thomas Palmer had tenderly nursed Martin Hammond who was wounded, despite having been wounded himself in the bitter fighting; Henry Slappey, who had been born in 1758 and fell wounded on the hill of death two days before his twenty-second birthday; Josiah Tanner, who was married in December 1771 to a woman named Martha, was wounded in the right arm; John Dobson, one of McDowell's Burke County, North Carolina, men, fell with multiple wounds; North Carolina-born Captain John Tubb Senior was wounded in the side and right arm; Robert Walker, who had been born around 1736 and was an experienced fighter against the Cherokee, "was shot through the body near the heart," but survived to serve again; William Bradley, who suffered a serious arm wound that permanently disabled him from future service to his country; and Joseph Rogers of the Burke County, North Carolina, militia was felled by bullets in both legs.[41] Again, these were just a few of the men of Colonel James Williams's and Colonel Edward Lacey's commands from York and Chester counties (South Carolina Districts) who were cut down on that bloody afternoon.

Fortunate to have survived the vicious contest that resulted in the most important Patriot victory of the war in South Carolina, Moses Shelby, brother of the colonel from Sapling Grove in the South Holston River country, described how "I received two wounds . . . the last wound, through my thigh near my body [and] I was assisted down to a branch, some distance from the foot of the Mountain."[42] In the words of a teenage citizen-soldier about the losses in his volunteer company: "We had two badly wounded; one lieutenant, by the name of Watson, the other a private, named Caldwell; we carried them to their own homes, in the evening, where they both died in a few days. Poor fellows! They were raised together; fought together; died nearly at the same time in the same house, and lie buried together."[43]

Ireland-born John Copeland described how Colonel Edward Lacey's South Carolina command, which had attacked to Colonel Williams's left, "suffered severely in the battle."[44] However, the amount of destruction among the Patriot ranks paled in comparison to the hard-hit Loyalists, who had been decimated. Private James Collins described how the Tories "lay dead in heaps, while others lay wounded or dying."[45] Indeed, in the words of Captain William Lenoir about the sad fate of the most seriously wounded Loyalists, "about forty of whom afterwards died of their wounds," especially head shots from the steady aim of the long rifles.[46] The highest-ranking South Carolina Loyalist, Colonel Daniel Plummer, whose South Carolina estate had been confiscated by the Patriots and who commanded around two hundred men of the Fair Forest Regiment of militia, "was probably killed at King's Mountain," in the words of historian Lyman C. Draper, which was not the case, however.[47] Indeed, Plummer had only been severely wounded when shot out of the saddle during Ferguson's escape attempt and eventually recovered from his serious wounds, although he was initially reported to have been killed, after having been left for dead on the field.[48] Another fine officer whose lands and property had been confiscated with considerable relish by Patriots, Captain Samuel Ryerson, who was third in command of Ferguson's task force, suffered a severe wound in the left hand and wrist, while Ensign John McGinnis was killed in leading the desperate counterattack against Ensign Robert Campbell's flanking force as ordered by Ferguson.[49]

Patriots like Captain William Lenoir were most fortunate in surviving their wounds. He "received two wounds from bullets one in his side and the other in his arm and a third bullet passed through his hair above where it was tied."[50] Colonel Shelby's concern about the welfare of his injured men began immediately after the firing stopped. Israel Hayter, who was a member of Ireland-born Captain James Dysart's company, Campbell's Virginia regiment, wrote how "Col. Isaac Shelby held him until the ball was extracted from his thigh."[51] Captain Robert Sevier, the brother of Colonel John Sevier, had been mortally wounded. He was destined to die nine days after the battle before reaching his Overmountain homeland along the clear and cold waters of the spring-fed Watauga River.[52]

The Spoils of War

Like the leading officers, the men of the lower ranks obtained their fair share of the booty to celebrate the one-sided success. Before his faithful orderly, Elias Powell, and other men had moved the body of their beloved dead commander from the north slope of the northeastern summit to a more secure location, Major Ferguson's bloodstained body was systematically looted by the victors and his possessions distributed to those leaders, who were most responsible for winning the day, in the true frontier tradition. The first arrivals took whatever they desired from the body of the fallen major who would never again see his beloved Scotland. For instance, Samuel Talbot "turned Ferguson over and got his pocket pistol," in the words of Robert Henry.[53] Symbolically and according to the conqueror's right, Colonel Shelby took Ferguson's maroon silken uniform sash, which he had worn over his shoulder under his lengthy duster.[54] Shelby also obtained the major's prized large silver whistle, while Elias Powell secured the smaller whistle used by Ferguson during the hard-fought battle.[55] Major Ferguson's long whistle had dictated the precise movements of his well-trained troops and was no ordinary trophy of war. Indeed, this exquisite "foot-long whistle, the piercing note of which had been heard again and again above the clamor and din of battle, fell to Shelby's lot."[56]

Gaining his fair share, Burke County's Major Joseph McDowell Jr., who was the brother of Colonel Charles McDowell, was given six porcelain plates, decorated with a red floral motif of a popular Oriental style of the day, from Ferguson's headquarters tent along with a cup and saucer from his dining table.[57] Because his horse had been killed in battle, Colonel Benjamin Cleveland secured the most coveted prize of all, Ferguson's white charger.[58] Because his own horse had been killed from under him, Colonel Edward Lacey, who would be left behind with a detachment of his South Carolina men after the main task force departed on October 8 to complete the process of having prisoners sign paroles, also secured one of Ferguson's horses—a "black English charger."[59] In a symbolic acquisition, Colonel Sevier gained Ferguson's major's commission and his nice mahogany field glass, which was an expensive astronomical telescope made in London.[60] And Colonel William Campbell secured Ferguson's stack of personal papers and correspondence that were taken from his headquarters tent, not far from the eastern slope of the northeastern spur.[61] Captain Joel Lewis, of Welsh heritage, who led a Virginia company in Campbell's regiment, secured Ferguson's "jewel-hilted poniard" and other items.[62]

Almost as soon as he had fallen on the timbered northern slope during his suicidal charge to break through the Patriot lines and before his body had been moved by his orderly and other survivors, Ferguson's body had drawn a crowd of curious Patriot soldiers who wanted to view what was left of the military man whom they had feared would march over the mountains to attack and burn down the Overmountain settlements. Even wounded Patriots were curious to see Ferguson's blood-splattered corpse. Injured Lieutenant Samuel Johnson's friends, including Colonel Cleveland, whose sizable bulk made the task relatively easy, carried him a good distance just to see Ferguson and gloat over his cruel demise on an obscure hill in the middle of nowhere. Clearly, the talented major had come a long way from his Scottish homeland in a true Celtic odyssey, which had come to a tragic and inglorious end like a classic Greek tragedy. But some of these rural "crackers," as they were called in disgust by the aristocratic elitists on both sides, were more than just curious, because they also desired a war trophy for themselves to take back home. Like a dead ancient Greek or Trojan warrior whose armor was considered the ultimate prize and trophy on the bloodstained plains before the high walls of the City of Troy long ago, Ferguson's body was stripped naked by the victors. His clothing, duster, checkered shirt, and uniform were torn to pieces for souvenirs by the motley conquerors of Kings Mountain.[63] Revealing a morbid fascination as if a hunter who had just felled a big white-tailed buck, elk, or buffalo, Silas McBee was one man who gloated over the exhilarating sight of Major Ferguson's gory remains, writing how after "the action I counted nine bullet holes through Ferguson."[64]

Persistent rumors have it that the first Patriots who discovered Ferguson's bloodied body performed a shameful act that represented the epitome of disrespect and contempt: While laughing and smiling, they allegedly took turns urinating on the major's body. In a supreme irony, Ferguson's last proclamation to raise North Carolina recruits in the western North Carolina Piedmont had contained an insulting taunt: "If you choose to be pissed upon forever and ever by a set of mongrels, say so at once and let your women turn their backs upon you and look out for real men to protect them."[65] Based on what he later learned from Loyalists who had been in the battle, Lieutenant Colonel Banastre Tarleton later wrote how the "mountaineers, it is reported, used every insult and indignity, after the action, towards the dead body of Major Ferguson."[66]

Even Colonel Shelby could not resist mocking the once-feared fallen leader who had long terrified Patriots far and wide. Not long after Ferguson had been cut down, a jubilant Colonel Shelby had ridden up in triumph and could not resist declaring in his elation: "Colonel, the fatal blow is struck—we have Burgoyned you"—a reference to the decisive defeat of General "Gentleman Johnny's" entire army at Saratoga, New York, in October 1777.[67] As noted, the spoils of war, including other personal possessions of Major Ferguson, like his cup towel of white linen, were then auctioned off like the selling of a splendid racehorse on the frontier. In the Southern tradition, the slaves of some Loyalist officers, who hailed from North and South Carolina, were part of the auction held on the mountaintop strewn with fallen men, going to the highest bidder. Exercising his ancient right as a victor like a victorious Greek warrior after the fall of ancient Troy when captured women were a primary prize of the leaders, including Achilles, Colonel Shelby purchased a slave woman named Rachel.[68] Ironically, in America's first civil war and unlike in the Civil War of 1861–1865, the men of both sides were slaveowners: one of the great paradoxes about the Battle of Kings Mountain long ignored by generations of historians, because it has been an uncomfortable truth of America and the Revolutionary War experience in general.

The victors "divided all booty, including much needed shoes and clothing. Isaac [Shelby] received, among other items, Ferguson's foot-long silver whistle and also a fine Irish linen tablecloth, five yards by three, with an unusual design of grapes, white sheaves, and acorn garlands."[69] James Collins described his share of the spoils: "In the evening [of October 7], there was a distribution made of the plunder . . . My father and myself drew two fine horses, two guns, and some articles of clothing with a share of powder and lead."[70] One of the first arrivals at the scene where Major Ferguson's body lay on the northern slope of the summit, one of Colonel's Lacey's South Carolina men had secured Ferguson's large silver watch.[71] In disgust, Loyalist Lieutenant Anthony Allaire wrote bitterly how "these villains divided our baggage, although they had promised on their word we should have it all."[72] Surgeon Uzal Johnson was likewise sickened by the Patriots claiming the spoils of war with considerable enthusiasm, writing in this journal how he and his comrades "had the Mortification to see our Baggage, divided to the difft. Corps."[73]

Ironically, not even the thrill and excitement of victory were enough to diminish the sheer hatred that the Patriots felt for the Loyalists and vice versa, including not only for the wounded men but also wounded relatives. As mentioned earlier, when one wounded Loyalist saw his brother-in-law, Captain James Withrow, among the victors, he pitifully asked for help in his hour of need. Without hesitation, Withrow then gave a heartless response filled with contempt: "Look to your [Tory] friends for help."[74] Even Colonel Shelby felt much the same but to a lesser extent, summarizing how when the firing finally stopped: "three hundred and seventy five of them [Loyalists] were left weltering in their Gore upon Kings Mountain among the latter Major Ferguson himself, he fell in the close of the action—about the same time or shortly before Colonel Williams was mortally wounded of which he died." As a fate would have it, Williams, who had led his South Carolinians of the Little River Regiment with distinction, was the highest-ranking Patriot leader who gave his life for winning the sparkling victory at Kings Mountain.[75]

Without ceremony or much respect, and certainly without the traditional honors, the body of the naked Major Ferguson was hastily wrapped in a cowhide by orderly Elias Powell and other remaining devoted followers of the Scotsman. His remains were then quickly buried in a wooded "draw" near the summit of Kings Mountain, where it has remained to this day. Symbolically, the major was buried beside the body of the red-haired, attractive Virginia Sal, who joined the major in death, as she had lived intimately, according to legend, with him on this campaign.[76]

When the smoke had first cleared and a count was taken, the men of Kings Mountain were astounded at how few Patriot men, only twenty-eight, had been killed in the battle. In the words of Colonel Arthur Campbell, "It has been remarked why so small a number of Americans were killed at Kings Mountain, compared to the loss of the enemy. Our officers accounted for it in this way: The tories occupied much the least space of ground, and of course were more thickly planted than the extended circle of Americans around them, so that the fire of our men seldom failed doing execution."[77]

Sheer luck had saved other Patriots, including Scotch-Irishman John McCutchen of the Ninety-Six District in the western South Carolina back-country, during the heat of battle. He had been one of Ferguson's captives atop the mountain, but "was deserted by his captors during the battle at Kings Mountain."[78] In addition, the Patterson boys, William and Thomas, whose Ireland-born father, Arthur, was killed in the fight in a bid to save them, and several Patriot women, who had refused to answer questions about the exact whereabouts of their rebel husbands who may have fought at Kings Mountain, were held as captives in Ferguson's encampment until "liberated" by the victors.[79]

Because the battle had closed just before sundown on a short autumn day and everyone was thoroughly exhausted, the weary Patriots lay on the ground on the battlefield for the night. Benjamin Sharp described how "we had to encamp on the ground, with the dead and wounded and pass the night amid the groans and lamentations."[80] Men like John Spelts were sickened by what they heard throughout the night, which was horrifying and never ceased hour after hour. He described how "the groans of the wounded and dying on the mountain were truly affecting—begging piteously for a little water; but in the hurry confusion, and exhaustion of the Whigs, these cries, when emanating from the Tories, were little heeded."[81]

Hundreds of men of both sides were treated by the capable Surgeon Uzal Johnson, the well-educated Loyalist native of New Jersey and the best medical man in Ferguson's command. He had been a respected physician before having decided to cast his fate with the Loyal Americans. As the only surviving British surgeon on Kings Mountain and with "some assistants," Johnson worked frantically throughout the night and well into the next morning of the Sabbath in attempting to save the lives of wounded men on both sides.[82] However, in Benjamin Sharp's words, Johnson only "attend[ed] their wounded; but the wounded Tories were unprovided for," which was only an order of priorities as ordered by the victors.[83] All the while, wounded Patriots continued to succumb to their battle injuries, far from home and families. Ensign Henry Dickenson described his own personal ordeal: "I understood that James Lairds, another intimate acquaintance was badly wounded, and who occupied me in removing him, and attending upon him, almost exclusively until he died."[84] After the battle, William Snodgrass walked over the body-strewn battleground and wrote how "Campbell's and Shelby's regiments lost principally all the men that were killed. . . . The greatest contact [of antagonists] was . . . on top of the mountain, where it was very narrow, where . . . most of the slain were, as there were but a few steps between us and the Enemy."[85] Indeed, a price for victory had been paid in full among relatives. For example, "Colonel Sevier lost his brother, Robert, and although Colonel Shelby's brother, Moses was badly wounded, he survived. While Colonel Campbell had several kinsmen in his command, they all survived the battle."[86]

The Sunday after the battle was certainly no day of rest for the exhausted victors. The morning of October 8 dawned bright and clear, which raised Patriot spirits because they knew that downpours of rain would not now slow their upcoming withdrawal back to the mountains. It was time to move northwest toward Gilbert Town and the Blue Ridge at a brisk pace, before the arrival of Cornwallis's reinforcements, especially Tarleton and his hard-hitting dragoons. This was the first full sunny day for what seemed like an eternity to the Overmountain and backcountry men. Because they had to hurry northwest to escape to the mountains to the west, the Patriots were up early that morning. Ferguson's seventeen wagons and tents were torched so they could not again be used by the enemy.

Out of urgent necessity because of shortages of everything, the victors ransacked the captured wagons for provisions but they were surprised to find little rations for the forthcoming long journey back to their homeland. Most of the wagons were filled with thousands of cartridges and Brown Bess muskets to supply the large number of new recruits Ferguson had envisioned rushing to his ranks—the primary reason why the major had made the mistake of having dispatched a two-hundred-man foraging party on the morning of the battle, when every man was needed in the ranks. Wounded Patriots were gingerly assisted onto horses' backs or blanket litters that stretched between two horses for the long journey ahead. These skilled frontiersmen also hurriedly crafted Indian litters, which were made from green tree limbs, known as travois, to drag behind horses. Everyone was working fast because of the rumor that Tarleton and his much-feared British Legion of Americans were on the way. Even worse, another rumor—a persistent one because nothing was more dreaded by these citizen-soldiers than the massacre of families in their absence—circulated that the Cherokee were again raiding the frontier settlements on the mountains' west side.

In one of the most tragic scenes played out at Kings Mountain, the tearful wives, children, and families from the local area arrived atop the mountain on Sunday morning to claim dead bodies of their Tory husbands and fathers and to nurse wounded Loyalists. After signing paroles given by the small command of South Carolinians from the Chester District (today's Chester County) under Colonel Edward Lacey, more than seven hundred Loyalist prisoners were directed to form a single file line with each man carrying two unloaded muskets over their shoulders, after the Patriots gathered around 1,500 or more captured muskets from both the prisoners and the supply wagons—a great windfall that needed to be transported to safety for later usage. The sturdiest Tories were then ordered to carry three muskets, of course without rounds or flints, which had been carefully removed by the victors. Even wounded and sick Tory prisoners were assigned the job of carrying off captured muskets from Ferguson's abundant supply, but they were forced to only carry one apiece. Just getting the frontier and backwater army off the mountain as soon as possible and once again on the move by mid-morning of October 8 with such a multitude of sullen prisoners was exasperating for frustrated officers.

Even the usually taciturn, mild-mannered Colonel Shelby, who was now single-minded in the need to hurriedly escape before it was too late, lost his temper with the endless phony delays of the balking prisoners, who were attempting to buy time, partly because he knew that they had to move on at a fast pace if Cornwallis had dispatched Tarleton in pursuit. When an older and somewhat feeble Loyalist claimed that he could not carry even a single musket on the long march northwest to the mountains, Shelby finally snapped. The colonel rode up and slapped the man on the shoulders with the flat of his sword and yelled that he had possessed sufficient strength to carry a musket to the top of Kings Mountain and then shoot down Patriots. Colonel Shelby's blow from the flat of the sword and convincing argument shortly hurried the disgruntled Loyalist, who had attempted to slow the march, into the ranks with an empty musket on his shoulder.[87]

Benjamin Sharp described the precarious situation in which considerable danger still lurked for the victors, it was feared, writing how "the next day, as soon as we could bury our dead, and provide litters to carry our wounded, we marched off to regain the upper country for fear of being intercepted by a detachment from the army of lord Cornwallis, for we were partly behind their quarters, being between him and the British garrison of Ninety-Sixth [to the southwest after the Loyalist] dead [were] left for their bones to bleach upon the mountain."[88] Lieutenant Samuel Newell wrote of his ordeal in only a few words that disguised the pain and the extent of the challenge for a wounded man in a ragtag frontier army without a medical department: "I was carried from the Mountain on a litter to the Catawba" River to his home east of Kings Mountain.[89]

Relatively few Patriots wrote anything about the hasty burial process of tossing bodies into two lengthy burial trenches—one Loyalist and one Patriot—partly because of its extremely haphazard nature. However, William Snodgrass, a citizen-soldier from the timbered hills of southwest Virginia, was one of the few survivors who described the totally inadequate burial process in some detail: "There were a few men left of our troops [after the departure northwest of the main task force], and the few of the British—each buried their own dead [and] they dug large pits and that in a number of them together, threw their blankets over them . . . it will be very difficult to ascertain where they were buried; or whether our men, and the British and Tories, were buried near the same place."[90] Ironically, this was perhaps the most symbolic act of all that was played out at Kings Mountain—the burying of Patriots and Loyalists together to lie forever side by side in South Carolina soil, since they were all Americans who died for what they believed was right, just like the fallen Union and Confederate soldiers at Antietam, Fredericksburg, and Gettysburg.

During the frantic march to reach the safety of the Blue Ridge Mountains before Tarleton and his green-coated hellions struck the withdrawing Patriot force that might well have resulted in a slaughter like in the tragic case of Colonel Abraham Buford's ill-fated Virginia command of Continentals, a host of ugly developments transpired. During the northwestern push, the life of Colonel James Williams came to an inglorious end. Joseph Kerr, of Scotch-Irish heritage, was a highly effective Patriot spy who had performed his key intelligence mission for the now mortally wounded Colonel Williams, a hero of the sparkling victory at Musgrove's Mill. The dying Colonel Williams had been brought from Kings Mountain in the hope of eventually transporting him to his Little River plantation in the South Carolina backcountry. Kerr wrote about the colonel's loss that sent a gloom throughout the army: "A mortal wound in the groin . . . terminated his life on the next day [Sunday October 8] after the battle before 12 O'clock [and in] conversing with him after the battle [Williams] knew he must die, and did so, cheerfully resigned to his fate."[91] Tearful members of his Little River Regiment from the South Carolina backcountry, who had carried him from atop Kings Mountain as gently as possible, laid their beloved colonel to rest.[92]

Prudently, Colonel Williams had made out his last will and testament on June 12, 1780, less than four months before the Battle of Kings Mountain, in which he specified that "My body to be Decently buried [by] My Executors."[93] In one of his last letters to his wife, Mary Wallace, Colonel Williams had emphasized for her to try to keep faith not only in God but also in the righteous cause that he considered sacred. He had penned heartfelt words to his wife, who had already been persecuted by Ferguson and his men like other members of the Williams family: "The uncertainly of your situation is my great mortification; but let our joint prayers meet in Heaven for each other and our bleeding country . . . I am with great regard your loving husband till death."[94]

As could be expected, the British and Loyalists had an entirely different view from that of Colonel James Williams. For instance, in a diary entry on July 10, 1780, Lieutenant Anthony Allaire described Williams as "a very violent, persecuting scoundrel."[95] By the colonel's side at his life's end were his teenage sons Daniel and Joseph, who had also fought at Kings Mountain and were destined not to survive this brutal war because the tragic fate of the hangman's noose of revenge-seeking Loyalists awaited them in the future. Colonel James Williams died beside the dusty road under the comforting shade of a large chestnut tree. Williams's death put the men of the frontier and Overmountain army in an especially nasty mood, and officers and men were angry. Worried that Tarleton might suddenly strike like a whirlwind, Colonel Campbell had already issued harsh orders that if he struck the column, then "immediately to fire on Captain De Peyster and his officers, who were in front, and then a second volley on the men."[96]

Chapter IX

Forgotten Decisive Turning Point of the American Revolution

Lord Charles Cornwallis and British leaders were stunned by the shocking news of the disaster at Kings Mountain and the swift elimination of one of the best commanders in the British Army and his entire task force of more than a thousand men. Perhaps Ireland-born Francis Rawdon, known as Lord Rawdon, said it best in regard to the unbelievable news of the vanquishing of Major Patrick Ferguson by a ghost army of country rustics that was not known to have existed: "A numerous army [had] appeared on the frontier, drawn from Nolachucky [sic], and other settlements beyond the mountains, whose very names had been unknown to us."[1] Equally surprised by the unexpected success on October 7, 1780, were American leaders, military and political, far and wide. Commanding the Continental Army in the South, Major General Nathanael Greene, who was stunned by the improbable success in the South Carolina backcountry, now came to the novel realization in this war how "the militia of the back country are formidable."[2] Perhaps none other than Colonel Isaac Shelby said it best in regard to the crucial importance of perhaps the most remarkable victory of the war on the decisive afternoon of October 7: "This battle happened at the most gloomy and critical period of the Revolutionary War, and was the first link in the great chain of events in the South that established the independence of the United States. It was achieved by raw and undisciplined riflemen without any authority from the Government under which they lived. It completely dispirited the Tories and so much alarmed Lord Cornwallis . . . that on being informed of Ferguson's total defeat and overthrow by the riflemen from the west [that] he ordered an immediately retreat [back into South Carolina]; marched all night in the utmost confusion and retrograded as far back [on October 14] as Winnsborough [sic] seventy or eighty miles."[3]

Indeed, as emphasized by one North Carolina historian who was right on target in his analysis:

> The battle of King's Mountain was decisive in its effect—shattering the plans of Cornwallis which till then appeared certain of success, and putting a full stop to the invasion of North Carolina, then well under way. Lord Charles Cornwallis abandoned his prepared campaign and left the State. The initiative of the [western] borderers, the loyalty of the militia, the energy of the pursuit, the perfection of the surprise . . . were the controlling factors in this overwhelming victory, and pivotal contest of the Revolution. The pioneers of the Old Southwest—the independent and aggressive yeomanry of North Carolina [including today's East Tennessee], Virginia, [Georgia] and South Carolina—had risen in their might; and without the authority of the blundering State governments, had created an army of frontiersmen, Indian fighters, and big game hunters which found no parallel or equal on the continent since [the battle of Point Pleasant in October 1774].[4]

In overall strategic terms, the victory at Kings Mountain sabotaged the British plan that if the South could be conquered, which had seemed inevitable, then "the Northern could thereafter be reduced by isolation and exhaustion [by the] Cut[ting of] the rebellious Union in two.[5]

Without exaggeration or hyperbole, one historian concluded how the "destruction of Ferguson and his entire command . . . was the turning point in the American Revolution in the South [and] Even though the redcoats continued to pursue the elusive goal of quelling the rebellion in the two Carolinas and Virginia for two more years, the fate of the King's fortunes in the South had been sealed by the utter annihilation of the Loyalist militia at Kings Mountain."[6] The ambitious British strategic plan of conquest was now in shambles because of defeat at Kings Mountain, because Lord Cornwallis had "counted on Ferguson to keep intact this force that was supposed to be the nucleus for a great popular uprising, and [now] it was irrevocably gone" forever.[7] Indeed, the astonishing victory at Kings Mountain was "the real turning point of the Revolution. Never again would the British be able to make a large-scale recruiting drive in the South [and] Part of the reason for the inhibited recruiting was the vengeance taken on the Loyalists by the over-the-mountain men."[8] Historian Benson Lossing concluded with insight how "no battle during the war, was more obstinately contested . . . it completely crushed the spirits of the Loyalists, and weakened beyond recovery the royal power in the Carolinas."[9] Colonel Robert Gray, a leader of the South Carolina Provincial Militia, revealed as much in regard to taking the crucial Loyalist equation out of the war in the South, writing: "Had our militia been certain of being treated as prisoners of war by the enemy [then] many more would have aided the royal standard."[10] Historian Robert Stansbury Lambert made the correct conclusion about how the dramatic victory at Kings Mountain "marked the turning point of the war in South Carolina, for before [Yorktown], the rebels had regained control of the state."[11] Indeed, an undeniable truth was expressed by a leading Loyalist officer in what was also a fitting tribute to the combat prowess of the Overmountain men and the skills of their incomparable popular leaders of the western frontier. In the words of Lieutenant Colonel Zacharias Gibbs, from the Fair Forest Creek region and who led the Spartan Regiment, which fought at Kings Mountain under Colonel Ambrose Mills, to Lord Cornwallis: "The opinion of the most experienced men is that the [Loyalist] militia cannot hold the back country as long as Holstein's [sic] River, Nolachucky [sic] and the Western Water People remained unconquered."[12]

Indeed, knowledgeable contemporaries like Gibbs accurately placed Kings Mountain in a proper historical perspective. Patriot Colonel William Hill, who had been born in Belfast, north Ireland, in 1740, saw Providence at work because of the miraculous rising of a frontier army and then the ultimate victory won at Kings Mountain: "As the result of that battle, was one grand link to the great chain of Providence & events that broke the plans of the enemy, to hold the Southern states as British provinces."[13] Major General Horatio Gates declared that the astonishing success at Kings Mountain was "Great and Glorious!"[14] In his revealing memoirs, Lieutenant Colonel Banastre Tarleton described the stunning setback in the remote South Carolina Piedmont at an obscure mountaintop: "The destruction of Ferguson and his corps marked the period and the extent of [Cornwallis's] first expedition into North Carolina. Added to the depression and fear it communicated to the loyalists upon the borders, and to the southward, the effect of such an important event was sensibly felt by Earl Cornwallis at Charlotte town, [especially] the total ruin of his militia, presented a gloomy prospect at the commencement of the campaign."[15]

In overall strategic terms, one modern historian concluded how the remarkable victory at Kings Mountain

> destroyed the British center of gravity, a well-organized Loyalist militia capable of securing South Carolina in the absence of British regulars. Not only did the disaster at Kings Mountain demoralize the surviving Loyalists, but it convinced [Cornwallis] to curtail attempts to recruit additional Loyalist militia regiments. Absent an effective Loyalist militia, the British did not have the manpower to both pacify South Carolina and continue the process of conquering the vast territory that lay between Charleston and the Chesapeake . . . The unexpected Patriot success halted the string of British victories in the south [while] Recruiting of Patriot militiamen improved enough to embolden [General Nathanael Greene] to take the offensive, leading to Brigadier General Daniel Morgan's victory at Cowpens, South Carolina, in January 1781.[16]

Another American historian emphasized the engagement's extreme importance, writing how "the battle of King's Mountain . . . turned the tide of Southern warfare. The destruction of Ferguson and his corps gave a complete check to the expedition of Cornwallis [because] he began to fear for the safety of South Carolina, liable to such sudden irruptions [sic] from the mountains; lest, while he was facing to the north, these hordes of stark-riding warriors might throw themselves behind him" to deal another devastating blow.[17] In the end, the defeat at Kings Mountain was very much a case of Major Patrick Ferguson's folly. Most of all, Ferguson "had paid a terrible price for underestimating the fighting abilities of his rebel foe and overestimating the security of his position atop Kings Mountain. Not only had he lost his life but also through the loss of his army of loyalists he had cost Cornwallis a vital offensive arm. Cornwallis would now have to rethink his strategy for overcoming the south."[18]

With a great deal of pride that was mixed with relief, therefore, a jubilant Patriot colonel wrote the good news to a fellow colonel on October 20, 1780: "Ferguson and his party are no more in circumstances to injure the citizens of America."[19] General William Davidson presented the joyous news that seemed unbelievable to General Thomas Sumter, the South Carolina "Gamecock": "Ferguson, the great Partizan, has miscarried" to ensure his doom.[20] Even before the Battle of Kings Mountain and especially after the unprecedented British disaster, Lord Cornwallis viewed the Loyalist militia as totally ineffective—an entirely unfair judgment (they fought extremely well on October 7) based partly on deep-seated British prejudices and contempt for the American fighting man on both sides—and doubted the validity of the entire Southern Strategy for winning the war based on raising Loyalist units to fight their war ("Americanization") to subdue fellow Americans.[21] Indeed, the concept upon which the whole British strategy for winning the war was based, of the Loyalists serving as an effective fighting force, had been punctured, like the bursting of a grossly inflated bubble, because Loyalists now correctly sensed that the tide had turned because of Ferguson's defeat and, therefore, they became much more hesitant to link themselves to a losing cause at such great risk to themselves.[22]

The great gathering of the Celtic clans in the Overmountain region and in the Southern backcountry had resulted in "not merely defeat" of the enemy, but "they had totally destroyed them" in incredibly short order and in record time.[23] Indeed, it had achieved more "than simply strip[ping] Cornwallis of his Loyalist light infantry and Major Ferguson, a promising and talented if overly rash officer [because it] had ultimately disastrous consequences for the royal cause," in the words of one modern historian, Stanley D. M. Carpenter.[24] In the future, Lord Cornwallis was fated to confront an even larger number of rebels across the South. They had rallied to the cause because they were now more confident about winning the ultimate victory after what happened on October 7, 1780. The elimination of Ferguson's entire command removed one of Cornwallis's best light commands (second only to Tarleton's British Legion) from the British Army, which was invaluable in performing reconnaissance, intelligence gathering, quick-strike capabilities, tactical mobility, and providing a highly visible force of well-trained men upon which large numbers of Loyalists could rally: All of these qualities were key for the Patriots to achieve decisive victory in the end and in thwarting the ambitious Southern Strategy. Indeed, the remarkable success on October 7 boldly advertised the dismal British strategic failure of utilizing large numbers of Loyalists to win the war—the central foundation of the entire Southern Strategy and the key to winning the war in the South.[25] Quite simply, the remarkable victory at Kings Mountain resulted in "the ruin of the Loyalist militia concept," which was the most important component of the British strategic plan for not only winning the war in the South but also later farther north, if everything had gone according to plan.

Conversely, the validation of the concept of effectively employing Patriot militia had been proven invaluable because "if properly led and given tactical tasks within their capabilities, [the militia] could be highly effective in battle."[26]

All in all, the remarkable success at Kings Mountain heralded nothing less than the end of Great Britain's bid to subjugate not only the South, but also the United States and the American people, while serving as "the grave of the last British hope of subduing the United States" for force of arms.[27] The news of the stunning Patriot victory that effectively wiped out about one-third of Lord Cornwallis's Army shocked Loyalists across the land, especially in the South; this was actually the beginning of the end of Great Britain's determined bid to retain its thirteen colonies. With considerable understatement, the *New York Packet* reported on November 23, 1780, how "Colonels Campbell and Sevier have taken a great part of Cornwallis' army, and a precious crew of Tories, at Kings Mountain."[28] Indeed, this most amazing Patriot success of the American Revolution in the South before Yorktown shattered the morale of the backcountry Loyalists and "undermined British strategy in the south, both in enlisting support and in subduing the backcountry [and] It left vulnerable to attack the chain of army posts that Cornwallis had established during his advance through the Carolinas. Cornwallis had to abandon his ambitious plans to launch a winter offensive in North Carolina and was forced to retreat sixty miles back to Winnsboro, South Carolina, to support his posts at Camden and Ninety-Six. He was unable to resume his planned attack for four months which allowed time for General Nathanael Greene to reconstitute a southern detachment of the Continental Army in North Carolina," while fueling the rise of greater resistance of the partisans, militia commands, and Continental troops across South Carolina.[29]

The astonishing repercussions of what happened at Kings Mountain in barely an hour entirely changed not only the course of the war in the South but also the overall strategic equation well beyond its borders and well into the future. Quite simply, the struggle of possession of Kings Mountain "was a requiem for Tories in America."[30] Ireland-born Lord Francis Rawdon, one of his lordship's top lieutenants, sensed as much, reporting to Lord Cornwallis how "the defeat of Ferguson was so dispirited this part of the country [the Carolinas], and indeed the loyal subjects were so wearied by the long continuance of the campaign, that Lieutenant Colonel John Harris Cruger [commanding at Ninety-Six] sent information to Lord Cornwallis, that the whole district had determined to submit as soon as the rebels should enter it."[31] He also wrote with disgust about the North Carolina Loyalists who later failed to rally to British service after the stunning defeat at Kings Mountain: "Not a single man attempted to improve the favourable moment [Cornwallis's invasion of North Carolina] or obeyed that summons for which they had been so impatient."[32] But Cornwallis said it best in regard to the disastrous strategic situation that existed for Great Britain after the fiasco at Kings Mountain: "The constant incursions of refugees, North Carolinians, Back Mountain men, and the perpetual risings in different parts of this Province, the invariable successes of all those parties against our militia, keep the whole country in constant alarm, and render the assistance of regular troops everywhere necessary."[33]

By any measure, the most surprising victory of this war in the South, and perhaps in all the Revolutionary War, represented "the finest hour" of the Southern fighting man, especially the Scotch-Irish, who were the finest mounted light infantry and citizen-soldiers in America during the all-important struggle in the South.[34] Most important, the Battle of Kings Mountain represented nothing less than a minor miracle that reversed the course of the American Revolution in dramatic fashion. Even more, "in that dismal autumn [for American fortunes in 1780] a rare event had occurred to lift rebel spirits during this long war—a victory by America. It had happened almost by accident, had been achieved by the kind of irregular forces [Major General Nathanael] Greene most despised, and had largely been brought about through overconfident blundering by a British commander [and] at the time it was an isolated and freak success."[35] Indeed, the high-stakes showdown at Kings Mountain was unique because perhaps "no battle in the Revolution was so picturesque or so furiously fought as that at Kings Mountain [and because] Not a regular soldier was in the American ranks [and] They fought under leaders of their own choosing" in the democratic tradition.[36] Ironically, it was the forest itself that proved the greatest advantage that had never been realized by Major Ferguson until it was too late. In the on-target words of Ireland-born Captain Alexander Chesney: "Kings Mountain from its height would have enabled us to oppose a superior force with advantage, had it not been covered with wood which sheltered the Americans and enabled them to fight in their favorite manner."[37]

Two of the greatest ironies and myths about the American Revolution and the war in the South were that the backcountry settlers were either mostly neutral or Loyalist after Charles Town's fall in late May 1780 and that the American militia—an old stereotype that possessed considerable validity beyond the South and farther north—was the worst fighting force in America. The much-maligned American militia had a record of average or poor performances in the campaigns with George Washington's Continental Army far to the north. However, like during the 1776 Cherokee War, the mounted Southern militia fought superbly dismounted as light infantry at Kings Mountain, thanks to the long rifle, the lessons learned from years of Indian fighting, and good horses that blessed these citizen-soldiers with an unmatched swift mobility. In truth, and although a long-ignored reality, the Southern militiamen, especially from the Overmountain region, might very well have been the finest fighters, experts at Indian and guerrilla warfare from years of combat, in America during the course of the American Revolution, which made them superior to not only the much-touted Continental regulars but also British regulars.[38]

General William Moultrie, the South Carolina lowcountry member of the privileged planter class, summarized the supreme importance of the climactic showdown at Kings Mountain: "This affair at King's mountain revived the drooping spirits of the Americans, and at the same time it was a very severe blow to Lord Cornwallis, to lose a brave, experienced and confidential officer, and eleven hundred men, was a serious consideration to him; after which he was obliged to contract his plans into very narrow limits, and he lost all hopes of recruiting his army from that part of the country. . . . The defeat of Colonel Ferguson, and the retreat of Lord Cornwallis to Winnsborough [sic], encouraged the American militia to collect and repair to the camps of their respective commanders; their turning out again obliged them to submit to strict discipline, and fight bravely."[39] But perhaps one shocked Loyalist partisan said it best: "The militia . . . was so totally disheartened by the defeat of Ferguson, that of that whole District, we could with difficulty assemble one hundred, and even those [militiamen] would not have made the smallest resistance if they had been attacked."[40]

Clearly, and to their everlasting credit, the homespun victors of Kings Mountain were the extremely tough, hard men who Governor John Rutledge, like so many others, never dreamed would rise up as one on such short notice, because they were in elitist and aristocratic minds nothing more than a "Pack of Beggars," as if they were nothing more than dirty London street urchins scouring around for crumbs from England's upper class.[41] Most important, it was these mostly lower-class and middle-class men of the backcountry and Overmountain region who delivered the stunning blow that "crippled" Cornwallis's Army at Kings Mountain and turned the tide to pave the way for the final chapter at Yorktown by sabotaging the British plan for winning the war by "Americanization" of the war effort.[42] Quite simply, the tide had been turned by the common man, not only in the war in the South, but also in the American Revolution by what had happened in barely an hour on Kings Mountain. Without the sparkling success at Kings Mountain, there would have been no winning of the struggle for independence.[43] Indeed, the Patriots had permanently gained the crucial initiative and momentum that would never be lost in the South for the war's remainder: a legacy of victory that continued all the way to Yorktown by the resurgent Patriots.[44]

However, unlike generations of Americans, including historians at the time and all the way to the twenty-first century, the most insightful British statesmen of the day prophetically understood that the unexpected "mongrel" victory by unschooled lower-class "barbarians" at Kings Mountain heralded dark portents ahead for British fortunes in America. As revealed in the pages of the *Maryland Gazette* on March 8, 1781, and in the month following the amazing one-sided success at Kings Mountain, a British member of the House of Commons declared with accurate insight and in no uncertain terms before the end of November: "The American war, a subject, which, unhappily, far from making us unanimous, which has formerly made us respectable and successful, seems now to have banished from us all future hopes" for success in America.[45] In the same newspaper published in Annapolis, Maryland, W. Davidson wrote a letter to Maryland Governor Thomas Sim Lee on October 10, 1780—which was published in the *Maryland Gazette* ten days later—from a camp on "Rocky River" by way of Thomas Sumter with an analysis that was right on target: "Sir, I have the pleasure of handing you very agreeable intelligence from the west—Ferguson [has been vanquished by the surprise attack at Kings Mountain which] lasted 47 minutes [and] This blow will certainly affect the British considerably . . . The above is true; the blow is great."[46]

In his journal on October 20, 1780, Dr. James Thacher of the Continental Army under Washington wrote how

> official intelligence is received of a very brilliant exploit of our militia in North Carolina. The famous royal partizan, Major Ferguson, was at

> the head of about one thousand and four hundred British troops and tories [but the Patriots] came up with him advantageously posted, at a place called King's mountains [sic]. No time was lost in making a vigorous attack, and giving the enemy a total defeat, in which Major Ferguson and one hundred and fifty of his men were killed, eight hundred made prisoners, and fifteen hundred stands of arms taken, with a trifling loss on our side, excepting the brave Colonel Williams, who received a mortal wound after being crowned with honor.[47]

A young soldier from Rhode Island, Private Jeremiah Greenman, penned in his journal intoxicating news that seemed too good to be true to greatly encourage Washington's Continental Army:

> This day we have an Extract from Genl. Orders Congratulating the Troops on an important advantage obtain'd in North [South] Carolina over a Corps of fourteen hundred Men, British Troops & New Levies, command by Colo. [sic] Ferguson, the Militia under Command of Colo. Williams & Shelby, who having colected [sic] to the amount of three thousand Men, detached Sixteen Hundred of their Number on hors [sic] back, to fall in with Fergisons [sic] party which they came up with at a place called Kings Mountain, advantageous posted & gave them at Total Defeat in which Colo. Forgerson [sic] with one hundred & fifty of his Men was killed & Eight-hundred made Prisoners [and] we took 15 hundred Stand of arms, in the attack we lost Colo. Williams & a very few men in proportion to that of the Enemies.[48]

Historian Jim Piecuch summarized the wide-ranging results stemming from the climactic showdown at Kings Mountain and its immense strategic consequences:

> What Ferguson intended is unclear, but it appears from his earlier operations that he hoped to induce the Rebels to attack him, so that while they were engaged they could be attacked in the rear by the reinforcements he had requested from Cornwallis. But the earl, however skilled he was in battlefield tactics, had limited abilities when it came to coordinating the operations of widely separated units. He sent

> no aid to Ferguson, who was only forty miles away. . . . The victory inspired the Whigs, demoralized the Loyalists and forced Cornwallis to abandon Charlotte and retreat to South Carolina. The advantage Cornwallis had won at Camden [in August 1780 by destroying Horatio Gates's army] was now completely lost, and British fortunes began to dim.[49]

Indeed, with the wiping out of his entire left flank task force and about one-third of his army, Cornwallis's fighting force had now essentially become a "dead whale upon the Sea Shore" at Charlotte, North Carolina.[50] Indeed, for the success of his much-anticipated united advance into North Carolina and farther north that had been the planned first stage for winning the war, Lord Cornwallis had desperately needed both his left and right wings of light troops to have advanced north simultaneously with the main army in the center from Charlotte. Consequently, the invasion of North Carolina came to an abrupt end with the shocking news of the Patriot victory at Kings Mountain. Now, Cornwallis, "instead of having a subdued population at his back," was "forced to allocate precious manpower on quelling districts he nominally controlled" in a stark reversal of strategic realities and the fortunes of war of a highly professional army recently thought to have been invincible by one and all.[51]

Using his prudent good judgment when he learned of the defeat at Kings Mountain, Cornwallis hastily retreated for fear that the Overmountain and backcountry men, who moved swiftly and with remarkable stealth over wide distances on their horses, might suddenly strike again on his left, or western, flank or even the rear. Near the end of October an astonished Patriot wrote with considerable disbelief about what seemed like nothing less than a miracle: "Cornwallis is retreating, and left his kettles boiling and about twenty or thirty wagons loaded."[52] Clearly, the surprising victory at Kings Mountain stopped Cornwallis's planned invasion of North Carolina and beyond far to the north in its tracks. The aristocratic lord was now out on a limb in his isolation amid a hostile North Carolina backcountry inhabited by far too many Scotch-Irish Presbyterians and with his left now dangling in midair after Ferguson's swift elimination. In short order and out of urgent necessity, a gloomy Cornwallis, who saw his dreams crushed, abandoned his North Carolina prize of Charlotte, the springboard for pushing north into Virginia and beyond. He then hurriedly retired all the way back to Winnsboro, South Carolina, and established winter quarters a good distance south of Kings Mountain to end active operations. But in truth and entirely unknown to him, or anyone else for that matter, Cornwallis was already doomed to a steady, continuous attrition that placed him on the road to Yorktown and the greatest British defeat of the war that was to ensure the winning of the American Revolution, thanks largely to what had happened at Kings Mountain.[53] In the end and inadvertently bestowing the greatest compliment to the Overmountain men, Lord Cornwallis reported to Sir Henry Clinton, who was headquartered in New York City, on December 29, 1780, "When the numerous and formidable body of the Back Mountain men came down to attack Major Ferguson [they] showed themselves to be our most inveterate enemies."[54] Even the often victorious and positive Tarleton was downbeat, lamenting "the total ruin of the [Loyalist] militia presented a gloomy prospect."[55]

As never before, the Loyalists across the Carolinas were now cowed by the unexpected victory of the war that caught both sides completely by surprise. The center of Loyalist resolve in the backcountry was virtually eliminated by an exodus of Loyalists east to the lowcountry with the startling news of Kings Mountain, until that center shifted to the low country and primarily to Charles Town because of the shocking reversal of fortunes in the backcountry, which no one had imagined possible in their wildest imaginations except a handful of frontier Patriot leaders, especially Colonel Shelby.[56] As noted, Lord Cornwallis gave up his hopes of utilizing an effective Loyalist militia that had been the primary basis of the Southern Strategy for winning the war. The psychological repercussions of the Kings Mountain victory steadily raised the level of resistance to a new high, which had vast repercussions that would echo around him month after month and all the way to Yorktown. As he penned to Clinton in New York City on January 6, 1781: "The perpetual risings in different parts of this province, the invariable successes of all these parties against our militia, keep the whole country in continued turmoil and render the assistance of regular troops every where necessary."[57]

Perhaps the words of one Loyalist partisan said it best in regard to the *lasting* meaningful aftereffects of the Kings Mountain victory: "The [Loyalist] militia was so totally disheartened by the defeat of Ferguson, that of that whole district [Ninety-Six], we could with difficulty assembled one hundred, and even those would not have made the smallest resistance if they had been attacked."[58] One of the smooth-faced teenage victors of Kings Mountain, Private James Collins, recorded the changed mood of the backcountry, where Loyalist sentiment faded away: "After the result of the battle was known, we seemed to gather strength, for many that before lay neutral, through fear or some other cause, shouldered their guns, and fell in the ranks."[59] Clearly, the tide had been permanently turned in the Southern war and in a decisive way because the amazing success at Kings Mountain "struck terror into the ranks of the Tories in the Ninety Six district" and across South Carolina and the South.[60] For the most part, the resolve of the Loyalists, who had been becoming formidable before October 7, and their widespread participation in this war had been effectively and forever eliminated by the stirring events at Kings Mountain. The removal of the centerpiece of the British strategy for winning the war to that point left Cornwallis and his army of mostly regulars more on their own than ever before: the strategic equation that eventually spelled his doom at Yorktown. Even diehard Loyalist partisan leader Robert Cunningham, who was the top leader in his South Carolina district in the backcountry, prudently advised his Tory relatives to relocate before it was too late, precisely because the tide had been turned for good in the backcountry and additional humiliating defeats were only a matter of time.[61]

Commanding British forces in Virginia and setting the stage for Yorktown, Brigadier General Alexander Leslie wrote to Cornwallis on October 24, 1780, about the new strategic realities ushered forth because of the most unexpected victory of the war at Kings Mountain: "By the Williamsburg [Virginia] papers sorry to hear of Major Ferguson's fate. It may, I am afraid, stop your Lordship's progress [north] towards us [in Virginia], and you are at such a distance it is not adviseable for me to penetrate [south] towards you, not knowing your situation, and the nature of troops under your command."[62] On December 9, 1780, Leslie penned the following to Lord Cornwallis from Portsmouth, Virginia, on the Chesapeake Bay: "The Williamsbourg [Williamsburg] papers of the 22nd October mentioned Ferguson's unhappy fate. This made us determine to establish a post here, for we foresaw your army under those circumstances could not penetrate so [far north and anywhere] near to Petersbourgh [Petersburg, Virginia] as I expected."[63] Most important, the powerful ripples from the total Loyalist defeat at Kings Mountain were felt by British leadership at the highest levels on both sides of the Atlantic for the remainder of 1780 and well beyond to the final showdown at Yorktown in October 1781. On November 4, 1780, a fearful, if not somewhat paranoid, Lord Cornwallis was still shaken by the breadth and thoroughness of Major Ferguson's defeat, writing to Lieutenant

Colonel Nesbit Balfour, who commanded the Charles Town garrison at the strategic port city on the Atlantic, about basically having to now buy loyalty to secure Loyalists, who were anything but highly motivated after what happened at Kings Mountain: "The 96 [South Carolina] militia must have considerable encouragement; I mean to give three month's back pay to those [Loyalists] who have been in constant service with Ferguson . . . I foresee that it will draw us into a great expence [sic] but I cannot help it, for should the [Loyalist] militia of this country absolutely refuse to serve, the consequences would indeed be fatal."[64]

Like Lord Cornwallis, Balfour was beset by a sense of panic because of the rise of resistance due to the most surprising of victories at Kings Mountain, as he revealed on November 1, 1780, to Lord Rawdon: "I have received many accounts of the numbers of the different rebell partys [sic] having increased considerably, and that they had cross the Santee both above and below Nielson's Ferry in small but many partys [and] the numbers and spirits [elevated by the Kings Mountain success] of the rebell partys so far unbalances that of our [Loyalist] militia [and] I fear much that they are become so formidable" as to prove unbeatable.[65] But from his headquarters at Charlestown on November 5, 1780, and barely a month after Kings Mountain, Lieutenant Colonel Balfour presented the ugliest realities for British fortunes in the South to Cornwallis that revealed how the great Patriot victory on October 7, 1780, had sabotaged the entire strategy upon which the conquest of the South was based: "The idea of [Loyalist] militia being of consequence or use as a military force I own I have now given up [and] I am at present from experience convinced that no militia of this province will be of any use to us as a military force."[66] In the same letter and never far from his mind, Balfour encountered all sorts of problems that stemmed, in his words of utter astonishment, "upon the whole unfortunate insurrection of the mountaineers, Ferguson's defeat and all the other bad consequences" of a conflict that was spiraling out of control at a rapid rate.[67]

Thanks to the defeat at Kings Mountain and as mentioned, Cornwallis was forced to call off his planned invasion of North Carolina until 1781. On November 12, 1780, barely a month after the dramatic showdown at Kings Mountain, he detailed the strategic situation to Balfour in a letter to reveal that he had cancelled, much to his disappointment, his planned triumphant march into North Carolina: "I have just received your letter of the 10th and Leslie's

[and] It convinces me that I was right not to go on. . . . The state of affairs at 96 absolutely require immediate offensive measures in that quarter or every thing will be lost."[68] On November 17, Lord Cornwallis described in another letter to Balfour the increasingly alarming situation in South Carolina caused by the Patriot success at Kings Mountain: "The situation of things in the 96 District was very unpleasant and distressing, our [Loyalist] friends terrified beyond expression, either flying down the country or submitting tamely to the insults and cruelties of the enemy, all the disaffected and many who had been neutral and some pretended friends flocking to the enemy's standard . . . I have no cavalry [after Ferguson's mounted task force had been eliminated and Tarleton on assignment] and am a little afraid of being alone in the part of the country you mention," and perhaps falling prey to the hard-hitting Overmountain men from regions not yet known at British headquarters.[69]

An increasingly gloomy Cornwallis, who admitted that he was "a little afraid" because of the extent of the disaster at Kings Mountain and the steadily deteriorating strategic situation across much of South Carolina, feared that if the garrison at the advanced post of Ninety-Six fell, then "not only South Carolina but Georgia must have fallen [and] Indeed, the carrying any of our post must be attended with fatal consequences."[70] At the end of his November 17 letter to Lieutenant Colonel Balfour, Cornwallis presented a gloomy assessment rooted in the undeniable realities stemming from Kings Mountain: "Either with Sumpter [sic], with Mecklenburg County, or with the Back Mountain men, we are sure of having perpetual war as long as the independence of America is in dispute."[71] Most of all, in overall strategic terms, the war's most remarkable and surprising victory at Kings Mountain "broke up the royal interest in the upper section of Carolina; it enabled our General [Nathanael Greene] to concentrate their forces upon great objects [and paved the way to] the splendid achievement at Yorktown."[72] Near the end of November 1780 when the first taste of winter in the backcountry had been felt, Lord Cornwallis was still worried where and when the Overmountain men might unexpectedly rise up once again to deliver a powerful blow and destroy British garrisons and independent task forces like in Ferguson's swift annihilation. In a November 27 letter to Balfour, Cornwallis feared that "the Back Mountain men were expected to join Sumpter [sic]" in still another swift uniting of highly mobile Patriots from both sides of the mountains like at Kings Mountain.[73]

In the citizen-soldier tradition and after fulfilling their vital mission, the ragtag victors of Kings Mountain returned to their families and homelands on both sides of the mountains. Upon reaching their isolated log cabins in the wilderness of the lush Holston, Nolichucky, and Watauga River Valleys of extraordinary natural beauty, these citizen-soldier volunteers, who had never worn a military uniform in their lives, once again hugged and kissed their wives and children, whom they feared they might never see again if the Cherokee had struck in their absence. In the balmy days of a mild Indian summer, young men and boys in hunting attire and civilian clothing now more fully thoroughly appreciated the meaning of Reverend Doak's inspirational words of "The Sword of the Lord and Gideon" as had been spoken at Sycamore Shoals, which had become their battle cry at Kings Mountain to inspire them to win the final victory. The victors saw new meaning in their Holy Bibles, especially the wisdom and moral lessons of the Old Testament, which were read more intently than before October 7, 1780, and the hand-carved wooden crucifixes that adorned the walls of their log cabins in the wilderness, because they realized that God had blessed them with a great victory second to none in the history of the Southern war.[74]

Hatred Continues to Fuel Patriotism

As mentioned, the most forgotten key to the victories at Kings Mountain and Cowpens, which were less than three months apart, was the great motivation of the common men in the ranks that stemmed from the seemingly endless list of British and Loyalist brutalities and cruelties of the war, which inspired desire for revenge and a determination to succeed at all costs. The situation developed because the British effort was caught in a fatal contradiction that was never resolved—no realistic solution existed at all—because of the inherent complexities and ambiguities in the nature of warfare and human nature: The pacification of a guerrilla war at the same time they were attempting to win hearts and minds and enlisting large numbers of Loyalist troops was an entirely paradoxical and impossible situation for them.

No atrocity after the Battle of Kings Mountain more incensed the Patriots of the South than the most infamous action of Bloody Bill Cunningham, who was now a major, on fateful November 19, 1781. On that day, he lived up to his infamous reputation while commanding a mounted partisan task force, including some men who had been members of Colonel Patrick Cunningham's regiment that fought at Kings Mountain, when he had raided the Saluda River Valley. Colonel Joseph Haynes, second in command of South Carolina's Little River Regiment and Colonel James Williams's friend, and around thirty-five of his followers were stationed at a blockhouse or "fort," which was located either at or near the colonel's Edgehill Plantation. Caught by surprise when the revenge-seeking members of the command of Bloody Bill, who was leading an especially hardened group of partisan Loyalists who had been driven from their homes primarily in Saluda County, South Carolina, the Patriots prudently barricaded themselves in the defensive structure in the nick of time. After a brief skirmish, the Loyalists set the structure on fire, which forced Haynes to surrender his command on the condition of decent treatment as prisoners. Of course, Cunningham had no desire whatsoever to bestow leniency or mercy in keeping with the viciousness of the war in the South. Reneging on his solemn promise to spare their lives, Cunningham proceeded to hang the prisoners as soon as they had laid down their weapons. He hanged Haynes, who had earlier led South Carolina militiamen against the Cherokee and later took command of the Little River Regiment after Colonel Williams's mortal wounding at Kings Mountain. Cunningham also hanged the sons of Colonel Williams, eighteen-year-old Captain Daniel Williams and fourteen-year-old Joseph Williams, who had fought at Kings Mountain and served in the Little River Regiment. Fourteen Patriots were killed in the Haynes massacre in the most brutal manner. Captain Williams's little son, Joseph, had requested of Cunningham in the most desperate of pleas, "Capt. Cunningham, how shall I go home and tell my mother that you have hanged brother Daniel." Bloody Bill promptly solved Joseph's personal dilemma by hanging the young man and fighter at Kings Mountain. The two sons of one of the foremost heroes of Kings Mountain and the highest-ranking Patriot leader who lost in life in leading the way to victory on October 7 were hanged by Cunningham.[75]

In June 1779, Daniel, before joining his father's Little River Regiment and now managing the Mount Pleasant plantation in his father's absence, had received a touching letter from his colonel father, who was in his late thirties: "I commit you to the care of Providence, begging that you will try to obtain that peculiar blessing. May God bless you, my son, and give you grace to conduct yourself, in my absence, as becomes a dutiful son to a tender mother and the family [and] I hope in God this will find you, my son, and your dear mother and the children, all well."[76]

Epilogue

The Battle of Kings Mountain, the greatest Patriot militia victory of the war, was the decisive turning point of the war in the South that reversed the course of the American Revolution. The completely unexpected success on the afternoon of October 7, 1780, "radically changed" the war by dramatically lifting the spirits of the often-defeated Patriots who became emboldened across the South, which caused many more men to join the resistance effort, while taking the war to the Loyalists with zeal. The fighting spirit and Patriot resistance effort of partisans, militiamen, and Continentals were not only solidified to a remarkable degree, but also strengthened on a continuous basis with each passing day until additional successes were won and everything came to fruition in the final showdown at Yorktown. In this regard, the sparkling success at Kings Mountain eventually translated directly into a host of other successes and set the stage for future victories for the war's remainder, including at Yorktown. Quite simply, the Kings Mountain victory was the most forgotten critical moment of the American Revolution in what was a "rare [battle] in the annals of warfare": the primary thesis of this book.[1]

In a December 3, 1780, letter to Sir Henry Clinton, Lord Charles Cornwallis lamented the disastrous fate of "poor Major Ferguson" and his entire command, knowing that he was now fighting an uphill battle because of the initiative and momentum that had been gained by the Patriots from the October 7 success.[2] To his superior in New York City, Cornwallis described the situation that led to the fiasco at Kings Mountain and the turning point of the American Revolution without ever realizing that his own tragic fate had already been sealed: Major Patrick Ferguson

> obtained my permission to make an incursion into Tryon County whilst the sickness of my army prevented my moving. As he had only militia and the small remains of his own corps without baggage or

> artillery, and as he promised to come back [to Charlottesville] if he heard of any superior fore, I thought he could do no harm and might help to keep alive the spirits of our friends [Loyalists] in North Carolina, which might be dampened by the slowness of our motions. The event [at Kings Mountain] proved unfortunate without any fault of Major Ferguson. A numerous and unexpected enemy came from the mountains. As they had good horses, their movements were rapid. Major Ferguson was tempted to stay near the mountains longer than he intended in hopes of cutting off Colonel [Elijah] Clarke on his return from Georgia. He was not aware that the enemy was so near him, and in endeavouring to execute my orders of passing the Catawbaw [River] and joining me at Charlottetown, he was attacked by a very superior force and totally defeated on King's [sic] Mountain.[3]

By any measure and although too often overlooked and minimized in traditional narratives of the American Revolution that have excessively focused on General Washington's less important campaigns (with the notable exceptions of the Trenton-Princeton campaign of 1776–1777 and the Yorktown campaign of 1781), the Battle of Kings Mountain was one of the most important and decisive engagements of the American Revolution, reversing the tide and changing the war's course in one of America's darkest hours, while paving the way for the final showdown and the surrender of Lord Cornwallis's Army at Yorktown. Unfortunately, however, the supreme importance of the Battle of Kings Mountain has long been obscured and silenced in traditional history books and by generations of historians, especially from the North, partly because this was a remarkable Southern victory, which then was ignored because Southerners became traitors to the nation when they seceded from the Union in 1860–61 and fought the bloodiest war in American history in 1861–1865.

Likewise, the dramatic story of the supreme importance of Scotch-Irish contributions to the South has also been tainted by demeaning racial and cultural stereotypes obscuring their crucial role in the winning of American independence and the making of America because they were nothing more than lowly "crackers" (a common view *both* then and today) entirely unworthy of acknowledgement in regard to having compiled one of the most distinguished and important military records in the annals of American history, especially at Kings Mountain. These were the men who made America—common, ordinary men who were citizen-soldiers of courage and faith who rose splendidly to the challenge, when the life of not only South Carolina, but also the very existence of their infant republic conceived in liberty was at stake.

In the end, the solemn prayer and fiery Old Testament words of Virginia-born Reverend Samuel Doak, the revered Scotch-Irish Presbyterian man of God from the Overmountain region, that were so eloquently spoken by him to the assembled citizen-soldiers in the picturesque setting of Sycamore Shoals on the Watauga River had inspired and fortified the moral resolve of those ordinary men who won the day at Kings Mountain. To the victors, this remarkable success had been ordained by God because they were righteous warriors of a holy cause second to none: just as Reverend Doak had promised by emphasizing that it was the most holy of wars that was biblical in nature and heralded a new vision for America in the future. At Kings Mountain, hundreds of attackers who sought to eliminate the greatest threat that they had ever known never forgot Reverend Doak's inspiring words, which had ultimately served as a forgotten catalyst that had played a role in reversing the course of a common people's revolution.

Doak's emotional benediction at Sycamore Shoals on the beautiful autumnal morning of September 26, 1780, had been answered with an intense righteous rage that was unleashed in full at Kings Mountain, which ultimately proved fatal to the determined British bid to subjugate the South, push farther north, and win the war. A major portion of England's finest army of conquest was vanquished in barely an hour by what was seen by the victors as resulting from the terrible "Sword of the Lord and of Gideon."[4] Like so many others, Reverend Doak firmly believed without any doubt whatsoever that a divine hand had brought forth the miraculous victory at Kings Mountain, because it was a righteous crusade and holy war against evil. In the representative words of a reflective Tennessee official: "I have thought how fate had named it King's Mountain [sic] and had placed the King's regulars on its summit, who shouted 'Long live the King!' as they looked down upon the advancing mountaineers . . . and I said God moves a mysterious way his wonders to perform."[5]

Equally symbolic to explain why they had fought with such tenacity and unbeatable spirit at Kings Mountain, the marble headstone of South Carolina's Private Samuel Shelton, a backcountry Patriot, was graced by words that were made possible by the victors of Kings Mountain and became a beautiful reality in the end: "He saw the last gasp of tyranny and the first breath of freedom."[6]

Likewise, the gravestone of Private Joseph White, who had been born in the largely Scotch-Irish community of Waxhaws, South Carolina, in 1763, was distinguished by the words: "With powder and ball he made the air to smoke and helped to free us from Britain's Yoke."[7] These are just some of the forgotten common men, frontiersmen, and backcountry settlers who were behind the true birth of the nation, which had to be won on the battlefield and not in the halls of the Continental Congress in Philadelphia, as these ordinary men realized and demonstrated on decisive October 7, 1780.

Appropriately and according to legend, it was an experienced Scotch-Irish fighting man named Joseph Greer, who was exceptionally tall and wore a coonskin hat, who was dispatched by Colonel John Sevier to ride more than five hundred miles northeast and all the way to Philadelphia to report the unbelievable news of an astonishing Kings Mountain victory in faraway South Carolina. Here, in November 1780 after the lengthy journey by way of Indian trails and a trusty compass, the illiterate, homespun Greer, who proudly wore frontier buckskin, boldly entered the chambers of the Continental Congress on his own and unannounced in defiance of standard political and upper-class protocol. Greer's towering presence and rugged frontier appearance of the Watauga settlement awed the smooth-talking and well-educated politicians in expensive powdered wigs and stylish silk clothing, including congressmen who had never fired a gun in battle or to put food on the table like this rustic messenger from the Overmountain region. Greer then presented the first news of the amazing victory at Kings Mountain to Congress, earning renown as "the Kings Mountain Messenger." Thanks to Greer, the astonishing news about the remarkable victory at Kings Mountain spread far and wide across America to cause widespread rejoicing.[8] According to tradition, General George Washington reportedly said of the Scotch-Irish fighting man in a glowing tribute: "With soldiers like that, no wonder the frontiersmen won."[9]

In a correct analysis, Major General Horatio Gates wrote how the "turning point of the American Revolution" victory had been won at Kings Mountain. Meanwhile, Washington knew that this incredible success of October 7, 1780, represented "an important objective gained" for the infant nation. But perhaps Thomas Jefferson said it best: "That memorable victory was the joyful annunciation of that turn in the tide of success that terminated the Revolutionary War with the seal of independence."[10] In London, British politician Horace Walpole informed sullen members of Parliament about the key demographic that had turned the tide, because of the dominant role and contributions of the Scotch-Irish Presbyterians, who were ever eager to reap revenge against their historic oppressors: "There is no use crying about it Cousin America has run off with a Presbyterian parson, and that's the end of it."[11] Sir Henry Clinton emphasized the overall importance of the climactic showdown at Kings Mountain, which "proved to be the first link in a chain of evils that followed each other in regular succession until they at last ended in the total loss of America."[12] Indeed, the Patriot success at Kings Mountain began the crucial process of effectively eroding the collective morale and the will of not only the British Parliament and ministry, but also King George III, that ultimately ensured the independence of the United States of America.[13]

For ample good reason, far more distinguished Americans of past generations thoroughly recognized the remarkable success at Kings Mountain than today, including even historians, because the victory "made us a nation of free and independent people" in an earthshaking development that changed the world.[14] And no leader was more responsible for this most remarkable and unexpected Patriot success of the American Revolution than Colonel Isaac Shelby, who was thereafter known as "Old Kings Mountain" because he symbolized the great October 7 victory for the rest of his life. Indeed, "he instigated the campaign leading to Kings Mountain, he drove it on, he shaped it" in its final magnificent form.[15] Indeed, in leading his homespun "mountain lads" to victory at only twenty-nine, Shelby was the man who had "conceived the goal of catching Ferguson and with boundless energy and single-mindedness drove the rude backwoods army to victory."[16] In the end, "the chief credit for inaugurating the entire campaign belongs to Shelby," because no commander was more responsible for the ultimate victory on October 7, 1780.[17]

Indeed, Colonel Shelby was the dynamic frontier leader who conceived the winning tactics that had allowed his "little army of mountain men," in the colonel's words of October 12, 1780, to surround Ferguson and then prevail by employing Indian-style tactics born of the frontier experience. A letter from John Sevier to Shelby revealed as much about the fruits of the informal decision-making process that was ultra-democratic in the frontier tradition, which had paid immense dividends in the end: "As to the plan of attacking the enemy, yourself was the only person that named the mode to me, and the same was acceded to unanimously . . . we [had previously] argued on the manner of attack immediately after Ferguson's spies were taken, while we were a little in front of our army, and as we were returning back to Campbell and the other officers."[18]

When all of the existing historical evidence and documentation has been weighed about what happened at Kings Mountain, a simple conclusion can be deducted: that the incredible success of the Overmountain and backcountry men in the most challenging military campaign of their lives might well have been justifiably called "Shelby's Victory" from beginning to end. Quite simply, if not for Colonel Isaac Shelby's many notable contributions throughout the campaign, then there might well have been no decisive victory on October 7, 1780. Indeed, because of an entirely unfair obscurity to this day, Colonel Shelby was the forgotten "father of the Patriot victory at Kings Mountain."[19]

In the beginning, it was Shelby who had conceived and then orchestrated in person what was nothing less, in the words of Colonel Arthur Campbell, than what proved to be the war's turning point: "It was Ferguson's defeat that was the first link in a grand chain of causes, which finally drew down ruin on the British interests in the Southern States, and finally terminated the war of the Revolution."[20] For these reasons, Orderly Sergeant William Delany, of Scotch-Irish descent, wrote how "it was generally said by those whom I heard speak of it at the time, that [Shelby] was entitled to more credit than any other officer at the mountain."[21] After the greatest victory of his career, Colonel Shelby returned to his beloved home of Sapling Grove nestled in the pristine wilderness of the South Holston River Valley—the land that he loved and fought to save during the climactic showdown at Kings Mountain. Neither Shelby nor his frontiersmen, who were all volunteer citizen-soldiers, or any of the victors at Kings Mountain were ever paid by the government for their distinguished services in the ultimate irony and one of the greatest possible injustices.[22]

The Most Forgotten Men Who Made America

Colonel Isaac Shelby paid tribute to his younger brother Moses Shelby, which was representative of the severe sufferings and hardships of the Overmountain men. In Shelby's admiring words about his brother, named after the most famous Hebrew prophet and "father" of the Israelites, who was just one of many forgotten and unsung heroes who rose to the challenge at Kings Mountain: "Moses was in his nineteenth year when he left his father's house to join the expedition against Ferguson and had never before . . . been more than forty miles from home [and] our march was too rapid for a youth of that age [because] the army having marched two or three hundred miles, and fought the battle in twelve days [and] Moses was severely wounded at the Mountain, and the bone of one thigh being fractured, he could be carried but a short distance from the battle-ground, where he lay on his back nearly three months, and was only able to ride out a few days." He then almost immediately joined the forces of Brigadier General Daniel Morgan just before the dramatic Battle of Cowpens in January 1781, where Moses was more seriously wounded than during the swirling combat at Kings Mountain.[23]

Today, the marble headstone of Lieutenant Thomas McCulloch, of Scotch-Irish descent and a member of Colonel William Campbell's Virginia Regiment who died on the long march away from Kings Mountain, eloquently said it best in regard to the true meaning of the victory at Kings Mountain for America. In the graveyard of Brittain Presbyterian Church, organized in 1768 and the first church established west of the Catawba River, Lieutenant McCulloch's tombstone reads in a fitting epitaph how he "lost his life in and for the honorable Just and virtious [sic] cause of liberty at the defeating Col. Ferguson's infamous company of bandity."[24] A dying Loyalist left his own scribbled last epitaph in his diary, which was found on his dead body on Sunday, October 8, by a Patriot soldier amid the carnage of Kings Mountain: "The cursed rebels came upon us killed and took every soul and so my dream friends I bid you farewell for I am started to the Warm Country" of hell.[25] Colonel William Campbell described with absolute delight in his official report about the decisive battle to Colonel Arthur Campbell from an encampment on Briar Creek in Wilkes County on October 20, 1780: "Ferguson and his party are no more in circumstances to injure the citizens of America."[26]

However, it should not be forgotten that the men who were defeated at Kings Mountain were fellow Americans, although almost always called "British," which has too often been the case in traditional and standard historical narratives, especially of a nationalist nature, that have focused on American exceptionalism and glorification. Colonel Shelby paid a compliment to the Loyalists and their martyred brash commander from faraway Scotland: "Ferguson did all that an officer could do under the circumstances. His men too fought bravely."[27] But in the words of one astounded Loyalist, it was not enough to simply outfight these mostly Scotch-Irish citizen-soldiers because the "'crackers' had no fear."[28] One disbelieving British general wrote to Cornwallis about the tenacity and fighting spirit of Southern Patriots that especially applied to the victors of the Battle of Kings Mountain: "I never saw such fighting since God made me. The Americans fought like demons."[29]

In a deeply personal letter written to his family in Scotland not long before his death on this hilltop of destiny, the religious-minded Major Patrick Ferguson, who was described by Lieutenant Antony Allaire as "brave, humane, and an agreeable companion," wrote heartfelt words of a philosophical nature that were among his last:

> I thank God more for this than for all his other blessings, that in every call of danger, or honor, I have felt myself collected and equal to the occasion. . . . The length of our lives is not at our command, however much the manner of them may be. If our Creator enables us to act the part of men of honor, and to conduct ourselves with spirit, probity, and humanity, the change to another world, whether now, or 50 years hence, will not be for the worse.[30]

At the height of America's miseries during the Great Depression and without exaggeration or hyperbole, President Herbert Hoover gave hope for a brighter future to the American people amid severe adversity in a radio broadcast to the country in which he emphasized how "there need be no fear for the future of a Republic that seeks inspiration from the spirit of the men who fought at the Battle of Kings Mountain."[31]

Today, the body of Major Patrick Ferguson rests in eternal peace in a draw situated on a wooded slope of Kings Mountain, and his final resting place has been symbolically marked by a clump of rocks of a traditional Scottish burial cairn. Like Ferguson, the more than two hundred Loyalists who died in the hard-fought battle should not be forgotten, nor the nine Tories, including high-ranking officers, who bravely went to their deaths at the Patriots' hanging tree on the march from Kings Mountain and "died like Romans," as penned Lieutenant Anthony Allaire with pride in his diary.[32]

As mentioned, these Overmountain and backcountry fighters who won the day on October 7 were certainly held in more absolute contempt and disgust by *both* friend and foe of the upper classes on both sides of the Atlantic before and during the war than any other white inhabitants of North America. Throughout the entirety of the colonial period and during the people's struggle for independence from 1775 to 1783, these Westerners of mostly lower-class origins—primarily immigrant roots from mostly Celtic nations, especially Ireland, long conquered by England in brutal fashion—without financial standing, economic prospects, or even the most basic educations were the most forgotten common men in America, but they nevertheless accomplished the impossible at Kings Mountain as America's most extraordinary fighting men of their day. Early banished to society's most remote margins and considered the lowest of the low by the elites of their ever-class-conscious, hierarchical world, these ordinary men of the frontier were mostly illiterate but they knew right from wrong, thanks to their Holy Bibles and revered men of God like Reverend Doak. After all, formal educations were not necessary for survival in their wilderness world, and most of them had never read the revered Age of Enlightenment works of the famous French philosophers, Thomas Paine's *Common Sense*, or even Thomas Jefferson's stirring words in the Declaration of Independence.

In the ultimate irony, if these common men of the Southern frontier from both sides of the Blue Ridge Mountains had depended upon the national or state governments or America's most famous leaders for assistance to deliver them from a true crisis situation and the enemy, then there would have been no United States of America today—the first government of the common people who overturned the rule of an autocratic European monarchy by a successful people's revolution for the first time in human history. In the end and as noted, what these ordinary men of the backcountry and Overmountain region reaped was nothing less than the real, but forgotten, turning point of the American Revolution. The dramatic victory at Kings Mountain played a vital role in the common people successfully cutting the links to the old planter-class world of the East Coast and to the Old World across the sea by opening the door to future westward expansion. This is a crucial, but forgotten, development because America's future and great promise lay in the seemingly endless lands of the North American continent that stretched to the Pacific, and these frontiersmen believed that they were the vanguard of the push west: a sacred right bestowed by God. In this sense, the men who won the day at Kings Mountain after some of the most savage combat of the American Revolution were also fighting for America's future that lay toward the setting sun. In this regard, the enemy at Kings Mountain represented stubborn obstacles and barriers that had to be removed at all costs to win the coveted opportunity to fulfill the promise of America for them and future generations, which equated to a limitless westward expansion and the conquest of an entire continent. For Colonel Shelby's men at Kings Mountain, America's very future and destiny were at stake, and they knew it to fuel their combat prowess on October 7, 1780.

Consequently, the climactic showdown at Kings Mountain was altogether different from other Revolutionary War battles that raged from 1775 to 1783 because much more was actually at stake for the Western pioneers on both sides of the mountains than simply another typical battle. Indeed, the bloody fight at Kings Mountain was about more than the struggle to win independence, the Continental Congress, and the Founding Fathers; it was actually about something altogether different: the historic and burning desire of the American people to fulfill their own personal destiny and that of their nation by pushing ever farther west, where there were no more redcoats, arbitrary rules, or regulations from kings on the Atlantic's other side to limit their ambitions that they viewed as deemed by God and the natural rights of man.

In the end, there would have been no great victory at Yorktown without the decisive victory at Kings Mountain that paved the way and made decisive success in 1781 possible. By any measure, Kings Mountain was one of the most remarkable victories in the annals of American history, especially because this triumphant frontier army had not been authorized by the national government in Philadelphia or drilled or trained like a conventional army as George Washington had long advocated. Instead in a raw, untamed land that had no laws, organized army, or Continental troops to protect the Western settlers, an ad hoc frontier army had formed by word of mouth from cabin to cabin in the wilderness to suddenly appear like magic to turn the tide of the American Revolution and save the day.

Consequently, by the disastrous summer of 1780, it had been left solely to the common people of the western frontier in the South to defend and save themselves because no one else would in a brutal Darwinian struggle that was one of life or death.

This book was written partly in the hope that the American people might be able to rediscover and better understand their own true heritage and most formative roots in regard to what it took for the common people of the frontier to overcome the odds and success in the making of America—self-reliance, resourcefulness, boldness, courage, and God-fearing to the end, which are all-important qualities that unfortunately are in short supply in today's America. The aristocratic Major Ferguson and Lord Cornwallis, who were Old World elitists to the core, learned the hard way about the fundamental truths of the backwoods and western character of these now forgotten American settlers and frontiersmen, who were mostly of the lower class and of the most humble of origins, not only at Kings Mountain on October 7, 1780, but also in the overall making of America.

Endnotes

Chapter I

1 Wade S. Kolb III, and Robert M. Weir, eds., *Captured at Kings Mountain, The Journal of Uzal Johnson, A Loyalist Surgeon* (Columbia: University of South Carolina Press, 2011), pp. 29–30; Harold Allen Skinner Jr., *The Staff Ride Handbook for the Battle for Kings Mountain* (Washington, DC: Combat Studies Institute Press, 2020) pp. 36, 80; Robert W. Brown Jr., *Kings Mountain and Cowpens, Our Victory Was Complete* (Charleston: The History Press, 2009), p. 48; John Buchanan, *The Road to Guilford Courthouse, The American Revolution in the Carolinas* (New York: John Wiley Press, 1999), p. 208; Archibald Henderson, *Isaac Shelby, Revolutionary Patriot and Border Hero*, The North Carolina Booklet, part 1, p. 142.

2 William T. Graves, *Backcountry Revolutionary, James Williams (1740–1780) with source documents* (Lugoff, SC: Woodward Corporation, 2012), p. 255.

3 Skinner, *The Staff Ride Handbook for the Battle for Kings Mountain*, p. 80; Brown, *Kings Mountain and Cowpens*, p. 48; Buchanan, *The Road to Guilford Courthouse*, p. 208.

4 Henderson, *Isaac Shelby*, TNCB, part 1, p. 142.

5 Kolb and Weir, eds., *Captured at Kings Mountain*, pp. 29–30; Lyman C. Draper, *Kings Mountains and Its Heroes, History of the Battle of Kings Mountain, October 7, 1780 and the Events which Led to It* (Johnson City: Overmountain Press, 1996), pp. 169, 488, 508–9, 541, 562; Skinner, *The Staff Ride Handbook for the Battle for Kings Mountain*, pp. 36, 80; James Webb, *Born Fighting, How the Scots-Irish Shaped America* (New York: Crown Publishing, 2005), pp. 24–160; John S. Pancake, *This Destructive War: The British Campaign in the Carolinas* (Tuscaloosa: University of Alabama Press, 1985), pp. 116–17; Henderson, *Isaac Shelby*, TNCB, part 1, pp. 142–43; Karen F. McCarthy, *The Other Irish, The Scots-Irish Rascals Who Made America* (New York: Sterling Publishing Company, 2011), p. 96; Brown, *Kings Mountain and Cowpens*, pp. 47–49; Sylvia Wrobel and George Grider, *Isaac Shelby, Kentucky's First Governor and Hero of Three Wars* (Cumberland: Cumberland Press, 1974), p. 43; Buchanan, *The Road to Guilford Courthouse*, pp. 208–11; Robert Stansbury Lambert, *South Carolina Loyalists in the American Revolution* (Columbia: University of South Carolina Press, 1987), p. 99; Brown, *Kings Mountain and Cowpens*, p. 48; Christopher Ward, *The War of the Revolution* (New York: Skyhorse Publishing, 2011), p. 740.

6 Dave Dameron, *King's Mountain, The Defeat of the Loyalists, October 7, 1780* (New York: Da Capo Press, 2003), p. 77.

7 Buchanan, *The Road to Guilford Courthouse*, pp. 210–11; Henderson, *Isaac Shelby*, TNCB, part 1, pp. 142–43.
8 Draper, *Kings Mountain and Its Heroes*, p. 507; Wrobel and Grider, *Isaac Shelby*, p. 45; Buchanan, *The Road to Guilford Courthouse*, p. 211.
9 Buchanan, *The Road to Guilford Courthouse*, pp. 226, 234–35; Skinner, *The Staff Ride Handbook for the Battle for Kings Mountain*, p. 80; Brown, *Kings Mountain and Cowpens*, p. 48.
10 Draper, *Kings Mountain and Its Heroes*, p. 474; Skinner, *The Staff Ride Handbook for the Battle for Kings Mountain*, pp. 57–58.
11 Brown, *Kings Mountain and Cowpens*, p. 48; Henderson, *Isaac Shelby*, TNCB, part 1, pp. 142–43.
12 Henderson, *Isaac Shelby*, TNCB, part 1, p. 143; Buchanan, *The Road to Charleston*, p. 29.
13 Henderson, *Isaac Shelby*, TNCB, part 1, p. 143; Draper, *Kings Mountain and Its Heroes*, p. 171.
14 Draper, *Kings Mountain and Its Heroes*, p. 563.
15 Buchanan, *The Road to Guilford Courthouse*, pp. 210–12; Henderson, *Isaac Shelby*, TNCB, part 1, p. 143; Dameron, *King's Mountain*, pp. 31–32.
16 Henderson, *Isaac Shelby*, TNCB, part 1, p. 144; Buchanan, *The Road to Guilford Courthouse*, p. 212.
17 Dameron, *King's Mountain*, p. 36; Henderson, *Isaac Shelby*, TNCB, part 1, p. 144; Buchanan, *The Road to Guilford Courthouse*, p. 212.
18 Buchanan, *The Road to Guilford Courthouse*, p. 212.
19 Dameron, *King's Mountain*, p. 34.
20 Buchanan, *The Road to Guilford Courthouse*, pp. 132–33, 142–44, 226; John F. Winkler, *Point Pleasant 1774* (New York: Osprey Publishing, 2014) pp. 73, 78–79.
21 Buchanan, *The Road to Guilford Courthouse*, pp. 226, 234–35; Skinner, *The Staff Ride Handbook for the Battle for Kings Mountain*, p. 23; Henderson, *Isaac Shelby*, TNCB, part 1, pp. 142–44; Wrobel and Gruder, *Isaac Shelby*, p. 46.
22 Brown, *Kings Mountain and Cowpens*, p. 48; Mary Adair Edwards Phifter, "Adair, John," NCpedia, https://www.ncpedia.org/biography/adair-john; Skinner, *The Staff Ride Handbook for the Battle for Kings Mountain*, p. 80; Buchanan, *The Road to Guilford Courthouse*, pp. 226, 234–35; Henderson, *Isaac Shelby*, TNCB, part 2, 3–4.
23 Draper, *Kings Mountain and Its Heroes*, p. 174.
24 Skinner Jr., *The Staff Ride Handbook for the Battle for Kings Mountain*, p. 23; Brown, *Kings Mountain and Cowpens*, p. 48; Henderson, *Isaac Shelby*, TNCB, part 2, p. 4.
25 Wrobel and Grider, *Isaac Shelby: Kentucky's First Governor and Hero of Three Wars* (Cumberland: Cumberland Press, 1974).
26 Benton Rain Patterson, *Washington and Cornwallis, The Battle for America* (Guilford: Lyon's Press, 2017), p. 246.
27 Brown, *Kings Mountain and Cowpens*, p. 49.

28 Patterson, *Washington and Cornwallis*, pp. 245–46; Wrobel and Grider, *Isaac Shelby*, p. 42.

29 Wrobel and Grider, *Isaac Shelby*, p. 42.

30 McCarthy, *The Other Irish*, p. 96.

31 Skinner Jr., *The Staff Ride Handbook for the Battle for Kings Mountain*, p. 20–21; Draper, *Kings Mountain and Its Heroes*, pp. 237–38.

32 Brown Jr., *Kings Mountain and Cowpens*, p. 64; Patterson, *Washington and Cornwallis*, p. 243.

Chapter II

1 Ward, *The War of the Revolution*, p. 741; Buchanan, *The Road to Guilford Courthouse*, p. 207.

2 Tara Mitchel Mielnik, "Arthur Campbell," Tennessee Encyclopedia, https://tennesseeencyclopedia.net/entries/arthur-campbell; Skinner, *The Staff Ride Handbook for the Battle for Kings Mountain*, p. 19; Buchanan, *The Road to Guilford Courthouse*, pp. 212–13; Gordon T. Belt and Traci Nichols-Belt, *John Sevier, Tennessee's First Hero* (Charleston: The History Press, 2014) p. 60.

3 Buchanan, *The Road to Guilford Courthouse*, p. 213; Henderson, *Isaac Shelby*, TNCB, part 2, p. 3; Wrobel and Grider, *Isaac Shelby*, pp. 45–46; McCarthy, *The Other Irish*, pp. 33–34, 100.

4 Skinner Jr., *The Staff Ride Handbook for the Battle for Kings Mountain*, p. 11; Buchanan, *The Road to Guilford Courthouse*, pp. 212–13.

5 Bobby G. Moss, *Roster of South Carolina Patriots in the American Revolution* (Baltimore: Genealogical Publishing Company, 1983), pp. 694–95.

6 Belt and Belt, *John Sevier*, p. 28.

7 Brown, *Kings Mountain and Cowpens*, p. 48.

8 Ibid.

9 Stanley D. M. Carpenter, *Southern Gambit, Cornwallis and the British March to Yorktown* (Norman: University of Oklahoma Press, 2019), p. 100; Michael C. Scoggins, *The Day It Rained Militia, Huck's Defeat and the Revolution in the South Carolina Backcountry, May-July 1780* (Charleston: Arcadia Press, 2005), p. 23–29.

10 Scoggins, *The Day It Rained Militia*, pp. 23–27.

11 Mielnik, "Arthur Campbell," Tennessee Encyclopedia; Draper, *Kings Mountain and Its Heroes*, p. 530.

12 Draper, *Kings Mountain and Its Heroes*, p. 563.

13 Carpenter, *Southern Gambit*, p. 97.

14 Ed Gilbert and Catherine Gilbert, *Patriot Militiaman in the American Revolution 1775–82* (New York: Osprey Publishing, 2015), pp. 14–17, 20, 24; Moss, *Roster of South Carolina Patriots in the American Revolution*, p. 968; Belt and Belt, *John Sevier*, p. 60; Wrobel and Grider, *Isaac Shelby*, p. 45; Dameron, *King's Mountain*, pp. 52–53; Thomas Fleming, *Cowpens* (Washington, DC: Department of the Interior, 1988), p. 12.

15 Gilbert and Gilbert, *Patriot Militiaman in the American Revolution 1775–82*, pp. 27–28.

16 Ibid., p. 30.
17 Skinner, *The Staff Ride Handbook for the Battle for Kings Mountain*, p. 58.
18 Patrick K. O'Donnell, *The Indispensables: The Diverse Soldier-Mariners Who Shaped the Country, Formed the Navy, and Rowed Washington Across the Delaware* (New York: Atlantic Monthly Press, 2021), pp. 41–47.
19 Robert M. Dunkerly, *The Battle of King's Mountain: Eyewitness Accounts* (Charleston: The History Press, 2007), p. 10.
20 Ibid; Abby Frye, "Mary Patton Undisputed Revolutionary War Hero, Historian Says," *Elizabethton Star*, August 4, 2015.
21 Draper, *Kings Mountain and Its Heroes*, p.507.
22 Dameron, *King's Mountain*, p. 34.
23 Leonard Hice, United States Government Pension Application, S8713, National Archives, Washington, DC.
24 Buchanan, *The Road to Charleston*, pp. 14; Carpenter, *Southern Gambit*, p. 100; Dan L. Morrill, *Southern Campaigns of the American Revolution* (Mount Pleasant: Nautical and Aviation Company of America, 1993), pp. 16–18; Wrobel and Gruder, *Isaac Shelby*, pp. 48–49; Rogers W. Young, *Rifles and Riflemen at the Battle of Kings Mountain*, pp. 15–18; Buchanan, *The Road to Guilford Courthouse*, p. 213–14; Brown, *Kings Mountain and Cowpens*, pp. 34–35; Draper, *Kings Mountain and Its Heroes*, p. 175; Pancake, *This Destructive War*, pp. 39, 51; Revolutionary War Soapstone Bullet Mold from North Carolina, Author's Collection; Gilbert and Gilbert, *Patriot Militiaman in the American Revolution 1775–82*, p. 26; Victor von Hagen, *The Germanic People in America* (Norman: University of Oklahoma Press, 1976), pp. 98–99.
25 Robert Bass, *Gamecock, The Life and Campaigns of General Thomas Sumter* (Orangeburg: Sandlapper Publishing Company, 2000), p. 60; Young, *Rifles and Riflemen at the Battle of Kings Mountain*, pp. 15–18.
26 Young, *Rifles and Riflemen at the Battle of Kings Mountain*, pp. 15–18; Buchanan, *The Road to Guilford Courthouse*, p. 241.
27 Gilbert and Gilbert, *Patriot Militiaman in the American Revolution 1775–82*, pp. 20, 22.
28 Ibid., pp. 16–18; Dunkerly, *The Battle of Kings Mountain*, p. 94.
29 Draper, *Kings Mountain and Its Heroes*, p. 70; Wrobel and Grider, *Isaac Shelby*, pp. 48–49.
30 Ibid.
31 Draper, *Kings Mountain and Its Heroes*, pp. 50, 70; Wrobel and Grider, *Isaac Shelby*, pp. 48–49.
32 Earle W. Crawford, *Samuel Doak: Pioneer Missionary of East Tennessee* (Limestone: Pioneer Printing, 1980), pp. 1, 3, 5–21, 24–25; Buchanan, *The Road to Guilford Courthouse*, p. 213.
33 Crawford, *Samuel Doak*, pp. 1–3; Belt and Belt, *John Sevier*, p. 62; Buchanan, *The Road to Guilford Courthouse*, pp. 226, 234–35.
34 John MacArthur, *The MacArthur Study Bible*, New King James Version (Nashville: Thomas Nelson, 1997), p. 343.
35 Ibid., p. 344.

36 Ibid., pp. 344–46.

37 Belt and Belt, *John Sevier*, pp. 60, 63–64; Crawford, *Samuel Doak*, pp. 1–3.

38 Crawford, *Samuel Doak*, p. 3; Draper, *Kings Mountain and Its Heroes*, p. 176.

39 Henderson, *Isaac Shelby*, TNCB, part 2, p. 4.

40 Brown, *Kings Mountain and Cowpens*, p. 49; Belt and Belt, *John Sevier*, pp. 62–64; Brown, *Kings Mountain and Cowpens*, p. 49; Crawford, *Samuel Doak*, pp. 1–3.

41 Charles Bracelen Flood, *Rise, and Fight Again: Perilous Times Along the Road to Independence* (New York: Dodd Mead and Company, 1976), pp. 352–53.

42 Dameron, *King's Mountain*, p. 36; Gilbert and Gilbert, *Patriot Militiaman in the American Revolution 1775–82*, pp. 16, 18; Wrobel and Grider, *Isaac Shelby*, pp. 46, 48; Buchanan, *The Road to Guilford Courthouse*, p. 214.

43 Draper, *Kings Mountain and Its Heroes*, p. 535; Dunkerly, *The Battle of Kings Mountain*, p. 19.

44 Dameron, *King's Mountain*, p. 36; Skinner, *The Staff Ride Handbook for the Battle for Kings Mountain*, p. 37; Draper, *Kings Mountain and Its Heroes*, pp. 471–72; Dunkerly, *The Battle of Kings Mountain*, p. 24; Patterson, *Washington and Cornwallis*, p. 246; Buchanan, *The Road to Guilford Courthouse*, pp. 214–15; Henderson, *Isaac Shelby*, TNCB, part 2, pp. 4–5; Wrobel and Grider, *Isaac Shelby*, p. 46; Robert Campbell Account, Lyman C. Draper Manuscript Collection, 17 DD 25, Wisconsin Historical Society, Madison, Wisconsin.

45 Buchanan, *The Road to Guilford Courthouse*, pp. 215–16; Randall Jones, *Before They Were Heroes at King's Mountain* (Daniel Boone Footsteps, 2011), pp. 427–28.

46 Jones, *Before They Were Heroes at King's Mountain* pp. 351–55.

47 Wrobel and Grider, *Isaac Shelby*, p. 46.

48 Buchanan, *The Road to Guilford Courthouse*, pp. 215–16; Jones, *Before They Were Heroes at King's Mountain*, p. 355.

49 McCarthy, *The Other Irish*, p. 100.

50 William T. Graves, *Backcountry Revolutionary*, p. 198.

51 Henderson, *Isaac Shelby*, TNCB, part 2, p. 4.

52 Ibid., p. 10.

53 Ibid., p. 4.

54 Agniel, *The American Revolution in the South 1780–1781*, p. 80; Buchanan, *The Road to Guilford Courthouse*, pp. 85–88.

55 Charles E. Hanson Jr., *The Plains Rifle* (Highland Park, NJ: The Gun Room Press, 1960), pp. 1–17; Belt and Belt, *John Sevier*, pp. 74, 77.

56 Hanson Jr., *The Plains Rifle*, pp. 13–17; John Buchanan, *The Road to Charleston, Nathanael Greene and the American Revolution* (Charlottesville: University of Virginia Press, 2019), pp. 3, 23; Young, *Rifles and Riflemen at the Battle of Kings Mountain*, pp. 15–18; Ward, *War of the Revolution*, p. 740; Skinner, *The Staff Ride Handbook for the Battle of Kings Mountain*, p. 2.

57 Brown, *Kings Mountain and Cowpens*, pp. 51, 56.

58 Skinner, *The Staff Ride Handbook for the Battle for Kings Mountain*, pp. 55–56.

59 Moss, *Roster of South Carolina Patriots in the American Revolution*, p. 941; Brown, *Kings Mountain and Cowpens*, p. 43.

60 Carol Berkin, *Revolutionary Mothers, Women's Struggle for America's Independence*, p. 37.
61 Norman Desmarais, ed., and annotated, *The Road to Yorktown, The French Campaign in the American Revolution, 1780–1783* (El Dorado Hills: Savas Beattie, 2021), pp. 160–61.
62 Buchanan, *The Road to Guilford Courthouse*, p. 206.
63 Belt and Belt, *John Sevier*, pp. 18–20.
64 Mary Hilliard Hinton, "Other North Carolina Heroines," *The North Carolina Booklet*, vol. 18, no. 1 (July 1918), p. 67.
65 Graves, *Backcountry Revolutionary*, p. 304; Draper, *Kings Mountain and Its Heroes*, pp. 86–87.
66 Draper, *Kings Mountain and Its Heroes*, pp. 86–87.
67 Ibid., p. 87.
68 Ibid.
69 Graves, *Backcountry Revolutionary*, pp. 138, 182.
70 Ibid., pp. 138, 142–43.
71 Ibid., p. 189.
72 Belt and Belt, *John Sevier*, p. 20.
73 Frank Moore, compiled, *The Diary of the American Revolution, From Newspapers to Original Documents* (New York: C. Scribner's, 1859), pp. 506–507.
74 Wrobel and Grider, *Isaac Shelby*, pp. 38–39.
75 Ward, *The War of the Revolution*, vol. 2, p. 740; Wrobel and Grider, *Isaac Shelby*, p. 39.
76 William Moultrie, *Memoirs of the American Revolution*, vol. 2 (Carlisle: Applewood Books, 2009), p. 219.
77 Draper, *Kings Mountain and Its Heroes*, p. 198.
78 Ibid., p. 488.
79 Holger Hoock, *Scars of Independence, America's Violent Birth* (New York: Crown Books, 2017), p. 267.
80 Buchanan, *The Road to Guilford Courthouse*, pp. 195, 200; Ward, *The War of the American Revolution*, vol. 2, p. 740; Morrill, *Southern Campaigns of the American Revolution*, p. 101.
81 Moultrie, *Memoirs of the American Revolution*, vol. 2, p. 237; Buchanan, *The Road to Guilford Courthouse*, p. 6.
82 Buchanan, *The Road to Guilford Courthouse*, p. 201.
83 Ibid., p. 202.
84 Ibid., p. 195.
85 Wrobel and Grider, *Isaac Shelby*, pp. 48–49; Skinner, *The Staff Ride Handbook for the Battle for Kings Mountain*, p. 11.
86 Patterson, *Washington and Cornwallis*, p. 243.
87 Lucien Agniel, *The American War in the South*, 1780–1781 (Riverside: Cheatham Press Inc., 1972), pp. 17–22, 52–53; Buchanan, *The Road to Charleston*, p. 1; Pancake, *This Destructive War*, p. 44; Buchanan, *The Road To Guilford Courthouse*, p. 226; Andrew Jackson O'Shaughnessy, *The Men Who Lost America: British*

Leadership, the American Revolution, and the Fall of Empire (New Haven: Yale University Press, 2014), pp. 6, 10, 215, 232, 249–55.

88 Flood, *Rise, and Fight Again*, p. 259.
89 Buchanan, *The Road to Guilford Courthouse*, p. 195.
90 Brown, *Kings Mountain and Cowpens*, p. 46.
91 Ibid., p. 48; Henderson, *Isaac Shelby*, TNCB, part 2, p. 5.

Chapter III

1 Lambert, *South Carolina Loyalists in the American Revolution*, pp. 147–48.
2 Moss, *Roster of South Carolina Patriots in the American Revolution*, p. 429.
3 Dameron, *King's Mountain*, p. 51; Lambert, *South Carolina Loyalists in the American Revolution*, pp. 24–25.
4 Lambert, *South Carolina Loyalists in the American Revolution*, p. 148; Andrew Ferguson, United States Governor Pension, Application, S32243, National Archives, Washington, DC.
5 Jacob Bealer Account, Draper Manuscript Collection, No. 2 DD 439–43, Wisconsin Historical Society, Madison, Wisconsin.
6 Moss, *Roster of South Carolina Patriots in the American Revolution*, p. 530.
7 Ibid., p. 668.
8 Ibid., p. 540.
9 Ibid., p. 503.
10 Ibid., p. 698.
11 Ibid., p. 937.
12 Louis B. Wright, *South Carolina, A History* (New York: W. W. Norton, 1977), p. 13.
13 Ibid., p. 147.
14 Moss, *Roster of South Carolina Patriots in the American Revolution*, p. 943.
15 Ibid., p. 1013.
16 Moultrie, *Memoirs of the American Revolution*, vol. 2, p. 242.
17 Flood, *Rise, and Fight Again*, pp. 264–65.
18 Buchanan, *The Road to Guilford Courthouse*, p. 217.
19 Carpenter, *Southern Gambit*, p. 169.
20 Dameron, *King's Mountain*, pp. 37–38; Buchanan, *The Road to Guilford Courthouse*, p. 217; Henderson, *Isaac Shelby*, TNCB, part 2, p. 5; Wrobel and Grider, *Isaac Shelby*, p. 47;
21 Skinner, *The Staff Ride Handbook for the Battle for Kings Mountain*, p. 10; Buchanan, *The Road to Guilford Courthouse*, p. 217.
22 Buchanan, *The Road to Guilford Courthouse*, pp. 217–18.
23 Ibid., 218.
24 Dameron, *King's Mountain*, p. 38; Henderson, *Isaac Shelby*, part 2, p. 5.
25 Dameron, *King's Mountain*, pp. 36, 38; Henderson, *Isaac Shelby*, TNCB, part 2, pp. 5–6.
26 Draper, *Kings Mountain and Its Heroes*, p. 564.
27 Skinner, *The Staff Ride Handbook for the Battle for Kings Mountain*, p.37; Henderson, *Isaac Shelby*, TNCB, part 2, p. 6; Patterson, *Washington and Cornwallis*, p. 247.

28 Skinner, *The Staff Ride Handbook for the Battle for Kings Mountain*, p. 37; Henderson, *Isaac Shelby*, TNCB, part 2, pp. 6–7; Buchanan, *The Road to Guilford Courthouse*, p. 218.
29 Buchanan, *The Road to Guilford Courthouse*, p. 218.
30 Graves, *Backcountry Revolutionary*, p. 255.
31 Buchanan, *The Road to Guilford Courthouse*, pp. 218, 226.
32 Ibid.; Henderson, *Isaac Shelby*, TNCB, part 2, p. 7.
33 Henderson, *Isaac Shelby*, TNCB, part 2, p. 7.
34 Ibid., pp. 7–8.
35 Skinner, *The Staff Ride Handbook for the Battle for Kings Mountain*, p. 37.
36 Benjamin Sharp Account, Lyman C. Draper Manuscript Collection, 17 DD 17, Wisconsin Historical Society, Madison, Wisconsin.
37 Henderson, *Isaac Shelby*, TNCB, part 2, p. 8; Wrobel and Grider, *Isaac Shelby*, p. 47.
38 Henderson, *Isaac Shelby*, TNCB, part 2, p. 9.
39 Henderson, *Isaac Shelby*, TNCB, part 1, p. 121; Winkler, *Point Pleasant 1774*, pp. 73, 78–79.
40 Wrobel and Grider, *Isaac Shelby*, p. 48.
41 Dameron, *King's Mountain*, p. 38; Wrobel and Grider, *Isaac Shelby*, p. 48; Buchanan, *The Road to Guilford Courthouse*, p. 220.
42 Kolb and Weir, eds., *Captured at Kings Mountain*, p. 30; Dameron, *King's Mountain*, p. 38; Wrobel and Grider, *Isaac Shelby*, pp. 48–49; Draper, *Kings Mountain and Its Heroes*, p. 509; Skinner, *The Staff Ride Handbook for the Battle for Kings Mountain*, p. 37; Phillip Thomas Tucker, *Alexander Hamilton's Revolution, His Vital Role as Washington's Chief of Staff* (New York: Skyhorse Publishing, 2017), pp. 9–11; Henderson, *Isaac Shelby*, TNCB, part 2, p. 9; Brown, *Kings Mountain and Cowpens*, pp. 51, 56; Buchanan, *The Road to Guilford Courthouse*, pp. 218–19.
43 Draper, *Kings Mountain and Its Heroes*, pp. 98, 124; Buchanan, *The Road to Guilford Courthouse*, p. 220; Wrobel and Grider, *Isaac Shelby*, pp. 48–49.
44 Buchanan, *The Road to Guilford Courthouse*, p. 219.
45 Skinner, *The Staff Ride Handbook for the Battle for Kings Mountain*, p. 37; Brown, *Kings Mountain and Cowpens*, p. 56; Henderson, *Isaac Shelby*, TNCB, part 2, p. 9.
46 Draper, *Kings Mountain and Its Heroes*, p. 509.
47 Skinner, *The Staff Ride Handbook for the Battle for Kings Mountain*, p. 37; Patterson, *Washington and Buchanan*, p. 247; Buchanan, *The Road to Guilford Courthouse*, pp. 214, 218–19; Wrobel and Grider, *Isaac Shelby*, pp. 48–49; Henderson, *Isaac Shelby*, TNCB, part 2, pp. 10–11.
48 Draper, *Kings Mountain and Its Heroes*, p. 509; Patterson, *Washington and Cornwallis*, p. 247; Buchanan, *The Road to Guilford Courthouse*, p. 219; Wrobel and Grider, *Isaac Shelby*, p. 46; Belt and Belt, *John Sevier*, pp. 63–64; Brown, *Kings Mountain and Cowpens*, p. 56.
49 Kolb and Weir, eds., *Captured at Kings Mountain*, pp. 30, 107; Skinner, *The Staff Ride Handbook for the Battle for Kings Mountain*, pp. 24, 37–38; Patterson, *Washington and Cornwallis*, p. 247; Buchanan, *The Road to Guilford Courthouse*, pp. 219–20, 223–24; Wrobel and Grider, *Isaac Shelby*, p. 49; Henderson, *Isaac Shelby*, TNCB, part 2, p. 10.

50 Patterson, *Washington and Cornwallis*, p. 247.
51 Kolb and Weir, eds., *Captured at Kings Mountain*, pp. 30–31.
52 Dunkerly, *The Battle of Kings Mountain*, p. 32.
53 Skinner, *The Staff Ride Handbook for the Battle for Kings Mountain*, p. 24; Henderson, *Isaac Shelby*, TNCB, part 2, pp. 9–10.
54 Henderson, *Isaac Shelby*, TNCB, part, 2, p. 10.
55 Ibid; Wrobel and Grider, *Isaac Shelby*, pp. 48–49.
56 Arnold J. Toynbee, trans., *Greek Historical Thought, From Homer to the Age of Heraclius* (New York: Mentor Book, 1952), pp. xxii, 72–73; Wrobel and Grider, *Isaac Shelby*, pp. 48–49; Nick Sekunda and John Warry, *Alexander the Great* (Oxford: Osprey Publishing Ltd., 2004), pp. 66–125.
57 Henderson, *Isaac Shelby*, TNCB, part 2, p. 11; Buchanan, *The Road to Guilford Courthouse*, p. 220; Skinner, *The Staff Ride Handbook for the Battle for Kings Mountain*, pp. 58–59.
58 Skinner, *The Staff Ride Handbook for the Battle for Kings Mountain*, p. 38; Patterson, *Washington and Cornwallis*, p. 247; Buchanan, *The Road to Guilford Courthouse*, pp. 220–21; Skinner, *The Staff Ride Handbook for the Battle for Kings Mountain*, pp. 24–25.
59 Graves, *Backcountry Revolutionary*, p. 255; Buchanan, *The Road to Guilford Courthouse*, pp. 221–23; Wrobel and Grider, *Isaac Shelby*, p. 45; Henderson, *Isaac Shelby*, TNCB, part 2, p. 13.
60 Benjamin Sharp Account, Lyman C. Draper Manuscript Collection, 17 DD 17, Wisconsin Historical Society, Madison, Wisconsin.
61 Draper, *Kings Mountain and Its Heroes*, p. 474; Buchanan, *The Road to Guilford Courthouse*, p. 222.
62 Buchanan, *The Road to Guilford Courthouse*, p. 222; Henderson, *Isaac Shelby*, TNCB, part 2, p. 13; Skinner, *The Staff Ride Handbook for the Battle for Kings Mountain*, p. 38.
63 Benjamin Sharp Account, Lyman C. Draper Manuscript Collection, 17 DD 17, Wisconsin Historical Society, Madison, Wisconsin.
64 Draper, *Kings Mountain and Its Heroes*, p. 459; Henderson, Isaac Shelby, TNCB, part, 2, p. 11.
65 Graves, *Backcountry Revolutionary*, p. 253.
66 Carl von Clausewitz, *On War*, indexed ed., trans. and eds. Michael Howard and Peter Paret (Princeton: Princeton University Press, 1989), p. 198.
67 Richard D. Blackmon, *Dark and Bloody Ground* (Yardley: Westholme Publishing, 2012), p. xxi; George MacDonald Fraser, *The Steel Bonnets, The Story of the Anglo-Scottish Border Reivers* (New York: Skyhorse Publishing, 2015), pp. 85–89.
68 O'Shaughnessy, *The Men Who Lost America*, pp. 256–59, 263, 265.
69 Blackmon, *Dark and Bloody Ground* p. xxi; John Knight, *War at Saber Point: Banastre Tarleton and the British Legion* (Yardley: Westholme, 2020), pp. 55–58, 133; Buchanan, *The Road to Guilford Courthouse*, pp. 58–59; Scott D. Aiken, *The Swamp Fox: Lessons in Leadership from the Partisan Campaigns of Francis Marion* (Annapolis: Naval Institute Press, 2012), pp. 27–193; Samuel A. Southworth,

Great Raids in History: From Drake to Desert One (Edison, NJ: Castle Books, 2002), pp. 1–3; Skinner, *The Staff Ride Handbook for the Battle for Kings Mountain*, p. 12.

70 Buchanan, *The Road to Charleston*, p. 16; Scoggins, *The Day It Rained Militia*, pp. 23–27.

71 Leonard Hice, United States Government Pension Record, S8713, National Archives, Washington, DC.

72 Draper, *Kings Mountain and Its Heroes*, p. 486.

73 Desmarais, *The Road to Yorktown*, p. 154.

74 Carl N. Degler, *Out of Our Past: The Forces that Shaped Modern America* (New York: Harper Touchbooks, 1967), p. 73; Morrill, *Southern Campaigns of the American Revolution*, pp. 5, 81; Buchanan, *The Road to Charleston*, pp. 14–15; Brown, *Kings Mountain and Cowpens*, p. 60; Buchanan, *The Road to Guilford Courthouse*, pp. 86, 88, 139, 222–23; Wrobel and Grider, *Isaac Shelby*, pp. 48–49.

75 Skinner, *The Staff Ride Handbook for the Battle for Kings Mountain*, pp. 1–2.

76 Buchanan, *The Road to Guilford Courthouse*, p. 222.

77 Graves, *Backcountry Revolutionary*, p. 296; Scoggins, *The Day It Rained Militia*, p. 99.

78 Buchanan, *The Road to Guilford Courthouse*, p. 220.

79 Moss, *Roster of South Carolina Patriots in the American Revolution*, pp. 694–95.

80 *Maryland Gazette*, Annapolis, Maryland, August 2, 1781.

81 Moss, *Roster of South Carolina Patriots in the American Revolution*, pp. 155, 753, 803, 818–20, 829, 834, 924, 929, 950, 959.

82 Charles Bowen Penson Application, Draper Manuscript Collection, No. 2 DD 228, Wisconsin Historical Society, Madison, Wisconsin.

83 Dameron, *King's Mountain*, pp. 38–39, 43–44; Dunkerly, *The Battle of Kings Mountain*, p. 64; Skinner, *The Staff Ride Handbook for the Battle for Kings Mountain*, pp. 25, 38; Henderson, *Isaac Shelby*, TNCB, Part 2, pp. 11, 13; Buchanan, *The Road to Guilford Courthouse*, pp. 114; 222–23; Thomas J. Fleming, *Cowpens: Official National Park Handbook* (Washington: Superintendent of Documents, 1998), p. 6; Graves, *Backcountry Revolutionary*, p. 125.

84 Benjamin Sharp Account, Lyman C. Draper Manuscript Collection, 17 DD 17, Wisconsin Historical Society, Madison, Wisconsin; Skinner, *The Staff Ride Handbook for the Battle for Kings Mountain*, p. 38; Henderson, *Isaac Shelby*, TNCB, part 2, p. 13.

85 Skinner, *The Staff Ride Handbook for the Battle for Kings Mountain*, p. 59.

86 Graves, *Backcountry Revolutionary*, pp. xi, xviii, xx–xxiii, 10, 19, 102–16, 125.

87 Ibid., pp. 15, 18.

88 Ibid., p. 121; Moss, *Roster of South Carolina Patriots in the American Revolution*, p. 994.

89 Graves, *Backcountry Revolutionary*, p. 121.

90 Draper, *Kings Mountain and Its Heroes*, pp. 86–87; Graves, *Backcountry Revolutionary*, p. 303.

91 Buchanan, *The Road to Guilford Courthouse*, p. 220; Henderson, *Isaac Shelby*, TNCB, part 2, pp. 10–11; Wrobel and Grider, *Isaac Shelby*, pp. 47–49.

92 Dunkerly, *The Battle of Kings Mountain*, p. 32.

93 Benjamin Sharp Account, Lyman C. Draper Manuscript Collection, 17 DD 17, Wisconsin Historical Society, Madison, Wisconsin; Buchanan, *The Road to Guilford Courthouse*, pp. 222–23.

94 Lambert, *South Carolina Loyalists in the American Revolution*, p. 100; Wrobel and Grider, *Isaac Shelby*, pp. 48–49.

95 Kolb and Weir, eds., *Captured at Kings Mountain*, p. 31.

96 Dunkerly, *The Battle of Kings Mountain*, p. 128.

97 Ibid., pp. 100, 136–37; William Seymour, *The Price of Folly: British Blunders in the War of American Independence* (Washington, DC: Potomac Books, 1995), p. 158; Draper, *Kings Mountain and Its Heroes*, pp. 510, 523; Skinner, *The Staff Ride Handbook for the Battle for Kings Mountain*, p. 38; Dameron, *King's Mountain*, p. 16.

98 Lambert, *South Carolina Loyalists in the American Revolution*, p. 100; Dunkerly, *The Battle of Kings Mountain*, p. 136; Dameron, *King's Mountain*, p. 16.

99 Dameron, *King's Mountain*, p. 16; Skinner, *The Staff Ride Handbook for the Battle for Kings Mountain*, p. 25.

100 Dunkerly, *The Battle of Kings Mountain*, pp. 137–38; Lambert, *South Carolina Loyalists in the American Revolution*, p. 86.

101 Skinner, *The Staff Ride Handbook for the Battle for Kings Mountain*, pp. 25–26.

102 Kolb and Weir, eds., *Captured at Kings Mountain*, p. 31; Seymour, *The Price of Folly*, p. 157–58; Lambert, *South Carolina Loyalists in the American Revolution*, pp. 85, 100, 112; Skinner, *The Staff Ride Handbook for the Battle for Kings Mountain*, p. 21; Buchanan, *The Road to Guilford Courthouse*, pp. 223–24; Wrobel and Grider, *Isaac Shelby*, pp. 48–49; Knight, *War at Saber Point*, p. 139; Brown, *Kings Mountain and Cowpens*, pp. 57–58; Jones, *Before They Were Heroes at King's Mountain*, p. 447; Dunkerly, *The Battle of Kings Mountain*, pp. 129, 137.

103 O'Shaughnessy, *The Men Who Lost America*, p. 264; Brown, *Kings Mountain and Cowpens*, p. 57; Wrobel and Grider, *Isaac Shelby*, p. 49; René Chartrand, *American Loyalist Troops 1775–84* (Oxford: Osprey Publishing Limited, 2008), pp. 4, 10; Dunkerly, *The Battle of Kings Mountain*, pp. 131, 133.

104 Skinner, *The Staff Ride Handbook for the Battle for Kings Mountain*, p. 35.

105 Ibid.

106 Patterson, *Washington and Cornwallis*, p. 247; Brown, *Kings Mountain and Cowpens*, p. 58.

107 Jones, *Before They Were Heroes at King's Mountain*, p. 448.

108 Brown, *Kings Mountain and Cowpens*, p. 57.

109 Ibid., p. 58; Skinner, *The Staff Ride Handbook for the Battle for Kings Mountain*, p. 121.

110 Dameron, *King's Mountain*, p. 49; Skinner, *The Staff Ride Handbook for the Battle of Kings Mountain*, pp. 20–21; Brown, *Kings Mountain and Cowpens*, p. 58.

111 1O'Shaughnessy, *The Men Who Lost America*, p. 224.

112 Patterson, *Washington and Cornwallis*, p. 248.

113 Ibid.

114 Ibid.

115 Graves, *Backcountry Revolutionary*, p. 256; "Colonel William Hill," Find a Grave, https://www.findagrave.com/memorial/133260248/william-hill; "The Patriot Leaders in South Carolina—Colonel William Hill," The American Revolution in South Carolina, https://carolana.com/SC/Revolution/patriot_leaders_sc_william_hill.html.
116 Skinner, *The Staff Ride Handbook for the Battle for Kings Mountain*, pp. 14, 18.
117 Buchanan, *The Road to Guilford Courthouse*, pp. 202–03; Knight, *War at Saber Point*, p. 108; O'Shaughnessy, *The Men Who Lost America*, p. 263.
118 Buchanan, *The Road to Guilford Courthouse*, p. 224.
119 Wrobel and Grider, *Isaac Shelby*, p. 49; Brown, *Kings Mountain and Cowpens*, p. 58.
120 Brown, *Kings Mountain and Cowpens*, p. 58.
121 Wrobel and Grider, *Isaac Shelby*, p. 49; Knight, *War at Saber Point*, p. 124.
122 Buchanan, *The Road to Charleston*, p. 2.
123 Knight, *War at Saber Point*, p. 128.
124 *Maryland Gazette*, November 3, 1780.
125 Mark Mayo Boatner III, *Encyclopedia of the American Revolution* (New York: David McKay Company, Inc., 1966), p. 582.
126 Moultrie, *Memoirs of the American Revolution*, vol. 2, p. 243, note.
127 Moss, *Roster of South Carolina Patriots in the American Revolution*, p. 980.
128 Ibid., p. 225.
129 Ibid., p. 596.
130 Ibid., p. 740.
131 Buchanan, *The Road to Guilford Courthouse*, p. 227; Brown, *Kings Mountain and Cowpens*, p. 59.
132 Henderson, *Isaac Shelby*, TNCB, part 2, p. 13; Wrobel and Grider, *Isaac Shelby*, pp. 1–2; Buchanan, *The Road to Guilford Courthouse*, pp. 226, 234–35.
133 Moss, *Roster of South Carolina Patriots in the American Revolution*, p. 241.
134 Ibid., p. 439.
135 Draper, *Kings Mountain and Its Heroes*, p. 70; Mark Mayo Boatner, *Encyclopedia of the American Revolution* (Philadelphia: David McKay and Company, 1966), p. 582.
136 Brown, *Kings Mountain and Cowpens*, p. 68; Si Sheppard, *Patriot Versus Loyalist, The American Revolution, 1775–1783* (New York: Osprey Publications, 2022), p. 65; Loretta Cozart, "Monument to African American Patriots at the Battle of Kings Mountain," Indiegogo, https://www.indiegogo.com/projects/monument-to-african-american-patriots-at-the-battle-of-kings-mountain#; Buskirk, *Standing in Their Own Light*, pp. 3–4.
137 Sheppard, *Patriot Versus Loyalist*, p. 65.
138 Andrew Ferguson, United States Government Pension Application, S32243, National Archives, Washington, DC.
139 John U. Rees, *'They Were Good Soldiers,' African-Americans Serving in the Continental Army, 1775–83* (Warwick: Helion and Company, 2019), pp. x-xi, 38, 108–17, 132–53.
140 Ibid., pp. 110–11.

141 Rees, *'They Were Good Soldiers,'* pp. 115–16; Cozart, "Monument to African American Patriots at the Battle of Kings Mountain."

142 Dameron, *King's Mountain*, pp. 31–32; Cozart, "Monument to African American Patriots at the Battle of Kings Mountain"; Jones, *Before They Were Heroes at King's Mountain*, p. 471; Rees, *'They Were Good Soldiers,'* pp. 114–16.

143 Cozart, "Monument to African American Patriots at the Battle of Kings Mountain"; Staff Reports, "Black American Hero of the Battle of Kings Mountain," August 11, 2012, *The Urban News*, https://theurbannews.com/communities/2012/black-american-hero-of-the-battle-of-kings-mountain.

144 Buchanan, *The Road to Guilford Courthouse*, pp. 206–07; Victor Wolfgang von Hagen, *The Germanic People in America* (Norman: University of Oklahoma Press, 1976), pp. 81–99.

145 James C. Kelly, *The Sword of the Lord and Gideon: A Catalog of Historical Objects Related to the Battle of Kings Mountain* (Boone: Appalachian Consortium Press, 1980), p. 19; Buchanan, *The Road to Guilford Courthouse*, p. 223; Gilbert and Gilbert, *Patriot Militiaman in the American Revolution 1775–82*, p. 47.

146 Draper, *Kings Mountain and Its Heroes*, p. 476.

147 Moss, *Roster of South Carolina Patriots in the American Revolution*, p. 522.

148 Ibid., pp. 180, 979.

149 History of Fincastle County, Va—Genealogy Trails, internet; "Philip Greever," Find A Grave, https://www.findagrave.com/memorial/74188981/philip-greever.

150 Von Hagen, *The Germanic People in America*, p. 160.

Chapter IV

1 Brown, *Kings Mountain and Cowpens*, pp. 59–60; Henderson, *Isaac Shelby*, TNCB, part 2, p. 13; Moss, *Roster of South Carolina Patriots in the American Revolution*, pp. 14–15; "Colonel John Moffet," Clan Moffat Genealogy Online, https://genealogy.clanmoffat.org/showmedia.php?mediaID=231&medialinkID=498.

2 Moss, *Roster of South Carolina Patriots in the American Revolution*, p. 315.

3 Ibid.

4 Ibid., p. 330.

5 Ibid., p. 544.

6 Henderson, *Isaac Shelby*, TNCB, part 2, p. 11.

7 Draper, *Kings Mountain and Its Heroes*, pp. 459, 552.

8 Brown, *Kings Mountain and Cowpens*, pp. 59–60.

9 Francis Marion Turner, *Life of General John Sevier* (Johnson City: Overmountain Press, 1997), p. 126.

10 Draper, *Kings Mountain and Its Heroes*, p. 553.

11 Ibid., pp. 292–93.

12 Samuel Newell Account, Lyman C. Draper Manuscript Collection, 3 DD 219, Wisconsin Historical Society, Madison, Wisconsin.

13 Benjamin Sharp Account, Lyman C. Draper Manuscript Collection, 17 DD 17, Wisconsin Historical Society, Madison, Wisconsin; Skinner, *The Staff Ride Handbook for the Battle for Kings Mountain*, p. 38; Henderson, *Isaac Shelby*, TNCB, part 2, p. 13; Buchanan, *The Road to Guilford Courthouse*, pp. 226, 234–35.

14 Gilbert and Gilbert, *Patriot Militiaman in the American Revolution 1775–82*, pp. 15–18; Buchanan, *The Road to Guilford Courthouse*, pp. 215, 237; Buchanan, *The Road to Guilford Courthouse*, pp. 226, 234–35.
15 Draper, *Kings Mountain and Its Heroes*, p. 552; Brown, *Kings Mountain and Cowpens*, p. 60; Buchanan, *The Road to Guilford Courthouse*, p. 223.
16 Benjamin Sharp Account, Lyman C. Draper Manuscript Collection, 17 DD 17, Wisconsin Historical Society, Madison, Wisconsin.
17 Dameron, *King's Mountain*, p. 34; Skinner, *The Staff Ride Handbook for the Battle for Kings Mountain*, pp. 38–39; Buchanan, *The Road to Guilford Courthouse*, p. 200.
18 Graves, *Backcountry Revolutionary*, pp. 254, 256.
19 Draper, *Kings Mountain and Its Heroes*, p. 212.
20 Belt and Belt, *John Sevier*, pp. 22, 93.
21 Ibid., p. 45.
22 Draper, *Kings Mountain and Its Heroes*, pp. 459, 552; Skinner, *The Staff Ride Handbook for the Battle for Kings Mountain*, p. 38; Buchanan, *The Road to Guilford Courthouse*, pp. 225–26, 234–35.
23 Dameron, *King's Mountain*, p. 43; Skinner, *The Staff Ridge Handbook for the Battle for Kings Mountain*, p. 38; Brown, *Kings Mountain and Cowpens*, p. 60; Buchanan, *The Road to Guilford Courthouse*, pp. 226, 234–35.
24 Dameron, *King's Mountain*, p. 43; Buchanan, *The Road to Guilford Courthouse*, pp. 226, 234–35.
25 Draper, *Kings Mountain and Its Heroes*, p. 552; Buchanan, *The Road to Guilford Courthouse*, pp. 225–26.
26 Moss, *Roster of South Carolina Patriots in the American Revolution*, p. 592; Buchanan, *The Road to Guilford Courthouse*, pp. 223, 226; Belt and Belt, *John Sevier*, p. 48; Roy McBee Smith, *Vardry McBee, Man of Reason in an Age of Extremes* (Spartanburg, SC: Laurel Heritage Press, 1997), pp. 37–40.
27 Brown, *Kings Mountain and Cowpens*, p. 60.
28 Buchanan, *The Road to Guilford Courthouse*, p. 336.
29 Draper, *Kings Mountain and Its Heroes*, p. 552; Wrobel and Grider, *Isaac Shelby*, p. 42.
30 Dameron, *King's Mountain*, p. 34; Skinner, *The Staff Ride Handbook for the Battle for Kings Mountain*, pp. 18–19, 62; Buchanan, *The Road to Guilford Courthouse*, pp. 225–26.
31 Draper, *Kings Mountain and Its Heroes*, pp. 479, 521; Brown, *Kings Mountain and Cowpens*, p. 60; Buchanan, *The Road to Guilford Courthouse*, pp. 226–27.
32 Draper, *Kings Mountain and Its Heroes*, pp. 302, 479.
33 Skinner, *The Staff Ride Handbook for the Battle for Kings Mountain*, p. 39; Buchanan, *The Road to Guilford Courthouse*, p. 227.
34 Buchanan, *The Road to Guilford Courthouse*, p. 227.
35 Ibid., pp. 224, 227.
36 Dameron, *King's Mountain*, pp. 43–44; Buchanan, *The Road to Guilford Courthouse*, p. 227; Kelly, *The Sword of the Lord and Gideon*, p. 19.

37 Moss, *Roster of South Carolina Patriots in the American Revolution*, p. 970; Gilbert and Gilbert, *Patriot Militiaman in the American Revolution 1775–82*, p. 44; Buchanan, *The Road to Guilford Courthouse*, pp. 227–28.
38 Gilbert and Gilbert, *Patriot Militiaman in the American Revolution 1775–82*, pp. 43–44; Draper, *Kings Mountain and Its Heroes*, pp. 292–93.
39 Dameron, *King's Mountain*, pp. 44, 49; Skinner, *The Staff Ridge Handbook for the Battle for Kings Mountain*, pp. 39, 63; Brown, *Kings Mountain and Cowpens*, p. 63; Buchanan, *The Road to Guilford Courthouse*, pp. 228.
40 Isaac Shelby and Hart Collection, No. 659z, University of South Carolina, Chapel Hill; Crawford, *Samuel Doak*, p. 21; Buchanan, *The Road to Guilford Courthouse*, pp. 226, 234–35.
41 Brown, *Kings Mountain and Cowpens*, p. 49.
42 Moss, *Roster of South Carolina Patriots in the American Revolution*, p. 547; Fred Anderson, *The War That Made America* (New York: Penguin Books, 2005), pp. 67–71; Sheppard, *Patriot Versus Loyalist*, p. 64.
43 Draper, *Kings Mountain and Its Heroes*, pp. 542–43; Sheppard, *Patriot Versus Loyalist*, p. 64; Buchanan, *The Road to Guilford Courthouse*, p. 228.
44 Sheppard, *Patriot Versus Loyalist*, p. 64,
45 Belt and Belt, *John Sevier*, p. 92.
46 Dameron, *King's Mountain*, p. 47; Buchanan, *The Road to Guilford Courthouse*, p. 228.
47 Henderson, *Isaac Shelby*, TNCB, part 2, p. 14; Belt and Belt, *John Sevier*, p. 92; Webb, *Born Fighting*, p. 160; Buchanan, *The Road to Guilford Courthouse*, pp. 226, 234–35.
48 Belt and Belt, *John Sevier*, p. 106; Henderson, *Isaac Shelby*, TNCB, part 2, p. 14.
49 Skinner, *The Staff Ride Handbook for the Battle for Kings Mountain*, pp. 39, 63; Buchanan, *The Road to Guilford Courthouse*, p. 228.
50 Dameron, *King's Mountain*, p. 47; Wrobel and Grider, *Isaac Shelby*, p. 50; Gilbert and Gilbert, *Patriot Militiaman in the American Revolution 1775–82*, p. 44; Skinner, *The Staff Ridge Handbook for the Battle for Kings Mountain*, p. 39.
51 Skinner, *The Staff Ride Handbook for the Battle for Kings Mountain*, pp. 64, 121.
52 Wrobel and Grider, *Isaac Shelby*, pp. 51, 60; Buchanan, *The Road to Guilford Courthouse*, pp. 226, 234–35.
53 Brown, *Kings Mountain and Cowpens*, p. 64; Dameron, *King's Mountain*, p. 49; Buchanan, *The Road to Guilford Courthouse*, pp. 228–29.
54 Skinner, *The Staff Ride Handbook for the Battle for Kings Mountain*, p. 35.
55 Ibid., pp. 39–40.
56 Lambert, *South Carolina Loyalists in the American Revolution*, p. 100.
57 Skinner, *The Staff Ride Handbook for the Battle for King Mountain*, pp. 24, 39; Lambert, *South Carolina Loyalists in the American Revolution*, p. 70.
58 Skinner, *The Staff Ride Handbook for the Battle for Kings Mountain*, p. 63.
59 Andrew Creswell Letter, December 5, 1822, Participant's File, Kings Mountain National Military Park, Blacksburg, South Carolina.
60 Draper, *Kings Mountain and Its Heroes*, p. 495; Dameron, *King's Mountain*, p. 49.
61 Fleming, *Cowpens*, p. 18.

62 Ibid.
63 Benjamin Sharp Account, Draper Manuscript Collection, No. 17 DD 17, Wisconsin Historical Society, Madison, Wisconsin; Skinner, *The Staff Ride Handbook for the Battle for Kings Mountain*, p. 80; Buchanan, *The Road to Guilford Courthouse*, pp. 226, 234–35; WHS; Graves, *Backcountry Revolutionary*, pp. 100–21, 225–26.
64 Benjamin Sharp Account, Draper Manuscript Collection, No. 17 DD 17, Wisconsin Historical Society, Madison, Wisconsin; Moss, *Roster of South Carolina Patriots in the American Revolution*, p. 970; Sheppard, *Patriot Versus Loyalist*, p. 64; Buchanan, *The Road to Guilford Courthouse*, pp. 227–29; Dameron, *King's Mountain*, pp. 48–49; Wrobel and Grider, *Isaac Shelby*, pp. 49, 51; Skinner, *The Staff Ride Handbook for the Battle for Kings Mountain*, p. 39.
65 Benjamin Sharp Account, Draper Manuscript Collection, No. 17 DD 17, Wisconsin Historical Society, Madison Wisconsin; Henderson, *Isaac Shelby*, part 2, p. 13.
66 Draper, *Kings Mountain and Its Heroes*, p. 524.
67 Henderson, *Isaac Shelby*, TNCB, part 2, pp. 13, 15; Buchanan, *The Road to Guilford Courthouse*, pp. 234–35.
68 Robert Campbell Account, Draper Manuscript Collection, No. 17 DD 25, Wisconsin Historical Society, Madison, Wisconsin.
69 Ibid.
70 Draper, *Kings Mountain and Its Heroes*, p. 543.
71 Dameron, *King's Mountain*, p. 47; Skinner, *The Staff Ride Handbook for the Battle for Kings Mountain*, p. 17.
72 Kelly, *The Sword of the Lord and Gideon*, p. 12; Draper, *Kings Mountain and Its Heroes*, pp. 242–43.
73 Kelly, *The Sword of the Lord and Gideon*, p. 14.
74 Moss, *Roster of South Carolina Patriots in the American Revolution*, pp. 6, 26.
75 Ibid., p. 757.
76 Ibid. p. 850; Fairfield, South Carolina, Irish history documents, author's collection.
77 Moss, *Roster of South Patriots in the American Revolution*, p. 894.
78 Ibid., pp. 427, 446; Sheppard, *Patriot Versus Loyalist*, p. 64.
79 Moss, *Roster of South Carolina Patriots in the American Revolution*, p. 658.
80 Ibid., p. 705.
81 Ibid., p. 986.
82 Draper, *Kings Mountain and Its Heroes*, p. 475.
83 Moss, *Roster of South Carolina Patriots in the American Revolution*, p. 705.
84 Lambert, *South Carolina Loyalists in the American Revolution*, pp. 99–101.
85 Wrobel and Grider, *Isaac Shelby*, pp. 48–49; Draper, *Kings Mountain and Its Heroes*, pp. 199, 204.
86 Draper, *Kings Mountain and Its Heroes*, pp. 312–13.
87 Field, "Battlefield Britain—Owain Glyn Dwr and the Battle for Wales," Battlefield Britain, September 24, 2004; Draper, *Kings Mountain and Its Heroes*, pp. 411, 460.
88 Draper, *Kings Mountain and Its Heroes*, pp. 247, 260–61, 304, 456–57.

89 Ibid., pp. 478–79.
90 Ibid., p. 461, 477–78.
91 Joshua Nichols, United States Government Pension Application, S32414, National Archives, Washington, DC.
92 Samuel Newell Account, Lyman C. Draper Manuscript Collection, 2 DD 219, Wisconsin Historical Society, Madison, Wisconsin; Draper, *Kings Mountain and Its Heroes*, p. 404.
93 "Kings Mountain," Georgia Sons of the American Revolution, 2021, https://gasocietysar.org/kings-mountain.
94 Ibid.
95 Skinner, *The Staff Ride Handbook for the Battle for Kings Mountain*, p. 18.
96 Agniel, *The South in the American Revolution*, p. 76.
97 Kolb and Weir, *Captured at Kings Mountain*, p. x; Lambert, *South Carolina Loyalists in the American Revolution*, pp. 58, 99–100, 104; Gilbert and Gilbert, *Patriot Militiaman in the American Revolution 1775–82*, p. 44; Dameron, *King's Mountain*, pp. 47, 50–52; Chartrand, *American Loyalist Troops 1775–84*, p. 10; Buchanan, *The Road to Guilford Courthouse*, pp. 228–29; Draper, *Kings Mountain and Its Heroes*, p. 527; Dameron, *King's Mountain*, p. 49; Wrobel and Grider, *Isaac Shelby*, pp. 48–51; Brown, *Kings Mountain and Cowpens*, p. 65; Philip Katcher, *The American Provincial Corps 1775–1784* (Reading, Berkshire, England: Osprey Publishing Limited, 1973), p. 23; Skinner, *The Staff Ride Handbook for the Battle for Kings Mountain*, pp. 14, 24; Daniel J. Brock, "Captain Samuel Ryerson," *Dictionary of Canadian Biography*, volume 5, (1801–1820); Stephen Foster and A. W. Putnam, "The Battle of King's Mountain," *The American Historical Magazine*, 1, no. 1 (January 1898): 27.
98 Fleming, *Cowpens*, p. 19.
99 Moss, *Roster of South Carolina Patriots in the American Revolution*, p. 486.
100 Draper, *Kings Mountain and Its Heroes*, p. 553
101 Henderson, *Isaac Shelby*, TNCB, part 2, pp. 7–8; Wrobel and Grider, *Isaac Shelby*, pp. 48–49.
102 Buchanan, *The Road to Guilford Courthouse*, p. 223; Draper, *Kings Mountain and Its Heroes*, p. 469.
103 Skinner, *The Staff Ride Handbook for the Battle for Kings Mountain*, pp. 41, 80.
104 Brown, *Kings Mountain and Cowpens*, p. 63.
105 Kelly, *The Sword of the Lord and Gideon*, p. 19; Buchanan, *The Road to Guilford Courthouse*, p. 227.
106 Buchanan, *The Road to Guilford Courthouse*, p. 227.
107 Brown, *Kings Mountain and Cowpens*, p. 65.
108 Dunkerly, *The Battle of Kings Mountain*, pp. 138–39; Jones, *Before They Were Heroes at King's Mountain*, p. 448.
109 Dunkerly, *The Battle of Kings Mountain*, pp. 138–39.
110 Ibid., p. 138.
111 Ibid., pp. 127–28.
112 John Franklin Account, Lyman C. Draper Manuscript Collection, R3756, Wisconsin Historical Society, Madison, Wisconsin.

113 Buchanan, *The Road to Guilford Courthouse*, p. 228.
114 Ibid.
115 Buchanan, *The Road to Guilford Courthouse*, p. 230.
116 Dameron, *King's Mountain*, p. 41; Henderson, *Isaac Shelby*, TNCB, part 2, p. 15; Buchanan, *The Road to Guilford Courthouse*, p. 229; Wrobel and Grider, *Isaac Shelby*, p. 49.
117 Henderson, *Isaac Shelby*, TNCB, part 2, p. 15.
118 Draper, *Kings Mountain and Its Heroes*, p. 524.
119 Dunkerly, *The Battle of Kings Mountain*, p. 92.
120 Dameron, *King's Mountain*, p. 43.
121 Buchanan, *The Road to Guilford Courthouse*, p. 229.
122 Graves, *Backcountry Revolutionary*, p. 320.

Chapter V

1 Dameron, *King's Mountain*, pp. 53–54; Brown, *Kings Mountain and Cowpens*, p. 65.
2 Dameron, *King's Mountain*, p. 54.
3 Ibid; Skinner, *The Staff Ride Handbook for the Battle for Kings Mountain*, pp. 17, 41, 92.
4 Foster and Putnam, "The Battle of King's Mountain," 27.
5 Draper, *Kings Mountain and Its Heroes*, p. 525.
6 Dunkerly, *The Battle of Kings Mountain*, p. 131.
7 Kolb and Weir, *Captured at Kings Mountain*, p. 31.
8 Skinner, *The Staff Ride Handbook for the Battle for Kings Mountain*, pp. 17 & 87, 41, 92; Brown, *Kings Mountain and Cowpens*, pp. 65–66; Benjamin Sharp Account, Draper Manuscript Collection, No. 17 DD 17, Wisconsin Historical Society, Madison, Wisconsin; Robert Campbell Account, Draper Manuscript Collection, No. 17 DD 25, Wisconsin Historical Society, Madison, Wisconsin; Wrobel and Grider, *Isaac Shelby*, pp. 51–52; Henderson, *Isaac Shelby*, TNCB, part 2, p. 15.
9 Dunkerly, *The Battle of Kings Mountain*, p. 131.
10 Kolb and Weir, *Captured at Kings Mountain*, p. 31.
11 Flood, *Rise, and Fight Again*, pp. 354–55.
12 Dameron, *King's Mountain*, p. 54; Draper, *Kings Mountain and Its Heroes*, pp. 246, 250, 525–26, 587; Skinner, *The Staff Ride Handbook for the Battle for Kings Mountain*, p. 17; Henderson, *Isaac Shelby*, TNCB, part 2, p. 15; Wrobel and Grider, *Isaac Shelby*, pp. 51–52; Winkler, *Point Pleasant 1774*, pp. 73, 78–79; Buchanan, *The Road to Guilford Courthouse*, pp. 234–35.
13 Henderson, *Isaac Shelby*, TNCB, part 2, p. 20.
14 Ibid.
15 Skinner, *The Staff Ride Handbook for the Battle for Kings Mountain*, p. 17; Henderson, *Isaac Shelby*, TNCB, part 2, p. 15.
16 Buchanan, *The Road to Guilford Courthouse*, pp. 234–35; Skinner, *The Staff Ride Handbook for the Battle for King Mountain*, pp. 17; Wrobel and Grider, *Isaac Shelby*, pp. 51–52; Henderson, *Isaac Shelby*, TNCB, part 2, p. 15.

17 Wrobel and Grider, *Isaac Shelby*, p. 52; Henderson, *Isaac Shelby*, TNCB, part 2, p. 20.
18 Wrobel and Grider, *Isaac Shelby*, p. 53.
19 Buchanan, *The Road to Guilford Courthouse*, p. 230.
20 Draper, *Kings Mountain and Its Heroes*, p. 418; Winkler, *Point Pleasant 1774*, pp. 73, 78–79: "Lt. John Sawyers," Geni biography, https://www.geni.com/people/Lt-John-Sawyers/6000000002932671614.
21 Henderson, *Isaac Shelby*, TNCB, part 2, p. 15; Wrobel and Grider, *Isaac Shelby*, p. 52.
22 Turner, *Life of General John Sevier*, p. 127.
23 Skinner, *The Staff Ride Handbook for the Battle for Kings Mountain*, pp. 121; Jones, *Before They Were Heroes at King's Mountain*, p. 449; Wrobel and Grider, *Isaac Shelby*, p. 52; Buchanan, *The Road to Guilford Courthouse*, pp. 210, 230; Sheppard, *Patriot Versus Loyalist*, p. 65.
24 Gilbert and Gilbert, *Patriot Militiaman in the American Revolution 1775–82*, p. 46; Buchanan, *The Road to Guilford Courthouse*, p. 229; Lambert, *South Carolina Loyalists in the American Revolution*, p. 100.
25 Buchanan, *The Road to Guilford Courthouse*, p. 230.
26 Draper, *Kings Mountain and Its Heroes*, p. 543.
27 Dunkerly, *The Battle of Kings Mountain*, p. 131.
28 Robert Campbell Account, Draper Manuscript Collection, No. 17 DD 25, Wisconsin Historical Society, Madison, Wisconsin.
29 Draper, *Kings Mountain and Its Heroes*, p. 543; Skinner, *The Staff Ride Handbook for the Battle for Kings Mountain*, p. 17; Gilbert and Gilbert, *Patriot Militiaman in the American Revolution 1775–82*, p. 44; Graves, *Backcountry Revolutionary*, pp. 225–26; Thomas Maxwell Account, Lyman C. Draper Manuscript Collection, 3 DD 236, Wisconsin Historical Society, Madison, Wisconsin.
30 Robert W. Gibbes, ed., *Documentary History of the American Revolution* (Columbia: Barnes Steam-Power Press, 1853), p. 140; Skinner, *The Staff Ride Handbook for the Battle for Kings Mountain*, p. 17; Wrobel and Grider, *Isaac Shelby*, pp. 51–52; Henderson, *Isaac Shelby*, TNCB, part 2, p. 15.
31 Draper, *Kings Mountain and Its Heroes*, p. 543.
32 Kolb and Weir, *Captured at Kings Mountain*, p. 31.
33 Philip Katcher, *The American Provincial Corps 1775–1784* (New York: Osprey Publishing, 1973), pp. 13, 18. 23; Graves, *Backcountry Revolutionary*, p. 256; Wrobel and Grider, *Isaac Shelby*, p. 52; Skinner, *The Staff Ride Handbook for the Battle for Kings Mountain*, pp. 14–15, 17, 41, 80–81, 90. Henderson, *Isaac Shelby*, TNCB, part 2, p. 20; Jones, *Before They Were Heroes at King's Mountain*, p. 449; Lambert, *South Carolina Loyalists in the American Revolution*, p. 99.
34 Skinner, *The Staff Ride Handbook for the Battle for Kings Mountain*, pp. 80–81.
35 Kolb and Weir, *Captured at Kings Mountain*, p. 31.
36 Gilbert and Gilbert, *Patriot Militiaman in the American Revolution 1775–82*; Skinner, *The Staff Ride Handbook for the Battle for Kings Mountain*, p. 14.
37 Draper, *Kings Mountain and Its Heroes*, p. 543; Skinner, *The Staff Ride Handbook for the Battle for Kings Mountain*, pp. 80–82.

38 Draper, *Kings Mountain and Its Heroes*, p. 543; Dameron, *King's Mountain*, p. 59.

39 Dameron, *King's Mountain*, p. 41; Draper, *Kings Mountain and Its Heroes*, pp. 494, 543.

40 Ibid., pp. 525–26, 587; Turner, *Life of General John Sevier*, p. 127; Wrobel and Grider, *Isaac Shelby*, pp. 51–52; Henderson, *Isaac Shelby*, TNCB, part 2, p. 15; Dameron, *King's Mountain*, p. 114.

41 Kelly, *The Sword of the Lord and Gideon*, p. 16; Henderson, *Isaac Shelby*, TNCB, part 2, p. 15; Wrobel and Grider, *Isaac Shelby*, pp. 51–52; Draper, *Kings Mountain and Its Heroes*, pp. 378, 589; Draper, *Kings Mountain and Its Heroes*, pp. 212, 242.

42 Dameron, *King's Mountain*, p. 32.

43 James Davison Account, Lyman C. Draper Manuscript Collection, No. 8 DD 68; Wisconsin History Society, Madison, Wisconsin; Draper, *Kings Mountain and Its Heroes*, p. 379; Sheppard, *Patriot Versus Loyalist*, p. 65; James (Davidson) Davison, II, WikiTree, internet.

44 Benjamin White Account, Lyman C. Draper Manuscript Collection, 3 DD 238, Wisconsin Historical Society, Madison, Wisconsin.

45 Draper, *Kings Mountain and Its Heroes*, p. 242.

46 Dunkerly, *The Battle of Kings Mountain*, p. 107.

47 "Rees Tate Bowen," WikiTree, https://www.wikitree.com/wiki/Bowen-936.

48 Robert Campbell Account, Lyman C. Draper Manuscript Collection, No. 17 DD 25, Wisconsin Historical Society, Madison, Wisconsin; Kelly, *The Sword of the Lord and Gideon*, p. 9; Dameron, *King's Mountain*, p. 57; Jones, *Before They Were Heroes at King's Mountain*, pp. 450–51; Brown, *Kings Mountain and Cowpens*, p. 66; Draper, *Kings Mountain and Its Heroes*, pp. 247, 456, 587; "Philip Greever," Find A Grave, https://www.findagrave.com/memorial/74188981/philip-greever; History of Fincastle County, Virginia, Genealogy Trails, https://genealogytrails.com/vir/fincastle/county_history_1.html; Skinner, *The Staff Ride Handbook for the Battle for Kings Mountain*, pp. 68, 87; Samuel Newell Account, Lyman C. Draper Manuscript Collection, 3 DD 129, Wisconsin Historical Society, Madison, Wisconsin.

49 Robert Campbell Account, Lyman C. Draper Manuscript Collection, No. 17 DD 25, Wisconsin Historical Society, Madison, Wisconsin; Jones, *Before They Were Heroes at King's Mountain*, p. 450–51.

50 Brown, *Kings Mountain and Cowpens*, p. 66.

51 Draper, *Kings Mountain and Its Heroes*, p. 242; Charles Bowen Account, Lyman C. Draper Manuscript Collection, No. 2 DD 228, Wisconsin Historical Society, Madison, Wisconsin.

52 Dunkerly, *The Battle of Kings Mountain*, p. 56; Draper, *Kings Mountain and Its Heroes*, pp. 404, 409.

53 Henry Dickenson Account, Lyman C. Draper Manuscript Collection, 3 DD 206, Wisconsin Historical Society, Madison, Wisconsin.

54 Draper, *Kings Mountain and Its Heroes*, pp. 251, 407; Dameron, *King's Mountain*, p. 57; Jones, *Before They Were Heroes at King's Mountain*, p. 451.

55 Draper, *Kings Mountain and Its Heroes*, pp. 251, 262, 305.

56 Jones, *Before They Were Heroes at King's Mountain*, p. 451.

57 Kolb and Weir, *Captured at Kings Mountain*, p. 31; Gibbes, *Documentary History of the American Revolution*, p. 140; Wrobel and Grider, *Isaac Shelby*, p. 52; Buchanan, *The Road to Guilford Courthouse*, p. 229; Skinner, *The Staff Ridge Handbook for the Battle for Kings Mountain*, p. 87.

58 Gilbert and Gilbert, *Patriot Militiaman in the American Revolution 1775–82*, p. 46.

59 Dunkerly, *The Battle of Kings Mountain*, pp. 85, 88.

60 Brown, *Kings Mountain and Cowpens*, p. 66–67; Emails from Lamar Tate, Kings Mountain National Military Park, Blacksburg, South Carolina, to author, May 14, 2021.

61 Henry Dickenson Account, Lyman C. Draper Manuscript Collection, 3 DD 206, Wisconsin Historical Society, Madison, Wisconsin; Dunkerly, *The Battle of Kings Mountain*, pp. 85, 88; Brown, *Kings Mountain and Cowpens*, p. 68; Skinner, *The Staff Ride Handbook for the Battle for Kings Mountain*, p. 87; Buchanan, *The Road to Guilford Courthouse*, p. 230; James Crow Account, Lyman C. Draper Manuscript Collection, 3 DD 198, Wisconsin Historical Society, Madison, Wisconsin.

62 James Crow Account, Lyman C. Draper Manuscript Collection, 3 DD 198, Wisconsin Historical Society, Madison, Wisconsin; Skinner, *The Staff Ride Handbook for the Battle for Kings Mountain*, p. 24; Jones, *Before They Were Heroes at King's Mountain*, pp. 451–52.

63 Jones, *Before They Were Heroes at King's Mountain*, p. 452.

64 Dunkerly, *The Battle of Kings Mountain*, p. 85.

65 Draper, *Kings Mountain and its Heroes*, pp. 255–56; Kelly, *The Sword of the Lord and Gideon*, p. 13; Brown, *Kings Mountain and Cowpens*, p. 69.

66 Dameron, *King's Mountain*, pp. 61–62.

67 Leonard Hice, United States Government Pension Application, S8713, National Archives, Washington, DC.

68 James Crow Account, Lyman C. Draper Manuscript Collection, 3 DD 198, Wisconsin Historical Society, Madison, Wisconsin; Brown, *Kings Mountain and Cowpens*, pp. 68–69.

69 Joseph Starns, United States Government Pension Application, S7600, National Archives, Washington, DC.

70 Skinner, *The Staff Ride Handbook for the Battle for Kings Mountain*, pp. 82, 87.

71 Ibid., p. 82.

72 Foster and Putnam, "The Battle of King's Mountain," p. 28.

73 Samuel Newell Account, Lyman C. Draper Manuscript Collection, 2 DD 129, Wisconsin Historical Society, Madison, Wisconsin.

74 Andrew Ferguson, United States Government Pension Application, S32243, National Archives, Washington, DC; Joseph Starns, United States Government Pension Application, S7600, National Archives, Washington, DC.

75 Dunkerly, *The Battle of Kings Mountain*, p. 141.

76 Kolb and Weir, *Captured at Kings Mountain*, p. 31; Skinner, *The Staff Ride Handbook for the Battle for Kings Mountain*, pp. 80, 82, 87; Jones, *Before They Were Heroes at King's Mountain*, p. 452.

77 Draper, *Kings Mountain and Its Heroes*, pp. 255, 257.

78 Ibid., p. 255.
79 Dameron, *King's Mountain*, p. 60.
80 Dunkerly, *The Battle of Kings Mountain*, pp. 85, 88.
81 Jones, *Before They Were Heroes at King's Mountain*, p. 452.
82 Draper, *Kings Mountain and Its Heroes*, p. 405.
83 Dameron, *King's Mountain*, p. 60.
84 Kolb and Weir, *Captured at Kings Mountain*, p. 31; Buchanan, *The Road to Guilford Courthouse*, p. 230; Jones, *Before They Were Heroes at King's Mountain*, pp. 451–52; Brown, *Kings Mountain and Cowpens*, p. 69; Dameron, *King's Mountain*, pp. 59–60.
85 Buchanan, *The Road to Guilford Courthouse*, p. 232.
86 Ibid.
87 Dameron, *King's Mountain*, p. 60; Skinner, *The Staff Ride Handbook for the Battle for Kings Mountain*, p. 81; Brown, *Kings Mountain and Cowpens*, pp. 68.
88 Dameron, *King's Mountain*, p. 60.
89 Draper, *Kings Mountain and Its Heroes*, p. 479.
90 Dameron, *King's Mountain*, p. 60; Skinner, *The Staff Ride Handbook for the Battle for Kings Mountain*, p. 81; Brown, *Kings Mountain and Cowpens*, p.68.
91 Joseph Starns, United States Government Pension Application, National Archives, Washington, DC; Dameron, *King's Mountain*, p. 60.
92 Dunkerly, *The Battle of Kings Mountain*, p. 88.
93 Unknown Author, Lyman C. Draper Manuscript Collection, 16 DD 66, Wisconsin Historical Society, Madison, Wisconsin.
94 Draper, *Kings Mountain and Its Heroes*, p. 543; Dameron, *King's Mountain*, pp. 60–61; Brown, *Kings Mountain and Cowpens*, pp. 68–69.
95 Dameron, *King's Mountain*, pp. 59, 61–62; Skinner, *The Staff Ride Handbook for the Battle for Kings Mountain*, p. 90.
96 Dameron, *King's Mountain*, p. 59; Skinner, *The Staff Ride Handbook for the Battle for Kings Mountain*, p. 90.
97 Skinner, *The Staff Ride Handbook for the Battle for Kings Mountain*, p. 92.
98 Draper, *Kings Mountain and Its Heroes*, p. 588.
99 Kolb and Weir, *Captured at Kings Mountain*, p. 31; Dameron, *King's Mountain*, p. 60.
100 Thomas Maxwell Account, Lyman C. Draper Manuscript Collection, 3 DD 236, Wisconsin Historical Society, Madison, Wisconsin; Draper, *Kings Mountain and Its Heroes*, p. 252.
101 Thomas Maxwell Account, Lyman C. Draper Manuscript Collection, 3 DD 236, Wisconsin Historical Society, Madison, Wisconsin.
102 Ibid., Draper, *Kings Mountain and Its Heroes*, p. 526; Dameron, *King's Mountain*, pp. 58, 61–62; Skinner, *The Staff Ride Handbook for the Battle for Kings Mountain*, pp. 48, 80, 83–84; Turner, *Life of General John Sevier*, p. 61.
103 Thomas Maxwell Account, Lyman C. Draper Manuscript Collection, 3 DD 236, Wisconsin Historical Society, Madison, Wisconsin; Draper, *Kings Mountain and Its Heroes*, pp. 104, 423, 543; Skinner, *The Staff Ride Handbook for the Battle for Kings Mountain*, pp. 42; 81–84; Gilbert and Gilbert, *Patriot Militiaman in the*

American Revolution, 1775–82, p. 46; Kelly, *The Sword of the Lord and Gideon*, pp. 15, 17; Dameron, *King's Mountain*, pp. 61–62; Turner, *Life of General John Sevier*, pp. 129–130; Jones, *Before They Were Heroes at King's Mountain*, pp. 460–461; "Episode 12—Jonathan Tipton," September 17, 2019, *OVM Podcast*, Mitchell County Historical Society, Bakersville, North Carolina.

104 Kolb and Weir, *Captured at Kings Mountain*, p. 31.

105 Draper, *Kings Mountain and Its Heroes*, p. 543.

106 Mark Derr, *The Frontiersman: The Real Life and the Many Legends of Davy Crockett* (New York: William Morrow, 1994), pp. 37–40.

Chapter VI

1 Brown, *Kings Mountain and Cowpens*, p. 75; Skinner, *The Staff Ride Handbook for the Battle for Kings Mountain*, p. 80–82, 84; Harvey, *A Few Bloody Noses*, p. 375.

2 Thomas Maxwell Account, Lyman C. Draper Manuscript Collection, 3 DD 236, Wisconsin Historical Society, Madison, Wisconsin.

3 Skinner, *The Staff Ride Handbook for the Battle for Kings Mountain*, pp. 42, 81–82, 84.

4 Ibid., pp. 81–82.

5 Draper, *Kings Mountain and Its Heroes*, p. 235.

6 Flood, *Rise, and Fight Again*, p. 355.

7 Kolb and Weir, *Captured at Kings Mountain*, p. 31; Dameron, *King's Mountain*, pp. 60–61; Skinner, *The Staff Ride Handbook for the Battle for Kings Mountain*, pp. 24, 81; Buchanan, *The Road to Guilford Courthouse*, p. 230.

8 Buchanan, *The Road to Guilford Courthouse*, p. 230.

9 Skinner, *The Staff Ride Handbook for the Battle for Kings Mountain*, p. 121; Buchanan, *The Road to Guilford Courthouse*, p. 231.

10 Buchanan, *The Road to Guilford Courthouse*, p. 232.

11 Graves, *Backcountry Revolutionary*, p. 241; Skinner, *The Staff Ride Handbook for the Battle for Kings Mountain*, p. 80.

12 Brown, *Kings Mountain and Cowpens*, p. 69.

13 Skinner, *The Staff Ride Handbook for the Battle for Kings Mountain*, pp. 14, 16.

14 Moss, *Roster of South Carolina Patriots in the American Revolution*, pp. 95, 106, 271, 356, 456, 508; "Major Thomas Young," South Carolina Militia in the Revolutionary War, https://www.nps.gov/articles/000/thomas-young.htm; Gilbert and Gilbert, *Patriot Militiaman in the American Revolution 1775–82*, pp. 42, 44, 46–47; Skinner, *The Staff Ride Handbook for the Battle for Kings Mountain*, p. 77; Brown, *Kings Mountain and Cowpens*, p. 65; Buchanan, *The Road to Guilford Courthouse*, p. 231; Jones, *Before They Were Heroes at King's Mountain*, p. 461; Graves, *Backcountry Revolutionary*, pp. 125, 138.

15 Buchanan, *The Road to Guilford Courthouse*, p. 231.

16 Moss, *Roster of South Carolina Patriots in the American Revolution*, p. 166; Gilbert and Gilbert, *Patriot Militiaman in the American Revolution 1775–82*, pp. 35, 47; "Major Thomas Young," South Carolina Militia in the Revolutionary War.

17 Graves, *Backcountry Revolutionary*, p. 138.

18 Ibid., pp. 14, 121, 195.
19 Ibid., p. 195.
20 Ibid., pp. 195, 328–31.
21 Skinner, *The Staff Ride Handbook for the Battle for Kings Mountain*, p. 77.
22 Draper, *Kings Mountain and Its Heroes*, pp. 271, 467.
23 Ibid., p. 469.
24 Foster and Putnam, "The Battle of King's Mountain," p. 32.
25 Skinner, *The Staff Ride Handbook for the Battle for Kings Mountain*, pp. 81–82; Buchanan, *The Road to Guilford Courthouse*, p. 229.
26 Buchanan, *The Road to Guilford Courthouse*, pp. 229–30.
27 Ibid., p. 230.
28 John Dobson Account, Lyman C. Draper Manuscript Collection, 2 DD 60, Wisconsin Historical Society, Madison, Wisconsin; Dameron, *King's Mountain*, p. 58.
29 John Duckworth, United States Government Pension Application, National Archives, Washington, DC.
30 Draper, *Kings Mountain and Its Heroes*, pp. 307, 471–72.
31 "John Dysart, Sr., (1749–1842)," WikiTree Genealogy, https://www.wikitree.com/wiki/Dysart-72; John Dysart Account, Lyman C. Draper Manuscript Collection, 2DD412.
32 Brown, *Kings Mountain and Cowpens*, p. 65; Buchanan, *The Road to Guilford Courthouse*, p. 231.
33 Draper, *Kings Mountain and Its Heroes*, pp. 243, 463–64; Brown, *Kings Mountain and Cowpens*, p. 72.
34 Benjamin Sharp Account, Lyman C. Draper Manuscript Collection, 17 DD 17, Wisconsin Historical Society, Madison, Wisconsin.
35 Joseph Phillips Account, Lyman C. Draper Manuscript Collection, 3 DD 215–216, Wisconsin Historical Society, Madison, Wisconsin.
36 Benjamin Sharp Account, Lyman C. Draper Manuscript Collection, 17 DD 17, Wisconsin Historical Society, Madison, Wisconsin.
37 Dameron, *King's Mountain*, p. 36; Skinner, *The Staff Ride Handbook for the Battle for Kings Mountain*, p. 74; Henderson, *Isaac Shelby*, TNCB, part 2, pp. 14–15; Jones, *Before They Were Heroes at King's Mountain*, pp. 21–24, 457–58.
38 Joseph Phillips Account, Lyman C. Draper Manuscript Collection, 3 DD 215–216, Wisconsin History Society, Madison Wisconsin; Benjamin Sharp Account, Lyman C. Draper Manuscript Collection, 17 DD 17, Wisconsin Historical Society, Madison, Wisconsin.
39 Benjamin Sharp Account, Lyman C. Draper Manuscript Collection, 17 DD 17, Wisconsin Historical Society, Madison, Wisconsin.
40 Dameron, *King's Mountain*, p. 36; Skinner, *The Staff Ride Handbook for the Battle for Kings Mountain*, p. 74.
41 Dameron, *King's Mountain*, p. 37; Draper, *Kings Mountain and Its Heroes*, p. 388; Skinner, *The Staff Ride Handbook for the Battle for Kings Mountain*, p. 74; *Jones, Before They Were Heroes at King's Mountain*, p. 457.
42 Dameron, *King's Mountain*, p. 37.

43 Draper, *Kings Mountain and Its Heroes*, p. 458.
44 Ibid.
45 Draper, *Kings Mountain and Its Heroes*, p. 195.
46 Jones, *Before They Were Heroes at King's Mountain*, p. 453.
47 Benjamin Sharp Account, Lyman C. Draper Manuscript Collection, 17 DD 17, Wisconsin Historical Society, Madison, Wisconsin; Skinner, *The Staff Ride Handbook for the Battle for Kings Mountain*, p. 74; Jones, *Before They Were Heroes at King's Mountain*, p. 458.
48 Draper, *Kings Mountain and Its Heroes*, pp. 261, 456–57; Dameron, *King's Mountain*, p. 66; Sheppard, *Patriot Versus Loyalist*, p. 69; *Yorker Observer*, Rock Hill, South Carolina, June 14, 1995.
49 Dameron, *King's Mountain*, p. 66.
50 Ibid.
51 Sheppard, *Patriot Versus Loyalist*, p. 69.
52 Ibid., pp. 65, 69.
53 "The Patriot Leaders of South Carolina—Colonel Edward Lacey," The American Revolution in South Carolina.
54 Skinner, *The Staff Ride Handbook for the Battle for Kings Mountain*, pp. 68, 70; Dameron, *King's Mountain*, pp. 37. 47–48; Brown, *Kings Mountain and Cowpens*, p. 65; Agniel, *The South in the American Revolution*, p. 77.
55 Henderson, *Isaac Shelby*, TNCB, part 2, p. 17; Skinner, *The Staff Ride Handbook for the Battle for Kings Mountain*, pp. 68–69.
56 Dameron, *King's Mountain*, p. 37; Henderson, *Isaac Shelby*, part 2, p. 17; Walter Clark, ed., *State Records of North Carolina* (Charleston: Nabu Press, 2010), p. 140.
57 Brown, *Kings Mountain and Cowpens*, pp. 71–73; Buchanan, *The Road to Guilford Courthouse*, pp. 230–31; Dameron, *King's Mountain*, p. 62, p. 64; Sheppard, *Patriot Versus Loyalist*, p. 69.
58 Henderson, *Isaac Shelby*, TNCB, part 2, pp. 16–17; Jones, *Before They Were Heroes at King's Mountain*, p. 443.
59 Dameron, *King's Mountain*, p. 62; Skinner, *The Staff Ride Handbook for the Battle for Kings Mountain*, pp. 70–71; Jones, *Before They Were Heroes at King's Mountain*, p. 457; Buchanan, *The Road to Guilford Courthouse*, p. 231.
60 Dunkerly, *The Battle of Kings Mountain*, p. 48.
61 Dameron, *King's Mountain*, p. 63.
62 Buchanan, *The Road to Guilford Courthouse*, p. 231; Skinner, *The Staff Ride Handbook for the Battle for Kings Mountain*, p. 70; Dameron, *King's Mountain*, p. 62.
63 Skinner, *The Staff Ride Handbook for the Battle for Kings Mountain*, p. 70; Jones, *Before They Were Heroes at King's Mountain*, p. 456; Turner, *Life of General John Sevier*, p. 129.
64 Turner, *Life of General John Sevier*, p. 129.
65 Dunkerly, *The Battle of Kings Mountain*, pp. 33–34; Dameron, *King's Mountain*, p. 64; Brown, *Kings Mountain and Cowpens*, p. 72; Skinner, *The Staff Ride Handbook for the Battle for Kings Mountain*, p. 71; "Capt. John Mattocks," Find A Grave, https://www.findagrave.com/memorial/13700227/john-mattocks.
66 Henderson, *Isaac Shelby*, TNCB, part 2, p. 17.

67 Draper, *Kings Mountain and Its Heroes*, p. 474; Skinner, *The Staff Ride Handbook for the Battle for Kings Mountain*, pp. 72–73.
68 Jones, *Before They Were Heroes at King's Mountain*, p. 456; Dunkerly, *The Battle of Kings Mountain*, p. 48.
69 Dunkerly, *The Battle of Kings Mountain*, p. 48; Jones, *Before They Were Heroes at King's Mountain*, p. 456.
70 Gilbert and Gilbert, *Patriot Militiaman in the American Revolution 1775–82*, p. 47; Buchanan, *The Road to Guilford Courthouse*, p. 231; Jones, *Before They Were Heroes at King's Mountain*, p. 456.
71 Buchanan, *The Road to Guilford Courthouse*, p. 231.
72 Ibid.
73 Moss, *Roster of South Carolina Patriots in the American Revolution*, p. 439.
74 Brown, *Kings Mountain and Cowpens*, p. 75; Dameron, *King's Mountain*, pp. 62, 64.
75 Joseph Phillips Account, Lyman C. Draper Manuscript, 3 DD 215–216, Wisconsin Historical Society, Madison, Wisconsin.
76 Dameron, *King's Mountain*, p. 63; Skinner, *The Staff Ride Handbook for the Battle for Kings Mountain*, p. 42; Henderson, *Isaac Shelby*, TNCB, part 2, p. 16.
77 Benjamin Sharp Account, Lyman C. Draper Manuscript Collection, 3 DD 214, Wisconsin Historical Society, Madison, Wisconsin.
78 Draper, *Kings Mountain and Its Heroes*, p. 543.
79 Ibid., pp. 277–78.
80 Andrew Ferguson, United States Government Pension Application, S32243, National Archives, Washington, DC; Jones, *Before They Were Heroes at King's Mountain*, pp. 471–72.
81 Draper, *Kings Mountain and Its Heroes*, p. 591.
82 Brown, *Kings Mountain and Cowpens*, p. 73.
83 Jones, *Before They Were Heroes at King's Mountain*, p. 455; Bowen Family History, Accounts of the Battle of Kings Mountain, FamilySearch, https://www.familysearch.org/en/memories/memory/8487185.
84 Ibid.
85 Bowen Family History, Accounts of the Battle of Kings Mountain.
86 Draper, *Kings Mountain and Its Heroes*, p. 554; "Lenoir, William," NCpedia, https://www.ncpedia.org/biography/lenoir-william; Jones, *Before They Were Heroes at King's Mountain*, p. 402.
87 Dameron, *King's Mountain*, pp. 52–53; Draper, *Kings Mountain and Its Heroes*, p. 263; Jones, *Before They Were Heroes at King's Mountain*, pp. 458–59.
88 Jones, *Before They Were Heroes at King's Mountain*, p. 458.
89 Ibid., p. 454; Kelly, *The Sword of the Lord and Gideon*, p. 29.
90 Dameron, *King's Mountain*, p. 62; Jones, *Before They Were Heroes at King's Mountain*, p. 463.
91 Henderson, *Isaac Shelby*, TNCB, part 2, p. 15.
92 Ibid., p. 17.
93 William Hill, *Col. William Hill's Memoirs of the Revolution* (Miami: HardPress Publishing, 2018), p. 23.

94 Draper, *Kings Mountain and Its Heroes*, p. 543.
95 Gilbert and Gilbert, *Patriot Militiaman in the American Revolution 1775–82*, p. 47; Brown, *Kings Mountain and Cowpens*, pp. 74–75.
96 Brown, *Kings Mountain and Cowpens*, pp. 74–75; Skinner, *The Staff Ride Handbook for the Battle for Kings Mountain*, p. 16.
97 Brown, *Kings Mountain and Cowpens*, p. 80.
98 Sheppard, *Patriot Versus Loyalist*, pp. 64, 68; Jones, *Before They Were Heroes at King's Mountain*, pp. 458–59; Wrobel and Grider, *Isaac Shelby*, p. 52.
99 Wrobel and Grider, *Isaac Shelby*, p. 52.
100 Ibid., pp. 52–53.
101 Ibid., p. 53.
102 Skinner, *The Staff Ride Handbook for the Battle for Kings Mountain*, p. 16; Jones, *Before They Were Heroes at King's Mountain*, p. 458.
103 Sheppard, *Patriot Versus Loyalist*, p. 75; Dameron, *King's Mountain*, p. 47; Gilbert and Gilbert, *Patriot Militiaman in the American Revolution 1775–82*, pp. 46–47; Buchanan, *The Road to Guilford Courthouse*, pp. 230–32.
104 Wrobel and Grider, *Isaac Shelby*, p. 52.
105 Brown, *Kings Mountain and Cowpens*, p. 75; Wrobel and Grider, *Isaac Shelby*, p. 53.
106 Skinner, *The Staff Ride Handbook for the Battle for Kings Mountain*, p. 42; Jones, *Before They Were Heroes at King's Mountain*, p. 463; Buchanan, *The Road to Guilford Courthouse*, p. 232; Henderson, *Isaac Shelby*, TNCB, part 2, pp. 14–15.
107 Emails from Tate to author, May 14, 2021; Brown, *Kings Mountain and Cowpens*, p. 66–67; Henderson, *Isaac Shelby*, TNCB, part 2, p. 15; Dunkerly, *The Battle of Kings Mountain*, p. 64; Jones, *Before They Were Heroes at King's Mountain*, pp. 462–63; Foster and Putnam, "The Battle of King's Mountain," p. 26.
108 Foster and Putnam, "The Battle of King's Mountain," pp. 26–27.
109 Draper, *Kings Mountain and Its Heroes*, pp. 409, 537; Skinner, *The Staff Ride Handbook for the Battle for Kings Mountain*, p. 89.
110 Draper, *Kings Mountain and Its Heroes*, p. 252; Dunkerly, *The Battle of Kings Mountain*, p. 64; Foster and Putnam, "The Battle of King's Mountain," p. 26.
111 Dunkerly, *The Battle of Kings Mountain*, p. 64; Foster and Putnam, King's Mountain, p. 26.
112 Jones, *Before They Were Heroes at King's Mountain*, pp. 462–63.
113 Draper, *Kings Mountain and Its Heroes*, p. 538.
114 Lambert, *South Carolina Loyalists in the American Revolution*, p. 101; Draper, *Kings Mountain and Its Heroes*, p. 253; Skinner, *The Staff Ride Handbook for the Battle for Kings Mountain*, p. 16.
115 Draper, *Kings Mountain and its Heroes*, p. 253.
116 Lambert, *South Carolina Loyalists in the American Revolution*, p. 101.
117 Skinner, *The Staff Ride Handbook for the Battle for Kings Mountain*, p. 27, note no. 8.
118 Dunkerly, *The Battle of Kings Mountain*, pp. 126–27.
119 Foster and Putnam, "The Battle of King's Mountain," p. 26; Skinner, *The Staff Ride Handbook for the Battle for Kings Mountain*, p. 16; Henderson, *Isaac Shelby*, part 2, p. 16; Lambert, *South Carolina Loyalists in the American Revolution*, p. 101.

120 Draper, *Kings Mountain and Its Heroes*, pp. 409–10; Foster and Putnam, "The Battle of King's Mountain," p. 26; Henderson, *Isaac Shelby*, TNCB, part 2, p. 19; Winkler, *Point Pleasant 1774*, pp. 73, 78–79.

121 Lambert, *South Carolina Loyalists in the American Revolution*, p. 101; Jones, *Before They Were Heroes at King's Mountain*, pp. 462–63; Patterson, *Washington and Cornwallis*, p. 243.

122 Lambert, *South Carolina Loyalists in the American Revolution*, p. 101; Jones, *Before They Were Heroes at King's Mountain*, pp. 462–63; Henderson, *Isaac Shelby*, part 2, p. 19; Winkler, *Point Pleasant 1774*, pp. 73, 78–79.

123 Henderson, *Isaac Shelby*, TNCB, part 2, p. 19.

124 Ibid., part 1, p. 121; Henderson, *Isaac Shelby*, TNCB, part 2, p. 21; Winkler, *Point Pleasant 1774*, 73, 78–79.

125 Foster and Putnam, "The Battle of King's Mountain," pp. 26, 28–29; Henderson, *Isaac Shelby*, TNCB, part 2, pp. 19–20; Draper, *Kings Mountain and Its Heroes*, p. 252–53; Ensign Robert Campbell Pension Application, Lyman C. Draper Manuscript Collection, No. 17 DD 25, Wisconsin History Society, Madison, Wisconsin.

126 Foster and Putnam, "The Battle of King's Mountain," p. 28.

127 Ibid., pp. 29.

128 Ibid.

129 Foster and Putnam, "The Battle of King's Mountain," pp. 26, 29; Dunkerly, *The Battle of Kings Mountain*, p. 64; "Silas McBee," Find A Grave, https://www.findagrave.com/memorial/95240444/silas-mcbee; "Silas Leroy McBee (1765–1845)," Geni, https://www.geni.com/people/Silas-McBee/6000000011379717694.

130 Dunkerly, *The Battle of Kings Mountain*, p. 64.

131 Lambert, *South Carolina Loyalists in the American Revolution*, p. 101; Draper, *Kings Mountain and Its Heroes*, pp. 252–53; Jones, *Before They Were Heroes at King's Mountain*, pp. 462–63; Henderson, *Isaac Shelby*, TNCB, part 2, p. 16; Wrobel and Grider, *Isaac Shelby*, p. 53; Foster and Putnam, "The Battle of King's Mountain," p. 29.

132 Ensign Robert Campbell Pension Application, Lyman C. Draper Manuscript Collection, No. 17 DD 25, Wisconsin Historical Society, Madison, Wisconsin; Henderson, *Isaac Shelby*, TNCB, part 2, p. 20.

133 Graves, *Backcountry Revolutionary*, p. 333; Skinner, *The Staff Ride Handbook for the Battle for Kings Mountain*, pp. 78–79; Jones, *Before They Were Heroes at King's Mountain*, pp. 462–63.

134 Ensign Robert Campbell Pension Application, Lyman C. Draper Manuscript Collection, No. 17 DD 25, Wisconsin Historical Society, Madison, Wisconsin.

135 Foster and Putnam, "The Battle of Kings Mountain," p. 30.

136 Dameron, *King's Mountain*, pp. 52, 76; Draper, *Kings Mountain and Its Heroes*, p. 314.

137 Draper, *Kings Mountain and Its Heroes*, p. 315 and unnumbered footnote.

138 Gilbert and Gilbert, *Patriot Militiaman in the American Revolution 1775–82*, p. 47.

139 Dameron, *King's Mountain*, p. 65; Draper, *Kings Mountain and Its Heroes*, pp. 145, 232, 259; Jones, *Before They Were Heroes at King's Mountain*, pp. 443, 457.

140 Draper, *Kings Mountain and Its Heroes*, p. 314.
141 Skinner, *The Staff Ride Handbook for the Battle of Kings Mountain*, p. 16; Draper, *Kings Mountain and Its Heroes*, pp. 314–15.
142 Jones, *Before They Were Heroes at King's Mountain*, p. 460.
143 Brown, *Kings Mountain and Cowpens*, p. 82.
144 Draper, *Kings Mountain and Its Heroes*, p. 479.
145 Dunkerly, *The Battle of Kings Mountain*, pp. 103–105; "David Beattie Captain," Rootsweb.com, https://sites.rootsweb.com/~celiadon/ps04/ps04_270.htm.

Chapter VII

1 Skinner, *The Staff Ride Handbook for the Battle for Kings Mountain*, pp. 78–79; Henderson, *Isaac Shelby*, part 2, pp. 14–15.
2 Joseph Phillips, Account, Lyman C. Draper Manuscript Collection, 3 DD 215–216, Wisconsin Historical Society, Madison, Wisconsin.
3 Benjamin Sharp Account, Lyman C. Draper Manuscript Collection, 17 DD 17, Wisconsin Historical Society, Madison, Wisconsin; "Benjamin Sharp (1762–1846)," WikiTree, https://www.wikitree.com/wiki/Sharp-1163; Joseph Phillips Account, Lyman C. Draper Manuscript Collection, 3 DD 215–216, Wisconsin Historical Society, Madison, Wisconsin.
4 Benjamin Sharp Account, Lyman C. Draper Manuscript Collection, 3 DD 214, Wisconsin Historical Society, Madison, Wisconsin.
5 Draper, *Kings Mountain and Its Heroes*, pp. 523.
6 William Edmondson Account, Lyman C. Draper Manuscript Collection, 3 DD 125, Wisconsin Historical Society, Madison, Wisconsin.
7 Samuel Newell Account, Lyman C. Draper Manuscript Collection, 3 DD 219, Wisconsin Historical Society, Madison, Wisconsin; Kolb and Weir, *Captured at Kings Mountain*, p. 31.
8 Dunkerly, *The Battle of Kings Mountain*, p.17.
9 Samuel Newell, Lyman C. Draper Manuscript Collection, 3 DD 219, Wisconsin Historical Society, Madison, Wisconsin.
10 Kolb and Weir, *Captured at Kings Mountain*, p. 31.
11 Ibid; Skinner, *The Staff Ride Handbook for the Battle for Kings Mountain*, pp. 78–79.
12 Skinner, *The Staff Ride Handbook for the Battle for Kings Mountain*, p. 79.
13 Ibid., p. 96.
14 James Crow Account, Lyman C. Draper Manuscript Collection, 3 DD 198, Wisconsin Historical Society, Madison, Wisconsin.
15 Kolb and Weir, *Captured at Kings Mountain*, p. 31; Dunkerly, *The Battle of Kings Mountain*, p. 142.
16 Andrew Creswell Letter, December 5, 1822, Participant's File, Kings Mountain National Military Park Archives, Blacksburg, South Carolina.
17 Kolb and Weir, *Captured at Kings Mountain*, p. 31; Dunkerly, *The Battle of Kings Mountain*, pp. 141–42.
18 Kolb and Weir, *Captured at Kings Mountain*, p. 31; Skinner, *The Staff Ride Handbook for the Battle for Kings Mountain*, pp. 16–17, 21–22, 42, 78–79; Brown,

Kings Mountain and Cowpens, pp. 74–76; Henderson, *Isaac Shelby*, part 2, pp. 14–15; Steven Eden, *Military Blunders: Wartime Fiascoes from the Roman Age Through World War I* (New York: MetroBooks, 1995), pp. 78–82.

19 James Davison Account, Lyman C. Draper Manuscript Collection, 8 DD 68, Wisconsin Historical Society, Madison, Wisconsin.

20 John Craig, United States Government Pension Application, S16740, National Archives, Washington, DC.

21 Draper, *Kings Mountain and Its Heroes*, p. 538.

22 Henry Dickenson, Lyman C. Draper Manuscript Collection, 3 DD 206, Wisconsin Historical Society, Madison, Wisconsin.

23 Kolb and Weir, *Captured at Kings Mountain*, p. 31; Foster and Putnam, "The Battle of King's Mountain," p. 33.

24 Henry Dickenson, Lyman C. Draper Manuscript Collection, 3 DD 206, Wisconsin Historical Society, Madison, Wisconsin; Draper, *Kings Mountain and Its Heroes*, p. 585; Kolb and Weir, *Captured at Kings Mountain*, p. 31.

25 Foster and Putnam, "The Battle of King's Mountain," p. 32.

26 Draper, *Kings Mountain and Its Heroes*, p. 585; Skinner, *The Staff Ride Handbook for the Battle for Kings Mountain*, pp. 21, 78–79.

27 Kolb and Weir, *Captured at Kings Mountain*, p. 31; Brown, *Kings Mountain and Cowpens*, p. 76; Lambert, *South Carolina Loyalists in the American Revolution*, pp. 100–101; Skinner, *The Staff Ride Handbook for the Battle for Kings Mountain*, p. 42.

28 Kolb and Weir, *Captured at Kings Mountain*, p. 31; Brown, *Kings Mountain and Cowpens*, pp. 74–75; Lambert, *South Carolina Loyalists in the American Revolution*, p. 100; Skinner, *The Staff Ride Handbook for the Battle for Kings Mountain*, p. 42.

29 Skinner, *The Staff Ride Handbook for the Battle for Kings Mountain*, pp. 78–79.

30 Draper, *Kings Mountain and Its Heroes*, pp. 277–78.

31 Robert Campbell Account, Lyman C. Draper Manuscript Collection, 17 DD 25, Wisconsin Historical Society, Madison, Wisconsin.

32 Ibid; Draper, *Kings Mountain and Its Heroes*, pp. 232, 280.

33 Kolb and Weir, *Captured at Kings Mountain*, p. 31; Dameron, *King's Mountain*, p. 69; Jones, *Before They Were Heroes at King's Mountain*, p. 456; Henderson, *Isaac Shelby*, TNCB, part 2, pp. 18–19; Lambert, *South Carolina Loyalists in the American Revolution*, p. 100.

34 Draper, *Kings Mountain and Its Heroes*, p. 196; Winkler, *Point Pleasant 1774*, pp. 73, 78–79.

35 Kolb and Weir, *Captured at Kings Mountain*, p. 31; Skinner, *The Staff Ride Handbook for the Battle for Kings Mountain*, pp. 21, 42, 78–79; Brown, *Kings Mountain and Cowpens*, p. 74.

36 Skinner, *The Staff Ride Handbook for the Battle for Kings Mountain*, p. 96.

37 Kolb and Weir, *Captured at Kings Mountain*, p. 31; Brown, *Kings Mountain and Cowpens*, p. 80.

38 Andrew Creswell Letter, December 5, 1822, Participant's File, Kings Mountain National Military Park, Blacksburg, South Carolina.

39 Draper, *Kings Mountain and Its Heroes*, p. 586.

40 Lambert, *South Carolina Loyalists in the American Revolution*, p. 99.

41 Kolb and Weir, *Captured at Kings Mountain*, p. 31; Skinner, *The Staff Ride Handbook for the Battle for Kings Mountain*, pp. 78–79, 101; Jones, *Before They Were Heroes at King's Mountain*, p. 463; Buchanan, *The Road to Guilford Courthouse*, p. 232.

42 Brown, *Kings Mountain and Cowpens*, p. 75; Jones, *Before They Were Heroes at King's Mountain*, p. 464

43 Jones, *Before They Were Heroes at King's Mountain*, p. 468.

44 Ibid., p. 463; Henderson, *Isaac Shelby*, TNCB, part 2, pp. 14–15.

45 James Crow Account, Lyman C. Draper Manuscript Collection, 3 DD 198, Wisconsin Historical Society, Madison, Wisconsin.

46 Skinner, *The Staff Ride Handbook for the Battle for Kings Mountain*, pp. 78–79; Jones, *Before They Were Heroes at King's Mountain*, pp. 463–64.

47 Skinner, *The Staff Ride Handbook for the Battle for Kings Mountain*, pp. 18, 42, 78–79.

48 Ibid., p. 95.

49 Ibid., pp. 78.

50 Draper, *Kings Mountain and Its Heroes*, p. 260.

51 James Crow Account, Lyman C. Draper Manuscript Collection, 3 DD 198, Wisconsin Historical Society, Madison, Wisconsin; Sheppard, *Patriot Versus Loyalist*, p. 70.

52 Skinner, *The Staff Ride Handbook for the Battle for Kings Mountain*, pp. 42, 95, 98; Dameron, *King's Mountain*, pp. 68–70.

53 Henderson, *Isaac Shelby*, TNCB, part 2, p. 18.

54 Ibid; Jones, *Before They Were Heroes at King's Mountain*, p. 464.

55 Robert Campbell Account, Lyman C. Draper Manuscript Collection, 17 DD 25, Wisconsin Historical Society, Madison, Wisconsin; Dameron, *King's Mountain*, p. 69; Sheppard, *Patriot Versus Loyalist*, p. 70.

56 Lambert, *South Carolina Loyalists in the American Revolution*, p. 99; Dameron, *King's Mountain*, pp. 68–70.

57 Kolb and Weir, *Captured at Kings Mountain*, p. 31; Kelly, *The Sword of the Lord and Gideon*, p. 121; Draper, *Kings Mountain and Its Heroes*, p. 525; Dameron, *King's Mountain*, pp. 68–70; Jones, *Before They Were Heroes at King's Mountain*, p. 464–65; Belt and Belt, *John Sevier*, pp. 64–65; Skinner, *The Staff Ride Handbook for the Battle for Kings Mountain*, pp. 98–99; Brown, *Kings Mountain and Cowpens*, p. 76; Robert Campbell Account, Lyman C. Draper Manuscript Collection, 17 DD 25, Wisconsin Historical Society, Madison, Wisconsin.

58 Peter McQueen, United States Government Pension Application, S30577, National Archives, Washington, DC; Wrobel and Grider, *Isaac Shelby*, p. 55; Gilbert and Gilbert, *Patriot Militiaman in the American Revolution, 1775–82*, p. 47.

59 Buchanan, *The Road to Guilford Courthouse*, p. 223; Dunkerly, *The Battle of Kings Mountain*, p. 64.

60 Kelly, *The Sword of the Lord and Gideon*, p. 21; Belt and Belt, *John Sevier*, pp. 64–65.

61 Dameron, *King's Mountain*, p. 70.

62 Henderson, *Isaac Shelby*, TNCB, part 2, p. 10, footnote 10; Wrobel and Grider, *Isaac Shelby*, pp. 48–49.
63 Kelly, *The Sword of the Lord and Gideon*, p. 6; Jones, *Before They Were Heroes at King's Mountain*, p. 465.
64 Skinner, *The Staff Ride Handbook for the Battle for Kings Mountain*, p. 99.
65 Sheppard, *Patriot Versus Loyalist*, p. 65; Draper, *Kings Mountain and Its Heroes*, p. 457.
66 Draper, *Kings Mountain and Its Heroes*, p. 525.
67 Benjamin Sharp Account, Lyman C. Draper Manuscript Collection, 17 DD 17, Wisconsin Historical Society, Madison, Wisconsin.
68 Skinner, *The Staff Ride Handbook for the Battle for Kings Mountain*, p. 99.
69 Dameron, *King's Mountain*, pp. 51, 70.
70 Ibid., p. 78.
71 Kolb and Weir, *Captured at Kings Mountain*, p. 31; Skinner, *The Staff Ride Handbook for the Battle for Kings Mountain*, pp. 21–22.
72 Foster and Putnam, "The Battle of King's Mountain," p. 31; Skinner, *The Staff Ride Handbook for the Battle for Kings Mountain*, pp. 95–96.
73 Lambert, *South Carolina Loyalists in the American Revolution*, p. 70; Skinner, *The Staff Ride Handbook for the Battle for Kings Mountain*, p. 102.
74 Skinner, *The Staff Ride Handbook for the Battle for Kings Mountain*, pp. 101–102, 121.
75 Draper, *Kings Mountain and Its Heroes*, p. 281; Skinner, *The Staff Ride Handbook for the Battle for Kings Mountain*, p. 102.
76 Draper, *Kings Mountain and Its Heroes*, p. 281.
77 Jones, *Before They Were Heroes at King's Mountain*, p. 466.
78 Dameron, *King's Mountain*, pp. 52–53; Brown, *Kings Mountain and Cowpens*, p. 81–82; Draper, *Kings Mountain and Its Heroes*, pp. 262, 281–82.
79 Dunkerly, *The Battle of Kings Mountain*, pp. 141–42.
80 Benjamin Sharp Account, Lyman C. Draper Manuscript Collection, 17 DD 17, Wisconsin Historical Society, Madison, Wisconsin.
81 Ibid; Jones, *Before They Were Heroes at King's Mountain*, p. 467; Henderson, *Isaac Shelby*, TNCB, part 2, pp. 20–21; Skinner, *The Staff Ride Handbook for the Battle for Kings Mountain*, pp. 94–95.
82 Henderson, *Isaac Shelby*, part 2, p. 21.
83 Draper, *Kings Mountain and Its Heroes*, p. 559.
84 Benjamin Sharp Account, Lyman C. Draper Manuscript Collection, 17 DD 17, Wisconsin Historical Society, Madison, Wisconsin.
85 Henderson, *Isaac Shelby*, part 2, p. 21; Brown, *Kings Mountain and Cowpens*, p. 82.
86 Skinner, *The Staff Ride Handbook for the Battle for Kings Mountain*, p. 102.
87 James Davison Account, Lyman C. Draper Manuscript Collection, 8 DD 68, Wisconsin Historical Society, Madison, Wisconsin; Foster and Putnam, "The Battle of King's Mountain," p. 31.
88 Dunkerly, *The Battle of Kings Mountain*, p. 92; Dameron, *King's Mountain*, p. 66.

89 John Craig United States Government Pension Application, S16740, National Archives, Washington, DC; Draper, *Kings Mountain and Its Heroes*, pp. 418, 566, 580–81, 280, 283; Skinner, *The Staff Ride Handbook for the Battle for Kings Mountain*, pp. 77, 101; Graves, *Backcountry Revolutionary*, pp. 134, 328–29; Henderson, *Isaac Shelby*, TNCB, part 2, pp. 21–22; Dunkerly, *The Battle of Kings Mountain*, pp. 132, 146; Turner, *Life of General John Sevier*, p. 129; Draper, *Kings Mountain and Its Heroes*, p. 416; Foster and Putnam, "The Battle of King's Mountain," p. 31; Jones, *Before They Were Heroes at King's Mountain*, pp. 467–68; Agniel, *The South in the American Revolution*, p. 79; Brown, *Kings Mountain and Cowpens*, p. 81; Andrew Creswell Letter, December 5, 1822, Participant's File, Kings Mountain National Military Park, Blacksburg, South Carolina; Joseph Hughes, United States Government Pension Application, S31764, National Archives, Washington, DC.
90 Draper, *Kings Mountain and Its Heroes*, p. 559.
91 William Moore Account, Lyman C. Draper Manuscript Collection, 3 DD 239, Wisconsin Historical Society, Madison, Wisconsin.
92 Draper, *Kings Mountain and Its Heroes*, p. 282.
93 Dunkerly, *The Battle of Kings Mountain*, pp. 92–93.
94 Ibid; Draper, *Kings Mountain and Its Heroes*, p. 282.
95 Draper, *Kings Mountain and Its Heroes*, p. 560.
96 Graves, *Backcountry Revolutionary*, pp. 138, 142.
97 Ibid., pp. 301–302.
98 Skinner, *The Staff Ride Handbook for the Battle for Kings Mountain*, pp. 99, 101
99 Dunkerly, *The Battle of Kings Mountain*, p. 16.

Chapter VIII

1 Benjamin Sharp Account, Lyman C. Draper Manuscript Collection, 17 DD 17, Wisconsin Historical Society, Madison, Wisconsin.
2 Robert Campbell Account, Lyman C. Draper Manuscript Collection, 17 DD 25, Wisconsin Historical Society, Madison, Wisconsin.
3 Buchanan, *The Road to Guilford Courthouse*, pp. 234–35; Skinner, *The Staff Ride Handbook for the Battle for Kings Mountain*, p. 80.
4 Draper, *Kings Mountain and Its Heroes*, p. 281.
5 Ibid., p. 282.
6 Ibid., p. 281.
7 Graves, *Backcountry Revolutionary*, pp. 328–29; Dameron, *King's Mountain*, p. 75.
8 Jones, *Before They Were Heroes at King's Mountain*, p. 468.
9 Samuel Newell Account, Lyman C. Draper Manuscript Collection, 2 DD 219, Wisconsin Historical Society, Madison, Wisconsin.
10 Draper, *Kings Mountain and Its Heroes*, pp. 292–93.
11 William Snodgrass Account, Lyman C. Draper Manuscript Collection, 3 DD 242, Wisconsin Historical Society, Madison, Wisconsin.
12 Jones, *Before They Were Heroes at King's Mountain*, p. 466; Dameron, *King's Mountain*, p. 79.

13 Dunkerly, *The Battle of Kings Mountain*, p. 142.
14 Skinner, *The Staff Ride Handbook for the Battle for Kings Mountain*, p. 26.
15 Kolb and Weir, *Captured at Kings Mountain*, p. 31.
16 James Crow Account, Lyman C. Draper Manuscript Collection, 3 DD 198, Wisconsin Historical Society, Madison, Wisconsin.
17 Young, *Rifles and Riflemen at the Battle of Kings Mountain*, p. 16; Dameron, *King's Mountain*, p. 51; Dunkerly, *The Battle of Kings Mountain*, p. 64; Buchanan, *The Road to Guilford Courthouse*, p. 228; Lambert, *South Carolina Loyalists in the American Revolution*, p. 102; Skinner, *The Staff Ride Handbook for the Battle for Kings Mountain*, p. 42.
18 Dunkerly, *The Battle of Kings Mountain*, p. 64.
19 Patterson, *Washington and Cornwallis*, p. 243.
20 Dunkerly, *The Battle of Kings Mountain*, pp. 140–41; Skinner, *The Staff Ride Handbook for the Battle for Kings Mountain*, p. 90; Dameron, *King's Mountain*, p. 69.
21 Kelly, *The Sword of the Lord and Gideon*, p. 27; Draper, *Kings Mountain and Its Heroes*, p. 281; Jones, *Before They Were Heroes at King's Mountain*, p. 467.
22 Dameron, *King's Mountain*, p. 51; Draper, *Kings Mountain and Its Heroes*, pp. 286–87, 479–80.
23 Kelly, *The Sword of the Lord and Gideon*, p. 31; Draper, *Kings Mountain and Its Heroes*, p. 459; Dameron, *King's Mountain*, p. 52.
24 Draper, *Kings Mountain and Its Heroes*, pp. 287.
25 Kelly, *The Sword of the Lord and Gideon*, p. 31; Buchanan, *The Road to Guilford Courthouse*, pp. 234–35; Dameron, *King's Mountain*, p. 69.
26 Henderson, *Isaac Shelby*, TNCB, part 2, pp. 18–19.
27 Graves, *Backcountry Revolutionary*, p. 305; Webb, *Born Fighting*, pp. 169–72.
28 Draper, *Kings Mountain and Its Heroes*, p. 543.
29 Ibid., p. 289.
30 Ibid., p. 519.
31 Foster and Putnam, "The Battle of King's Mountain," p. 32.
32 Dunkerly, *The Battle of Kings Mountain*, p. 35; Skinner, *The Staff Ride Handbook for the Battle for Kings Mountain*, pp. 17, 26, 42; Brown, *Kings Mountain and Cowpens*, pp. 68, 83; Belt and Belt, *John Sevier*, p. 71.
33 Brown, *Kings Mountain and Cowpens*, pp. 82–83.
34 Sheppard, *Patriot Versus Loyalist*, p. 70.
35 Dunkerly, *The Battle of Kings Mountain*, pp. 27–28.
36 Samuel Newell letter to Colonel David Campbell, August 4, 1823, Lyman C. Draper Manuscript Collection, 3 DD 231, Wisconsin Historical Society, Madison, Wisconsin.
37 Samuel Newell Account, Lyman C. Draper Manuscript Collection, 3 DD 219, Wisconsin Historical Society, Madison, Wisconsin.
38 Dunkerly, *The Battle of Kings Mountain*, p. 35.
39 Dameron, *King's Mountain*, p. 75; Skinner, *The Staff Ride Handbook for the Battle for Kings Mountain*, pp. 83–90, 103, 122–23; Kolb and Weir, *Captured at Kings Mountain*, p. 31.

40 Moss, *Roster of South Carolina Patriots in the American Revolution*, p. 271.

41 Moss, *Roster of South Carolina Patriots in the American Revolution*, pp. 183, 389, 408, 522, 530, 682, 721, 751, 870, 915, 940; William Bradley, United States Government Pension Application, W8399, National Archives, Washington, DC; John Dobson Account, Lyman C. Draper Manuscript Collection, 2 DD 60, Wisconsin Historical Society, Madison, Wisconsin; William Griffis, United States Government Pension Application, R4323, National Archives, Washington, DC; Joseph Rogers, United States Government Pension Application, S32340, National Archives, Washington, DC.

42 Draper, *Kings Mountain and Its Heroes*, p. 577.

43 Dunkerly, *The Battle of Kings Mountain*, p. 35.

44 John Copeland, United States Government Pension Application, S30966, National Archives, Washington, DC.

45 Dunkerly, *The Battle of Kings Mountain*, p. 34.

46 Draper, *Kings Mountain and Its Heroes*, p. 553.

47 Dameron, *King's Mountain*, pp 51, 70; Draper, *Kings Mountain and Its Heroes*, p. 483; Lambert, *South Carolina Loyalists in the American Revolution*, p. 100.

48 Lambert, *South Carolina Loyalists in the American Revolution*, p. 102; Dameron, *King's Mountain*, p. 70; Sheppard, *Patriot Versus Loyalist*, p. 70.

49 Brock, "Captain Samuel Ryerson," *Dictionary of Canadian Biography*, vol. 5, (1801–1820).

50 Clark, *State Records of South Carolina*, p. 140.

51 Israel Hayter Account, Lyman C. Draper Manuscript Collection, 3 DD 240, Wisconsin Historical Society, Madison, Wisconsin.

52 "Cpt Robert Sevier," Find A Grave, https://www.findagrave.com/memorial/12939087/robert-sevier.

53 Buchanan, *The Road to Guilford Courthouse*, p. 234; Dameron, *King's Mountain*, p. 70.

54 Kelly, *The Sword of the Lord and Gideon*, p. 33.

55 Buchanan, *The Road to Guilford Courthouse*, p. 234.

56 Henderson, *Isaac Shelby*, TNCB, part 2, p. 21.

57 Kelly, *The Sword of the Lord and Gideon*, pp. 32, 34–35; Buchanan, *The Road to Guilford Courthouse*, p. 234.

58 Draper, *Kings Mountain and Its Heroes*, p. 308; Buchanan, *The Road to Guilford Courthouse*, p. 234.

59 Dunkerly, *The Battle of Kings Mountain*, p. 142; Jones, *Before They Were Heroes at King's Mountain*, p. 477; Sheppard, *Patriot Versus Loyalists*, p. 65.

60 Kelly, *The Sword of the Lord and Gideon*, p. 36; Draper, *Kings Mountain and Its Heroes*, p. 308.

61 Turner, *Life of General John Sevier*, p. 133.

62 Draper, *Kings Mountain and Its Heroes*, p. 457.

63 Dameron, *King's Mountain*, p. 70; Jones, *Before They Were Heroes at King's Mountain*, pp. 469–70; Buchanan, *The Road to Guilford Courthouse*, p. 234.

64 Dunkerly, *The Battle of Kings Mountain*, p. 64.

65 Jones, *Before They Were Heroes at King's Mountain*, p. 470; Dameron, *King's Mountain*, p. 78.
66 Dunkerly, *The Battle of Kings Mountain*, p. 145.
67 Henderson, *Isaac Shelby*, TNCB, part 2, p. 21.
68 Kelly, *The Sword of the Lord and Gideon*, pp. 34–35; Wrobel and Grider, *Isaac Shelby*, p. 56.
69 Wrobel and Grider, *Isaac Shelby*, p. 56.
70 Dunkerly, *The Battle of Kings Mountain*, p. 35.
71 Draper, *Kings Mountain and Its Heroes*, p. 308.
72 Ibid., p. 510.
73 Kolb and Weir, *Captured at Kings Mountain*, p. 32.
74 Buchanan, *The Road to Guilford Courthouse*, p. 235.
75 Graves, *Backcountry Revolutionary*, pp. 234–35.
76 Skinner, *The Staff Ride Handbook for the Battle for Kings Mountain*, pp. 26, 42–43; Draper, *Kings Mountain and Its Heroes*, p. 292; Dameron, *King's Mountain*, p. 79.
77 Skinner, *The Staff Ride Handbook for the Battle for Kings Mountain*, p. 79.
78 Moss, *Roster of South Carolina Patriots in the American Revolution*, pp. 612–13.
79 Draper, *Kings Mountain and Its Heroes*, pp. 312–13; Dunkerly, *The Battle of Kings Mountain*, p. 10.
80 Benjamin Sharp Account, Lyman C. Draper Manuscript Collection, 17 DD 17, Wisconsin Historical Society, Madison, Wisconsin.
81 John Spelt Account, Lyman C. Draper Manuscript Collection, 2 DD 224, Wisconsin Historical Society, Madison, Wisconsin.
82 Kolb and Weir, *Captured at Kings Mountain*, p. 31; Benjamin Sharp Account, Lyman C. Draper Manuscript Collection, 17 DD 17, Wisconsin Historical Society, Madison, Wisconsin; Skinner, *The Staff Ride Handbook for the Battle for Kings Mountain*, pp. 122–23.
83 Benjamin Sharp Account, Lyman C. Draper Manuscript Collection, 17 DD 17, Wisconsin Historical Society, Madison, Wisconsin.
84 Henry Dickenson Account, Lyman C. Draper Manuscript Collection, 3 DD 206, Wisconsin Historical Society, Madison, Wisconsin.
85 William Snodgrass Account, Lyman C. Draper Manuscript Collection, 3 DD 242, Wisconsin Historical Society, Madison, Wisconsin.
86 Dameron, *King's Mountain*, p. 77.
87 "Account of Re-burial of Colonel Williams' Body," *Spartanburg Herald*, August 26, 1928; Wrobel and Grider, *Isaac Shelby*, p. 58; Gilbert and Gilbert, *American Militiaman in the American Revolution, 1775–82*, p. 48; Buchanan, *The Road to Guilford Courthouse*, p. 237; Jones, *Before They Were Heroes at King's Mountain*, pp. 470, 475–77; Skinner, *The Staff Ride Handbook for the Battle for Kings Mountain*, pp. 21–22, 26, 43; Dunkerly, *The Battle of Kings Mountain*, p. 34.
88 Benjamin Sharp Account, Lyman C. Draper Manuscript Collection, 17 DD 17, Wisconsin Historical Society, Madison, Wisconsin.
89 Samuel Newell Account, Lyman C. Draper Manuscript Collection, 3 DD 219, Wisconsin Historical Society, Madison, Wisconsin.

90 William Snodgrass Account, Lyman C. Draper Manuscript Collection, 3 DD 242, Wisconsin Historical Society, Madison, Wisconsin; Dameron, *King's Mountain*, p. 84.

91 Graves, *Backcountry Revolutionary*, pp. 133–34; Jones, *Before They Were Heroes at King's Mountain*, p. 478.

92 Wayne Lynch, "Death of a Patriot at King's Mountain," *Journal of the American Revolution*, January 30, 2014, https://allthingsliberty.com/2014/01/death-patriot-kings-mountain.

93 Graves, *Backcountry Revolutionary*, p. 191.

94 Ibid., p. 196; James Williams Biography, American Battlefield Trust, https://www.battlefields.org/learn/biographies/james-williams.

95 Draper, *Kings Mountain and Its Heroes*, p. 500.

96 Brown, *Kings Mountain and Cowpens*, p. 87; Jones, *Before They Were Heroes at King's Mountain*, p. 478.

Chapter IX

1 Draper, *Kings Mountain and Its Heroes*, p. 295.

2 Ibid., p. 374.

3 Henderson, *Isaac Shelby*, TNCB, part 2, p. 35.

4 Ibid.

5 Ibid; Henry P. Johnston, *The Yorktown Campaign and the Surrender of Cornwallis, 1781* (Williamstown, MA: Corner House Publishers, 1973 reprint of 1881 edition), p. 18.

6 Morrill, *Southern Campaigns of the American Revolution*, p. 111.

7 Flood, *Rise, and Fight Again*, p. 357.

8 Agniel, *The South in the American Revolution*, p. 78.

9 Draper, *Kings Mountain and Its Heroes*, p. 375.

10 Dunkerly, *The Battle of Kings Mountain*, pp. 140–41.

11 Lambert, *South Carolina Loyalists in the American Revolution*, p. 104.

12 Ibid., pp. 58, 104; Dameron, *King's Mountain*, p. 51.

13 Graves, *Backcountry Revolutionary*, p. 236; Moss, *Roster of South Carolina Patriots in the American Revolution*, p. 446.

14 Draper, *Kings Mountain and Its Heroes*, p. 377.

15 *Historical Statements Concerning the Battle of Kings Mountain and the Battle of Cowpens, South Carolina* (Washington, DC: United States Government Printing Office, 1928), p. 34.

16 Skinner, *The Staff Ride Handbook for the Battle for Kings Mountain*, p. 1.

17 Draper, *Kings Mountain and Its Heroes*, p. 376.

18 Patterson, *Washington and Cornwallis*, p. 251.

19 Gibbes, *Documentary History of the American Revolution*, p. 140.

20 Pancake, *This Destructive War*, p. 120.

21 Carpenter, *Southern Gambit*, pp. 169–72.

22 Skinner, *The Staff Ride Handbook for the Battle for Kings Mountain*, p. 1; Buchanan, *The Road to Guilford Courthouse*, p. 241.

23 Webb, *Born Fighting*, p. 171; Pancake, *This Destructive War*, p. 120.
24 Carpenter, *Southern Gambit*, p. 172.
25 Buchanan, *The Road to Guilford Courthouse*, p. 241; Carpenter, *Southern Gambit*, pp. 142, 147, 170–71.
26 Skinner, *The Staff Ride Handbook for the Battle for Kings Mountain*, p. 2.
27 Neal and Segars, *Churches in South Carolina Burned During the American Revolution*, p. 14.
28 *New York Packet*, New York, New York, November 23, 1780.
29 O'Shaughnessy, *The Men Who Lost America*, p. 265; Dameron, *King's Mountain*, p. 87.
30 Allen, *Tories*, p. 290.
31 Pancake, *This Destructive War*, p. 121.
32 Carpenter, *Southern Gambit*, p. 171.
33 Draper, *Kings Mountain and Its Heroes*, p. 377.
34 Scoggins, *The Day It Rained Militia*, p. 147.
35 Harvey, *A Few Bloody Noses*, p. 373.
36 Young, *Rifles and Riflemen at the Battle of Kings Mountain*, pp. 13–14.
37 Sheppard, *Patriot Versus Loyalist*, pp. 71–72.
38 Ibid; Scoggins, *The Day It Rained Militia*, pp. 155–59; Blackmon, *Dark and Bloody Ground*, p. xxi; Neal and Segars, *Churches in South Carolina Burned During the American Revolution*, p. 14.
39 Moultrie, *Memoirs of the American Revolution*, vol. 2, pp. 246–47; Buchanan, *The Road to Guilford Courthouse*, pp. 6–7.
40 Pancake, *This Destructive War*, p. 82.
41 Buchanan, *The Road to Guilford Courthouse*, p. 7.
42 Brendan Morrissey, *Yorktown 1781: The World Turned Upside Down* (New York: Osprey Publications, 1997), p. 19.
43 Young, *Rifles and Riflemen at the Battle of Kings Mountain*, pp. 6–7.
44 Buchanan, *The Road to Guilford Courthouse*, 241.
45 *Maryland Gazette*, November 27, 1780.
46 Ibid., October 20, 1780.
47 James Thacher, MD, *Military Journal, During the American Revolutionary War, from 1776 to 1783* (Cranbury, NJ: The Scholar's Bookshelf, 2005), pp. 235–36.
48 Robert Bray and Paul Bushnell, eds., *Diary of a Common Soldier in the American Revolution, 1775–1783 An Annotated Edition of the Military Journal of Jeremiah Greenman* (Dekalb: Northern Illinois University Press, 1978), p. 184.
49 Jim Piecuch, *The Battle of Camden: A Documentary History* (Charleston: The History Press, 2006), p. 142.
50 Knight, *War at Saber Point*, p. 139.
51 Ibid.
52 *Maryland Gazette*, November 3, 1780.
53 Knight, *War at Saber Point*, p. 139.
54 Ian Saberton, ed., *The Cornwallis Papers: The Campaign of of 1780 and 1781 in the Southern Theatre of the American Revolution*, vol. 3 (Uckfield: 2010), p. 30.
55 Knight, *War at Saber Point*, p. 139.

56 Ibid; George Smith McCowen, *The British Occupation of Charleston, 1780–82* (Columbia: University of South Carolina Press, 1972), pp. 47–48; Pancake, *This Destructive War*, p. 82.
57 Carpenter, *Southern Gambit*, p. 169.
58 Pancake, *This Destructive War*, p. 82.
59 Dunkerly, *The Battle of Kings Mountain*, p. 35.
60 Pancake, *This Destructive War*, p. 82.
61 Ibid.
62 Saberton, *The Cornwallis Papers*, vol. 3, pp. 37–38.
63 Ibid., p. 41.
64 Ibid., p. 60.
65 Ibid., pp. 61–62.
66 Ibid., p. 65.
67 Ibid., p. 66.
68 Ibid., p. 71.
69 Ibid., p. 75.
70 Ibid., pp. 73–74.
71 Ibid., p. 76.
72 Foster and Putnam, "The Battle of King's Mountain," p. 39.
73 Saberton, *The Cornwallis Papers*, vol. 3, p. 90.
74 Agniel, *The South in the American Revolution*, pp. 74–75.
75 Lambert, *South Carolina Loyalists in the American Revolution*, pp. 148–49; Graves, *Backcountry Revolutionary*, pp. 134, 138, 142–43; Jones, *Before They Were Heroes at King's Mountain*, pp. 461–62; Moss, *Roster of South Carolina Patriots in the American Revolution*, p. 429.
76 Graves, *Backcountry Revolutionary*, p. 185.

Epilogue

1 Belt and Belt, *John Sevier*, pp. 47, 59; Saberton, *The Cornwallis Papers*, vol. 3, pp. 8–9, 11, 24; Fleming, *Cowpens*, p. 21; Dameron, *King's Mountain*, p. 79.
2 Saberton, *The Cornwallis Papers*, vol. 3, p. 24.
3 Ibid., p. 24.
4 Crawford, *Samuel Doak*, p. 3; Gilbert and Gilbert, *Patriot Militiaman in the American Revolution 1775–82*, pp. 9–10; Belt and Belt, *John Sevier*, pp. 41, 47, 60–63, 77; Dunkerly, *Kings Mountain*, p. 94.
5 Belt and Belt, *John Sevier*, p. 83.
6 Moss, *Roster of South Carolina Patriots in the American Revolution*, p. 859.
7 Ibid., p. 986.
8 Belt and Belt, *John Sevier*, pp. 65–70.
9 James Dulley, "Kings Mountain Turned Tide of American Revolution," *The Tennessee Magazine*, updated November 1, 2022, https://www.tnmagazine.org/kings-mountain-turned-tide-of-american-revolution.
10 Belt and Belt, *John Sevier*, pp. 41, 47.
11 McCarthy, *The Other Irish*, p. 101.

12 Carpenter, *Southern Gambit*, p. 172.
13 Pancake, *This Destructive War*, p. 240.
14 Belt and Belt, *John Sevier*, p. 83.
15 Wrobel and Grider, *Isaac Shelby*, pp. 60–61; Buchanan, *The Road to Guilford Courthouse*, pp. 234–45.
16 Henderson, *Isaac Shelby*, TNCB, part 2, p. 10; Buchanan, *The Road to Guilford Courthouse*, pp. 234–35.
17 Henderson, *Isaac Shelby*, TNCB, part 2, p. 24.
18 Draper, *Kings Mountain and Its Heroes*, p. 525; Henderson, *Isaac Shelby*, TNCB, part 2, p. 22.
19 Skinner, *The Staff Ride Handbook for the Battle for Kings Mountain*, pp. 80; Winkler, *Point Pleasant 1774*, pp. 73, 78–79; Buchanan, *The Road to Guilford Courthouse*, pp. 234–35.
20 Draper, *Kings Mountain and Its Heroes*, p. 529; Buchanan, *The Road to Guilford Courthouse*, pp. 234–35.
21 Draper, *Kings Mountain and Its Heroes*, p. 579.
22 Dameron, *King's Mountain*, pp. 25, 89.
23 Henderson, *Isaac Shelby*, TNCB, part 2, p. 28.
24 Jones, *Before They Were Heroes at King's Mountain*, p. 483.
25 Skinner, *The Staff Ride Handbook for the Battle for Kings Mountain*, p. 96.
26 Dunkerly, *The Battle of Kings Mountain*, p. 27.
27 Skinner, *The Staff Ride Handbook for the Battle for Kings Mountain*, p. 90.
28 Draper, *Kings Mountain and Its Heroes*, p. 593.
29 Buchanan, *The Road to Guilford Courthouse*, p. 382.
30 Skinner, *The Staff Ride Handbook for the Battle for Kings Mountain*, pp. 102–104.
31 Hoock, *Scars of Independence*, p. 403.
32 Draper, *Kings Mountain and Its Heroes*, p. 511; Dameron, *King's Mountain*, p. 122.

Index